Interprocess Communications in UNIX®
The Nooks and Crannies

John Shapley Gray

For book and bookstore information

http://www.prenhall.com

Prentice Hall PTR
Upper Saddle River, NJ 07458

Library of Congress Cataloging-in-Publication Data

Gray, John Shapley.
  Interprocess communications in UNIX—the nooks and
  crannies / John Shapley Gray.
    p. cm.
  Includes bibliographical references and index.
  ISBN 0-13-186891-8 (paper)
  1. UNIX (Computer file) 2. Operating systems (Computers)
  I. Title.
  QA76.76.O63G729 1997
  005.2—dc20   96-9015
                                                        CIP

Editorial/production supervision: *BooksCraft, Inc., Indianapolis, IN*
Cover design director: *Jerry Votta*
Cover design: *Lundgren Graphics*
Acquisitions editor: *Greg Doench*
Editorial assistant: *Leabe Berman*
Manufacturing manager: *Alexis R. Heydt*

© 1997 by Prentice Hall PTR
Prentice-Hall, Inc.
A Simon & Schuster Company
Upper Saddle River, NJ 07458

The publisher offers discounts on this book when ordered in bulk quantities.
For more information, contact:

Corporate Sales Department
Prentice Hall PTR
One Lake Street
Upper Saddle River, NJ 07458
Phone: 800-382-3419   Fax: 201-236-7141
E-mail: corpsales@prenhall.com

Printed in the United States of America

10 9 8 7 6 5 4 3 2 1

ISBN: 0-13-186891-8

Prentice-Hall International (UK) Limited, *London*
Prentice-Hall of Australia Pty. Limited, *Sydney*
Prentice-Hall Canada Inc., *Toronto*
Prentice-Hall Hispanoamericana, S.A., *Mexico*
Prentice-Hall of India Private Limited, *New Delhi*
Prentice-Hall of Japan, Inc., *Tokyo*
Simon & Schuster Asia Pte. Ltd., *Singapore*
Editora Prentice-Hall do Brasil, Ltda., *Rio de Janeiro*

Interprocess Communications in UNIX®

Table of Contents

Introduction

UNIX is a large and complex operating system that continues to evolve to meet user demands. It is virtually impossible for a user to master all of UNIX in a short period of time. It is equally difficult to present, in a cogent, digestible manner, all of UNIX. However, numerous authors have made some very respectable attempts to do so.

Bach, M. J., *The Design of the UNIX Operating System*, Prentice Hall, 1986

Leffler, S. J., M. K. McKusick and J. S. Quarterman, *The Design and Implementation of the 4.3BSD UNIX Operating System*, Addison-Wesley - Benjamin/Cummings, 1989

Others have addressed the specifics of programming in a UNIX environment, most notably:

Rochkind, M. J., *Advanced UNIX Programming*, Prentice Hall, 1985

Stevens, W. R., *Advanced Programming in the UNIX Environment*, Addison-Wesley, 1992

I will make no attempt to duplicate their efforts. Instead, it is my hope to present to the reader one aspect of UNIX—the basics of processes and interprocess communications. It is assumed that the reader has a working knowledge of C programming. It is further assumed that, while not being an expert, the reader has worked in a UNIX-based environment and is reasonably familiar with a UNIX-based text editor such as **vi**.

This text makes extensive references to specific UNIX system calls and predefined library functions. The reader is encouraged to read the manual page for each system call/library function as they are encountered. The manual pages in UNIX are an unparalleled source of information. For the uninitiated, **Appendix A** covers the format and use of UNIX manual pages.

All programming references and examples were generated on a Sun SPARC 10 Model 41 running Sun Microsystems' Solaris 2.4. Sun Microsystems' C++ compiler, CC, was used to compile all source code. Solaris has its origins in AT&T UNIX. Prior to moving to Solaris, Sun Microsystems' platforms ran SunOS which is a BSD (Berkeley)-based version of UNIX. Many of the examples (and some of the exercises) have been run in a SunOS 4.1.3 setting, and on a PC platform using Slackware Linux. Linux, originally developed by Linus Torvalds, is a freely distributed PC-based hybrid UNIX. Linux system administration is BSD-like, while its programming environment has a definite AT&T flavor. In most cases, few, if any, modifications were needed to generate clean executable code. In these alternate environments the GNU C compiler, gcc, was used. In *any* UNIX setting, IPC (interprocess communication) support must be available for the user to pursue the materials covered in the chapters on semaphores, message queues and shared memory. Under Solaris, IPC support is enabled by default. However, in some versions of UNIX (such as SunOS and Linux) you may need to modify system configuration files and recompile the kernel to enable IPC support. Unless you are the current system administrator, you most likely will want to seek help when recompiling the UNIX kernel.

ACKNOWLEDGMENTS

While my name graces the cover of this text, I would be the first to admit that its creation has not been a singular task. My family, my wife Marie and son Bill, have figured prominently in my efforts. They unfailingly provided me with the moral support when my ardor to complete the task at hand waned, and often had to forgo their own activities so that I might pursue mine. I would also like to acknowledge those who helped me in numerous ways to refine my thoughts and class notes into the text that follows. Joe DiOrio, Robert Mela and John Kagan were my first line reviewers. Their feedback helped me smooth off the rough edges and put things right from the start. My UNIX Internals classes at the University of Hartford served as a test bed for all of the proposed exercises. I would also like to thank those who reviewed my work: Peter Collinson (Hillside Systems), Tim Gottleber (Dallas County Community College), Doug Langston (Fidelity Investments), and S. Lee Henry (Johns Hopkins University). The University of Hartford generously provided me with the sabbatical time to write the bulk of the text and the members of the Math/Physics/Computer Science department offered their ongoing collegial support. Special thanks to my department chairman, Joel Kagan, for his continued support. Kudos to Greg Doench, editor at Prentice Hall, who was handled all my neophyte concerns about the publication process with aplomb and finesse. I am indebted to Leabe Berman, who kept things on track when they went astray. My thanks would not be complete without a mention of my parents and grandparents who instilled in me from the beginning that anything is possible if you do not give up—I guess I listened. Last, but never least, my cat, Footsie, whose unerring ability to park herself on the most critical section of my paperwork never failed to amaze me.

Interprocess Communications in UNIX®

Programs and Processes

1.1 INTRODUCTION

Fundamental to all operating systems is the concept of a **process**. While somewhat abstract, a process consists of an executing (running) program, its current values, state information, and the resources used by the operating system to manage the execution of the process. A process is a dynamic entity. In a UNIX-based operating system, at any given point in time, multiple processes *appear* to be executing concurrently. From the viewpoint of each of the processes involved it *appears* they have access to, and control of, all system resources as if they were in their own stand-alone setting. Both viewpoints are an illusion. The majority of UNIX operating systems run on platforms that have a single processing unit capable of supporting many *active* processes. However, at any point in time only one process is actually being worked upon. By rapidly changing the process it is currently executing, the UNIX operating system gives the appearance of concurrent process execution. The ability of the operating system to multiplex its resources among multiple processes in various stages of execution is called **multiprogramming** (or **multitasking**). Systems with multiple processing units, which by definition can support true concurrent processing, are called **multiprocessing**.

As noted, part of a process consists of the execution of a **program**. A program is an inactive, static entity consisting of a set of instructions and associated data. If a

program is invoked multiple times it can generate multiple processes. We can consider
a program to be in one of two basic formats:

☞ **source program**—A source program is a series of valid statements for a specific
programming language (such as C). The source program is stored in a plain
ASCII text file. For purposes of our discussion we will consider a plain ASCII text
file to be one that contains characters represented by the ASCII values in the
range of 32–127. Such source files can be displayed to the screen or printed on
the line printer. Under most conditions, the access permissions on the source file
are marked as non-executable. A sample C language source program is shown in
Program 1.1.

☞ **executable program**—An executable program is a source program that, by way
of a translating program such as a compiler, assembler, etc., has been put into a
special format that the operating system can execute (run). The executable program is not a plain ASCII text file and, in most cases, is not displayable on the
terminal or printed by the user.

Program 1.1 A source program in C.

```
/*
 *        Display Hello World 3 times
 */
#include <stdio.h>
#include <string.h>
#include <sys/types.h>
#include <stdlib.h>
#include <unistd.h>

char            *cptr = "Hello World\n";  /* static by placement */
char             buffer1[25];

main(void){
  void            showit(char *);         /* function prototype  */
  int             i = 0;                  /* automatic variable  */
  strcpy(buffer1, "A demonstration\n");   /* library function    */
  write(1, buffer1, strlen(buffer1)+1);   /* system call         */
  for (; i < 3; ++i)
    showit(cptr);                         /* function call       */
}
void
showit(char *p){
  char            *buffer2;
  if ((buffer2=(char *) malloc((unsigned) (strlen(p)+1)))!= NULL){
    strcpy(buffer2, p);                   /* copy the string     */
    printf("%s", buffer2);                /* display string      */
    free(buffer2);                        /* release location    */
  } else {
    printf("Allocation error.\n");
    exit(1);
  }
}
```

1.2 LIBRARY FUNCTIONS

Programs of any complexity make use of **functions**. A function is a collection of declarations and statements that carries out a specific action and/or returns a value. Functions are either defined by the user, or have been previously defined and made available to the user. Previously defined functions that have related functionality (e.g., math or graphics routines) are stored in object code format in **library** (archive) **files**. Object code format is a special file format that is generated as an intermediate step when an executable program is produced. Like executable files, object code files are also not displayed to the screen or printed. Functions stored in library files are often called **library functions** or **run-time library routines**.

The standard location for library files in most UNIX systems is the directory /usr/lib. Ancillary library files may also be found in the /usr/local/lib directory. By convention the three-letter prefix for a library file is **lib** and the file extension is **.a**. The UNIX archive utility **ar**, which maintains library files, can be used to examine their contents[1]. For example, the command:

```
% ar t /usr/lib/libc.a | pr -4 -t
```

will pipe the table of contents (indicated by the -t command line option) of the standard C library file (libc.a) to the **pr** utility, which will display the output to the screen in a four-column format. The object code in this library is combined by default with all C programs when they are compiled. Therefore, in a C program when a reference is made to **printf**, the object code for the **printf** function is obtained from the /usr/lib/libc.a library file.

If your system supports the -k (keyword) option for the manual pages you may issue the following command to obtain a single-line synopsis, from the windex database, of all the library function calls on your system:

```
% man -k \(3
```

As shown, this command asks the **man** (manual) program to display the one-line summary of each of the entries in section 3 of the manual. Section 3 (with its several subsections) contains the subroutine and library function manual pages. The "\" is used in the command sequence to escape the parenthesis so the shell will pass the parenthesis on to the **man** command. Without the escape the shell would attempt to interpret the parenthesis which would then produce a syntax error. If your system indicates that the windex database has not been generated, the command:

```
% catman  -w
```

will, providing you have the proper access privileges, generate the windex database file.

A more expansive overview of the library functions may be obtained by viewing the **Intro** manual page entry for Section 3. On most systems the command:

---

1. The archive utility is one of the many exceptions to the rule that all command line options for system utilities begin with a "-".

```
% man -s3 Intro
```

will return the **Intro** manual pages. In this invocation the -s flag is used to notify **man** of the appropriate section. Some versions of the **man** command omit the "s" portion of the section flag (i.e., -3 would indicate Section 3). Additional manual page information addressing manual page organization and use can be found in Appendix A: **Using UNIX Manual Pages**.

1.3 SYSTEM CALLS

Some previously defined functions used by programs are actually **system calls**. While resembling library functions in format, system calls request the UNIX operating system to directly perform some work on behalf of the invoking process. The code that is executed by the operating system lies within the **kernel** (the central controlling program). The system call acts as a high/mid-level language interface to this code. To protect the integrity of the kernel, the process executing the system call must temporarily switch from **user mode** (with user privileges and access permissions) to **system mode** (with system/root privileges and access permissions). This switch in context carries with it a certain amount of overhead and may, in some cases, make a system call less efficient than a library function that performs the same task. Many library functions (such as those dealing with input and output) are fully buffered and thus allow the system some control as to when specific tasks are actually executed.

Section 2 of the manual contains the pages on system calls. Issuing a manual pages command similar to the ones previously presented but using the value 2 in place of 3 will generate information on all the system calls defined in the manual pages. It is important to remember that some library functions have embedded system calls. For example, the library calls **scanf** and **printf** make use of the system calls **read** and **write**.

The relationship of library functions and system calls is shown in Figure 1.1.

The arrows in the diagram indicate possible paths of communication. As shown, executable programs may make use of system calls directly to request the kernel to

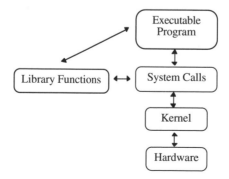

Fig. 1.1 Hardware and software layers.

perform a specific function. Or the executable programs may invoke a library function which in turn may perform system calls.

1.4 LINKING OBJECT CODE

Code from library files is combined with object code from the source program at compile time on an as-needed basis. When programming in C, additional library files containing the object code for system calls and library functions not contained in the standard C library can be specified at compile time. This is done by using the -1 compiler option, followed by the library name *without* the **lib** prefix and the .a extension. For example, the C compilation command:

```
% cc prgm.c -lm
```

would indicate to the link-loader portion of the **cc** compiler program that the math library object code found in libm.a should be combined with the object code created from the source program prgm.c. Be aware that library functions often require the inclusion of additional header files in the source program. The header files will contain the requisite function prototypes, macro definitions, defined constants, etc. Without the inclusion of the proper header files, the program will not compile correctly. In addition, the program will not compile correctly if you include the proper header file(s) and forget to link in the associated library containing the object code! Such omissions are often the source of cryptic compiler error messages of this ilk: *"Undefined symbol first referenced in file ... ld: fatal: Symbol referencing errors. No output written to a.out. Compilation failed."*

The synopsis section of the manual page (see Appendix A) will list the names of header file(s) if they are required. When multiple inclusion files are indicated, the order in which they are listed in the source program should match the order specified in the manual pages. The order of the inclusion is important, as occasionally the inclusion of a specific header file will *depend upon* the inclusion of the previously referenced header file. This dependency relationship is most commonly seen as the need for inclusion of the <sys/types.h> header file prior to the inclusion of other system header files. The notation <sys/types.h> indicates that the header file types.h can be found in the *usual place* (most often /usr/include on a UNIX-based system) in the subdirectory sys.

E X E R C I S E   1 – 1

Use the **ar** command to examine the contents of the standard C library (/usr/lib/libc.a). How many **printf**-*related* functions are archived in the standard C library?

E X E R C I S E   1 – 2

Are there any library functions/system calls that occur in more than one library? If so, name one and explain why this might be done.

1.5 MANAGING FAILURES

In most cases[2], if a system call or library function is unsuccessful it returns a value of
-1 and assigns a value to an external variable called **errno** to indicate what the actual
error is. The defined constants for all error codes can be found in the header file <sys/
errno.h>. It is a good habit to have the invoking program examine the return value
from a system call or library function to determine if it was successful. If the invocation fails, the program should take an appropriate action. A common action is to display a short error message and **exit** (terminate) the program. The library function,
perror, can be used to produce an error message.

For each system call and library function discussed in detail in the text, a summary table will be given. The summary table is a condensed version of UNIX manual
page information. The format of a typical summary table (the one for **perror**) is shown
in Figure 1.2.

The summary table for **perror** indicates the header file <stdio.h> must be
included if we are to use **perror**. Notice that the header file <sys/errno.h>, which

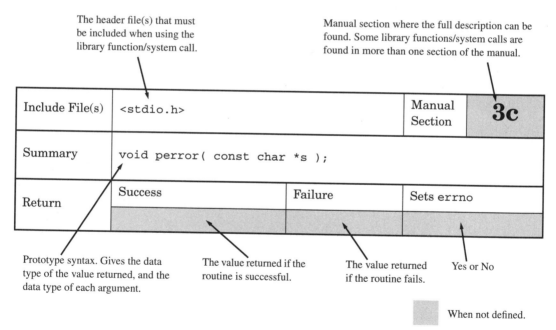

Fig. 1.2 Explanation of the summary table format.

---

2. This type of hedging is necessary since system calls that return an integer value usually return a
-1 on failure, while those that return a pointer to a character return a NULL pointer. However, as
system calls are written by a disjoint set of programmers with differing ideas on what should be
done, a return value that does not meet this rule of thumb is occasionally encountered.

was mentioned previously, is not referenced in the summary table. The <sys/errno.h> file is included *only* if the defined constants for specific error codes are to be referenced. The **perror** library function takes a single argument which is a pointer to a character string constant (i.e., const char *). In addition, the **perror** library function does not return a value (as indicated by the data type void) and will not modify **errno** if it fails.

A program example using systems calls that provides some error checking by **perror** and **errno** is shown in Program 1.2.

Program 1.2 Using errno and perror.

```
/*
 *   Checking errno and using perror
 */
#include <stdio.h>
#include <unistd.h>
#include <stdlib.h>
extern int         errno;
void
main(int argc, char *argv[ ]) {
  int               n_char = 0, buffer[10];
  /*
   *   Initially n_char is set to 0 -- errno is 0 by default
   */
  printf("n_char = %d \t errno = %d \n", n_char, errno);
  /*
   *   Display a prompt to stdout
   */
  n_char = write(1, "Enter a word ", 14);
  /*
   *   Use the read system call to obtain 10 characters from stdin
   */
  n_char = read(0, buffer, 10);
  printf("\nn_char = %d \t errno = %d \n", n_char, errno);
  /*
   *    If the read has failed ...
   */
  if (n_char == -1) {
    perror(argv[0]);
    exit(1);
  }
  /*
   *    Display the characters read
   */
  n_char = write(1, buffer, n_char);
}
```

Notice that to use the **errno** variable it must first be declared as an external (extern) integer. If this program is run, the initial output indicates that both n_char and **errno** contain the value 0. If the user enters the word *testing* when prompted, the output will be:

Fig. 1.3 Initial run of Program 1.2 with no errors.

```
% a.out
n_char = 0          errno = 0
Enter a word testing

n_char = 8          errno = 0
testing
```

In this case the **read** system call did not fail and has instead, as defined in the manual page, returned the number of characters read from standard input (the keyboard). Note, as we have used **read** in the program, not **scanf**, the newline will be one of the characters that is read and counted. As there was no error, the value in **errno** was not modified and remained at 0. If we run the program again and enter more than 10 characters when prompted (in hopes of generating an error) the output becomes:

Fig. 1.4 Second run of Program 1.2 with additional keyboard input.

```
% a.out
n_char = 0          errno = 0
Enter a word testing further

n_char = 10         errno = 0
testing fu%rther Command not found.
%
```

This time the program reads exactly 10 characters and displays them. The remaining characters are left in the input buffer and end up being processed by the system after the program finishes execution. This produces the output of the strange line: testing fu%rther Command not found. The characters: testing fu are displayed by the program. The Command not found message is generated by the operating system when it attempts to execute the leftover input, i.e., rther as a command. In this case, providing more input values than needed (i.e., extra characters) does not cause the **read** system call to fail and **errno** is not changed.

However, if we change the file number for the **read** system call to 3, (a file number that we have not opened, versus 0 [standard input] which is automatically opened for us by the operating system when the program runs) the **read** system call will fail and the program output will be:

Fig. 1.5 Third run of Program 1.2 with an induced error.

```
n_char = 0          errno = 0
Enter a word
n_char = -1              errno = 9
a.out: Bad file number
%
```

As expected, this time the return value from the **read** system call is -1. The external variable **errno** now contains the value 9 which is equivalent to the symbolic constant EBADF defined in the <sys/errno.h> file. If we call **perror** with a NULL argument: "", the message "Bad file number" will be displayed (the error message the system associates with error code 9). As noted, **perror** does take one argument: a character pointer. If passed a character pointer to a valid string, **perror** will display the referenced string followed by a colon ":" and then append its predefined error message. Programmers often use the argument to **perror** to qualify the error message (e.g., pass the name of the executing program as was done in the prior example) or in the case of file manipulation, pass the name of the current file. Unfortunately, **perror** issues a new line following the error message it produces, thus preventing the user from appending additional information to the **perror** display line. There are two ways around this oversight.

Associated with **perror** are two additional external variables. These variables are extern char *sys_errlist[ ] and extern int sys_nerr. The external variable sys_nerr contains the largest error message number value, while sys_errlist is a pointer to an external character array of error messages. In place of calling **perror** to return the specific error, we may (if we have provided the proper declarations) use the value in **errno** to index the sys_errlist[ ] array to obtain the error message directly. Another approach to error message generation is to use the library function, **strerror** (see Table 1.1).

Table 1.1 Summary of the **strerror** library function.

Include File(s)	<string.h>	Manual Section	**3c**
Summary	char *strerror(int errnum);		
Return	Success	Failure	Sets errno
	Pointer to error message		

The **strerror** function will map the integer errnum argument (which can be the **errno** value) to an error message and returns a pointer to the message. The error message generated by **strerror** should be the same as the message generated by **perror**.

Note that the system never clears the **errno** variable (even after a successful system call). It will always contain the value assigned by the system for the last failed call. Appendix B, **UNIX Error Messages**, contains additional information on error messages.

E X E R C I S E   1 – 3

Write a program to display all of the available system error messages in a numbered two-columns-per-line-format. Is there an error message for error number 0? Should there be?

E X E R C I S E   1 – 4

The first argument to the **read/write** system call is an integer value indicating the file descriptor. When a program executes, the operating system will automatically open three file descriptors: **stdin** (standard input which defaults to the keyboard and is referenced by the value 0), **stdout** (standard output which defaults to the terminal [screen] and is referenced by the value 1) and **stderr** (standard error which defaults to the console device and is referenced by the value 2). If the last **write** in Program 1.2 is written to 0 (standard input) the program will still compile, run, produce output and **NOT** generate an error message—why is this?

E X E R C I S E   1 – 5

Write your own error messaging function that is called when a file manipulation failure occurs. The function should provide a more descriptive, *user friendly* interface than **perror**. It might be helpful to examine the header file <sys/errno.h> and the manual page entry for **Intro** in section 2 (i.e., man -s2 Intro) prior to starting this assignment.

1.6 EXECUTABLE FILE FORMAT

In a UNIX environment, source files that have been compiled into an executable form to be run by the system are put into a special format called **a.out** format. Files in a.out format contain a header entry (for specifying hardware/program characteristics), program text, data, relocation information, symbol table and string table information. Files in a.out format are marked as executable by the operating system and may be run by entering their name on the command line. To make the issue no less confusing, when C program files are compiled the compiler, by default, places the executable file in a file called a.out.

E X E R C I S E   1 – 6

The layout of the header entry of an a.out format file is defined by the **exec** structure. Depending on the version of UNIX you are using, the form of this structure can be found in one of the following header files: <sys/a.out.h> or <sys/exec.h>. Write a short C program that will read the name of a file passed on the command line and determine if the file named is in a.out format and, if so, on what architecture (hardware) type the file will run. Note, the system utility **file**, which identifies file types, uses the information in the file /etc/magic to identify files. An alternate approach to this exercise would be to use the /etc/magic information to identify an a.out file and the architecture on which it will execute.

1.7 SYSTEM MEMORY

In UNIX, when an executable program is read into system memory by the kernel and executed, it becomes a process. We can consider system memory to be divided into two distinct regions or spaces. First is **user space**, which is where user processes will run. The system will manage individual user processes within this space and prevent them from interfering with one another. Processes in user space, termed **user processes**, are said to be in **user mode**. Second is a region called **kernel space,** which is where the kernel executes and provides its services. As noted previously, user processes can only access kernel space through system calls. When the user process runs a portion of the kernel code via a system call, the process is known temporarily as a **kernel process** and is said to be in **kernel mode.** While in kernel mode the process will have special (root) privileges and access to key system data structures. This change in mode, from user to kernel, is called a **context switch**.

1.8 PROCESS MEMORY

When residing in system memory, the user process, like Gaul, is divided into three segments or regions; **text**, **data** and **stack**.

☞ **text segment**—The text segment (sometimes called the instruction segment) contains the executable program code and constant data. The text segment is marked by the operating system as read-only and cannot be modified by the process. Multiple processes can share the same text segment. Processes share the text segment if a second copy of the program is to be executed concurrently. In this setting the system references the previously loaded text segment rather than reloading a duplicate. If needed, shared text, which is the default when using the C compiler, can be turned off by using the -N option on the compile line. In Program 1.1, the executable code for the functions **main** and **showit** would be found in the text segment.

☞ **data segment**—The data segment, which is contiguous (in a virtual sense) with the text segment, can be subdivided into initialized data (e.g., in C, variables that are declared as static or are static by virtue of their placement) and uninitialized data. In Program 1.1, the pointer variable **cptr** would be found in the initialized area and the variable **buffer1** in the uninitialized area. During its execution lifetime, a process may request additional data segment space. In Program 1.1 the call to the library routine **malloc** in the **showit** function is a request for additional data segment space. Library memory allocation routines (e.g., **malloc**, **calloc**, etc.) in turn make use of the system calls **brk** and **sbrk** to extend the size of the data segment. The newly allocated space is added to the end of the current uninitialized data area. This area of available memory is sometimes called the **heap**. In Figure 1.6 this region of memory is labeled as unmapped.

☞ **stack segment**—The stack segment is used by the process for the storage of automatic identifiers, register variables and function call information. The identifier i in the function **main,** buffer2 in the function **showit,** and stack frame information stored when the **showit** function is called within the **for** loop would be found in the stack segment. As needed the stack segment grows toward the uninitialized data segment. The area *beyond* the stack contains the command line arguments and environment variables for the process. The actual location of the stack is system dependent.

1.9 THE ᴜ AREA

In addition to the text, data and stack segments, the operating system also maintains for each process, a region called the **u area** (user area). The u area contains information specific to the process (e.g., open files, current directory, signal actions, accounting information, etc.) and a system stack segment for process use. If the process makes a system call (e.g., the system call to **write** in the function **main** in Program 1.1), the stack frame information for the system call would be stored in the system stack segment. Again, this information is kept by the operating system in an area that the process does not normally have access to. Thus, if this information is needed, the process must use special system calls to access it. Like the process itself, the contents of the u area for the process are paged in and out by the operating system. The layout of the u area is defined in detail in the header file <sys/user.h>.

The conceptual relationship of system and process memory is illustrated in Figure 1.6.

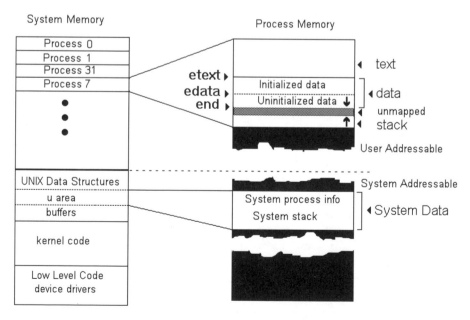

Fig. 1.6 System and process memory.

1.10 Process Memory Addresses

The system keeps track of the virtual addresses associated with each user process segment. This address information is available to the process and can be obtained by referencing the external variables etext, edata and end. The *addresses* (not the contents) of these three variables correspond respectively to the first valid address above the text, initialized data and uninitialized data segments. Program 1.3 shows how this information can be displayed.

Program 1.3 Displaying segment address information.

```
/*
 *  Displaying process segment addresses
 */
#include <stdio.h>
extern int      etext, edata, end;
void
main(void){
  printf("etext: %6X \t edata: %6X \t end: %6X \n",
       &etext, &edata, &end);
}
```

If we add a few lines of code to Program 1.1, we can verify the virtual address location of key identifiers in our program. Program 1.4 incorporates a macro, SHW_ADR( ), to display the address of an identifier.

Program 1.4 Confirming Program 1.1 address locations.

```
/*
 *  Program 1.1 modified to display identifier addresses
 */
#include <stdio.h>
#include <string.h>
#include <sys/types.h>
#include <stdlib.h>
#include <unistd.h>

#define SHW_ADR(ID,I) printf("The id %s \t is at adr:%8X\n",ID,&I)
extern int      etext, edata, end;

char            *cptr = "Hello World\n"; /* static by placement */
char            buffer1[25];

void
main(void){
  void          showit(char *);         /* function prototype  */
  int           i = 0;                   /* automatic variable  */
                                        /* display segment adr */
  printf("Adr etext: %8X \t Adr edata: %8X \t Adr end: %8X \n\n",
       &etext, &edata, &end);
  SHW_ADR("main", main);                /* display addresses   */
  SHW_ADR("showit", showit);
  SHW_ADR("cptr", cptr);
  SHW_ADR("buffer1", buffer1);
```

```
      SHW_ADR("i", I);
      strcpy(buffer1, "A demonstration\n");    /* library function */
      write(1, buffer1, strlen(buffer1) + 1); /* system call       */
      for (; i < 1; ++i)
         showit(cptr);                          /* function call     */
}
void
showit(char *p){
   char           *buffer2;
   SHW_ADR("buffer2", buffer2);
   if ((buffer2=(char *)malloc((unsigned)(strlen(p)+1))) != NULL){
      strcpy(buffer2, p);                      /* copy the string   */
      printf("%s", buffer2);                   /* display the string */
      free(buffer2);                           /* release location  */
   } else {
      printf("Allocation error.\n");
      exit(1);
   }
}
```

A run of this program produces output that verifies our assertions concerning the range of addresses for identifiers of different storage types. Note, the actual addresses displayed by the program are system dependent.

Fig. 1.7 Output of Program 1.4.

```
Adr etext: 2990 Adr edata:20108 Adr end: 20138
The id main       is at adr:    2326
The id showit     is at adr:    243E
The id cptr       is at adr:    200F0
The id buffer1    is at adr:   20108
The id i          is at adr: DFFFC18
A demonstration
The id buffer2    is at adr: DFFFC08
Hello World
```

The output of Program 1.4 is presented pictorially in Figure 1.8.

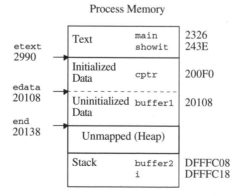

Fig. 1.8 Address locations in Program 1.4.

EXERCISE   1 – 7

Investigate the UNIX commands **limit** and **size**. How does the information these commands report relate to the values of etext, edata and end?

EXERCISE   1 – 8

In addition to etext, edata and end, all programs have a **break** value (the first valid address beyond the data segment for the program) which is initially set to the address of end. By definition the break value should change as the system allocates—frees memory. Is this true on your system? Does the break value change when **malloc** and **free** are used? Write a program that supports your answer. Read the manual pages on the system call, **sbrk,** *carefully* before doing this assignment. Is the warning in the manual page warranted?

1.11 CREATING A PROCESS

It is apparent that there must be some mechanism by which the system can create a new process. With the exception of some initial processes generated by the kernel during bootstrapping (e.g., **swapper, init** and **pagedaemon**) , all processes in a UNIX environment are created by a **fork** system call, shown in Table 1.2. The initiating process is termed the **parent** and the newly generated process the **child**.

Table 1.2 Summary of the **fork** system call.

Include File(s)	`<sys/types.h>` `<unistd.h>`		Manual Section	**2**
Summary*	`pid_t fork( void );`			
Return	Success	Failure	Sets errno	
	0 in child, child PID in parent	-1	Yes	

*The include file `<sys/type.h>` contains the definition of pid_t, and the include file `<unistd.h>` contains the declaration for the **fork** system call.

The **fork** system call does not take an argument. If the **fork** system call fails it will return a -1 and set the value in **errno** to indicate one of the error conditions shown in Table 1.3.

Otherwise, when successful, **fork** returns the process ID of the child process in the parent process, and it returns a 0 in the child process. By checking the return value from **fork,** a process can easily determine if it is a parent or child process. A par-

Table 1.3 `fork` error messages[*].

#	Constant	`perror` Message	Explanation
11	EAGAIN	Resource temporarily unavailable	• System limit for total number of processes for single user is exceeded. • Available system memory for raw I/O is insufficient.
12	ENOMEM	Not enough space	Insufficient swap space available to generate another process.

[*]If the library function/system call sets **errno** and can fail in *multiple* ways, the summary table will be followed by an error message table. This table will contain the error number (#), the equivalent defined constant, the message generated by a call to **perror**, and a brief explanation of the message in the current context.

ent process may generate multiple child processes, but each child process has only one parent. Figure 1.9 shows parent/child process relationships.

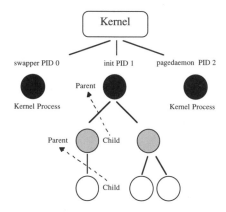

Fig. 1.9 The parent/child process relationship.

E X E R C I S E   1 – 9

When you check the process status table on a BSD-based UNIX system (see the UNIX process status command **ps**) the processes **swapper**, **init** and **pagedaemon** will be present (**sched**, **init** and **pageout** under Solaris). A search of the file system(s) will show that while there is a system program called **init** (most often found as /sbin/init) there is no system program file for these other processes. Why is this?

When a **fork** system call is made, the operating system generates a copy of the parent process which becomes the child process. The operating system will pass to the child process most of the parent's system information (e.g., open file descriptors, environment information, etc.). However, some information is unique to the child process:

☞ The child has its own process ID (PID).

☞ The child will have a different parent process ID (PPID) than its parent.

☞ System imposed process limits (e.g., amount of CPU time the process is allotted) are reset to zero.

☞ All record locks on files are reset.

☞ The action to be taken when receiving signals is different.

A program that uses the **fork** system call is shown in Program 1.5.

Program 1.5 Generating a child process.

```
/*
 *  First example of a fork system call (no error check)
 */
#include <stdio.h>
#include <sys/types.h>
#include <unistd.h>

void
main(void) {
  printf("Hello\n");
  fork( );
  printf("bye\n");
}
```

The output of the program is:

Fig. 1.10 Output of Program 1.5.

```
% a.out
Hello
bye
bye
```

Notice that the statement `printf("bye\n");` only occurs once in the program, but the run of the program produces the word "bye" twice—once by the parent process and once by the child process. A more detailed description of the **fork** system call and its uses can be found in Chapter 3, **Using Processes**.

1.12 SUMMARY

Processes are instances of executable programs that are run by the operating system. Programs make use of predefined functions to implement their tasks. Some of these predefined functions are actually system calls. System calls request the kernel to directly perform a task for the process. Other predefined functions are library functions. Library functions, which may indirectly contain system calls, also perform tasks for the process, but in a less intrusive manner. The object code for system calls and library functions is stored in object code format in library files. The object code for system calls and library functions is included, on an as-needed basis, when a program is compiled.

When a system call or library function fails, the external variable **errno** can be examined to determine the reason for failure. The library functions **perror** or **strerror** can be used to generate a descriptive error message.

Executing programs are placed in system memory. The executable code and constant data for the program are placed in a region known as the text segment. The initialized and uninitialized program data is placed in the data segment. The program stack segment is used to handle automatic program variables and function call data. In addition, the system will keep process specific information and system call data in the user area (u area) of memory.

Processes are generated by the **fork** system call. A newly generated process inherits the majority of its state information from its parent.

## CHAPTER 2

Processing Environment

2.1 INTRODUCTION

All processes have a processing environment (not to be confused with environment *variables* that are, as we will see, part of the processing environment). The processing environment consists of a unique set of information and conditions that is determined by the current state of the system and by the parent of the process. A process can access processing environment information and, in some cases, modify it. This is accomplished either directly or by using system calls or library functions.

2.2 PROCESS ID

Associated with each process is a unique positive integer identification number called a process ID (**PID**). As process IDs are allocated sequentially, when a system is booted a few system processes, which are initiated only once, will always be assigned the same unique process ID. In BSD-based UNIX, the **swapper** process (responsible for process scheduling) is process 0, **init** (whose basic responsibility is the managing of terminal lines and who is the parent process of all other UNIX processes) is process 1, and **pagedaemon** (responsible for paging) is process 2. In a Solaris environment, process 0 is **sched**, process 1 **init**, and process 2 **pageout**. While some of the process names are different they are similar in function to their BSD counterparts. Other pro-

cesses are assigned free **PID**s of increasing value until the maximum system value for
a process ID is reached. The maximum value for process IDs can be found as the
defined constant, MAXPID, in the header file <sys/param.h>. When the highest **PID**
has been assigned, the system will wrap around and begin to reuse lower **PID** numbers not currently in use.

    The system call **getpid** can be used to obtain the process ID (Table 2.1). The **get-
pid** system call does not accept an argument. If it is successful it will return the process ID number. If the calling process does not have the proper access permissions the
getpid call will fail, returning a value of -1 and setting **errno** to EPERM (1).

Table 2.1 Summary of the **getpid** system call.

Include File(s)	<sys/types.h> <unistd.h>		Manual Section	**2**
Summary	`pid_t getpid( void );`			
Return	Success	Failure	Sets errno	
	The process ID	-1	Yes	

    A process can determine its own process ID by use of the **getpid** system call as
shown in the following code segment:

```
printf("My PID is %d \n", getpid( ));
```

    The **getpid** system call is of limited use. Usually the process ID will be different
on each invocation of the program. The manual page entry for **getpid** notes that the
most common use for this system call is the generation of unique temporary file
names. However, for everyday use, the library functions **tmpnam** and **tempnam** are much
better suited for the production of unique temporary file names.

2.3 PARENT PROCESS ID

Every process has an associated parent process ID (**PPID**). The parent process is the
process that forked the child process. The parent process ID can be obtained by using
the system call **getppid** (Table 2.2).

    Like the **getpid** system call, **getppid** does not require an argument. If it is suc-
cessful it will return the process ID number of the parent process. The **getppid** call
will fail, returning a value of -1 and setting **errno** to EPERM (1) if the calling process
does not have the proper access permissions.

    The following code segment displays the parent process ID:

```
printf("My Parent Process ID is %d \n", getppid( ));
```

    Unfortunately, there is no system call that allows a parent process to determine
the process IDs of all its child processes. If such information is needed, the parent pro-

Table 2.2 Summary of the `getppid` system call.

Include File(s)	`<sys/types.h>` `<unistd.h>`		Manual Section	**2**
Summary	`pid_t getppid( void );`			
Return	Success	Failure	Sets `errno`	
	The parent process ID	-1	Yes	

cess should save the returned child process ID value from the **fork** system call as each child process is created.

EXERCISE   2 – 1

The manual page entry for the **getppid** system call does not specifically indicate what is returned by **getppid** if the parent process is no longer present when the **getppid** call is made. Write a program that displays the value returned by **getppid** when such an event occurs (the parent predeceases the child). How did you assure that the parent process was not present when the child process made its **getppid** call?

2.4 PROCESS GROUP ID

Every process belongs to a process group that is identified by an integer process group ID value. When a process generates child processes, the operating system will automatically create a process group. The initial parent process is known as the **process leader**. The process leader's process ID will be the same as its process group ID[1]. Additional process group members generated by the process group leader inherit the same process group ID. The operating system uses process group relationships to distribute signals to groups of processes. For example, should a process group leader receive a kill or hang-up signal causing it to terminate, then all processes in its group will also be passed the same terminating signal. A process can find its process group ID from the system call **getpgid**. In some versions of UNIX you may find the **getpgid** system call absent. In these versions the system call **getpgrp** (which requires no process ID argument) provides the same functionality as the **getpgid** system call. The **getpgid** system call is defined as shown in Table 2.3.

If successful, this call will return the process group ID for the pid that is passed. If the value of pid is 0, the call is for the current process (eliminating the need for a separate call to **getpid**). If the **getpgid** system call fails, a -1 is returned and the value in **errno** is set to one of the values in Table 2.4 to indicate the source of the error.

A short program using the **getpgid** system call is shown in Program 2.1.

---

1. Ah-ha—other than generating temporary file names, a place to use the **getpid** system call!

Table 2.3 Summary of the `getpgid` system call.

Include File(s)	`<sys/types.h>` `<unistd.h>`		Manual Section	**2**
Summary	`pid_t getpgid( pid_t pid );`			
Return	Success	Failure	Sets errno	
	The process group ID	-1	Yes	

Table 2.4 `getpgid` error messages.

#	**Constant**	`perror` **Message**	**Explanation**
1	EPERM	Not owner	Invalid access permissions for the calling process.
3	ESRCH	No such process	No such process ID as `pid`.

Program 2.1 Displaying process group IDs.

```
/*
 *       Displaying process group ID information
 */
#include <stdio.h>
#include <sys/types.h>
#include <unistd.h>

void
main( void ){
  int           i;
  printf("\n\nInitial process \t PID %6d \t PPID %6d \t GID %6d\n\n",
        getpid(), getppid(), getpgid(0));
  for (i = 0; i < 3; ++i)
    if (fork( ) == 0)                    /* Generate some processes */
      printf("New process     \t\t PID %6d \t PPID %6d \t GID %6d\n",
          getpid(), getppid(), getpgid(0));
}
```

When run, the output of the program is:

Fig. 2.1 Program 2.1 output.

```
Initial process            PID  22025   PPID  21292   GID 22025
New process                PID  22026   PPID  22025   GID 22025
New process                PID  22027   PPID  22026   GID 22025
New process                PID  22029   PPID  22026   GID 22025
New process                PID  22028   PPID  22027   GID 22025
New process                PID  22030   PPID  22025   GID 22025
New process                PID  22031   PPID      1   GID 22025
New process                PID  22032   PPID  22025   GID 22025
```

Note that the actual ID numbers will change each time the program is run. The relationship of the processes within the process group is shown in Figure 2.2.

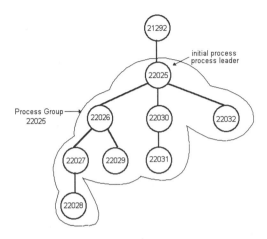

Fig. 2.2 Process ID relationships.

All of the processes generated by the program indicate that they belong to the same process group, i.e., the process group of the initial process 22025. Notice that the process identified as PID 22031 indicates a parent process ID (**PPID**) of 1, *not* 22030 as shown in Figure 2.2. If the parent of a process dies[2] (terminates), the process init (which is process ID 1) will inherit the process and become its *foster* parent. The process group ID for a process does not change if this inheritance occurs.

A process may change its process group by using the system call **setpgid**, which sets the process group ID (Table 2.5).

Table 2.5 Summary of the **setpgid** system call.

Include File(s)	<sys/types.h> <unistd.h>		Manual Section	**2**
Summary	pid_t setpgid(pid_t pid, pid_t pgrp);			
Return	Success	Failure	Sets errno	
	0	-1	Yes	

The **setpgid** system call will set the process group `pid` to that of `pgrp`. If the value for `pid` is 0, the call refers to the current process. Otherwise, the call refers to

---

2. There seems to be no end to the anthropomorphic references for parent/child processes, even when they border on the macabre!

the specified process ID. The value for pgrp represents the group to which the process will belong. If the value for pgrp is 0, the pid referenced process will become the process leader. For this call to be successful the invoking process must have the correct permissions to institute the requested change. The **setpgid** system call returns 0 if successful, or returns a -1 and sets **errno** if it fails. The value **errno** is assigned when **setpgid** fails is given in Table 2.6.

Table 2.6 setpgid error messages.

#	Constant	perror Message	Explanation
1	EPERM	Not owner	• Process pid already a session leader. • Process pid is not in same session as calling process. • Invalid process group specified
3	ESRCH	No such process	No such process ID as pid.
13	EACCES	Permission denied	Process pid has executed an exec.
22	EINVAL	Invalid argument	• The pgrp value is less than 0 or greater than PID_MAX-1.

Note, for those of us who talk fast or listen casually it is easy to confuse the *process group* ID with the process's *group* ID. A process's group ID is covered in the section on **Real and Effective User and Group IDs**.

In addition to process groups, UNIX also supports the concept of a session. A session is a collection of related and unrelated processes and process groups. As with process grouping, there are a number of system calls that can be used to create and manipulate a session.

E X E R C I S E   2 – 2

Modify Program 2.1 so that each new process becomes its own group leader.

2.5 PERMISSIONS

All UNIX files (executable and otherwise) have an associated set of owner permission bits that are used by the operating system to determine access. The permission bits are grouped into three sets of three bits each. Each bit within a set determines if a file can be read, written to or executed. The three sets correspond to three classes of users: the file **owner**, those in the file owner's **group** and all **other** users. We can think of the nine permission bits as representing a three-digit octal number as shown in Figure 2.3. This permission set would indicate that the file owner has read, write and execute permission; group members have read and write permission; and all others have execute-only permission.

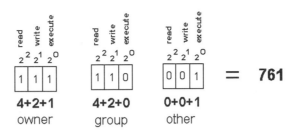

Fig. 2.3 File permissions as octal values.

At a system level, the permissions of a file are modified using the **chmod** command. The permissions of a file can be listed with the **ls** command using the -1 (long format) flag. For example, in the **ls** command output shown in Figure 2.4, the file owner (**root**) of the file (**vmunix**) has permission to read (**r**), write (**w**) and execute (**x**) the file. Members of the file owner's group can read and execute the file, as can users classified as other. The group name is not shown in this example. In some versions of UNIX, the group name is shown by default when issuing the **ls -1** command, and in other forms of UNIX (such as *true-blue* BSD), the **-g** flag must be added to the command (i.e., **ls -1g**) to obtain the group name.

Fig. 2.4 File permissions displayed by **ls**.

The interpretation of the permission bits for directories is slightly different than for files. When the file is a directory, setting the read bit indicates the directory can be read or displayed. Setting the write bit indicates files or links can be added or removed from the directory, and setting execute permission indicates traversal permission is granted. If traversal permission is *not* set, the directory name can only be used as part of a path name but cannot be examined directly.

E X E R C I S E   2 – 3

Is the owner of a file also a member of the class "other"? If the file protections on a file are set so that only those in the class "other" have read/write/execute access, does the owner still have access to the file? Is this reasonable? Why?

When generating files in UNIX, such as by I/O redirection, or compiling a source program into an executable, the operating system will assign permissions to the file.

The default permissions assigned to the file are determined by a bitwise operation on two three-digit octal mask values. These mask values are the **creation mask** and the **umask**. Unless otherwise specified (such as when creating or opening a file within a program), the creation mask used by the system is 777 for executable and directory files and 666 for text files. The default umask value is set by the system administrator and is most commonly 022. If you want to change the value of umask, and would like the value available to all your processes, insert the command **umask** nnn (where nnn is the new value for umask) in your startup .login (or .profile) file.

At a system level the current umask value may be displayed/modified by using the **umask** command. An example using the **umask** command follows:

Fig. 2.5 Using the **umask** command.

```
% umask
022
% umask 011
% umask
011
```

When a new file is created, the system will exclusive **OR** (**XOR**) the creation mask for the file with the current umask value. The exclusive **OR** operation acts the same as a subtract (without any borrow) of the umask value from the creation mask. The net result determines the permissions for the new file. For example, generating a text file called foo using command line I/O redirection, as shown:

Fig. 2.6 Generating a plain text file using I/O redirection.

```
% cat > foo
hello foo
^d
```

---

will set the permissions for the text file, foo, to 644 (666 minus 022). This is verified by the output of the **ls** command using the **-l** option:

Fig. 2.7 The default permissions of a plain text file.

```
% ls -l foo
-rw-r--r--  1 gray           10 Nov 15 10:41 foo
```

If we generate a directory (or executable file such as a.out using the C compiler), the default permissions, using the 022 umask, will be 755 (777 minus 022). For example:

Fig. 2.8 The default permission of a directory entry.

```
% mkdir bar
% ls -ld bar
drwxr-xr-x  2 gray          512 Nov 15 10:41 bar
```

The use of system calls **chmod**, **stat** (file status information) and **umask** which allow a process access to this information is presented in the section on **File System Information.**

2.6 REAL AND EFFECTIVE USER AND GROUP IDs

In UNIX, with the exception of a few special system processes, processes are generated by users (root and otherwise) who have logged on to the system. During the login process the system queries the password file[3] to obtain two identification (ID) numbers. The numbers the system obtains are in the third and fourth fields of the password entry for the user. These are, respectively, the **real user ID (UID)** and **real group ID (GID)** for the user. For example, in the sample password file entry:

```
drubin:ZRvOQccnuCFtw:118:25:Dan Rubin:/usr4/accounts/guest/drubin:/bin/csh
```

the user login drubin has a real user ID of 118 and a group ID of 25. The real user ID should be (if the system administrator is on the ball) a unique integer value, while the real group ID (also an integer value) may be common to several logins. Group ID numbers should map to the group names stored in the file /etc/group[4]. The maximum value for a user or group ID can be found as the defined constant value **MAXID** in the file <sys/param.h>. In general, IDs of less than 100 usually indicate user logins with special status.

For every process the system also keeps a second set of IDs called effective IDs, the **effective user ID** (EUID) and **effective group ID** (EGID). The operating system will use the real IDs to identify the *real user* for things such as process accounting or sending mail, and the effective IDs to determine what additional permissions should be granted to the process. Most of the time the real and effective IDs for a process are identical. However, there are occasions when non-privileged users on a system must be allowed to access/modify privileged files (such as the password file). To allow controlled access to key files, UNIX has an additional set of file permissions (known as set-user-ID (SUID) and set-group-ID (SGID) that can be specified by the file's owner. When indicated, these permissions tell the operating system that, when the program is run, the resulting process should have the privileges of the owner/group of the program (versus the real user/group privileges associated with the process). In these instances, the effective IDs for the process become those indicated for the file's owner. A listing for a **suid** program is shown below:

```
-rwsr-xr-x  5 root        32768 Oct 11  1990 /usr/bin/passwd
```

---

3. In older versions of UNIX the complete password file (passwd) was found in the /etc directory. In newer versions, for security reasons, the password file, while still present, may have some of its pertinent information stored elsewhere (such as in the file /etc/shadow). While the /etc/passwd file is readable by the ordinary user, supplemental password files usually are not.

4. If, for some reason, there is no group name for the assigned group number, the system will display the group number when you issue the **ls -lg** command.

As shown, this passwd program has its owner permissions set to **rws.** The letter **s** in the owner's category, found in place of the letter **x**, indicates that when this program is run, the process should have the privileges of the file owner (which is root). The set-user information is stored by the system in a tenth permission bit and can be modified using the system level command, **chmod.** The **suid** setting for the passwd program allows the non-privileged user running it to temporarily have root (superuser) privileges. In this case, the user running the program will be able to modify the system password file, as the permissions on the password file indicate that it is owned and can only be modified by root. Needless to say, programs that have the **suid** or **sgid** bit set should be carefully thought out, especially if the programs are owned by the superuser (root).

At a system level, the command **id** (as shown below) will display the current user, group ID and group affiliation information. Note that while a file can belong to only one group, a user can belong to many groups.

Fig. 2.9 Typical **id** information.

```
% id
uid=107(gray) gid=1(daemon) groups=1(daemon),0(wheel),101(laser)
```

In a programming environment, the system calls that return the user/group real and effective IDs for a process are given in Table 2.7.

Table 2.7 Summary of user/group real and effective ID system calls.

Include File(s)	`<sys/types.h>` `<unistd.h>`		Manual Section	**2**
Summary	`uid_t getuid(  void );` `uid_t geteuid( void );` `gid_t getgid(  void );` `gid_t getegid( void );`			
Return	Success	Failure	Sets errno	
	The requested ID			

There are corresponding system calls that can be passed ID values to set (change) the user/group real and effective IDs. However, these calls are of limited use since non-superusers are restricted to passing only the real or effective IDs of the current process.

2.7 FILE SYSTEM INFORMATION

In addition to process ID information, the process environment contains file system information. Associated with each open file is an integer file descriptor value that the operating system uses as an index to a 64-entry **file descriptor table** located in the u (user) area for the process. The per process file descriptor table references a **system file table** which is located in kernel space. In turn, the system file table maps to a **system inode table** that contains a reference to a more complete internal description of the file.

When a child process is generated, it receives a *copy* of its parent's file descriptor table (this includes the three descriptors—stdin, stdout and stderr) with the file pointer offset associated with each open file. If a file is marked as shareable, the operating system will need to save each file pointer offset separately. The relationship of process and system file tables are shown in Figure 2.10.

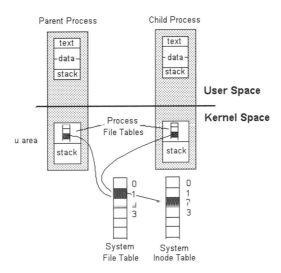

Fig. 2.10 Process/system file table relationships.

E X E R C I S E   2 – 4

Write a program that verifies that a parent and child process share the same file pointer and file pointer offset. The parent should open a text file and **fork** a child process. The child process should read from the text file and display what it has read. When the child terminates, the parent process should then read from the same file and display what it has read. At this juncture you may need to use the **sleep** system call to synchronize file access between the parent and child processes.

E X E R C I S E   2 – 5

Write a program that determines by *trial and error* the number of files a process can have simultaneously open (is it really 64 as mentioned?). Be sure to *remove* (investigate the **unlink** system call) any files that you generate.

2.8 FILE INFORMATION

There are a number of system calls that a process can use to obtain file information. Of these, the **stat** system calls provide the process with a comprehensive set of file-related information somewhat analogous to the information that can be obtained by using the system level **ls** command (Table 2.8).

Table 2.8 Summary of the **stat** system calls.

Include File(s)	`<sys/types.h>` `<sys/stat.h>`		Manual Section	**2**

Summary	`int stat (const char *path,`
	`            struct stat *buf);`
	`int lstat(const char *path,`
	`            struct stat *buf);`
	`int fstat(int fildes,`
	`            struct  stat *buf);`			

Return	Success		Failure	Sets errno
	0		-1	Yes

As its first argument, the **stat** system call takes a character pointer to a string containing the path for a file. The **lstat** system call is similar to **stat** except when the file referenced is a symbolic link. In the case of a symbolic link, **lstat** will return information about the link entry, while **stat** will return information about the actual file. The **fstat** system call takes an integer file descriptor value of an open file as its first argument.

All three **stat** system calls return, via their second argument, a pointer to a **stat** structure. The **stat** structure, which is defined in its entirety in the header file <sys/ stat.h>, normally contains members for:

```
dev_t     st_dev;      /* device file resides on */
ino_t     st_ino;      /* this file's number */
u_short   st_mode;     /* protection */
short     st_nlink;    /* number of hard links to the file */
short     st_uid;      /* user ID of owner */
short     st_gid;      /* group ID of owner */
dev_t     st_rdev;     /* the device identifier(special files only)*/
off_t     st_size;     /* total size of file, in bytes */
time_t    st_atime;    /* file data last access time */
time_t    st_mtime;    /* file data last modify time */
time_t    st_ctime;    /* file data last status change time */
long      st_blksize;  /* preferred blocksize for file system I/O*/
long      st_blocks;   /* actual number of blocks allocated */
```

The special data types (i.e., **dev_t**, **ino_t**, etc.) of individual structure members are mapped to standard data types in the header file <sys/types.h>. If the **stat** system calls are successful they return a value of 0. Otherwise they return a value of -1 and set **errno**. As these system calls reference file information there are numerous error situations that may be encountered. The value that **errno** may be assigned and an explanation of the associated **perror** message are shown in Table 2.9.

Table 2.9 stat error messages.

#	Constant	perror **Message**	Explanation
2	ENOENT	No such file or directory	File does not exist (or is NULL).
4	EINTR	Interrupted system call	Signal was caught during the system call.
9	EBADF	Bad file number	The value in fildes is not a valid open file descriptor.
13	EACCES	Permission denied	Search permission denied on part of file path.
14	EFAULT	Bad address	buf or path reference an illegal address.
20	ENOTDIR	Not a directory	Part of the specified path is not a directory.
67	ENOLINK	The link has been severed	The path value references a remote system that is no longer active.
71	EMULTIHOP	Multihop attempted	The path value requires multiple hops to remote systems but file system does not allow it.
78	ENAMETOOLONG	File name too long	The path value exceeds system path/file name length.
79	EOVERFLOW	Value too large for defined data type	A value for a member of the structure referenced by buf is too large.
90	ELOOP	Number of symbolic links encountered during path name traversal exceeds MAXSYMLINKS	The **perror** message says it all.

A program showing the use of the **stat** system call is shown in Program 2.2.

Program 2.2 Using the **stat** system call.

```
/*
   Using the stat system call
*/

#include <stdio.h>
#include <unistd.h>
#include <sys/types.h>
```

```
#include <sys/stat.h>
#include <stdlib.h>
#define  N_BITS 3
void
main(int argc, char *argv[ ]){
   unsigned int    i, mask = 0700;
   struct stat     buff;
   static char     *perm[] = {"---", "--x", "-w-", "-wx",
                              "r--", "r-x", "rw-", "rwx"};

   if (argc > 1) {
     if ((stat(argv[1], &buff) != -1)) {
       printf("Permissions for %s ", argv[1]);
       for (i = 3; i; --i) {
         printf("%3s",perm[(buff.st_mode & mask) >> (i-1)*N_BITS]);
         mask >>= N_BITS;
       }
       putchar('\n');
     } else {
       perror(argv[1]);
       exit(1);
     }
   } else {
     fprintf(stderr, "Usage: %s file_name\n", argv[0]);
   }
}
```

When this program is run and passed its own name on the command line, the output is:

Fig. 2.11 Output of Program 2.2.

```
% a.out a.out
Permissions for a.out rwxr-xr-x
```

The system command sequence **ls -l** for the same file produces the same set of permissions:

Fig. 2.12 Verifying Program 2.2 output with the **ls** command.

```
% ls -l a.out
-rwxr-xr-x  1 gray           24576 Nov 16 10:02 a.out
```

E X E R C I S E   2 − 6

Modify the example **stat** program so that its output is as *close* as possible to the **ls -l** output on your system when passed a file or directory name on the command line. Note, the **stat** call will not return the user's name (only the **UID**). The **UID** can be passed to the **getpwuid** library call. The **getpwuid** call will return the user's name (along with additional password entry information). A description of the **getpwuid** library call is found in section 3C of the manual. If needed, a second library call, **getgrgid**, can be used to map the **GID** value to the actual group name.

In a programming environment, the access permissions of a file can be modified with the **chmod/fchmod** system calls (Table 2.10).

Table 2.10 Summary of the **chmod/fchmod** system calls.

Include File(s)	`<sys/types.h>` `<sys/stat.h>`	Manual Section	**2**

Summary	`int chmod( const char *path,`
	`            mode_t mode );`
	`int fchmod( int fildes,`
	`            mode_t mode );`		

Return	Success	Failure	Sets errno
	0	-1	Yes

Both system calls accomplish the same action and only differ in the format of their first argument. The **chmod** system call takes a character pointer reference to a file path as its first argument, while **fchmod** takes an integer file descriptor value of an open file. The second argument for both system calls is the mode. The mode can be specified literally as an octal number (e.g., 0755) or by bitwise ORing together combinations of defined permission constants found in the header file `<sys/stat.h>`. Unless the effective user ID of the process is that of the superuser, the effective user ID and the owner of the file whose permissions are to be changed must be the same. If either system call is successful, it returns a 0. Otherwise, the call returns a -1 and sets the value in **errno**. As with the **stat** system calls the number of error conditions is quite extensive (see Table 2.11).

Table 2.11 **chmod/fchmod** error messages.

#	Constant	perror **Message**	**Explanation**
1	EPERM	Not owner	Not owner or file or superuser.
2	ENOENT	No such file or directory	File does not exist (or is NULL).
4	EINTR	Interrupted system call	Signal was caught during the system call.
5	EIO	I/O error	I/O error while attempting read or write to file system.
9	EBADF	Bad file number	The value in `fildes` is not a valid open file descriptor.
13	EACCES	Permission denied	Search permission denied on part of file path.
14	EFAULT	Bad address	`path` references an illegal address.

Table 2.11 `chmod/fchmod` error messages. (Continued)

#	Constant	`perror` **Message**	**Explanation**
20	ENOTDIR	Not a directory	Part of the specified `path` is not a directory.
30	EROFS	Read-only file system	File referenced by `path` is on read-only file system.
67	ENOLINK	The link has been severed	The `path` value references a remote system that is no longer active.
74	EMULTIHOP	Multihop attempted	The `path` value requires multiple hops to remote systems but file system does not allow it.
78	ENAMETOOLONG	File name too long	The `path` value exceeds system path/file name length.
90	ELOOP	Number of symbolic links encountered during path name traversal exceeds MAXSYMLINKS	The **perror** message says it all.

The umask mask value, which is inherited from the parent process, may be modified by a process with the **umask** system call (Table 2.12).

Table 2.12 Summary of the **umask** system call.

Include File(s)	`<sys/types.h>` `<sys/stat.h>`		Manual Section	**2**
Summary	`mode_t umask( mode_t cmask );`			
Return	Success	Failure	Sets `errno`	
	The previous umask			

When invoked, **umask** both changes the umask value to the integer value passed and returns the old (previous) umask value[5]. If you use the **umask** system call to determine the *current* umask setting, you should call **umask** a second time, passing it the value returned from the first call, to restore the settings to their initial state.

---

5. This system call appears to have been written before such techniques were frowned upon (i.e., both changing the state of the umask and returning its current value).

EXERCISE   2 − 7

The **umask** system call will never generate an error or set the value in **errno**. Why is this?

The library function **getcwd** is used to find the current working directory of a process. The function is defined as shown in Table 2.13. It will return a pointer to the current directory pathname. The function expects two arguments. The first is a pointer to the location where the pathname should be stored. If this argument is set to NULL, **getcwd** will use **malloc** to automatically allocate storage space. The second argument is the length of the pathname to be returned (plus 1 for the \0 to terminate the string). The include file <sys/parm.h> contains the defined constant **MAXPATHLEN** that could be used to assure a buffer of sufficient size (i.e., **MAXPATHLEN**+1). If **getcwd** fails, it will return a NULL and will set **errno** (Table 2.13).

Table 2.13 Summary of the **getcwd** library function.

Include File(s)	<unistd.h>		Manual Section	**3c**
Summary	extern char *getcwd(char *buf, size_t size);			
Return	Success	Failure	Sets errno	
	A pointer to the current directory name	NULL	Yes	

Table 2.14 **getcwd** error messages.

#	Constant	perror **Message**	**Explanation**
13	EACCES	Permission denied	Search permission denied on part of file path.
22	EINVAL	Invalid argument	The value for size is less than or equal to 0.
34	ERANGE	Result too large	The value for size is greater than 0 but less than the length of the path plus 1.

The system call **chdir** is used to change the current working directory (as is the **cd**[6] command at system level). See Table 2.15.

The **chdir** system call takes a character pointer reference to a valid pathname (the process must have search permission for all directories referenced) as its argu-

---

6. The **cd** command, unlike many other system level commands, is not run as a child process so its change will take effect for the current process.

Table 2.15 Summary of the **chdir/fchdir** system calls.

Include File(s)	<unistd.h>		Manual Section	**2**
Summary	int chdir(const char *path); int fchdir(int fildes);			
Return	Success	Failure	Sets errno	
	0	-1	Yes	

ment. The **fchdir** system call takes an open file descriptor of a directory as its argument. If successful, the system call will return a 0 and the new working directory for the process will be the one specified. If the call fails, a -1 is returned and **errno** is set (Table 2.16).

Table 2.16 chdir/fchdir error messages.

#	Constant	perror **Message**	**Explanation**
2	ENOENT	No such file or directory	File does not exist (or is NULL).
4	EINTR	Interrupted system call	Signal was caught during the system call.
5	EIO	I/O error	I/O error while attempting read or write to file system.
9	EBADF	Bad file number	The value in fildes is not a valid open file descriptor.
13	EACCES	Permission denied	Search permission denied on part of file path.
14	EFAULT	Bad address	path references an illegal address.
20	ENOTDIR	Not a directory	Part of the specified path is not a directory.
67	ENOLINK	The link has been severed	The path value references a remote system that is no longer active.
74	EMULTIHOP	Multihop attempted	The path value requires multiple hops to remote systems but file system does not allow it.
78	ENAMETOOLONG	File name too long	The path value exceeds system path/file name length.
90	ELOOP	Number of symbolic links encountered during path name traversal exceeds MAXSYMLINKS	The **perror** message says it all.

E X E R C I S E   2 – 8

Predict what will happen when a process forks a child process and the child process issues a **chdir** system call—will the current directory for the parent be changed as well? Write a program that substantiates your answer.

2.9 PROCESS RESOURCE LIMITS

As system resources are finite, every process is restrained by certain operating system imposed limits. At the command line, the **limit** command (which is actually a built-in command found in the C shell [/bin/csh]) provides the user with a means to display and modify current system limits. The command **limit -h** will display the hard limits for the system. The hard limits can only be *increased* by the superuser. The command **limit**, without the **-h** flag, will display the limits (also known as soft limits) for the current process and any child process it generates. The **limit** command displays the resource *maximums* for the following categories:

cputime	- number of cpu seconds allowed for the process
filesize	- size (number of bytes) when generating a single file
datasize	- the data plus stack segment size
stacksize	- the stack segment size
coredumpsize	- core dump file size
descriptors	- the number of file descriptors

An example showing the hard limits of a system is shown below:

Fig. 2.13 Typical hard limits on a Sun system.

```
% limit -h
cputime          unlimited
filesize         unlimited
datasize         229376 kbytes
stacksize        131072 kbytes
coredumpsize     unlimited
memoryuse        unlimited
descriptors      256
```

The limits for the current process on this system are slightly less for stack size and number of file descriptors:

Fig. 2.14 Individual process resource limits.

```
% limit
cputime          unlimited
filesize         unlimited
```

```
datasize          229376 kbytes
stacksize         2048 kbytes
coredumpsize      unlimited⁷
memoryuse         unlimited
descriptors       64
```

Resource limit information for a process can be obtained in a programming environment as well. Historically the **ulimit** system call was used to obtain part of this information. In more recent versions of UNIX the **ulimit** system call has been superseded by the **getrlimit/setrlimit** calls described below. However, **ulimit** still bears investigation (Table 2.17).

Table 2.17 Summary of the **ulimit** system call.

Include File(s)	`<ulimit.h>`		Manual Section	**2**
Summary	`long ulimit(int cmd,` `/* long newlimit */);`			
Return	Success	Failure	Sets errno	
	Non-negative long integer	-1	Yes	

The argument `cmd` can take one of four different values:

1   Obtain file size limit for this process. The value returned is in units of 512-byte blocks.

2   Set the file size limit to the value indicated by `newlimit`. Non-superusers only can decrease the file size limit. This is the only command in which the argument `newlimit` is used.

3   Obtain the maximum break value.

4   Obtain the maximum size of the file descriptor table for the process.

If **ulimit** is successful, it returns a positive integer value; otherwise it returns a -1 and sets the value in **errno** (Table 2.18).

Table 2.18 **ulimit** error messages.

#	Constant	perror **Message**	**Explanation**
13	EPERM	Not owner	Calling process is not superuser.
22	EINVAL	Invalid argument	The value for `cmd` is invalid.

---

7. In many UNIX environments, at the system level you can issue the command **limit core-dumpsize 0** to inhibit the generation of a core file.

The newer **getrlimit/setrlimit** system calls provide the process more complete access to system resource limits (Table 2.19).

Table 2.19 Summary of the **getrlimit/setrlimit** system calls.

Include File(s)	`<sys/time.h>` `<sys/resource.h>`		Manual Section	**2**

Summary	`int getrlimit(int resource,`
	`            struct rlimit *rlp);`
	`int setrlimit(int resource,`
	`            const struct rlimit *rlp);`			

Return	Success	Failure	Sets errno	
	0	-1	Yes	

The rlimit structure:

```
struct rlimit {
        int  rlim_cur;   /* current (soft) limit */
        int  rlim_max;   /* hard limit          */
    };
```

along with a number of defined constants used by the two functions:

```
#define RLIMIT_CPU     0         /* cpu time in milliseconds */
#define RLIMIT_FSIZE   1         /* maximum file size in bytes */
#define RLIMIT_DATA    2         /* data size in bytes */
#define RLIMIT_STACK   3         /* stack size in bytes */
#define RLIMIT_CORE    4         /* core file size in bytes */
#define RLIMIT_RSS     5         /* resident set size in bytes */
#define RLIMIT_NOFILE  6         /* maximum descriptor index + 1 */
#define RLIM_NLIMITS   7         /* number of resource limits */
#define RLIM_INFINITY  0x7fffffff /* actual value of "unlimited" */
```

are found in the header file `<sys/resource.h>`. A program using the **getrlimit** system call is shown in Program 2.3.

Program 2.3 Displaying resource limit information.

```
/*
 *  Using getrlimt to display system resource limits
 */
#include <stdio.h>
#include <sys/time.h>
#include <sys/resource.h>
void
main( void ){
  struct rlimit plimit;
  int          resource;
  static char  *label[RLIM_NLIMITS]={"CPU time", "File size",
                      "Data segment", "Stack segment",
                      "Core size","Resident set size",
```

```
                                 "File descriptors"};
   for (resource = 0; resource < RLIM_NLIMITS; ++resource) {
     getrlimit(resource, &plimit);
     printf("%-20s \t Current: %10i \t Max: %10i\n",
             label[resource], plimit.rlim_cur, plimit.rlim_max);
   }
}
```

The output sequence from this program is comparable to the output of the system level **limit** command shown earlier:

Fig. 2.15 Program 2.3 output.

```
% a.out

CPU time                    Current: 2147483647      Max: 2147483647
File size                   Current: 2147483647      Max: 2147483647
Data segment                Current:  234881024      Max:  234881024
Stack segment               Current:    2097152      Max:  134217728
Core size                   Current: 2147483647      Max: 2147483647
Resident set size           Current: 2147483647      Max: 2147483647
File descriptors            Current:         64      Max:        256
```

The **setrlimit** system call, like the **ulimit** call, can only be used by the non-superuser to *decrease* resource limits. If these system calls are successful, they return a 0; otherwise they return a -1 and set the value in **errno** (Table 2.20).

Table 2.20 getrlimit/setrlimit error messages.

#	Constant	perror Message	Explanation
13	EPERM	Not owner	Calling process is not superuser.
22	EINVAL	Invalid argument	The value for resource is invalid.

EXERCISE   2 – 9

How do you explain the apparent difference in the values reported by **limit** and **getrlimit** for the size of the stack segment?

Additional process limit information can be obtained from the **sysconf** library function (Table 2.21).

The **sysconf** function is passed an integer name value that indicates the limit requested and if successful, returns the long integer value associated with the limit. If the **sysconf** function fails, it returns a -1 and sets the value in **errno**. The limits that **sysconf** *knows about* are defined as constants in the header file <unistd.h>. In past versions of UNIX, some of these limit values were found in the header file <sys/parm.h>. A portion of <unistd.h> is shown below:

Table 2.21 Summary of the `sysconf` library function.

Include File(s)	`<unistd.h>`		Manual Section	**3c**
Summary	`long sysconf(int name);`			
Return	Success	Failure	Sets errno	
	Non-negative long integer	-1	Yes	

```
/* WARNING: _SC_CLK_TCK and sysconf() are also defined /declared
                                          in <time.h>. */

#define _SC_ARG_MAX           1       /* space for argv & envp */
#define _SC_CHILD_MAX         2       /* max children per process */
#define _SC_CLK_TCK           3       /* clock ticks / sec */
#define _SC_NGROUPS_MAX       4       /* numb of groups if supp. */

#define _SC_OPEN_MAX          5       /* max open files per process */

#define _SC_JOB_CONTROL       6       /* do we have job control */
#define _SC_SAVED_IDS         7       /* do we have saved uid/gids */
#define _SC_VERSION           8       /* POSIX version supported */
```

Program 2.4, which displays the values associated with the limits for a system, is shown below.

Program 2.4 Displaying system limits.

```
/*
 *  Using sysconf to display system limits
 */
#include <stdio.h>
#include <unistd.h>
void
main( void ){
  static char    *limits[] = {"Max size of argv + envp",
                              "Max # of child processes",
                              "Ticks / second",
                              "Max # of groups",
                              "Max # of open files",
                              "Job control supported?",
                              "Saved IDs supported?",
                              "Version of POSIX supported",
                              0};
  register        i;
  for (i = 0; limits[i]; ++i) {
    printf("%-35s %d\n", limits[i], sysconf(i+1));
  }
}
```

When run on a local system, Program 2.4 produced the output shown in Figure 2.16.

Fig. 2.16 Output of Program 2.4.

```
% a.out

Max size of argv + envp              1048320
Max # of child processes             997
Ticks / second                       100
Max # of groups                      16
Max # of open files                  64
Job control supported?               1
Saved IDs supported?                 1
Version of POSIX supported           199309
```

If the **sysconf** function fails due to an invalid name value, a -1 will be returned and **errno** will be set to ENIVAL (22) for which, if invoked, **perror** will display the message "*Invalid argument*".

2.10 SIGNALING PROCESSES

When events out of the ordinary occur, a process may receive a signal. Signals are generated when an event occurs that requires attention. They can be thought of as a software version of a hardware interrupt and may be generated by various sources:

☞ **Hardware**—Such as when a process attempts to access addresses outside its own address space or divides by zero.

☞ **Kernel**—Notifying the process that an I/O device for which it has been waiting (say, input from the terminal) is available.

☞ **Other processes**—A child process notifying its parent process that it has terminated.

☞ **User**—Pressing keyboard sequences that generate a quit, interrupt or stop signal.

Signals are numbered and are defined in the header file <signal.h>. Signal definitions have been further refined in newer versions of UNIX in the header file <sys/signal.h>. The process that receives a signal can take one of three courses of action:

1. **Perform the system-specified default for the signal.** For *most* signals the default action (what will be done by the process if nothing else has been specified) is to: a) notify the parent process that it is terminating, b) generate a **core** file (a file containing the current memory image of the process) and c) terminate.

2. **Ignore the signal.** A process can do this with all but two special signals: SIG-STOP (signal 23) a stop-processing signal which was not generated from the terminal and SIGKILL (signal 9), which indicates the process is to be killed (terminated). The inability of a process to ignore these special signals ensures the operating system the ability to remove errant processes.

3. **Catch the signal.** As with ignoring signals, this can be done for all signals except the SIGSTOP and SIGKILL signals. When a process catches a signal it

invokes a special signal handling routine. After executing the code in the signal handling routine, the process, if appropriate, resumes where it was interrupted.

A child process inherits the actions associated with specific signals from its parent. However, should the child process overlay its process space with another executable image, such as with an **exec** system call (see the chapter on **Using Processes**), all signals that were associated with signal catching routines at specific addresses in the process are reset to their default action in the new process. This resetting to the default action is done by the system, as the address associated with the signal catching routine is no longer valid in the new process image. In most cases (except for I/O on slow devices such as the terminal) when a process is executing a system call and a signal is received, the interrupted system call will generate an error (usually returning -1) and set the global **errno** variable to the value EINTR. The process issuing the system call is responsible for re-executing the interrupted system call. As the responsibility for checking each system call for signal interrupts carries such a large overhead, it is rare that once a signal is caught the process resumes normal execution. More often than not the process will use the signal catching routine to perform housekeeping duties (such as closing files, etc.) before exiting on its own. Signals sent to a process/session group leader will also be passed to the members of the group. Signals and signal catching routines are covered in greater detail in the chapter on **Primitive Communications**.

E X E R C I S E   2 – 1 0

The system specified default for signals 1-31 is given in the general manual pages on **signal** (section 5 of the manual). As a default action, how many signals a) produce core dumps, b) cause the process to stop, c) are discarded?

2.11 COMMAND LINE VALUES

Part of the processing environment of every process are the values passed to the process in the function **main**. These values can be from the command line or may be passed to a child process from the parent via an **exec** system call. These values are stored in a ragged character array referenced by a character pointer array that, by tradition, is called argv. The number of elements in the argv array is stored as an integer value which (again by tradition) is referenced by the identifier argc. Program 2.5, which displays command line values:

Program 2.5 Displaying command line arguments.

```
/*
 *  Displaying the contents of argv[ ] (the command line)
 */
#include <stdio.h>

void
main(int argc, char *argv[ ]){
```

```
    for ( ; *argv; ++argv )
      printf("%s\n", *argv);
}
```

takes advantage of the fact that in newer ANSI standard versions of UNIX, the last element of the `argv` array (i.e., `argv[argc]`) is guaranteed to be a NULL pointer. However, in most programming situations, especially when backward compatibility is a concern, it is best to use the value in `argc` as a limit when stepping through `argv`. If we run the above program as `a.out` and place some arbitrary values on the command line we obtain the output shown below:

Fig. 2.17 Output of Program 2.5.

```
% a.out this is a test
a.out
this
is
a
test
```

We can envision the system as storing these command line values in `argc` and `argv` as shown in Figure 2.18.

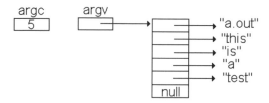

Fig. 2.18 Storage of command line values.

In this situation (where the system fills the `argv` array), `argc` will always be greater than 0, and the first value referenced by `argv` will be the name of the program that is executing. The system automatically terminates each string with a null character.

In programs, it is a common practice to scan the command line to ascertain its contents (such as when looking for command line options). At one time programmers wishing to check the contents of the command line for options had to write their own command line parsing code. However, there is a general purpose library function called **getopt** that will do this[8]. The **getopt** library function is somewhat analogous to

---

8. For those who do shell programming, you should find that your system supports a shell version of this library function which historically was called **getopt**, but in more current versions of UNIX is called **getopts** (with an "s").

the Swiss army knife—it can do lots of things, but to the uninitiated, upon first exposure, it appears unduly complex (Table 2.22).

Table 2.22 Summary of the `getopt` library function.

Include File(s)	`<stdlib.h>`		Manual Section	**3c**

Summary	`int getopt( int argc, char **argv,`
	`            char *optstring );`
	`extern char *optarg;`
	`extern int   optind, opterr;`			

Return	Success		Failure	Sets errno
	Next option letter		-1 or '?'	

The **getopt** function requires three arguments. The first is an integer value `argc` (the number of elements in the second argument). The second argument is a pointer to a pointer to a character (usually this is the array of character strings referenced by `argv`). The third argument is a pointer to a string of valid option letters (characters) that `getopt` should recognize. As noted, in most settings the values for `argc` and `argv` are the same as those for main's first and second argument. However, nothing prevents users from generating these two arguments to **getopt** on their own.

The format of `optstring`'s content bears further explanation. If an option letter *expects* a following argument, the option letter in `optstring` is followed by a colon. For example, if the option letter "s" (which, say, stands for *size*) is to be followed by an integer size value, the corresponding `optstring` entry would be "s:". On the command line the user would enter `-s 200` to indicate a *size* of 200. For a command line option to be processed properly by **getopt** it must be preceded with a "-" while the argument(s) to the option should have no leading "-" and should be separated by whitespace from the option.

The **getopt** function will return, as an integer, one of three values:

☞ -1 indicating all options have been processed, *or* the first non-option argument (something that does not start with a "-" or is not an argument to another option) has been reached.

☞ ? indicating an option letter has been processed that was not in the `optstring` or an option argument was specified (with the ":" notation in the `optstring`) but none was found when processing the command line. When a "?" is returned **getopt** also displays an error message on standard error. The automatic display of the error message can be disabled by changing the value stored in the external identifier **opterr** to 0 (it is set to 1 by default).

☞ The next option letter in `argv` that matches a letter in `optstring`. If the letter matched in `optstring` is followed by a colon, then the external character pointer optarg will reference the argument value. Remember that if the argument value is to be treated as a numeric value (versus a string), it must be converted.

The external integer optind is initialized by the system to 1 before the first call to **getopt**. It will contain the index of the next argument in argv to be processed. A comparison of the value in optind to the value in argc can be used to determine if all items on the command line have been processed. A program demonstrating the use of **getopt** is shown in Program 2.6.

Program 2.6 Using the library function **getopt**.

```
/*  Processing the command line using getopt
 */
#include <stdio.h>
#include <stdlib.h>
extern char     *optarg;
extern int       optind, opterr;
void
main(int argc, char *argv[ ]){
  int            c;
  static char    optstring[] = "abs:";
  opterr = 0;                  /* turn off automatic error messages */
  while ((c = getopt(argc, argv, optstring)) != -1)
    switch (c) {
    case 'a':
      printf("Found option a\n");
      break;
    case 'b':
      printf("Found option b\n");
      break;
    case 's':
      printf("Found option s with an argument of: %d\n",
             atoi(optarg));
      break;
    case '?':
      printf("Found an option that was not in optstring\n");
    }
if (optind < argc)
    printf("Left off at: %s \n", argv[optind]);
}
```

A run of the program with some *sample* command line options:

Fig. 2.19 Output of Program 2.6.

```
% a.out -abc -s 34 -b joe -a
Found option a
Found option b
Found an option that was not in optstring
Found option s with an argument of: 34
Found option b
Left off at: joe
```

shows that **getopt** can process options in groups (e.g., -abc), or as singletons (e.g., -b), is not concerned with the alphabetic order of options, and stops when it encounters the first non-option argument (i.e., "joe").

Modify Program 2.3 to accept command line options that will be processed with the library call **getopt**. Where appropriate, allow the user to specify arguments to change values of specific limits (use the **setrlimit** system call).

2.12 Environment Variables

Each process also has access to a list of environment variables. The environment variables, like the command line values, are stored as a ragged array of characters. Environment variables, which are most commonly set at the shell level, are passed to a process by its parent when the process begins execution. Environment variables can be accessed in a program by using an external pointer called environ which is defined as:

```
extern char **environ;
```

In most older (and in some current) versions of UNIX, the environment variables could also be accessed by using a *third* argument in the function **main** called envp. When used, the envp argument to main is defined as:

```
main(int argc,char *argv[],char **envp /* OR as *envp[]*/)
```

As environ and envp can both be used to accomplish the same thing, and current standards discourage the use of envp, only the use of the external pointer environ will be discussed in detail.

The contents of the environment variables can be obtained in a manner similar to the command line arguments:

Program 2.7 Displaying environment variables.

```
/*  Using the environ pointer to display the command line
*/
#include <stdio.h>

extern char **environ;

void
main( void ){
  for (  ; *environ; ++environ)
    printf("%s\n", *environ);
}
```

A *partial* listing of the output of this program run on a local system:

Fig. 2.20 Output of Program 2.7.

```
% a.out
HOME=/usr4/accounts/facstaff/gray
SHELL=/bin/csh
TERM=vt102
USER=gray
PATH=/usr/lang/SC1.0:/usr0/applications:/bin:/usr/bin:/usr/ucb:/etc:/usr/etc:/usr/
local/bin:/usr/local/bin/news:/usr/sunlink/dni/bin:/usr/openwin/bin:/usr/openwin/
demo:/usr/local/bin/pbmplus:/usr/CC/sun4:/usr9/dstool/bin:.
LOGNAME=gray
OPENWINHOME=/usr/openwin
EXINIT=set showmode redraw
.
.
.
```

shows that all environment variables are stored as strings in the format name=value.
Many of the environment variables shown here are common to all UNIX systems (e.g.,
USER, PATH, etc.), while others are system dependent (e.g., OPENWINHOME). For
the more curious, the manual page on **environ** (% man -s5V environ) furnishes a
detailed description of the environment variables which are commonly found and
their uses.

The two library calls shown in Tables 2.23 and 2.24 can be used to manipulate
environment variables.

Table 2.23 Summary of the **getenv** library function.

Include File(s)	<stdlib.h>		Manual Section	**3c**
Summary	char *getenv(char *name);			
Return	Success	Failure	Sets errno	
	Pointer to the value in the environment	NULL		

Table 2.24 Summary of the **putenv** library function.

Include File(s)	<stdlib.h>		Manual Section	**3c**
Summary	int putenv(char *string);			
Return	Success	Failure	Sets errno	
	0	Non-negative integer		

The first library call, **getenv,** will search the environment list for the first occurrence of a specified variable. The character string argument passed to **getenv** should be of the format name= where name is the *name* of the environment variable to find with an appended "=". Note that name is case sensitive (environment variables are often in UPPER case) and there should be no intervening blank between name and the "=". If **getenv** is successful, it will return a pointer to the string assigned to the environment variable specified; otherwise it will return a NULL pointer. For example, in Program 2.8:

Program 2.8 Using **getenv.**

```
/*
 *  Displaying the contents of the TERM variable
 */
#include <stdio.h>
#include <stdlib.h>
void
main( void ){
  char          *c_ptr;
  c_ptr = getenv("TERM=");
  printf("The variable TERM is %s\n", c_ptr==NULL ?
         "NOT found" : c_ptr );
}
```

---

the output (shown below) indicates that, in this case, the environment variable TERM has been found and that its current value is vt102. Notice that only the string to the right of the equals was returned by **getenv.**

Fig. 2.21 Checking the output of Program 2.8.

```
% echo $TERM
vt102

% a.out
The variable TERM is vt102
```

Modifying or adding environment variable information, which is usually accomplished with the library function **putenv,** is a little trickier. The environment variables, along with the command line values, are stored by the system in the area just beyond the stack segment for the process (see the section on **Process Memory**). This area is accessible by the process and can be modified by the process, but *not* expanded. When environment variables are added, or an existing environment variable is modified so it is larger (storage-wise) than its initial setting, the system will move the environment variable information from its stack location to the text segment of the process (the **putenv** function uses **malloc** to allocate additional space). To further complicate the issue in this situation, envp (if supported) will still point to the table on the stack when referencing the original environment variables, but will point to the text segment for the *new* environment variable. This is yet another reason to stay clear of envp!

One last caveat appears in the **putenv** manual page, which goes something like this:

" ... A potential error is to call putenv with an automatic variable as the argument, then exit the calling function while the string is still part of the environment..."

This warning indicates that after the calling function (which for discussion has made the **putenv** call) has finished, its stack space (where automatic variables are stored) is freed. If the process continues, the freed stack space will be reused for other purposes, ensuring the referenced string stored by **putenv** will be overwritten.

Program 2.9 demonstrates the **putenv** function:

Program 2.9 Using **putenv**.

```
/*
  Using putenv to modify the environment as seen by parent --
  child processes
*/
#include <stdio.h>
#include <sys/types.h>
#include <unistd.h>
#include <stdlib.h>
extern char **environ;
void
main( void ){
  int numb, show_env( char ** );
  printf("Parent before any additions *********\n");
  (void) show_env( environ );
  putenv("PARENT_ED=parent");
  printf("Parent after one addition    *********\n");
  (void) show_env( environ );
  if (fork( ) == 0 ){                /* In the CHILD now        */
    printf("Child before any additions ********\n");
    (void) show_env( environ );
    putenv("CHILD_ED=child");
    printf("Child after one addition   ********\n");
    (void) show_env( environ );
    exit( 0 );
  }                                  /* The PARENT              */
  sleep( 10 );                       /* make sure child is done */
  printf("Parent after child is done  *********\n");
  numb = show_env( environ );
  printf("... and at address [%8X] is ... %s\n",environ+numb,
         *(environ+numb) == NULL ? "Nothing!" : *(environ+numb));
}
/*
   Display the contents of the passed list ... return number found
*/
int show_env( char **cp ){
  int i = 0;
  for ( ; *cp; ++cp, ++i)
    printf("[%8X] %s\n",cp, *cp);
  return i;
}
```

The abridged output (some of the intervening lines of output were removed for clarity) of this program, when run on a local system, was:

Fig. 2.22 Output of Program 2.9.

```
% a.out
Parent before any additions **********
[EFFFFF14] HOME=/usr4/accounts/facstaff/gray
.
.
.
[EFFFFF38] USER=gray
Parent after one addition   **********
[    61B0] HOME=/usr4/accounts/facstaff/gray
.
.
.
[    61D4] USER=gray
[    61D8] PARENT_ED=parent
Child before any additions ********
[    61B0] HOME=/usr4/accounts/facstaff/gray
.
.
.
[    61D4] USER=gray
[    61D8] PARENT_ED=parent
Child after one addition   ********
[    61D0] HOME /usr4/accounts/facstaff/gray
.
.
.
[    61D4] USER=gray
[    61D8] PARENT_ED=parent
[    61DC] CHILD_ED=child
Parent after child is done  **********
[    61B0] HOME=/usr4/accounts/facstaff/gray
.
.
.
[    61D4] USER=gray
[    61D8] PARENT_ED=parent
... and at address [    61DC] is ... Nothing!
```

There are several important concepts that can be gained by examining this program and its output. First, it is clear that the addresses associated with the environment variables are changed (from the stack segment to the text segment) when a new environment variable is added. Second, the child process inherits a *copy* of the environment variables from its parent. Third, as each process has its own address space, it is not possible to pass information back to a parent process from a child process[9].

---

9. I am sure that many *human* children would say this is also true for their parent/child relationship—everything (especially tasks) seems to flow one way.

Fourth, when adding an environment variable, the `name=value` format should be adhered to. While it is not checked in the example program, **putenv** will return a 0 if it is successful and a non-zero value if it fails to accomplish its mission.

E X E R C I S E   2 – 1 2

If a child process modifies (without changing the storage size and without using **putenv**) an environment variable that was initially found in the parent, is the change available to the parent a) while the child exists? b) after the child has terminated? Would this be a reliable way for parent/child processes to communicate? Write a program that supports your answer.

2.13 SUMMARY

The framework in which a process carries on its activities is its processing environment. The processing environment consists of a number of components. A series of identification numbers, process ID, parent process ID and process group ID, are used to reference the individual process, its parent and the group with which the process is affiliated. In its environment a process has access to resources (i.e., files and devices). Access to these resources is determined by permissions that are initially set when the resource is generated. When accessing files a process can obtain additional system information about the resource. All processes are constrained by system-imposed resource limits. A process can obtain limit information using the appropriate system call or library function. Processes may receive signals which in turn may require a specific action. The values passed via the command line to the process can be obtained. In addition, the process has access to, and may modify (in some settings), environment variables.

Using Processes

3.1 Introduction

Processes are at the very heart of the UNIX operating system. As we have seen, all but a very few special processes are generated by the **fork** system call. If successful, the **fork** system call produces a child process that continues its execution at the point of its invocation in the parent process. In this chapter, we will explore the generation and use of child processes in detail.

3.2 The fork System Call Revisited

The **fork** system call is unique in that, while it is called once, it returns twice. As noted in Chapter One, if the **fork** system call is successful, it will return a value of 0 to the child process and the process ID of the child to the parent process. If the **fork** system call fails, it will return a -1 and set the global variable, **errno**. The failure of the system to generate a new process can be traced, by examination of the **errno** value, to either exceeding the limits on the number of processes (system-wide or for the specific user) or to the lack of available swap space for the new process. It is interesting to note that in theory UNIX is always supposed to leave room in the process table for at least one superuser process which could be used to remove (kill) hung or runaway processes. Unfortunately, on many UNIX systems it is still relatively easy to write a program that will fill the system with dummy processes, effectively locking out system access by anyone including the superuser.

After the **fork** system call, both the parent and child processes are running and continue their execution at the next statement after the **fork**. The return from the **fork** system call can be examined and the process can make a decision as to what code is executed next. The process receiving a 0 from the **fork** system call *knows* it is the child, as 0 is the process ID of **swapper** (or **sched** under Solaris) and thus is not valid as a PID. Conversely, the parent process will receive the PID of the child. An example of a **fork** system call is shown in Program 3.1:

Program 3.1 Generating a child process.

```
/*
 *   Generating a child process
 */
#include <stdio.h>
#include <sys/types.h>
#include <unistd.h>

void
main( void ){

  if (fork(  ) == 0)
    printf("In the CHILD process\n");
  else
    printf("In the PARENT process\n");
}
```

There is no guarantee as to the output sequence that will be generated by this program. If the program is run numerous times, sometimes the statement "In the CHILD process" will be displayed before the "In the PARENT process" and other times it will not. The output sequence is dependent upon the scheduling algorithm used by the kernel. The effects of process scheduling are further demonstrated by Program 3.2:

Program 3.2 Multiple activities parent/child processes.

```
/*
 *   Multiple activities PARENT -- CHILD processes
 */
#include <stdio.h>
#include <sys/types.h>
#include <unistd.h>
#include <string.h>
void
main(void) {
  int            i;
  static char    buffer[10];
  if (fork(  ) == 0) {          /* In the child process   */
    strcpy(buffer, "CHILD\n");
  } else {                      /* In the parent process  */
    strcpy(buffer, "PARENT\n");
  }
  for (i = 0; i < 5; ++i) {     /* Both processes do this */
```

```
    sleep(1);                          /* 5 times each.          */
    write(1, buffer, sizeof(buffer));
  }
}
```

When run, the output of this program on a local system was:

Fig. 3.1 Output of Program 3.2.

```
% a.out
PARENT
PARENT
CHILD
PARENT
CHILD
PARENT
CHILD
PARENT
CHILD
% CHILD
```

There are several interesting things to note about this program and its output. First, the **write** system call was used in the program, not the library function **printf**. The **printf** function is buffered and, if used, would have resulted in the five-message output from each process being displayed all at one time without any interleaving of messages. Second, the system call **sleep** (sleep a specified number of seconds) was used to prevent the process from running to completion within one time slice (which again would produce a homogenous output sequence). Third, one process (in the case shown, it happens to be the parent process) will always end before the other. If there is sufficient intervening time before the second process ends, the system will redisplay the prompt, thus producing the last line of output where the output from the child process is appended to the prompt (i.e., % CHILD).

E X E R C I S E   3 – 1

When the following program is run:

```
/*
 *  A funny C program ...
 */
#include <stdio.h>
#include <sys/types.h>
#include <unistd.h>
void
main( void ) {
  fork( );      printf("hee\n");
  fork( );      printf("ha\n");
  fork( );      printf("ho\n");
}
```

assuming all **fork** system calls are successful, how many lines of output will be produced?
Is it ever possible for a ho to be output before a hee? Why? Would the number of hee's, ha's
and ho's be different if the newline was left out of each of the **printf** statements? Why?

3.3 **exec's** MINIONS

Processes generate child processes for a number of reasons. In UNIX, there are several long-lived processes which run continuously in the background and provide system services upon demand. These processes, called **daemon**[1] processes, frequently
generate child processes to carry out the requested service. Some daemon processes
commonly found in a UNIX environment are **lpd**, the line printer daemon, **inetd**, the
Internet services daemon, and **routed**, the network routing daemon. Some problems
(such as with databases) lend themselves to concurrent type solutions that can be
effected via multiple child processes executing the same code. More commonly, a process generates a child process because it would like to transform the child process by
changing the program code the child process is executing. There is a set of six system
calls[2] under the generalized heading **exec** which allow the process to do just this. It is
important to remember that when a process issues any **exec** call, if the call is successful, the existing process is overlaid with a new set of program code. The text, data and
stack segment of the process are replaced and only the **u** (user) area of the process
remains the same. The new program code begins its execution at the function **main**.
Since the system is now executing a different set of code for the same process, some
things, by necessity, must change.

☞ Signals that were specified as being caught by the process (i.e., associated with a
signal catching routine) are reset to their default action, as the addresses for the
signal catching routines are no longer valid.

☞ In a similar vein, if the process was profiling (determining how much time is
spent in individual routines), the profiling will be turned off in the overlaid process.

☞ If the new program has its **SUID** bit set, the effective **EUID** and **EGID** are set
accordingly.

If successful, the **exec** calls do *not* return as the calling image is lost.

Before we delve into these system calls we should take a quick look at what normally transpires when a valid command is issued at the system (shell) level, as this
process will reflect the functionality available in a program. If the command issued is:

```
% cat file.txt > file2.txt
```

---

1. As in deity (of old English origins), not demon.
2. In the past, these were listed as five library functions that acted as an interface to the **execve**
system call.

the shell parses the command line and divides it into valid tokens (e.g., **cat**, file.txt, etc.). The shell (via a call to **fork**) then generates a child process. After the **fork**, the shell will close standard output and open the file file2.txt, mapping it to standard output in the child process. Next, by calling **execve**, the shell overlays the current program code with the program code for the command (in this case, the code for **cat**). When the command is finished, the shell redisplays its prompt. Figure 3.2 shows the process creation and command execution sequence.

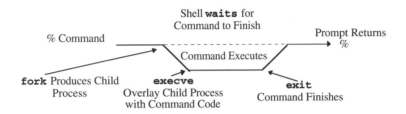

Fig. 3.2 Process creation and command execution at the shell level.

While the command is executing, the shell, by default, waits in the background. As we will see, there is a **wait** system call that allows the shell, or any other process, to wait. Should the user place an "&" at the end of the command (to indicate to the shell that the command be placed in background), the shell will not wait and will return immediately with its prompt. When the command is finished, it may perform a call to **exit** or **return** when in the function **main**. The integer value passed to these calls is made available to the parent process via an argument to the **wait** system call. When on the command line, the returned value is stored in the system variable named **status**. If you issue the command:

```
% echo $status
```

the system will display the value returned by the last command executed. As the mapping of standard output to the file **file2.txt** was done in the child process and not in the shell, the I/O redirection has no further impact on ensuing command sequences.

We should note that it is possible for a user at the command line to issue an **exec** system call. The syntax would be:

```
% exec command [arguments]
```

However, most users would *not* do this. The current process (the shell) would be overlaid with the program code for the command. Once the command was finished, the user would be logged out, as the original shell process would no longer exist!

In a programming environment, the **exec** system calls can be used to execute another program. The prototypes for the **exec** system calls, listed in their entirety, are:

Table 3.1 The **exec** system call prototypes.

```
#include <unistd.h>

int execl  ( const char *path, const char *arg0, ...,
             const char *argn, char * /*NULL*/);

int execv  ( const char *path, char *const argv[]);

int execle ( const char *path, char *const arg0[],... ,
             const char *argn, char * /*NULL*/,
             char *const envp[ ]);

int execve ( const char *path, char *const argv[],
             char *const envp[ ]);

int execlp ( const char *file, const char *arg0, ...,
             const char *argn, char * /*NULL*/);

int execvp ( const char *file, char *const argv[]);
```

The naming convention for these system calls reflects their functionality. Each call starts with the letters **exec**. The next letter in the call name indicates if the call takes its arguments in a list format (i.e., literally specified as a series of arguments) or as a pointer to an array of arguments (analogous to the argv structure discussed earlier). The presence of the letter "**l**" indicates a list arrangement, "**v**" the array or vector arrangement. The next letter of the call name (*if present*) is either an "**e**" or "**p**". The presence of an "**e**" indicates the programmer will construct (in the array/vector format) and pass their own environment variable list. The passed environment variable list will become the third argument to the function **main** (i.e., **envp**). As noted in the section on environment variables, **envp** is of limited practical value. When the programmer is responsible for the environment the current environment variable list is *not* passed. The presence of a "**p**" indicates the current PATH string should be used when the system searches for executable files[3]. In the four system calls where the PATH string is not used (**execl**, **execv**, **execle** and **execve**), the path to the program to be executed must be fully specified.

The functionality of the **exec** system calls is best summarized by Table 3.2.

Of the six variations, **execlp** and **execvp** system calls are used most frequently (as automatic environment passing and path searching are usually desirable) and will be explained in detail.

3.3.1 execlp

The **execlp** system call (Table 3.3) is used when the number of arguments to be passed to the program to be executed is known in advance. When using **execlp,** the

---

3. If the executable file is a script, the Bourne shell (**/bin/sh**) is invoked to execute the script. The shell is then passed the specified argument information.

Table 3.2 `exec` system call functionality.

Library Call Name	Argument Format	Pass Current Environment Variables ?	Search of PATH Automatic?
execl	list	yes	no
execv	array	yes	no
execle	list	no	no
execve	array	no	no
execlp	list	yes	yes
execvp	array	yes	yes

Table 3.3 Summary of the `execlp` system call.

Include File(s)	<unistd.h>		Manual Section	**2**

Summary	`int execlp ( const char *file,`
	`            const char *arg0,`
	`            ...,`
	`            const char *argn,`
	`            char *  /*NULL*/ );`			

Return	Success		Failure	Sets errno
	Does not return		-1	Yes

initial argument, file, is a pointer to the file that contains the program code to be executed. If this file reference begins with a "/", it is assumed that the reference is an absolute path to the file. In this circumstance, it would appear that the "**p**" specification (**execlp**) is superfluous, however, the PATH string is still used if other arguments are file names or if the code to be executed contains file references. If no initial "/" is found, each of the directories specified in the PATH variable will be, in turn, preappended to the file name specified and the *first* valid program reference found will be the one executed. It is a good practice to fully specify the program to be executed in all situations to prevent a program with the same name, found in a prior PATH string directory, from being inadvertently executed. For the **execlp** call to be successful, the file referenced must be found and be marked as executable. If the call fails, it will return a -1 and set **errno** to indicate the error. As the overlaying of one process image with another is very complex, the possibilities for failure are numerous (as shown in Table 3.4).

Argument 0 (arg0) through argument n (argn) of this call are pointers to the arguments that would be normally passed by the system to the program, if it were invoked on the command line. That is, argument 0 (arg0), by convention, should be the name of the program that is executing. This is usually the same as the value in

Table 3.4 `exec` error messages.

#	Constant	`perror` **Message**	**Explanation**
2	ENOENT	No such file or directory	One or more parts of path to new process file does not exist (or is NULL).
4	EINTR	Interrupted system call	Signal was caught during the system call.
7	E2BIG	Arg list too long	New process argument list plus exported shell variables exceeds the system limits.
8	ENOEXEC	Exec format error	New process file contains invalid magic number.
11	EAGAIN	Resource temporarily unavailable	Total system memory while reading raw I/O is temporarily insufficient.
12	ENOMEM	Not enough space	New process memory requirements exceed system limits.
13	EACCES	Permission denied	• Search permission denied on part of file path. • The new file to process is not an ordinary file. • No execute permission on the new file to process.
14	EFAULT	Bad address	path references an illegal address.
20	ENOTDIR	Not a directory	Part of the specified path is not a directory.
67	ENOLINK	The link has been severed	The path value references a remote system that is no longer active.
74	EMULTIHOP	Multihop attempted	The path value requires multiple hops to remote systems but file system does not allow it.
78	ENAMETOOLONG	File name too long	The path value exceeds system path/file name length.
90	ELOOP	Number of symbolic links encountered during path name traversal exceeds MAXSYMLINKS	The **perror** message says it all.

`file`, although the program referenced by `file` may include an absolute path, while the value in argument 0 most often would not. Argument 1 (`arg1`) would be the first parameter to be passed to the program (which, using `argv` notation, would be `argv[1]`), argument 2 (`arg2`) the second, etc. The last argument to the **execlp** library call is a NULL that is, for portability reasons, cast to a character pointer. The following program, which invokes the **cat** utility program, demonstrates the use of the **execlp** library call:

Program 3.3 Using the **execlp** system call.

```
/*
 *  Running the cat utility via an exec system call
 */
#include <stdio.h>
#include <unistd.h>
#include <stdlib.h>
int
main(int argc, char *argv[ ]){

  if (argc > 1) {
    execlp("/bin/cat", "cat", argv[1], (char *) NULL);
    perror("exec failure ");
    exit(1);
  }
  fprintf(stderr, "Usage: %s text_file\n", *argv);
  exit(1);
}
```

When passed a text file name on the command line, this program will display the contents of the file to the screen. The program accomplishes this by overlaying its process image with the program code for the **cat** utility program. The program passes the **cat** utility program the name (referenced by argv[1]) of the file to display. If the **execlp** system call fails, the call to **perror** would be made and the program would exit, and return the value 1 to the system. If the call is successful, the **perror** and **exit** statements are never reached, as they are replaced with the program code for the **cat** utility.

A sample run of the program is shown below:

Fig. 3.3 Output of Program 3.3.

```
% a.out test.txt
This is a sample text
file for a program to
display!
```

EXERCISE   3 – 2

What value is used by the system to generate a system process table entry when the **execlp** call is issued? Is it the value referenced by file, or the value referenced by arg0? What happens if arg0 is set to NULL (""), or if arg0 is omitted entirely (we follow the file value immediately with (char *) NULL)? Is it possible, in a case like this, for the value of argc to be 0? Write a program that substantiates your findings.

3.3.2 execvp

If the number of arguments for the program to be executed is dynamic, then the system call **execvp** is used (Table 3.5). As with the **execlp** system call, the initial argument to **execvp** is a pointer to the file that contains the program code to be executed. However, *unlike* **execlp,** there is only one additional argument that **execvp** requires. This second argument, defined as:

```
char *const argv[ ]
```

specifies that a reference to an array of pointers to character strings should be passed. The format of this array parallels that of argv and, in many cases, is argv. If the reference is not the argv values for the current program, the programmer is responsible for constructing and initializing a *new* argv array. If this second approach is taken, the last element of the new argv array should contain a NULL address value. If **execvp** fails it will return a value of -1 and set the value in **errno** to indicate the source of the error (see Table 3.5).

Table 3.5 Summary of the **execvp** system call.

Include File(s)	<unistd.h>		Manual Section	**2**
Summary	int execvp (const char *file, char *const argv[ ]);			
Return	Success		Failure	Sets errno
	Does not return		-1	Yes

Program 3.4 makes use of the argv values for the current program:

Program 3.4 Using **execvp** with argv values.

```
/*
 *   Using execvp to execute the contents of argv
 */
#include <stdio.h>
#include <unistd.h>
#include <stdlib.h>
int
main(int argc, char *argv[ ]) {

  execvp(argv[1], &argv[1]);
  perror("exec failure");
  exit(1);
}
```

The program will execute, via **execvp**, the program passed to it on the command line. The first argument to **execvp**, argv[1], is the reference to the program to execute. The second argument, &argv[1], is the reference to the remainder of the command line argv array. Notice that both of these references began with the second element of argv (that is, argv[1]), as argv[0] is the name of the current program (e.g., a.out). The following output shows that the program does work as expected:

Fig. 3.4 Output of Program 3.4 when passed the **cat** command.

```
% a.out cat test.txt
This is a sample text
file for a program to
display!
```

If we place additional information on the command line when running Program 3.4, we find the program will pass the information on. For example:

Fig. 3.5 Output of Program 3.4 when passed the **cat** command with the **-n** option.

```
% a.out cat -n test.txt
     1  This is a sample text
     2  file for a program to
     3  display!
```

If argv values of the current program are not used with **execvp,** then the programmer must construct a new argv to be passed. An example of how this can be done is shown in Program 3.5:

Program 3.5 Using **execvp** with a programmer-generated argument list.

```
/*
 *  Generating our own argv type list for execvp
 */
#include <stdio.h>
#include <unistd.h>
#include <stdlib.h>
int
main( void ){
   static char    *new_argv[ ] = {"cat",
                                   "test.txt",
                                   (char *) 0
                                   };
   execvp("/bin/cat", new_argv );
   perror("exec failure ");
   exit(1);
}
```

When compiled and run as a.out, the output of this program will be the same as the output from the first run of Program 3.4.

3.4 USING `fork` AND `exec` TOGETHER

In most programs, the `fork` and `exec` system calls are used in conjunction with one another (in some operating systems, the `fork` and `exec` calls are packaged as a single `spawn` system call). The parent process generates a child process which it then overlays by a call to `exec`. For example:

Program 3.6 Using `fork` with `execlp`.

```
/*
 *  Overlaying a child process via an exec
 */
#include <stdio.h>
#include <unistd.h>

void
main(void){

   static char    *mesg[ ] = {"Fie", "Foh", "Fum"};
   int             display_msg(char *), i;

   for (i = 0; i < 3; ++i)
     (void) display_msg(mesg[i]);
   sleep(2);
}

int
display_msg(char *m) {
   char            err_msg[25];
   switch (fork( )) {
   case 0:
     execlp("/usr/bin/echo", "echo", m, (char *) NULL);
     sprintf(err_msg, "%s Exec failure", m);
     perror(err_msg);
     return (1);
   case -1:
     perror("Fork failure");
     return (2);
   default:
     return (0);
   }
}
```

Program 3.6 will display three messages (the contents of the array `mesg`). This action is accomplished by calling the `display_msg` function three times. Once in the `display_msg` function, the program forks a child process and then overlays the child process code with the program code for the `echo` command. The output of the program will be:

Fig. 3.6 Output of Program 3.6.

```
% a.out
Foh
Fie
Fum
```

Due to scheduling, the order of the messages may change when run successive times.

It is interesting to observe what happens if the **execlp** call in display_msg fails. If we purposely sabotage the **execlp** system call by changing it to:

```
execlp("/usr/bin/no_echo", "echo", m , (char *) NULL );
```

and assuming there is not an executable file called no_echo to be found, the output[4] of the program becomes:

Fig. 3.7 Output of Program 3.6 when **execlp** fails.

```
% a.out
Foh Exec failure: No such file or directory
Fum Exec failure: No such file or directory
Fie Exec failure: No such file or directory
Foh Exec failure: No such file or directory
Fum Exec failure: No such file or directory
Fum Exec failure: No such file or directory
Fum Exec failure: No such file or directory
```

Surprisingly, when the **exec** call fails, we end up with a total of *eight* processes—the initial process and its seven children. Most likely this was not the intent of the original programmer. One way to correct this is within the display_msg function: in the **case 0:** branch of the **switch** statement, replace the **return** statement with a call to **exit**.

E X E R C I S E   3 – 3

In its current implementation, Program 3.6 does not make use of the value returned by the display_msg function. Should it? Should the program continue if either the **fork** or the **exec** call fails? Is the failure of one of these calls less *fatal* than the other?

Combining what we have learned so far, we can produce, in relatively few lines of code, a shell program that restricts the user to a few basic commands (in this example **ls**, **ps** and **df**). The code for the shell program[5] is shown in Program 3.7.

This program could be considered a *very* stripped-down version of a restricted[6] shell. The main thrust of the program is pedagogical, and improvements and expan-

---

4. The program uses a common programming trick (i.e., **sprintf**) to create a message string "on-the-fly" to pass to the **perror** routine.

5. For reasons that become obvious when the program is run, this is nicknamed the **huh?** shell.

6. Most UNIX environments come with a predefined restricted shell, **/usr/lib/rsh** (not **/usr/bin/rsh**, the remote shell command). The restricted shell is sometimes specified as a login shell for users (such as **ftp**) that require a more controlled environment.

sions (of which there can be many) will be addressed in ensuing sections of the text
and in a number of exercises.

Program 3.7 The **huh**? shell.

```c
/*
 *  A limited shell program
 */
#include <stdio.h>
#include <unistd.h>
#include <string.h>
#include <stdlib.h>
#define MAX     256
#define CMD_MAX 10

char            *valid_cmds = " ls  ps  df ";
int
main(void){
  char            line_input[MAX], the_cmd[CMD_MAX];
  char            *new_args[CMD_MAX], *cp;
  int             i;
  while (1) {
    printf("cmd> ");
    if (gets(line_input) != NULL) {
      cp = line_input;
      i = 0;
      if ((new_args[i] = strtok(cp, " ")) != NULL) {
        sprintf(the_cmd, "%s ", new_args[i]);
        if ((strstr(valid_cmds, the_cmd) - valid_cmds) % 4 == 1) {
          do {
            ++i;
            cp = NULL;
            new_args[i] = strtok(cp, " ");
          } while (i < CMD_MAX - 1 && new_args[i] != NULL);
          new_args[i] = NULL;
          switch (fork( )) {
          case 0:
            execvp(new_args[0], new_args);
            perror("exec failure");
            exit(1);
          case -1:
            perror("fork failure");
            break;
          default:
            /* wait for child to finish */
            ;
          }
        } else
          printf("huh?\n");
      }
    }
  }
}
```

The commands the user is permitted to issue when running the program are
found in the global character string called `valid_cmds`. In the `valid_cmds` string,

each two-letter command is preceded and followed by a space. By delimiting the commands in this manner a predefined C string searching function **strstr** can be used to determine if a user has entered a *valid* command. While this technique is simplistic, it is effective when a limited number of commands need to be checked. The program then issues a shell-like prompt, cmd>, and uses the C input function **gets** to store user input in a character array buffer called line_input. The **gets** function will read a line of input, including intervening whitespace, that is terminated by a newline. If the **gets** function fails (such as when the user just presses return), the program loops back around and re-prompts the user for additional input. Upon entry of input, the program uses the C string function **strtok** to obtain the first valid token from the line_input array. The **strtok** function, which will divide a referenced character string into tokens, requires a pointer to the array it is to parse and a list of delimiting characters that delimit tokens (in this case only a blank " " has been indicated). The **strtok** function is a wonderful example of the idiosyncratic nature of functions in UNIX. When **strtok** is called successive times and passed a reference to NULL, it will continue to parse the initial input line starting each time where it left off previously. The **sprintf** function is used to add a trailing blank to this first token, and the resulting string is stored in a character array called the_cmd.

The next line of the program checks for the presence of the command in the valid_cmds string at a mod-4-based offset (see Figure 3.8).

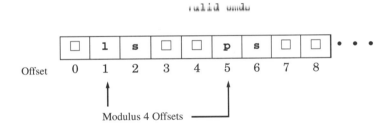

Fig. 3.8 Character offsets in the valid_cmds string.

If the command is found, a **do-while** loop is used to obtain the remaining tokens (up to the limit CMD_MAX). These tokens are stored in successive elements of the previously declared new_args array. Upon exiting the loop, we assure that the last element of the **new_args** array contains the requisite NULL value. A **switch** statement, in concert with **fork** and **exec** system calls, is used to execute the command.

E X E R C I S E   3 – 4

In Program 3.7, why was new_args[0] passed to the **execvp** system call rather than the reference the_cmd?

EXERCISE   3 – 5

When running Program 3.7, we can specify options to commands. For example:

    df -t

will work just as if we were running the regular shell. However, if we indicate that the output of a command is to be redirected to a file, say, /tmp/ps_out (i.e., df -t > /tmp/ps_out), the command no longer works as expected. Why is this?

EXERCISE   3 – 6

Restructure Program 3.7 into functional units. Add (as part of the valid_cmds string) the **pwd** (print working directory), **lo** (logout) and **cd** (change directory) commands. Submit evidence that these *new* commands have been implemented successfully.

3.5 ENDING A PROCESS

Eventually all things must come to an end. Now that we have generated processes, we should take a closer look at how to end a process. Under its own power (assuming the process does not receive a terminating signal and the system has not crashed!) a process normally terminates in one of three ways. In order of preference these are:

1. It issues (at any point in its code) a call to either **exit** or **_exit**.
2. It issues a **return** in the function **main**.
3. It *falls off the end* of the function **main** ending implicitly.

C programmers routinely make use of the C library function **exit** to terminate programs. This function, which does not return a value, is defined as:

Table 3.6 Summary of the **exit** library function.

Include File(s)	<stdlib.h>		Manual Section	**3c**
Summary	void exit(int status);			
Return	Success	Failure	Sets errno	
	No return	No return		

In earlier versions of C the inclusion of a specific header file was not required when using **exit**. More recent versions of C require the inclusion of the file <stdlib.h> which contains the **exit** function prototype. The **exit** function accepts a single parameter, an integer **status** value, that will be returned to the parent process[7]. By convention, a 0 value is returned if the program has terminated normally, otherwise a non-zero value is returned[8]. For those who wish to standardize the value returned by **exit** when terminating, the header file <stdlib.h> contains two defined constants, EXIT_SUCCESS and EXIT_FAILURE, which can be used to indicate program success and failure respectively. In some versions of C, the **exit** function (or return statement) can be invoked without passing an exit status value (i.e., **exit( );** or **return;**). In these cases, the value returned to the parent process is *technically* undefined.

Upon invocation, the **exit** function performs three actions. Figure 3.9 shows the relationship of the actions taken.

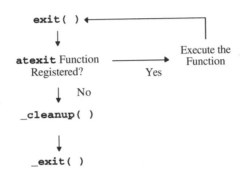

Fig 3.9 Actions taken by library function **exit**.

First, **exit** will call, in *reverse* order, all functions that have been registered using the **atexit** library function. The **atexit** function is relatively new. Some older Sun OS-based versions of C supported a library function called **on_exit** that offered a similar functionality. A brief description of the **atexit** function is in order. The definition of **atexit**, shown in Table 3.7, indicates that functions to be called (when the process terminates normally[9]) are registered by passing the **atexit** function the address of the function. The registered functions should not have any parameters. If **atexit** is successful in registering the function, **atexit** will return a 0; otherwise, it returns a non-zero value[10].

Program 3.8 demonstrates the use of **atexit**.

---

7. I know, I know—what if the parent is no longer around? Remember that **init** inherits processes whose parents are gone. The handling of status values is discussed further in the section, **Waiting on Processes.**

8. Only the low-order eight bits are returned, thus values range from 0-255. (Hum ... should **exit(-1)** actually return a 255?)

9. A normal termination is considered a call to **exit** or a **return** in main. On our Solaris-based system, **atexit** registered functions will be called even if the program ends implicitly.

10. This is one of the rare cases where no explanation of **errno** values is provided by system designers.

Table 3.7 Summary of the **atexit** library function.

Include File(s)	`<stdlib.h>`		Manual Section	**3c**
Summary	`int atexit( void (*func) (void));`			
Return	Success	Failure	Sets errno	
	0	Non-zero	Yes	

Program 3.8 Using the **atexit** library function.

```
#include <stdio.h>
#include <stdlib.h>
int
main( void ){
  void            f1(void), f2(void), f3(void);
  atexit(f1);
  atexit(f2);
  atexit(f3);
  printf("Getting ready to exit\n");
  exit(0);
}

void
f1(void){
  printf("Doing F1\n");
}
void
f2(void){
  printf("Doing F2\n");
}

void
f3(void){
  printf("Doing F3\n");
}
```

When run, the output of the program shows that the registered functions are called in inverse order (Figure 3.10).

Fig. 3.10 Output of Program 3.8.

```
% a.out
Getting ready to exit
Doing F3
Doing F2
Doing F1
```

EXERCISE   3 – 7

Explore the **atexit** function. What happens if one of the functions registered with **atexit** contains a call to **exit**? What if the registered function (with the **exit** call) is called directly rather than having the program **exit** in main—are things handled correctly?

The second action taken by the C library function, **exit**, is to call the standard I/O library function **_cleanup**. After **_cleanup** has been executed, the third and final action of **exit** is to call the system call **_exit** (passing on to it the value of status).

Programmers may call **_exit** directly, if they wish to circumvent the invocation of **atexit** registered functions and **_cleanup**.

Table 3.8 Summary of the **_exit** system call.

Include File(s)	<unistd.h>		Manual Section	2
Summary	void _exit(int status);			
Return	Success	Failure	Sets errno	
	Does not return	Does not return		

The **_exit** system call, like its relative, **exit**, does not return (Table 3.8). This call also accepts an integer status value which will be made available to the parent process. When terminating a process the system performs a number of housekeeping operations.

☞ All open file descriptors are flushed and closed.

☞ The parent of the process is notified (via a SIGCHLD signal) that the process is terminating.

☞ Status information is returned to the parent process (if it is waiting for it). If the parent process is not waiting, the system stores the status information until a **wait** by the parent process is effected.

☞ All child processes of the terminating process have their parent process ID (**PPID**) set to 1 the process ID of **init**.

☞ If the process was a group leader, process group members will be sent SIGHUP/ SIGCONT signals.

☞ Shared memory segments and semaphore references are readjusted.

☞ If the process was running accounting, the accounting record is written out to the accounting file.

3.6 WAITING ON PROCESSES

> They also serve who only stand and wait.
>
> *John Milton 1608–1674 On His Blindness [1652]*

More often than not, a parent process needs to synchronize its actions by waiting until a child process has either stopped or terminated its actions. The **wait** system call allows the parent process to suspend its activity until one of these actions has occurred (Table 3.9). The activities of **wait** are summarized in Figure 3.11.

Table 3.9 Summary of the **wait** system call.

Include File(s)	<sys/types.h> <sys/wait.h>		Manual Section	**2**
Summary	pid_t wait(int *stat_loc);			
Return	Success	Failure	Sets errno	
	Child PID	-1	Yes	

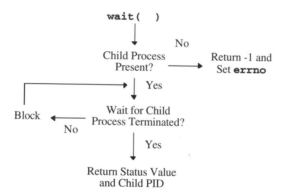

Fig. 3.11 Summary of **wait** activities.

The **wait** system call accepts a single argument, which is a pointer to an integer, and returns a value defined as type pid_t. Data type pid_t is found in the header file <sys/types.h>, and is most commonly a long int. If the calling process does not have any child processes associated with it, **wait** will return immediately with a value of -1 and **errno** will be set to ECHILD (10). However, if *any* child processes are still active, the calling process will block (suspend its activity) until a child process terminates. When a waited-for child process terminates, the status information for the child and its process ID (PID) are returned to the parent. The status information is stored as an integer value at the location referenced by the pointer, stat_loc. The low-order 16 bits of the location contain the actual status information, and the high-order bits (assuming a 32-bit machine) are set to zero. The low-order bit information can be further subdivided into a low- and high-order byte. This information is interpreted in one of two ways:

1. If the child process terminated normally, the low-order byte will be 0 and the high-order byte will contain the exit code (0-255):

byte 3	byte 2	byte 1	byte 0
		exit code	0

2. If the child process terminated due to an uncaught signal, the low-order byte will contain the signal number and the high-order byte will be 0:

byte 3	byte 2	byte 1	byte 0
		0	signal #

In this second situation, if a core file has been produced the leftmost *bit* of byte 0 will be a 1. If a NULL argument is specified for **wait**, the child status information is *not* returned to the parent process, the parent is only notified of the child's termination.

Here are two programs, a parent (Program 3.9) and child (Program 3.10), that demonstrate the use of **wait**.

Program 3.9 The parent process.

```
/*
 *  A parent process that waits for a child to finish
 */
#include <stdio.h>
#include <sys/types.h>
#include <unistd.h>
#include <sys/wait.h>
#include <stdlib.h>
int
main( void ){
  pid_t          pid, w;
  int            i, status;
  char           value[3];    /* place to store index as string */
  for (i = 0; i < 3; ++i) {   /* generate 3 child processes      */
    if ((pid = fork( )) == 0) {
      sprintf(value, "%d", i);
      execl("child", "child", value, (char *) 0);
    } else                    /* assuming no failures here ...   */
      printf("Forked child %d\n", pid);
  }
/*
 *      Wait for the children
 */
  while ((w = wait(&status)) && w != -1) {
    if (w != -1)
      printf("Wait on PID: %d returns status of : %04X\n", w, status);
  }
  exit(0);
}
```

The parent program forks three child processes. Each child process is overlaid with the executable code for the child (found in Program 3.10). Via the command line, the child process is passed (as a string) the value of the loop counter. As each child process is produced, the parent process displays the child process ID. After all three processes have been generated, the parent process initiates a loop to wait for the child processes to finish their execution. As each child process terminates, the value returned to the parent process is displayed.

Program 3.10 The child process.

```
/*
 *   The child process
 */
#include <stdio.h>
#include <sys/types.h>
#include <unistd.h>
#include <stdlib.h>
#include <signal.h>

int
main(int argc, char *argv[ ]){

  pid_t           pid;
  int             ret_value;

  pid = getpid( );
  ret_value = (int) (pid % 256);
  srand((unsigned) pid);
  sleep(rand( ) % 5);
  if (atoi(*(argv + 1)) % 2) {      /* assuming argv[1] exists!  */
    printf("Child %d is terminating with signal 0009\n", pid);
    kill(pid, 9);                   /* commit hara-kiri          */
  } else {
    printf("Child %d is terminating with  exit(%04X)\n", pid, ret_value);
    exit(ret_value);
  }
}
```

In the child program, the child process obtains its own process ID (PID) using the **getpid** call. The PID value is used to generate a unique value to be returned when the process exits. In addition, the PID value is used as a *seed* value to initialize the **srand** function. The child process then sleeps a random number of seconds (0-4). After sleeping, if the argument passed to the child process on the command line is even (i.e., divisible by 2), the child process kills itself by issuing a signal 9 (SIGKILL) to its own process ID. If the argument on the command line is odd, the child process exits normally returning the previously calculated return value. In both cases, the child process displays a message indicating what it will do before it actually executes the statements.

The programs are run by calling the parent program. Two sample output sequences are shown in Figure 3.12.

Fig. 3.12 Two runs of Programs 3.9 and 3.10.

```
% parent
Forked child 4727
Child 4728 is terminating with signal 0009
Forked child 4728
Child 4729 is terminating with    exit(0079)
Forked child 4729
Wait on PID: 4729 returns status of : 7900
Wait on PID: 4728 returns status of : 0009
Child 4727 is terminating with    exit(0077)
Wait on PID: 4727 returns status of : 7700

% parent
Forked child 4731
Forked child 4732
Forked child 4733
Child 4732 is terminating with signal 0009
Wait on PID: 4732 returns status of : 0009
Child 4733 is terminating with    exit(007D)
Wait on PID: 4733 returns status of : 7D00
Child 4731 is terminating with    exit(007B)
Wait on PID: 4731 returns status of : 7B00
```

There are several things of interest to note in this output. In the first output sequence, two of the child processes (PID 4728 and 4729) have terminated before the parent has finished its process generation. Processes that have terminated but have not been **waited** upon by their parent process are called *zombie* processes. Zombie processes occupy a slot in the process table and will be marked with the letter "Z" when a process status command is issued (e.g., ps -alx or ps -el). A zombie process cannot be killed[11] even with the standard Teflon bullet (e.g., at a system level: **kill -9** process_id_number). Zombies are put to rest when their parent process performs a **wait** to obtain the process status information. When this occurs the remainder of the system resources allocated for the process are recovered by the kernel. Should the child process become an orphan before its parent issues the **wait**, the process will be inherited by **init** which, by design, will issue a **wait** for the process. On some very *rare* occasions, even this will not cause the zombie process to "die". In these cases, a system reboot may be needed to clear the process table of the entry.

Both sets of output clearly show that when the child process terminates normally, the exit value returned by the child is stored in the second byte of the integer value referenced by argument to the **wait** call in the parent process. Likewise, if the child terminates due to an uncaught signal, the signal value is stored in the first byte of the same referenced location. It is also apparent that **wait** will return with the information for the first child process that terminates, which may or may not be the first child process generated.

---

11. This miraculous ability is the source of the name "zombie."

E X E R C I S E   3 – 8

Add the **wait** system call to the **huh?** shell program (Program 3.7).

E X E R C I S E   3 – 9

Write a program that produces three zombie processes. Submit evidence, via the output of the **ps** command, that these processes are truly generated and are eventually destroyed.

E X E R C I S E   3 – 1 0

In Program 3.10 if the child process uses a signal 8 (versus 9) to terminate, what is returned to the parent as the signal value? Why?

It is easy to see that the interpretation of the status information can be cumbersome to say the least. In older versions of UNIX, programmers wrote their own macros to interrogate the contents of status. In newer versions of UNIX, a series of macros, found under the manual heading **wstat,** have been defined for this purpose. These macros are shown in Table 3.10.

Table 3.10 The **wstat** macros.

```
#include <sys/wait.h>

WIFEXITED(stat)
WEXITSTATUS(stat)

WIFSIGNALED(stat)
WTERMSIG(stat)

WIFSTOPPED(stat)
WSTOPSIG(stat)

WIFCONTINUED(stat)
WCOREDUMP(stat)
```

The argument to each of these macros is the integer status value that is returned to the **wait** call. The macro WIFEXITED evaluates to a non-zero (true) if the child process terminated normally. With normal termination, the WEXITSTATUS macro will return the exit value of the child process. The WIFSIGNALED macro returns a non-zero if the child process terminated due to an uncaught signal, and the macro WTERMSIG will return the actual signal value. As shown below, these macros could be incorporated in the wait loop in the parent Program 3.6 to obtain the child status information:

```
    while ((w = wait(&status)) && w != -1) {
        if (w != -1) {
```

```
            if (WIFEXITED(status))        /* use wstat macros     */
              printf("Wait on PID: %d returns value of  : %04X\n",
                      w, WEXITSTATUS(status));
            else if (WIFSIGNALED(status))
              printf("Wait on PID: %d returns signal of : %04X\n",
                      w, WTERMSIG(status));
        }
     }
```

There are several other **wstat** macros. The WIFSTOPPED macro returns a true
if the child process is currently stopped, and the WSTOPSIG macro returns the signal
that caused the child to stop. The macro, WIFCONTINUED, returns a non-zero if the
child process has continued. The macro WCOREDUMP returns a true if a core dump
file has been generated.

E X E R C I S E   3 – 1 1

Write your own version of the WCOREDUMP macro. Show that the macro works when a
process receives a terminating signal that generates/does not generate a core image file.

While the **wait** system call is helpful, it does have some limitations. It will
always return the status of the *first* child process that terminates or stops. Thus, if the
status information returned by **wait** is *not* from the child process we want, the information may need to be stored on a temporary basis for possible future reference, and
additional calls to **wait** made. An additional limitation of **wait** is that it will always
block if status information is not available. Fortunately, another system call, **waitpid**,
which is more flexible (and thus more complex), addresses these shortcomings. In
most invocations, the **waitpid** call will block the calling process until one of the specified child processes changes state. The **waitpid** system call summary is shown in
Table 3.11.

Table 3.11 Summary for the **waitpid** system call.

Include File(s)	<sys/types.h> <sys/wait.h>		Manual Section	**2**

Summary	`pid_t waitpid( pid_t pid,`
	             `int *stat_loc,`
	             `int options );`			

Return	Success	Failure	Sets errno	
	Child PID or 0	-1	Yes	

The first argument of the **waitpid** system call, pid, is used to stipulate the set of
child process identification numbers that should be waited for (Table 3.12).

Table 3.12 Interpretation of `pid` values by **waitpid**.

pid Value	Wait for
< -1	Any child process whose **process group** ID equals the absolute value of **pid.**
-1	Any child process—in a manner similar to **wait**.
0	Any child process whose **process group** ID equals the caller's process group ID.
> 0	The child process with this process ID.

The second argument, `*stat_loc`, as with the **wait** call, references an integer status location where the status information of the child process will be stored if the **waitpid** call is successful. This location can be examined directly or with the previously discussed **wstat** macros.

The third argument, `options`, may be 0 (don't care), or it can be formed by a bitwise OR of one or more of the flags listed in Table 3.13 (these flags are defined in the `<sys/wait.h>` header file). The flags are applicable to the specified child process set discussed previously.

Table 3.13 Flag values for **waitpid**.

FLAG Value	Specifies
WCONTINUED	Any unreported continued child process.
WNOHANG	Do not block if the status cannot be obtained—return a value of **0 not the PID.**
WNOWAIT	Keep the process in *waitable* state (thus it can be waited on again with possibly the same results).
WUNTRACED	Any unreported stopped child process (the macro WIFSTOPPED can be used for this).

If the value given for `pid` is -1 and the option flag is set to 0, the **waitpid** and **wait** system call will act in a similar fashion. If **waitpid** fails it will return a value of -1 and set **errno** to indicate the source of the error (Table 3.14).

Table 3.14 **waitpid** error messages.

#	Constant	perror Message	Explanation
4	EINTR	Interrupted system call	Signal was caught during the system call.
10	ECHILD	No child process	Process specified by `pid` does not exist.
22	EINVAL	Invalid argument	Invalid value for `options`.

If we modify (the changes in the program are in **highlighted** text) a few lines in our current version of the parent process (Program 3.9) to save the generated child process IDs in an array, we can use this information with the `waitpid` system call to coerce the parent process into displaying status information from child processes in the order of child process generation versus their termination order.

Program 3.11 A parent program using `waitpid`.

```
#include <stdio.h>
#include <sys/types.h>
#include <unistd.h>
#include <sys/wait.h>
#include <stdlib.h>

int
main(   ){
  pid_t           pid[3], w;   /* pid is now an array of PID's    */
  int             i, status;
  char            value[3];    /* place to store index as string */

  for (i = 0; i < 3; ++i) {    /* generate 3 child processes      */
    if ((pid[i] = fork()) == 0) {/* store each PID                */
      sprintf(value, "%d", i);
      execl("child", "child", value, (char *) 0);
    } else
      printf("Forked child %d\n", pid[i]);
  }
/*  Wait for the children ... in order of generation
*/
  for( i=0; (w = waitpid( pid[i], &status, 0)) && w != -1; ++i ) {
    if (w != -1) {

      if (WIFEXITED(status))  /* use wstat macros       */
        printf("Wait on PID: %d returns value of  : %04X\n", w,
                WEXITSTATUS(status));
      else if (WIFSIGNALED(status))
        printf("Wait on PID: %d returns signal of : %04X\n", w,
                WTERMSIG(status));
    }
  }
  exit(0);
}
```

A run of this program (using the same child process—Program 3.10) confirms that the status information returned to the parent is indeed ordered based on the sequence of child processes generation, not the order in which the processes terminated. Also note that as the `wstat` macros are used to evaluate the return from `waitpid,` the returned signal information has been adjusted from its second byte location.

Fig. 3.13 Output of Program 3.11.

```
% parent
Forked child 1151
Forked child 1152
Forked child 1153
Child 1152 is terminating with signal 0009
Child 1153 is terminating with    exit(0081)
Child 1151 is terminating with    exit(007F)
Wait on PID: 1151 returns value of  : 007F
Wait on PID: 1152 returns signal of : 0009
Wait on PID: 1153 returns value of  : 0081
```

E X E R C I S E   3 – 1 2

The discussion in the text centers on a parent process *waiting* for a child process to terminate/stop. We already have the tools necessary for a child process to determine if its parent process has terminated. Show how this can be done. What are the advantages/disadvantages of your implementation?

On some occasions, the information returned from **wait** or **waitpid** may be insufficient. Additional information on resource usage by a child process may be sought. There are two BSD compatibility library functions, **wait3** and **wait4**[12], that can be used to provide this information (Table 3.15).

Table 3.15 Summary of the **wait3/wait4** library functions.

Include File(s)	<sys/types.h> <sys/wait.h> <sys/time.h> <sys/resource.h>		Manual Section	**3b**

Summary	`pid_t wait3( int *stat_loc,`
	 `              int options,`
	 `              struct rusage *rusage );`
	 `pid_t wait4( pid_t pid,`
	 `              int *stat_loc,`
	 `              int options,`
	 `              struct rusage *rusage );`			

Return	Success	Failure	Sets errno	
	Child PID or 0	-1	Yes	

---

12. It is not clear if these functions will be supported in subsequent versions of Sun OS, and they may limit the portability of programs that incorporate them.

The **wait3** and **wait4** functions only differ in their ability to specify the process ID to wait for. The **wait3** function will wait for the first child process to terminate or stop. The **wait4** function will wait for the specified process ID (pid). In addition, should the pid value passed to the **wait4** function be set to 0, **wait4** will wait on the first child process in a manner similar to **wait3**. Both functions accept option flags to indicate whether or not they should block and/or report on stopped child processes. These option flags are shown in Table 3.16.

Table 3.16 Option flag values for **wait3**/**wait4**.

FLAG Value	Specifies
WNOHANG	Do not block if the status cannot be obtained—return a value of **0 not the PID.**
WUNTRACED	Any unreported stopped child process (the macro WIFSTOPPED can be used for this).

Both functions contain an argument that is a reference to an rusage structure. This structure is defined in the header file <sys/resource.h>[13]. If the rusage argument is non-null, the system will fill the rusage structure with the current information from the specified child process. If these system calls are successful they return a 0, otherwise they return a -1 and set **errno**. See Table 3.17.

Table 3.17 **wait3**/**wait4** error messages.

#	Constant	perror **Message**	Explanation
4	EINTR	Interrupted system call	Signal was caught during the system call.
10	ECHILD	No child process	Process specified by pid does not exist.
14	EFAULT	Bad address	Illegal address reference in rusage.
22	EINVAL	Invalid argument	Invalid value for options.

3.7 SUMMARY

Processes are generated by the **fork** system call. The process that issues the **fork** system call is known as the parent and the new process as the child. Child processes may have their executable code overlaid with other executable code via an **exec** system call. When a process finishes executing its code, performs a return in the function

---

13. On some systems, you may need the header file **<sys/rusage.h>** instead of **<sys/resource.h>** and you may need to explicitly link in the BSD library that contains the object code for the **wait3** / **wait4** functions.

main, or makes an `exit` system call the process terminates. Parent processes may `wait` for their child processes to terminate. Terminating processes return status information that can be examined by the parent process.

Primitive Communications

4.1 INTRODUCTION

Now that we have covered the basics of process structure and generation, we can begin to address the topic of interprocess communications. It is common for processes to need to coordinate their activities (e.g., such as when accessing a non-shareable system resource). Conceptually, this coordination is implemented via some form of passive or active communication between processes. As we will see, there are a number of ways in which interprocess communications can be carried out. The remaining chapters will address a variety of interprocess communication techniques. As the techniques become more sophisticated, they will become more complex, and hopefully more flexible and reliable. We start off discussing primitive communication techniques which, while they get the job done, will have certain limitations.

4.2 LOCK FILES

A lock file (which should not be confused with file/record locking which is an I/O technique covered in the next section) can be used by processes as a way to communicate with one another. The processes involved may be different programs or multiple instances of the same program. The use of lock files has a long history in UNIX. Early versions of UNIX (as well as some current versions) use lock files as a means of communication. Lock files are sometimes found in line printer and **uucp** implementations.

The theory behind the use of a lock file as an interprocess communication technique is rudimentary. In brief, by using an agreed-upon file-naming convention, a process examines a prearranged location for the presence or absence of a lock file. Often the location is a temporary directory (e.g., /tmp) where the files are automatically cleared when the system reboots (or by periodic housecleaning by the system administrator) and where all users normally have read/write/execute permission. If the file is present, the process takes one set of actions, and if the file is missing, it takes another. For example, suppose we have two processes, Process_One and Process_Two, that seek access to a single non-shareable resource (e.g., a printer or disk). A lock file based communication convention for the two processes could be as shown in Figure 4.1.

Process_One checks for the presence of the lock file. If no lock file is found, Process_One creates the lock file using the agreed-upon naming convention. Process_One then uses the resource. When Process_One is done with the resource, it releases the resource and removes the lock file. However, if upon inspection the lock file was present (indicating, in this case, that Process_Two has access to the resource), Process_One would, repeatedly, *wait* a specified amount of time and then check again for the presence of the lock file, etc. Process_Two would act in a manner similar to Process_One.

Fig. 4.1 Using a lock file for communication with two processes.

It is clear that communication implemented in this manner only conveys a minimal amount of information from one process to another. In essence, the processes are using the presence or absence of the lock file as a binary semaphore. The file's presence or absence communicates, from one process to another, the availability of a resource.

Such a communication technique is fraught with problems. The most apparent problem is that the processes must agree upon the naming convention for the lock file. However, additional, perhaps unforeseen, problems may arise as well. For example:

1. What if one of the processes fails to remove the lock file when it is finished with the resource?

2. Polling (constant checking to determine if a certain event has occurred) is expensive (CPU-wise) and is to be avoided. How does the process that does not obtain access to the resource *wait* for the resource to become free?

3. Race conditions whereby both processes find the lock file absent at the same time and, thus, both attempt to simultaneously create it should not happen. Can we make the generation of the file atomic (non-divisible, i.e., non-interruptible)?

As we will see, we will be able to address some of these concerns and others we will only be able to limit in scope. A program that implements communications using a lock file is discussed below. The code for the main portion of the program is shown in Program 4.1A.

Program 4.1A Using a lock file—the main program.

```
/*
 *  Using a lock file as a process communication technique.
 */

#include <stdio.h>
#include <stdlib.h>
#include <limits.h>
#include <string.h>
#include <unistd.h>
#include <fcntl.h>
#include <errno.h>
#include <stdlib.h>

#define NTRIES   5    /* default values  */
#define SLEEP    5
#define PATH     "/tmp/"
#define LFILE    "TEST.LCK"
enum boolean {  FALSE, TRUE  };

void
main(int argc, char *argv[]){
   int            numb_tries,i = 5;
   unsigned int   sleep_time;
   char           *fname;
   void           set_defaults(int, char *[], int *,
                               unsigned *, char **);
   boolean        acquire(char *, int, unsigned);
   boolean        release(char *);
   /*
    *  Assign values
    */
   set_defaults(argc, argv, &numb_tries, &sleep_time, &fname);
                                /* Obtain lock file   */
   if (acquire(fname, numb_tries, sleep_time)) {
     while (i--) {
       printf("%d\n", i);            /* Use resource       */
       sleep(sleep_time);
     }
     release(fname);                 /* Remove lock file   */
   } else
     printf("Unable to obtain lock file\n");
}
```

The first few lines of the program have numerous **include** statements for header files. These contain function declarations and defined constants that will be needed in the program. Unfortunately, as implementations of C have become more complex, the number of requisite header files has increased. Following the **include** statements are several locally defined constants. These **define** statements establish four default values for: the number of tries the program will make when attempting to create the lock file, the amount of time to wait in seconds between attempts, the path where the lock file will reside, and the name of the lock file. The program will allow the user to change some or all of the default values by passing alternate values on the command line when the program is invoked. While it was not done in this example, the default **define** statements could be placed in their own header file which, in turn, would be included in the program. If this was done, it would ensure that any program including the header file would have the same default definitions. Following the declaration of local variables and functions the program calls the set_defaults function. The code for this function is shown in Program 4.1B.

Program 4.1B Using a lock file—the set_defaults function.

```
/*
 * Assign the values for the number of tries, the amount of sleep
 * time between tries, the path to the lock file and the lock file
 * name.
 */
void
set_defaults(int ac, char *av[], int *n, unsigned *s, char **f){

  static char full_name[PATH_MAX];

  *n = NTRIES;                      /* Start with defaults     */
  *s = SLEEP;
  strcpy(full_name, PATH);
  strcat(full_name, LFILE);

  switch (ac) {
  case 5:                           /* File name was specified */
  case 4:                           /* Path name was specified */
    full_name[0] = '\0';            /* "clear" the string      */
    strcpy(full_name, av[3]);       /* Add the passed in path  */
    if (ac == 5)                    /* If file name passed     */
      strcat(full_name, av[4]);     /* Add the file name       */
    else                            /* otherwise               */
      strcat(full_name, LFILE);     /* Add the dflt file name  */
  case 3:
    if ((*s = atoi(av[2])) <= 0)    /* Seconds of sleep time   */
      *s = SLEEP;
  case 2:
    if ((*n = atoi(av[1])) <= 0)    /* Number of times to try  */
      *n = NTRIES;
  case 1:                           /* Use the defaults        */
    break;
  default:
    fprintf(stderr, "Usage: %s
                    [[tries][sleep][path][lockfile]]\n",av[0]);
    exit(1);
  }
  *f = full_name;                   /* The full PATH+FILE name */
}
```

The set_defaults function is used to assign values to the four program variables. Upon entry to the function, the default values are assigned. Next, the number of arguments passed on the command line (which was passed to the set_defaults function as the variable ac) is examined and a **switch** statement used to determine if changes in the default assignments will be made. The set_defaults function assumes the command line arguments are arranged as:

```
% program  numb_of_tries  sec_to_sleep  path  lck_file_name
```

The value for numb_of_tries and the sec_to_sleep should be non-zero. The path value should be the name of a valid accessible path (ending with a trailing "/"). The lck_file_name is the name to be used for the lock file. As written, the set_defaults function does not validate the passed-in path and lock file values.

Once the default values have been assigned, the program attempts to generate the lock file by calling the function acquire. If the program is successful in creating the lock file it then accesses the resource. In the case of this program the resource to be used is the screen. When access to the screen is acquired, the program will display a series of integer values on the screen. Once the program is finished with the resource (all values have been displayed), the lock file is removed via the release function. The acquire and release functions are shown in Program 4.1C.

Program 4.1C Using a lock file—the acquire and release functions.

```
/*
 * Create the lock file (0 bytes *without* RWX permissions).
 * If successful return a TRUE.  If unable to create the file as
 * the file already exists(errno == EACCES), wait a specified
 * numbhr of nnnnndn and try ngnin.  Aftnr n nnh numbhr of trirn
 * OR if unable to generate the file for other reasons (e.g.,
 * incorrect path name specification)return a FALSE.
 */

boolean
acquire(char *file, int numb_tries, unsigned sleep_time){
  int    fd, count = 0;

  while ((fd = creat(file, 0)) == -1 && errno == EACCES)
    if (++count < numb_tries)        /* If still more tries  */
      sleep(sleep_time);             /* sleep for a while    */
    else
      return ((boolean) FALSE);      /* Unable to generate   */
  close(fd);                         /* Close it (0 bytes)   */
  return ((boolean) (fd != -1));     /* OK if actually done  */
}
/*
 * Attempt to remove the lock file.  If successful return a TRUE
 * else return a FALSE.
 */
boolean
release(char *file){
  return ((boolean) (unlink(file) == 0));
}
```

The program function acquire relies on the system call **creat** (note there is no trailing "**e**"), to generate the lock file (Table 4.1). By definition **creat** is used to create a

Table 4.1 Summary of the **creat** system call.

Include File(s)	`<sys/types.h>`
	`<sys/stat.h>`
	`<fcntl.h>`
		Manual
		Section
			2

Summary	`int creat( const char *path,` `                mode_t mode );`		
Return	Success	Failure	Sets errno
	Lowest available integer file descriptor	-1	Yes

new file or rewrite a file that already exists (first truncating it to 0 bytes). The **creat** system call will open a file for writing only.

creat requires two arguments. The first argument, `path`, is a character pointer to the file to be created and the second argument, `mode`, is a value of type **mode_t** (in most cases defined as type **int** in the `<sys/types.h>` file) which specifies the mode (access permissions) for the created file. The header file `<fcntl.h>` contains a number of predefined constants that may be ORed bitwise to specify the `mode` for the file. The **creat** system call in the program function `acquire` creates a file whose access mode is 0. In the program, if **creat** is successful, the file generated will not have read, write or execute permission for any user groups (this excludes the superuser root[1]).

An alternate approach to creating the file would be to use the **open**[2] system call. The equivalent statement using **open** would be:

```
open( path, O_WRONLY | O_CREAT | O_TRUNC, 0 );
```

If the **creat** call is successful, it will return an integer value that is the lowest available file descriptor. If **creat** fails, it will return a -1 and set **errno**. Table 4.2 contains the errors that may be encountered when using the **creat** system call.

As shown, a number of things can cause **creat** to fail, including too many files open, an incorrectly specified file and/or path name, etc. The failure we test for in the **while** loop of our program is EACCES[3]. The failure of **creat**, and the setting of **errno** to EACCES, indicates the file to be created already exists and write permission to the file is denied (remember, the file was generated with a `mode` of 0).

As noted, the **while** loop in the `acquire` function tests to determine if a file can be created. If the file can be created, the loop is exited and the file descriptor is closed (leaving the file at 0 bytes in length). When the file cannot be created and the error code in **errno** is EACCES, the **if** statement in the body of the loop is executed. In the

---

1. As the superuser has special privileges, the lock file implementation shown here would not work for the superuser.
2. At one time the **open** system call did not support the O_CREAT (create) option.
3. EACCES is a defined constant found in the `<sys/errno.h>` header file.

Table 4.2 `creat` error messages.

#	Constant	perror **Message**	**Explanation**
2	ENOENT	No such file or directory	One or more parts of path to new process file does not exist (or is NULL).
4	EINTR	Interrupted system call	Signal was caught during the system call.
11	EAGAIN	Resource temporarily unavailable	The file is currently locked by another process.
13	EACCES	Permission denied	• Search permission denied on part of file path. • The directory where file is to be created does not permit writing. • No write permission on the file to process.
14	EFAULT	Bad address	path references an illegal address.
20	ENOTDIR	Not a directory	Part of the specified path is not a directory.
21	EISDIR	Is a directory	The referenced file is a directory.
23	ENFILE	File table overflow	System file table is full.
24	EMFILE	Too many open files	Process has exceeded the limit for number of open files.
28	ENOSPC	No space left on device	File system has no inodes left for file generation.
30	EROFS	Read-only file system	Referenced file is (or would be) on a read-only file system.
67	ENOLINK	The link has been severed	The path value references a remote system that is no longer active.
74	EMULTIHOP	Multihop attempted	The path value requires multiple hops to remote systems but file system does not allow it.
78	ENAMETOOLONG	File name too long	The path value exceeds system path/file name length.
90	ELOOP	Number of symbolic links encountered during path name traversal exceeds MAXSYMLINKS	The **perror** message says it all.

if statement the value for count is tested against the designated number of tries for creating the file. If sufficient tries have not been made, a call to **sleep**, to suspend processing, is made.

sleep is a library function that suspends the invoking process for the number of seconds indicated by its argument seconds. See Table 4.3. If **sleep** is interrupted (such as by a signal), the number of unslept seconds is returned. If the amount of time slept is equal to the argument value passed, **sleep** will return a 0. Using **sleep** in the polling loop to have the process *pause* is a compromise. It is not an elegant way to reduce CPU intensive code but, at this point, is better than no built-in wait. In later chapters we will discuss alternate solutions to this problem.

Table 4.3 Summary of the **sleep** library function.

Include File(s)	<unistd.h>		Manual Section	**3c**
Summary	unsigned sleep(unsigned seconds);			
Return	Success	Failure	Sets errno	
	Amount of unslept time remaining			

If, in the program function acquire, the number of tries has been exceeded, a FALSE value, indicating a failure, is returned. A boolean TRUE type value is returned if the **while** loop is exited because the **creat** call was successful. If the **creat** fails for any other reason, a FALSE type value is returned.

The release function attempts to remove the file using the system call **unlink** (Table 4.4). In the program the release function is coded to return the success or failure of **unlink**'s ability to accomplish its task. As written, the program discards the value returned by the release function.

Table 4.4 Summary of the **unlink** system call.

Include File(s)	<unistd.h>		Manual Section	**2**
Summary	int unlink(const char *path);			
Return	Success	Failure	Sets errno	
	0	-1	Yes	

If the **unlink** system call fails it returns a value of -1 and sets **errno** to one of the values found in Table 4.5. If **unlink** is successful it returns a value of 0.

Table 4.5 `unlink` error messages.

#	Constant	perror **Message**	**Explanation**
1	EPERM	Not owner	The referenced file is a directory and calling process is not the superuser.
2	ENOENT	No such file or directory	One or more parts of `path` to the file to process does not exist (or is NULL).
4	EINTR	Interrupted system call	Signal was caught during the system call.
13	EACCES	Permission denied	• Search permission denied on part of file path. • The directory where file is to be removed does not permit access. • Parent directory where file is located has sticky bit set and current process does not have access permissions to parent directory and file to remove.
14	EFAULT	Bad address	`path` references an illegal address.
16	EBUSY	Device busy	Referenced file is a mount point and mounted file system is in use.
20	ENOTDIR	Not a directory	Part of the specified `path` is not a directory.
30	EROFS	Read-only file system	Referenced file is (or would be) on a read-only file system.
67	ENOLINK	The link has been severed	The `path` value references a remote system that is no longer active.
74	EMULTIHOP	Multihop attempted	The `path` value requires multiple hops to remote systems but file system does not allow it.
78	ENAMETOOLONG	File name too long	The `path` value exceeds system path/file name length.
90	ELOOP	Number of symbolic links encountered during path name traversal exceeds MAXSYMLINKS	The **perror** message says it all.

A sample run of the program is shown below:

Fig. 4.2 Output of Program 4.1.

```
% a.out 1 5&; a.out 2 2
4
[1] 5203
Unable to obtain lock file
% 3
2
1
0
[1]    Exit 3              a.out 1 5
```

The program, a.out, is invoked twice. To allow the two processes to execute *concurrently* the first invocation of the program is placed in the background (via the trailing "&" after the 5). The first process creates the lock file and gains access to the screen. This process is responsible for generating the five values (4, 3, 2, 1, 0) that are displayed on the screen. The second process, after two tries with two-second intervals between each try, exits and produces the message Unable to obtain lock file.

E X E R C I S E   4 – 1

Write a program where a parent process **fork**s three child processes. The child processes are to be similar to the example program just given. Each child process should be passed the name of a text file to display on the screen. Show output whereby all processes eventually gain access to the file, and show output when at least one of the processes fails. The parent process should remove any *leftover* lock files that may have existed from previous invocations before forking the child processes.

E X E R C I S E   4 – 2

A classic operating system problem is that of coordinating a producer and consumer process. The producer *produces* a value and stores the value (such as in a common buffer or file) that can *only hold one* of the items produced. The consumer obtains (in a non-destructive manner) the value from the storage location and *consumes* it. The producer and consumer work at different rates. To guarantee integrity, each value *produced* must be *consumed* (not lost via overwriting by a speedy producer with a slow consumer) and no value should be *consumed* twice (such as when the consumer is faster than the producer). Write a producer/consumer process pair that uses a lock file communication technique to coordinate their activities. To ensure that no data is lost or duplicated, the producer process should *produce* its values by reading them from an input file—storing them in the common location. The consumer should append the values it *consumes* (reads from the common location) to an output file. After processing, say, 100 unique values, both the input file for the producer and the output file for the consumer should be identical. Use the **sleep** library call with small random values to simulate the producer and consumer working at different rates.

One way to solve the problem is to use *two* lock files. When using two lock files, one file would indicate whether or not the number has been produced and the second file would indicate if the number has been consumed. The activities of the two processes to be coordinated can be summarized as follows:

```
Producer
do
   sleep random amount
   read a number from input file
   if # has been consumed
     write number to common buffer
     indicate new # produced
until 100 numbers produced
```

```
Consumer
do
   sleep random amount
   if a new # produced
     read number from common buffer
     indicate # was consumed
     append number read to output file
until 100 numbers produced
```

Hint: When using lock files we test as to whether or not we can create a lock file. Thus, we could use the successful creation of the lock file as an indication of access and the inability to create the lock file as a prohibition of access. Using this approach initially, the lock file indicating a number has been consumed would be absent, and the lock file indicating a new number produced would be present.

4.3 LOCKING FILES

A second basic communication technique, similar in spirit to using lock files, can be implemented by using some of the standard file protection routines found in UNIX. UNIX allows the locking of records. As there is no real record structure imposed on a UNIX file, a record (which is sometimes called a segment or section) is considered to be a specified number of contiguous bytes of storage starting at an indicated location. If the starting location for the record is the beginning of a file, and the number of bytes equals the number found in the file, then the entire file is considered to be the record in question. Locking routines can be used to impose **advisory** or **mandatory** locking. In advisory locking the operating system keeps track of which processes have locked files. The processes that are using these files cooperate and only access the record/file when they determine the lock is in the appropriate state. When advisory locking is used, rogue processes can still ignore the lock, and if permissions permit, modify the record/file. In mandatory locking the operating system will check lock information with every **read** and **write** call. The operating system will ensure that the proper lock protocol is being followed. While mandatory locking offers added security it is at the expense of additional system overhead. Locks become mandatory if the file being locked is a plain file (not executable) and the set-group-ID is on and the group execution bit is off. At a system level the **chmod** command can be used to specify a file support mandatory locking. For example, in Figure 4.3, the permissions on the data file x.dat are set to support mandatory file locking. The **ls** command displays the letter "l" in the group execution bit field of files that support a mandatory lock.

Fig. 4.3 Specifying mandatory locking with **chmod**.

```
% ls -l x.dat
-rw-r--r--   1 gray        faculty        6 Jun 16 11:12 x.dat
% chmod +l x.dat
% ls -l x.dat
-rw-r-lr--   1 gray        faculty        6 Jun 16 11:12 x.dat
```

The topic of record locking is expansive. We will focus on one small aspect of it. We will use file locking routines to place and remove an advisory lock on an entire file as a communication technique with cooperating processes.

There are several ways to set a lock. The two most common approaches will be presented: the **fcntl** system call and the **lockf** library function. We will begin with **fcntl** (Table 4.6).

Table 4.6 Summary of the **fcntl** system call.

Include File(s)	`<sys/types.h>` `<fcntl.h>`		Manual Section	**2**

Summary	`int fcntl( int fildes,`
	`            int cmd,`
	`            /* arg */ ... );`			

Return	Success	Failure	Sets errno	
	Value returned depends upon the cmd argument passed	-1	Yes	

As its first argument the **fcntl** system call is passed a valid integer file descriptor of an open file. The second argument, cmd, is an integer command value that specifies the action that **fcntl** should take. The command values for locking are specified as defined constants in the header file `<sys/fcntl.h>` which is included by `<fcntl.h>`. The more frequently used constants are shown in Table 4.7.

Table 4.7 Lock specific defined constants used with the **fcntl** system call.

Defined Constant	Action Taken by fcntl
F_SETLK	Set or remove a lock. Specific action is based on the contents of the flock structure which is passed as a third argument to **fcntl**.
F_SETLKW	Same as F_SETLK, but block if the indicated record/segment is not available—the default is not to block.
F_GETLK	Return lock status information via the flock structure which is passed as the third argument to **fcntl**.
F_RSETLK F_RSETLKW F_RGETLK	Similar to actions above, but for NSF files.

The third argument for **fcntl** is optional for some invocations. However, when working with locks the third argument references an flock structure which is defined as:

```
typedef struct flock {
        short     l_type;      /* the lock type              */
        short     l_whence;    /* starting position          */
        off_t     l_start;     /* relative offset            */
        off_t     l_len;       /* length (0 == end of file   */
        long      l_sysid;     /* distributed process ID     */
        pid_t     l_pid;       /* process ID assoc with file */
        long      pad[4];      /* for future use             */
    } flock_t;
```

The flock structure is used to pass information to, and return information from, the **fcntl** call. The type of lock, l_type, is indicated by using one of the defined constants shown in Table 4.8.

Table 4.8 Defined constants used in the flock l_type member.

Defined Constant	Lock Specification
F_RDLCK	Read lock
F_WRLCK	Write lock
F_UNLCK	Remove lock(s)
F_UNLKSYS	Remove remote lock(s)

The l_whence, l_start and l_len flock members are used to indicate the starting location (0, the beginning of the file; 1, the current location; and 2, the end of the file), relative offset and size of the record (segment). If these values are set to 0 the entire file will be operated upon. The l_sysid and l_pid are used to return process ID information of the process associated with the lock. The l_sysid value is only valid in a distributed architecture environment.

When dealing with locks, if **fcntl** fails to carry out an indicated command it will return a value of -1 and set **errno**. Error messages associated with locking are shown in Table 4.9.

Program 4.2 demonstrates the use of file locking.

Table 4.9 **fcntl** error messages relating to *locking*.

#	Constant	perror **Message**	Explanation
4	EINTR	Interrupted system call	Signal was caught during the system call.
5	EIO	I/O error	I/O error while attempting **read** or **write.**
9	EBADF	Bad file number	• fildes is not a valid open file descriptor. • cmd is F_SETLK or F_SETLKW and the type of lock is F_RDLCK or F_WRLCK and fildes is not opened for the correct mode.

11	EAGAIN	Resource temporarily unavailable	• The cmd is F_SETLK and:
			  1. a write lock has been set and a read lock is attempted.
			  2. a read or write lock has been set and a write lock is attempted.
			  NOTE: Previously fcntl returned the value EACCES for these error conditions.
			• The cmd is F_SETLK or F_SETLKW, mandatory locking is set and file is currently mapped to memory.

14	EFAULT	Bad address	cmd is F_GETLK, F_SETLK or F_SETLKW and arg contains an invalid address.
22	EINVAL	Invalid argument	• cmd invalid. • cmd is F_GETLK, F_SETLK or F_SETLKW and arg or data in arg is invalid. • fildes does not support locking.
46	ENOLCK	No record lock available	System has reached the maximum for number of record locks.
56	EDEADLK	File locking deadlock	cmd is F_SETLKW and requested lock is blocked by lock from another process. If **fcntl** blocks the calling process waiting for lock to be free, deadlock would occur.
67	ENOLINK	The link has been severed	The fildes value references a remote system that is no longer active.
79	EOVERFLOW	Value too large for defined data type	cmd is F_GETLK and returned l_pid value is too large to be stored.

Program 4.2 Using **fcntl** to lock a file.

```
/*
 *  Locking a file
 */
#include <stdio.h>
#include <stdlib.h>
#include <unistd.h>
#include <fcntl.h>
#include <errno.h>
#include <stdlib.h>
#define MAX 5
main(int argc, char *argv[ ]) {
  int            f_des, pass = 0;
  pid_t          pid = getpid();
  struct flock   lock;           /* for fcntl info                  */
  if (argc < 2) {                /* File to lock                    */
    fprintf(stderr, "Usage %s lock_file_name\n", *argv);
    exit(1);
  }
  sleep(1);                      /* don't start immediately         */
  if ((f_des = open(argv[1], O_RDWR)) < 0) {
    perror(argv[1]);    exit(2);
  }
  lock.l_type   = F_WRLCK;       /* set a write lock                */
  lock.l_whence = 0;             /* start at beginning              */
  lock.l_start  = 0L;            /* with a 0 offeset                */
  lock.l_len    = 0L;            /* whole file                      */
  while (fcntl(f_des, F_SETLK, &lock) < 0) {
    switch (errno) {
    case EAGAIN:
    case EACCES:
      if (++pass < MAX)
        sleep(1);
      else {
        fcntl(f_des, F_GETLK, &lock);
        fprintf(stderr,"Process %d found file locked by %d\n",
                       pid, lock.l_pid);
        exit(3);
      }
      continue;
    }
    perror("fcntl");
    exit(4);
  }
  fprintf(stderr, "\nProcess %d has the file\n", pid);
  sleep(3);
  fprintf(stderr, "Process %d done with the file\n", pid);
  exit(0);
}
```

In this program the name of the file to be locked is passed on the command line. A call to **sleep** is placed at the start of the program to slow down the processing (for demonstration purposes only). The designated file is opened for reading and writing. The lock structure is assigned values that indicate a **write** lock is to be applied to the entire file. In the while loop that follows, a call to **fcntl** requests the lock be placed. If

fcntl fails and errno is set to either EAGAIN or EACCES (values that indicate the lock could not be applied), the process will **sleep** for one second and try to apply the lock again. To be safe the EACCES constant is grouped with EAGAIN, as in some versions of UNIX this is the value that is returned when a lock cannot be applied. If the MAX number of tries (passes) has been exceeded another call to **fcntl** is made to obtain information about the process that has locked the file. In this call the address of the lock structure is passed to **fcntl**. The process ID of the locking process is displayed and the program exits. If an error other than EAGAIN or EACCES is encountered when attempting to set the lock, **perror** is called, a message displayed and the program exits. If the process successfully obtains the lock the process prints an informational message, sleeps three seconds (to simulate some sort of processing) and prints a second message as it terminates. When the process terminates the system removes the lock on the file. If the process was not to terminate, the process would set the l_type member to F_UNLCK and reissue the **fcntl** call to clear the lock.

If we run three copies of Program 4.2 in rapid succession, using the file x.dat as the lock file, their output will be similar to that shown in Figure 4.4.

Fig. 4.4 Running multiple copies of Program 4.2—locking a file.

```
% p42 x.dat &; p42 x.dat &; p42 x.dat &
[1] 9386
[2] 9387
[3] 9388
%
Process 9386 has the file
Process 9386 done with the file
[1]    Done                  p42 x.dat
Process 9387 has the file
Process 9388 found file locked by 9387
[3]    Exit 3                p42 x.dat
Process 9387 done with the file
[2]    Done                  p42 x.dat
```

Notice that the last process, PID 9388 in this example, is unable to place a lock on the file and returns the process ID of the process that currently has the lock on the file. The second process, PID 9387, through repeated retries (with intervening calls to **sleep**) is able to lock the file once the first process is finished with it.

E X E R C I S E   4 – 3

Change the F_SETLK constant in Program 4.2 to F_SETLKW. Recompile the program and rerun it as shown in Figure 4.4. What sequence of messages are produced now? Why?

The **lockf** library function may also be used to lock a file. The **lockf** library function is summarized in Table 4.10.

The fildes argument is a file descriptor of a file that has been opened for either writing (O_WRONLY) or for reading and writing (O_RDWR). The function argument

Table 4.10 Summary of the `lockf` library call.

Include File(s)	`<unistd.h>`		Manual Section	**3c**

Summary	`int lockf( int fildes,`
	`           int function,`
	`           long size );`			

Return	Success	Failure	Sets errno	
	0	-1	Yes	

for `lockf` is similar to the `cmd` argument used with `fcntl`. The `function` value indicates the action to be taken. The actions that `lockf` will take are summarized in Table 4.11 (as specified in the include file `<unistd.h>`).

Table 4.11 Defined `function` constants.

Defined Constant	Lock Specification
F_ULOCK	Unlock a previously locked section of a file.
F_LOCK	Lock a section of a file for exclusive use if it is available.
F_TLOCK	Test and, if successful, lock a section of a file for exclusive use if it is available.
F_TEST	Test a section of a file for the presence of other locks.

The `size` argument indicates the number of contiguous bytes to lock or unlock. A value of zero indicates the section should be from the present location to the end of the file.

If the `lockf` call is successful it returns a value of 0. If the call fails it will set errno and return the value -1 (Table 4.12).

Of the two techniques, `lockf` is simpler but less flexible than using `fcntl`. Note that when using the `lockf` call the user must issue a separate `lseek` system call to position the file pointer to the proper location prior to the call. Also, when generating parent/child process pairs, each shares the same file pointer. If locks are to be used in both processes it is sometimes best to close and reopen the file in question so that each process has its own separate file pointer.

E X E R C I S E   4 – 4

Write Exercise 4.1 using the `lockf` system call.

Table 4.12 `lockf` error messages.

#	Constant	`perror` Message	Explanation
9	EBADF	Bad file number	`fildes` is not a valid open file descriptor.
11	EAGAIN	Resource temporarily unavailable	The `cmd` is F_TLOCK or F_TEST and the specified section is already locked.
56	EDEADLK	File locking deadlock	• `cmd` is F_LOCK and deadlock has occurred. • `cmd` is F_LOCK, F_TLOCK or F_ULOCK and maximum number of system locks has been reached (an ENOLCK condition for **fcntl** call).
70	ENCOMM	Communication error on send	The `fildes` value references a remote system that is no longer active. (This was ENOLINK with the **fcntl** call).

4.4 SIGNALS—CONTINUED

A second primitive interprocess communication technique involves the use of signals. As previously indicated, signals occur asynchronously (with no specified timing or sequencing). Signals, which can be sent by processes or by the kernel, serve as notification that an event has occurred. Signals are *generated* when the event first occurs and are considered to be *delivered* when the process takes action on the signal. The delivery of most signals can be *blocked* so that the signal can be acted upon at a later time.

The symbolic name for each signal can be found in several places. Usually the manual pages for **signal** (% man -s5 signal) or the header file <sys/signal.h> contain a list of each signal name, its underlying integer value, the default action to be taken upon receipt, and what event the signal signifies. The first 33 signals, as described in manual section 5, are shown in Table 4.13.

Table 4.13 The first 33 signals.

Symbolic Name	Value	Default	Event Signaled
SIGABRT	6	Core & Exit	Abort
SIGALRM	14	Exit	Alarm Clock
SIGBUS	10	Core & Exit	Bus Error
SIGCHLD	18	Ignore	Child Status Changed
SIGCONT	25	Ignore	Continued
SIGEMT	7	Core & Exit	Emulation Trap

Table 4.13 The first 33 signals. (Continued)

Symbolic Name	Value	Default	Event Signaled
SIGFPE	8	Core & Exit	Arithmetic Exception
SIGHUP	1	Exit	Hangup
SIGILL	4	Core & Exit	Illegal Instruction
SIGINT	2	Exit	Interrupt
SIGKILL (*)	9	Exit	Killed
SIGLWP	33	Ignore	Special signal used by thread library
SIGPIPE	13	Exit	Broken Pipe
SIGPOLL	22	Exit	Pollable Event
SIGPROF	29	Exit	Profiling Timer Expired
SIGPWR	19	Ignore	Power Fail / Restart
SIGQUIT	3	Core & Exit	Quit
SIGSEGV	11	Core & Exit	Segmentation Fault
SIGSTOP (*)	23	Stop	Stopped (signal)
SIGSYS	12	Core & Exit	Bad System Call
SIGTERM	15	Exit	Terminated
SIGTRAP	5	Core & Exit	Trace / Breakpoint Trap
SIGTSTP	24	Stop	Stopped (user)
SIGTTIN	26	Stop	Stopped (tty input)
SIGTTOU	27	Stop	Stopped (tty output)
SIGURG	21	Ignore	Urgent Socket Condition
SIGUSR1	16	Exit	User Signal 1
SIGUSR2	17	Exit	User Signal 2
SIGVTALRM	28	Exit	Virtual Timer Expired
SIGWAITING	32	Ignore	Process's LWPs are blocked
SIGWINCH	20	Ignore	Window Size Change
SIGXCPU	30	Core & Exit	CPU time limit exceeded
SIGXFSZ	31	Core & Exit	File size limit exceeded

Note that all signals begin with the prefix SIG and end with a semi-mnemonic suffix. For the sake of portability when referencing signals, it is usually best to use their symbolic names rather than their assigned integer values. Signals marked with (*) cannot be caught or ignored. The defined constants, SIGRTMIN and SIGRT-MAX, are also found in `<sys/signal.h>` and allow the generation of additional real time signals.

For each signal, a process may take one of the following three actions:

1. **Perform the default action.** This is the action that will be taken unless otherwise specified. The default action for each signal is listed in the previous table. Specifically these actions are:

   Exit   Perform all the activities associated with the **exit** system call.

   Core   Produce a core image (file) and then perform exit activities.

   Stop   Suspend processing.

   Ignore   Disregard the signal.

2. **Ignore the signal.** If the signal to be ignored is currently blocked, it is discarded. The SIGKILL and SIGSTOP signals cannot be ignored.

3. **Catch the signal.** In this case, the process supplies the address of a function (often called a *signal catcher*) that is to be executed when the signal is received. In most circumstances, the signal catching function will have a single integer parameter. The parameter value, which is assigned by the system, will be the number of the signal caught. When the signal catcher function finishes, the interrupted process will, unless otherwise specified, resume its execution where it left off.

A discussion of the implementation details for ignoring and catching signals are covered in the following section, **Signal and Signal Management Calls**.

Signals are generated in a number of ways:

1. By the kernel indicating:

   Hardware conditions—The most common of which are SIGSEGV, when there has been an addressing violation by the process and SIGFPE, indicating a division by zero.

   Software conditions—Such as SIGIO, indicating I/O is possible on a file descriptor.

2. By the user at a terminal:

   Keyboard—The user produces keyboard sequences that will interrupt or terminate the currently executing process. For example, the interrupt signal, SIGINT, is usually mapped to the key sequence CTRL+"C" and the terminate signal, SIGQUIT, to the key sequence CTRL+"\". The command **stty -a** will display the current mappings of keystrokes for the interrupt and quit signals.

kill command—By using the **kill** command, the user, at the command line, can generate any of the previously listed signals for any process that has the same effective ID. The syntax for the **kill** command is:

```
% kill [ -signal ] pid . . .
```

When issued, the **kill** command will send the specified signal to the indicated process ID. The signal can be an integer value or one of the symbolic signal names with the SIG prefix removed. If no signal number is given, the default is SIGTERM (terminate). The process ID(s) (multiple process IDs are separated with whitespace) are the IDs of the processes that will be sent the signal. If needed, the **ps** command can be used to obtain current process IDs for the user.

It is possible for the pid value to be less than 1 and/or for the signal value to be 0. In these cases, the **kill** command will carry out the same actions as specified for the **kill** system call described in the following section. As would be expected, the **kill** command is just a command line interface to the **kill** system call.

3. **The kill system call** (Table 4.14). The **kill** system call is used to send a signal to a process or a group of processes.

Table 4.14 Summary of the **kill** system call.

Include File(s)	`<sys/types.h>` `<signal.h>`		Manual Section	**2**
Summary	`int kill( pid_t pid, int sig );`			
Return	Success	Failure	Sets errno	
	0	-1	Yes	

Notice that the argument sequence for the **kill** system call is the *reverse* of that of the **kill** command. The value specified for the pid argument indicates which process or process group will be sent the signal. Table 4.15 below summarizes how to specify a process or process group:

Table 4.15 Interpretation of pid values by the **kill** system call.

pid	Process(es) Receiving the Signal
> 0	Process whose process ID is the same as pid
0	Processes in the same process group as the sender
-1	Not superuser: All processes whose real ID is the same as the effective ID of the sender Superuser: All processes excluding special processes
< -1	Processes whose process group is abs (-pid)

The value for `sig` can be any of the symbolic signal names (or the equivalent integer value) found in the signal header file. If the value of `sig` is set to 0, the `kill` system call will perform an error check of the specified process ID, but will not send the process a signal. Sending a signal of 0 to a process ID and checking the return value of the `kill` system call is sometimes used as a way of determining if a given process ID is present. This technique is not foolproof, as the process may terminate on its own immediately after the call to check on it has been made. Remember that UNIX will reuse process ID values once the maximum process ID has been assigned.

If the `kill` system call is successful it returns a 0, otherwise it returns a value of -1 and sets **errno** as indicated in Table 4.16.

Table 4.16 `kill` error messages.

#	Constant	`perror` Message	Explanation
1	EPERM	Not owner	• Calling process does not have permission to send signal to specified process(es). • Process is not superuser and its effective ID does not match real or save user ID.
3	ESRCH	No such process	No such process, or process group, as `pid`.
22	EINVAL	Invalid argument	Invalid signal number specified.

E X E R C I S E   4 – 5

The `kill` command also accepts the option `-l` (the letter "L" in lowercase) which lists the defined signals that `kill` *knows* about. At the system level issue the command :

`% kill -l`

Find the integer value, default action and the event signaled for at least two signals that are known to the `kill` command but were *not* described in the previous signal table (Table 4.12).

E X E R C I S E   4 – 6

Write a parent program that **fork**s several child processes that each **sleep** a random number of seconds. The parent process should then **wait** for the child processes to terminate. Once a child process has terminated, the parent process should terminate the remaining children by issuing a SIGTERM signal to each. Be sure to verify (via the **wait** system call) that each child process terminated received the SIGTERM signal.

4. **The alarm system call** (Table 4.17). The **alarm** system call sets a timer for the issuing process and generates a SIGALRM signal when the specified number of real time seconds have passed.

Table 4.17 Summary of the **alarm** system call.

Include File(s)	<unistd.h>		Manual Section	**2**
Summary	unsigned alarm(unsigned sec);			
Return	Success		Failure	Sets errno
	Amount of time remaining			No

If the value passed to **alarm** is 0, the timer is reset. Processes generated by a **fork** have their alarm values set to 0, while processes created by an **exec** will inherit the **alarm** with its remaining time. **Alarm** calls cannot be stacked—multiple calls will reset the alarm value. A call to **alarm** returns the amount of time remaining on the alarm clock.

4.5 SIGNAL AND SIGNAL MANAGEMENT CALLS

In the previous section we noted that a process can handle a signal by doing nothing (thus allowing the default action to occur), ignoring the signal, or catching the signal. Both the ignoring and catching of a signal entail the association of a signal catching routine with a signal. In brief, when this is done the process automatically invokes the signal catching routine when the designated signal is received. There are two basic system calls that can be used to modify what a process will do when a signal has been received. These two calls are **signal** and **sigset**. The **signal** system call has been present in all versions of UNIX (Table 4.18). The **sigset** call is somewhat more recent and is part of a series of calls often grouped under the rubric of simplified signal management calls (Table 4.19).

Table 4.18 Summary of the **signal** system call.

Include File(s)	<signal.h>		Manual Section	**2**
Summary	void (*signal (int sig, void (*disp) (int))) (int);			
Return	Success		Failure	Sets errno
	Signal's previous disposition		SIG_ERR (-1)	Yes

Table 4.19 Summary of the `sigset` system call.

Include File(s)	`<signal.h>`		Manual Section	**2**
Summary	`void (*sigset (int sig,` `            void (*disp) (int))) (int);`			
Return	Success	Failure	Sets `errno`	
	SIG_HOLD if the signal was blocked else the signal's previous disposition	SIG_ERR (-1)	Yes	

The most difficult part of using **signal/sigset** is deciphering their prototype. In essence, the prototype declares **signal**, as well as **sigset**, to be a function that accepts two arguments, an integer `sig` value and a pointer to a function which will be called when the signal is received. If the invocation of **signal** is successful it will return a pointer to a function that returns nothing (**void**). This is the previous disposition for the signal. The **sigset** system call, if successful, will return a similar value providing the indicated signal was not blocked. If **sigset** is successful and the signal was blocked, then the value SIG_HOLD is returned. The mysterious (**int**) found at the far right of the prototype indicates the referenced function has an integer argument. This argument is automatically filled by the system and, if examined, will contain the signal number. Either system call will fail and return the value SIG_ERR (-1) setting the value in **errno** to EINVAL (22) if the value given for `sig` is not valid.

While the prototypes for **signal** and **sigset** are similar, the functionality of each is slightly different. Let's begin with the **signal** system call.

The first argument to the **signal** system call is the signal that we intend to associate with a new action. The signal value can be an integer or a symbolic signal name. The `sig` value cannot be SIGKILL or SIGSTOP. The second argument to **signal** is the address of the signal catching function. The signal catching function can be a user-defined function or one of the defined constants SIG_DFL or SIG_IGN. Specifying SIG_DFL for a signal resets the action to be taken to its default action when the signal is received. Indicating SIG_IGN for a signal means the process will ignore the receipt of the specified signal.

An examination of the signal header files will show that SIG_DFL and SIG_IGN are defined as integer values that have been appropriately cast to non-valid address locations. The declaration most commonly found for SIG_DFL and SIG_IGN is shown below. There are two other defined constants that can be used by **signal** and **sigset**. These constants are SIG_ERR, the value returned by **signal** and **sigset** if they fail, and SIG_HOLD, the value returned by **sigset** if it is successful and the indicated signal was blocked. See Figure 4.5.

Program 4.3 uses the **signal** system call to show how a signal can be ignored.

Fig. 4.5 Defined constants used by **signal** and **sigset**.

```
#define SIG_DFL  (void(*)()) 0
#define SIG_ERR  (void(*)())-1
#define SIG_IGN  (void(*)()) 1
#define SIG_HOLD (void(*)()) 2
```

Program 4.3 Pseudo **nohup**—ignoring a signal.

```
/*
 *  Using the signal system call to ignore a hangup signal
 */
#include <stdio.h>
#include <signal.h>
#include <fcntl.h>
#include <unistd.h>
#include <stdlib.h>

const char      *file_name = "nohup.out";

int
main(int argc, char *argv[]){
  int           new_stdout;

  if (argc < 2) {
    fprintf(stderr, "Usage: %s command [arguments]\n", *argv);
    exit(1);
  }

  if (isatty( 1 )) {
    fprintf(stderr, "Sending output to %s\n", file_name);
    close( 1 );
    if ((new_stdout = open(file_name, O_WRONLY | O_CREAT |
                         O_APPEND, 0644)) == -1)          {
      perror(file_name);
      exit(2);
    }
  }
  if (signal(SIGHUP, SIG_IGN) == SIG_ERR) {
    perror("SIGHUP");
    exit(3);
  }
  ++argv;
  execvp(*argv, argv);
  perror(*argv);          /* Should not get here unless  */
  exit(4);                /* the exec fails.             */
}
```

Program 4.3 is a *limited* version of the **/usr/bin/nohup** command found on most UNIX systems. In UNIX, the **nohup** command can be used to run commands which will be immune to hangups and quits. If the standard output for the current process is associated with a terminal the output from **nohup** will be sent to the file nohup.out. The **nohup** command is often used with the command line background specifier "&" to allow a command to continue its execution in the background even after the user has logged out.

Like **nohup**, our pseudo **nohup** program (Program 4.3) will execute the command (with optional arguments) that is passed to it on the command line. After checking the number of command line arguments, the file descriptor associated with stdout is evaluated. The assumption here is that the file descriptor associated with stdout is 1. If needed, there is a standard I/O function named **fileno** that can be used to find the actual file descriptor value. The library function **isatty** is used to determine if the descriptor is associated with a terminal device.

Table 4.20 Summary of the **isatty** library function.

Include File(s)	`<stdlib.h>` OR `<unistd.h>`		Manual Section	**3c**
Summary	`int isatty( int fildes );`			
Return	Success	Failure	Sets errno	
	1	0		

The **isattty** library function takes a single integer fildes argument. If fildes is associated with a terminal device **isatty** returns a 1, otherwise it returns a 0. In the program if the **isatty** function returns a 1, an informational message is displayed to standard error to tell the user where the output from the command passed to the pseudo **nohup** program can be found. Next, the file descriptor for stdout is closed. The **open** statement which follows the **close** will return the first free file descriptor. As we have just closed stdout, the descriptor returned by the **open** will be that of stdout. Once this reassignment has been done, any information written to stdout by the program will, in turn, be appended to the file nohup.out. Notice that the call to **signal** to ignore the SIGHUP signal is done within an if statement. Should the **signal** system call fail (return a SIG_ERR), then a message would be displayed to standard error and the program would exit. If the **signal** call is successful, the argv pointer is incremented to step by the name of the current program. The remainder of the command line is then passed to the **execvp** system call. Should the **execvp** call fail, **perror** will be invoked and a message displayed. If **execvp** is successful, the current process will be overlaid by the program/command passed from the command line.

The output in Figure 4.6 shows what happens when the pseudo **nohup** program is run on a local system and passed a command that takes a long time to execute (e.g., **find**, starting at the root directory, all file names and display each name to the screen).

Fig. 4.6 Output of Program 4.3 when passed a command that takes a long time to execute.

```
% a.out find / -name \* -print &
Sending output to nohup.out
[1] 10919
% find: cannot read dir /lost+found: Permission denied
find: cannot read dir /usr0/lost+found: Permission denied
```

```
% jobs
[1]  + Running                a.out find / -name * -print
% kill -HUP %1
% jobs
[1]  + Running                a.out find / -name * -print
% kill -KILL %1
%
[1]     Killed                a.out find / -name * -print
% jobs
%
```

When the program was placed in the background, the system reported the job number (in this case [1]) and the process ID (10919). The **jobs** command confirms that the process is still running. As can be seen, the **kill** -HUP %1 command (send a hangup signal to job 1) did not cause the program to terminate. This is not unexpected, as the SIGHUP signal was being ignored. The command **kill** -KILL %1 was used to terminate the job.

EXERCISE   4 – 7

When the **find** command was run by Program 4.3, the error messages from **find** (such as it not having permission to read certain directories), which are written to stderr, were still displayed. Modify Program 4.3 so that error messages from the program being run (such as **find** or **cc**) are discarded. What are the pros and cons of such a modification?

As noted, if a signal catching function name is supplied to the **signal** system call, the process will automatically call this function when the process receives the signal. However, prior to calling the function, if the signal is not SIGKILL, SIGPWR or SIGTRAP, the system will reset the signal's disposition to its default. This means that if two of the same signals are received successively, it is entirely possible that, before the signal catching routine is executed, the second signal may cause the process to terminate (if that is the default action for the signal). It is possible to reduce, but not entirely eliminate, this window of opportunity for failure by resetting the disposition for the signal in the catching routine. Program 4.4 catches signals and attempts to reduce this window of opportunity.

Program 4.4 Catching SIGINT and SIGQUIT signals.

```
/*
 *  Catching a signal
 */
#include <stdio.h>
#include <signal.h>
#include <unistd.h>
#include <stdlib.h>

int
main(void) {
  int             i;
  void            signal_catcher(int);
```

```
  if (signal(SIGINT , signal_catcher) == SIG_ERR) {
    perror("SIGINT");
    exit(1);
  }
  if (signal(SIGQUIT , signal_catcher) == SIG_ERR) {
    perror("SIGQUIT");
    exit(2);
  }
  for (i = 0;   ; ++i) {      /* Forever ...          */
    printf("%i\n", i);        /* display a number     */
    sleep(1);
  }
}

void
signal_catcher(int the_sig){
  signal(the_sig, signal_catcher);  /* reset       */
  printf("\nSignal %d received.\n", the_sig);
  if (the_sig == SIGQUIT)
    exit(3);
}
```

In an attempt to avoid taking the default action (which in this case is to terminate) for either of the two caught signals, the first statement in the program function signal_catcher is a call to **signal** to reestablish the association between the signal being caught and the signal catching routine.

When run on a local system, the output of the program was:

Fig. 4.7 Output of Program 4.4.

```
% a.out
0
1
2
^C
Signal 2 received.
3
^C^C^C
Signal 2 received.
4
^C^C
Signal 2 received.
^\
Signal 3 received.
%
```

From this output we can see that each time CTRL+"C" was pressed, it was echoed back to the terminal as ^C. Even if CTRL+"C" was struck in quick succession, as shown by multiple ^Cs, the program responded just once with the signal 2 received. message. On this system it is clear that some of the signals were *lost* (the signals were not queued). When a SIGQUIT signal was generated, a message was displayed and the program exited.

EXERCISE   4 – 8

Experiment with Program 4.4. In the program function signal_catcher, where must
the statement

signal(the_sig, signal_catcher);

be placed to have it *fail* to reset the action when successive CTRL+"C" sequences are
entered?

EXERCISE   4 – 9

Remove the statement:

if (the_sig == SIGQUIT)

    exit(3);

from Program 4.4. Recompile the program and run it in the background (i.e., a.out &).
How did you stop the program from displaying numbers on the screen?

EXERCISE   4 – 1 0

Write a program that **forks** a child process. The parent and child process should generate
and send random signals to each other. In each process, display the signal being sent and
the signal caught. Be sure both processes **exit** gracefully and that neither remains active
if the other has terminated due to the receipt of a SIGKILL signal. *Hint:* Remember that
you can, with **kill**, determine if a process is still present.

The **sigset** system call, like the **signal** system call, can be used to associate an
alternate action for the receipt of a signal. The **sigset** system call makes use of a signal mask. For each process, the system records which signals should be blocked. The
record of signals to be blocked is stored in the process's signal mask. On most systems
the signal mask is implemented as the defined data type sigset_t, which is an array
of long integers. When a **sigset** call is made, the system will add the sig value to the
process's current signal mask before it executes the signal catching function. As soon
as the signal catching function is finished, the process will return to where it was previously, and the system will restore the signal mask to its previous state. Thus, *unlike*
signal, **sigset** installed signal catching routines remain installed even after they
have been invoked. When successful, **sigset** returns either the defined constant,
SIG_HOLD, (indicating the signal was previously blocked), or the disposition previously associated with the signal.

Program 4.5, which is similar to Program 4.4, shows the use of the **sigset** system call.

Again, notice that in the program function signal_catcher, it is no longer necessary to reset the association for the signal caught to the signal catching routine.

Program 4.5 Using the **sigset** system call.

```
/*
 *  Catching signals with sigset
 */
#include <stdio.h>
#include <signal.h>
#include <unistd.h>
#include <stdlib.h>
int
main(void){
  int               i;
  void              signal_catcher(int);

  if (sigset(SIGINT, signal_catcher) == SIG_ERR) {
    perror("Sigset can not set SIGINT");
    exit(SIGINT);
  }
  if (sigset(SIGQUIT, signal_catcher) == SIG_ERR) {
    perror("Sigset can not set SIGQUIT");
    exit(SIGQUIT);
  }
  for (i = 0;; ++i) {
    printf("%i\n", i);
    sleep(1);
  }
}
void
signal_catcher(int the_sig){

  printf("\nSignal %d received.\n", the_sig);
  if (the_sig == SIGQUIT)
    exit(1);
}
```

There are four other signal-related system calls that can be used for signal management. These calls are shown in Table 4.21.

Table 4.21 Summary of the **sighold**, **sigrelse**, **sigignore** and **sigpause** system calls.

Include File(s)	<signal.h>		Manual Section	**2**

Summary	`int sighold  ( int sig );`
	`int sigrelse ( int sig );`
	`int sigignore( int sig );`
	`int sigpause ( int sig );`			

Return	Success	Failure	Sets errno	
	0	-1	Yes	

Each of the functions returns a 0 if it is successful, otherwise it returns a -1 and sets the value in **errno** (Table 4.22).

Table 4.22 `sighold`, `sigrelse`, `sigignore` and `sigpause` error messages.

#	Constant	`perror` Message	Explanation
4	EINTR	Interrupted system call	Signal was caught during the **sigpause** system call.
22	EINVAL	Invalid argument	Invalid signal number specified.

The process's signal mask can be manipulated with the **sighold** and **sigrelse** system calls. The **sighold** system call will add the indicated signal to the calling process's signal mask, while the **sigrelse** system call will remove the signal. The **sigignore** system call will cause the indicated signal to be ignored (this call is somewhat redundant as the same functionality can be accomplished by using the **sigset** or **signal** system call with the defined constant SIG_IGN). The **sigpause** system call will remove the signal from the process's signal mask and suspend the process until the indicated signal is received.

The use of the **sighold** and **sigrelse** system calls is shown in Program 4.6.

Program 4.6 Using **sighold** and **sigset**.

```
/*
 *  Demonstration of the sighold and sigset system calls.
 */
#include <stdio.h>
#include <signal.h>
#include <unistd.h>
int
main( void ) {
  void          sigset_catcher(int);
  sighold(SIGUSR1);
  sigset(SIGUSR2, sigset_catcher);
  printf("Waiting for signal\n");
  pause( );
  printf("Done\n");
  exit(0);
}
void
sigset_catcher( int n ) {
  printf("Received signal %d will release SIGUSR1\n", n);
  sigrelse(SIGUSR1);
  printf("SIGUSR1 released!\n");
}
```

In Program 4.6, we use the **sighold** system call to *hold* (block) incoming SIGUSR1 signals. The SIGUSR1 and SIGUSR2 signals are two user-defined signals whose default action is termination of the process. The **sigset** system call is used to associate the receipt of SIGUSR2 with the signal catching routine and a message is displayed. Following this, a call to **pause** is made. The **pause** system call suspends a process until it receives a signal that has not been ignored (Table 4.23).

Table 4.23 Summary of the `pause` system call.

Include File(s)	`<unistd.h>`		Manual Section	**2**
Summary	`int pause( void );`			
Return	Success	Failure	Sets errno	
	If the signal does not cause termination then -1 returned	Does not return	Yes	

The `pause` system call will return a -1 if the signal received while pausing does not cause termination. The value in errno will be EINTR (4). If the received signal causes termination `pause` will not return (which is to be expected!).

In the program function sigset_catcher, the `sigrelse` system call is used to release the pending SIGUSR1 signal. Notice that a `printf` statement was placed *before* and *after* the `sigrelse` call. A sample run of this program run locally is shown in Figure 4.8.

Fig. 4.8 Output of Program 4.6.

```
% a.out &
[1] 5245
% Waiting for signal
% kill -USR1 5245
% kill -USR2 5245
% Received signal 17 will release SIGUSR1
[1]    User Signal 1        a.out
```

When run, the program is placed in background so the user can continue to issue commands from the keyboard. The system displays the job number for the process and the process ID. The program begins by displaying the Waiting for signal message. The user, via the `kill` command, sends the process a SIGUSR1 signal. This signal, while received by the process, is not acted upon as the process has been directed to block this signal. When the SIGUSR2 signal is sent to the process, the signal is caught by the process and the program function **sigset_catcher** is called. The initial **printf** statement in the signal catching routine is executed and its message about receiving signals is displayed. The following **sigrelse** call then unblocks the pending SIGUSR1 signal that was issued earlier. As the default action for SIGUSR1 is termination, the process terminates and the system produces the trailing information indicating the process was terminated via user signal 1. As the process terminates normally the second **printf** statement in the signal catching routine and the **printf** in the main of the program are not executed.

The **sigpause** system call is used to pause (suspend) a process until the specified signal is received. Program 4.7 demonstrates the use of the **sigpause** system call.

E X E R C I S E   4 – 1 1

In Program 4.6, replace all occurrences of SIGUSR1 with SIGPWR (SIGPWR indicates a power failure, but by default this signal is ignored). Recompile the program, run it in the background, and issue several SIGPWR signals to the process from the keyboard before issuing the SIGUSR2 signal. How many times is the message `SIGPWR released!` displayed? Why?

Program 4.7 Using **sigpause**.

```
/*
 *  Pausing with sigpause
 */
#include <stdio.h>
#include <signal.h>
#include <unistd.h>
void
main(void){
  void          sigset_catcher(int);
  sigset(SIGUSR1, sigset_catcher);

  while (1) {
    printf("Waiting for signal %d\n", SIGUSR1);
    sigpause(SIGUSR1);    /* Wait for USR1 signal    */
  }
}

void
sigset_catcher(int n){
  sighold(SIGINT);        /* Hold interrupt          */
  sighold(SIGTERM);       /* Hold terminate          */
  printf("Beginning important stuff\n");
  sleep(10);              /* Simulate work ....      */
  printf("Ending important stuff\n");
  sigrelse(SIGTERM);      /* Release interrupt        */
  sigrelse(SIGINT);       /* Release terminate        */
}
```

In main, signal SIGUSR1 is associated with the signal catching function `sigset_catcher`. Then, in an endless loop, the program pauses, waiting for the receipt of the SIGUSR1 signal. Once the SIGUSR1 signal is received (caught) the signal catching function is executed. While in the signal catching function, the signals SIGINT and SIGTERM are held. A set of messages indicating the beginning and end of an *important* section of code are displayed. The SIGINT and SIGTERM signals are then released. In summary, the program defers the execution of an interrupt-protected section of code until it receives a SIGUSR1 signal.

A run of the program produces the following output:

Fig. 4.9 Output of Program 4.7.

```
% a.out &
[1] 8589
% Waiting for signal 16
kill -USR1 8589
% Beginning important stuff
kill -INT  8589
% jobs
[1]   + Running                 a.out
% Ending important stuff
[1]      a.out
```

The process was first sent a SIGUSR1 signal which caused it to begin the program function `sigset_catcher`. While it was in the `sigset_catcher` function, an interrupt signal was sent to the process. This signal did not cause the process to immediately terminate, as the process had indicated that this signal was to be held. The **jobs** command confirms that the process is still active. However, once the SIGINT and SIGTERM signals are released, the pending SIGINT signal is acted upon and the process terminates.

E X E R C I S E   4 – 1 2

Write a program that generates a parent and child process that solves the producer/consumer problem presented in Exercise 4.2. Make the parent process the producer and the child process the consumer. In place of a lock file, use signals to coordinate the activities of the processes. One approach would be to use SIGUSR1 to indicate the resource is available to be accessed and use signal SIGUSR2 to indicate a new value is available. Do signals provide a reliable way of solving the problem? What problems are inherent in their use?

4.6 SUMMARY

As we have seen, lock files, the locking of files and signals, can be used as a primitive means of communication between processes. Lock files require the participating processes to agree upon file names and locations. The creation of a lock file carries with it a certain amount of system overhead characteristic of all file manipulations. In addition, the problems associated with the removal of "leftover" invalid lock files and the implementation of non-system intensive polling techniques must be addressed. On the positive side, lock file techniques can be used in any UNIX environment that supports the **creat** system call, and cooperating processes do not need to be related.

UNIX has predefined routines that can be used to lock a file. We can use the presence of a lock on a file to indicate that a resource is unavailable. Advisory locking is less system intensive than mandatory locking and is thus more common. As with lock files, the participating processes using advisory locking must cooperate to effectively communicate.

Signals provide us with another basic communication technique. While signals do not carry any information content, they can be, as we have seen, used to communicate from one process to another. From a system implementation standpoint, signals are more efficient than using lock files. However, participating processes must have access to each other's process IDs (in most cases the processes will be parent/child pairs). In most environments, the number of user-designated signals are limited. Cooperating processes must agree upon the "meaning" of each signal. When a signal is sent from one process to another, unless the receiving process acknowledges the receipt of the signal, there is no way for the sending process to know if its initial signal was received. Signal manipulation can be tricky and its implementation from one version of UNIX to another may vary (this is one of the last areas of UNIX to be standardized). All of these techniques are easy to understand and to implement. However, all approaches have a number of limitations that remove them from serious consideration when reliable communication between processes is needed.

Pipes

read
We have discussed ... ◀ *PIPE*
PIPE
PIPE

write
◀ the previous ...

5.1 INTRODUCTION

We have discussed the nature and generation of processes. In the previous chapter we addressed primitive techniques for communicating between two or more processes. These techniques were limited in scope and suffered from a lack of reliable synchronization. Beginning with this chapter, we will explore interprocess communication techniques using system designed interprocess facilities. We will start with **pipes** that will provide processes with a simple, synchronized way of passing information.

We can think of the pipe as a special file that can store a limited amount of data in a first-in-first-out (FIFO) manner. On most systems pipes are limited to 10 logical blocks, each of 512K bytes. The include file <limits.h> or <sys/param.h> contains a defined constant PIPE_BUF that specifies the maximum number of bytes a pipe may hold. On our system the value for PIPE_BUF is 5120 (i.e., 10 blocks of 512 bytes each). As a general rule, one process will write to the pipe (as if it were a file), while another process will read from the pipe.

As shown in Figure 5.1, conceptually we can envision the pipe as a conveyor belt composed of 10 logical data blocks that are continuously filled (written to) and emptied (read). The system keeps track of the current location of the last read/write location. Data is written to one end of the pipe and read from the other. From an implementation standpoint, an actual file pointer (as associated with a regular file) is not defined for a pipe.

Fig. 5.1 Conceptual data access using a pipe.

The system provides the synchronization between the writing and reading processes. By default, if a writing process attempts to **write** to a full pipe, the system will automatically block the process until the pipe is able to receive the data. Likewise, if a **read** is attempted on an empty pipe, the process will block until data is available. In addition, the process will block if a specified pipe has been opened for reading, but another process has not opened the pipe for writing.

Data is written to the pipe using the unbuffered I/O **write** system call (Table 5.1).

Table 5.1 Summary of the **write** system call.

Include File(s)	<unistd.h>		Manual Section	**2**

Summary	ssize_t write(int fildes,
	                    const void *buf,
	                    size_t nbyte);			

Return	Success	Failure	Sets errno	
	Number of bytes written	-1	Yes	

Using the file descriptor specified by `fildes`, the **write** system call will attempt to write `nbyte` bytes from the buffer referenced by `buf`. If the **write** system call is successful, the number of bytes actually written is returned. Otherwise a -1 is returned and the global variable, **errno,** is set to indicate the nature of the error. As shown in Table 5.2, the number of ways in which **write** can fail is impressive indeed!

`write`s to a pipe are similar to those for a file except that:

☞ Each file **write** request is always *appended* to the end of the pipe.

☞ **Write** requests of PIPE_BUF size or less are guaranteed not to be interleaved with other **write** requests to the same pipe[1].

☞ When the O_NONBLOCK and O_NDELAY flags are clear a **write** request may cause the process to block. The defined constants O_NONBLOCK and O_NDELAY are found in the header file <sys/fcntl.h> and can be set with the **fcntl** system call. By default, these values are considered to be cleared, thus **write** will block if the device is busy and **write**s will be delayed (written to an

---

1. While **write** will still work if the number of bytes is greater than PIPE_BUF, it is best to stay within this limitation to guarantee the integrity of data.

Table 5.2 `write` error messages.

#	Constant	`perror` **Message**	**Explanation**
4	EINTR	Interrupted system call	Signal was caught during the system call.
5	EIO	I/O error	Background process cannot write to its controlling terminal.
6	ENXIO	No such device or address	Hangup occurred while writing to a stream.
9	EDADF	Bad file number	`fildes` is an invalid file or not open for writing.
11	EAGAIN	Resource temporarily unavailable	• O_NDELAY or O_NONBLOCK is set and the file is currently locked by another process. • System memory for raw I/O is temporarily insufficient • Attempted **write** to pipe of `nbytes` but less than `nbytes` is available.
14	EFAULT	Bad address	`buf` references an illegal address.
22	EINVAL	Invalid argument	Cannot **write** to a stream linked below a multiplexor.
27	EFBIG	File too large	Attempt to **write** a file that exceeds the current system limits.
28	ENOSPC	No space left on device	File system has no space left for file **write**.
32	EPIPE	Broken pipe	• Attempt to `write` to a pipe that is not opened for reading on one end (in this case a SIGPIPE signal also generated). • Attempt to `write` to a FIFO that is not opened for reading on one end. • Attempt to **write** to a pipe with only one end open.
34	ERANGE	Result too large	`nbyte` value is less than 0 or greater than system limit.
45	EDEADLK	Deadlock situation detected/avoided	The **write** system call would have gone to sleep generating a deadlock situation.
46	ENOLCK	No record locks available	• Locking enabled but region was previously locked. • System lock table is full.
63	ENOSR	Out of streams resources	Attempt to **write** to stream but insufficient stream memory available.
67	ENOLINK	The link has been severed	The `path` value references a remote system that is no longer active.

internal buffer which is written out to disk by the kernel at a later time). Once the **write** has completed it will return the number of bytes successfully written.

☞ When the O_NONBLOCK or O_NDELAY flags are set, and the request to **write** PIPE_BUF bytes or less is not successful, the value returned by the **write** system call can be summarized as:

O_NONBLOCK	O_NDELAY	Value Returned
set	clear	-1
clear	set	0

If both O_NONBLOCK and O_NDELAY flags are set, **write** will not block the process.

☞ If a **write** is made to a pipe that is not open for reading by any process, a SIG-PIPE signal will be generated and the value in **errno** will be set to EPIPE (broken pipe). The default action (if not caught) for the SIGPIPE signal is termination.

Data is read from the pipe using the unbuffered I/O **read** system call summarized in Table 5.3.

Table 5.3 Summary of the **read** system call.

Include File(s)	`<sys/types.h>`
	`<sys/uio.h>`
	`<unistd.h>`
			Manual
			Section
				2

Summary	`ssize_t read( int fildes,`
	`                void *buf,`
	`                size_t nbyte );`			

Return	Success	Failure	Sets errno	
	Number of bytes read	-1	Yes	

The **read** system call will read `nbyte` bytes from the open file associated with the file descriptor `fildes` into the buffer referenced by `buf`. If the **read** call is successful the number of bytes actually read is returned. If the number of bytes left in the pipe is less than `nbytes`, the value returned by **read** will reflect this. When at the end of the file, a value of 0 is returned. If the **read** system call fails a -1 is returned and the global variable, **errno**, is set. The values that **errno** may take when **read** fails are shown in Table 5.4.

In other aspects, **reads** performed on a pipe are similar to those on a file except that:

☞ All **reads** are initiated from the current position (i.e., no seeking is supported).

☞ If both O_NONBLOCK and O_NDELAY flags are clear, then a **read** system call

Table 5.4 `read` error messages.

#	Constant	`perror` **Message**	**Explanation**
4	EINTR	Interrupted system call	Signal was caught during the system call.
5	EIO	I/O error	Background process cannot **read** from its controlling terminal.
6	ENXIO	No such device or address	File pointer reference is invalid.
9	EDADF	Bad file number	`fildes` is an invalid file or not open for reading.
11	EAGAIN	Resource temporarily unavailable	• O_NDELAY or O_NONBLOCK is set and the file is currently locked by another process. • System memory for raw I/O is temporarily insufficient. • O_NDELAY or O_NONBLOCK is set but no data waiting to be **read**.
14	EFAULT	Bad address	`buf` references an illegal address.
22	EINVAL	Invalid argument	Cannot **read** to a stream linked below a multiplexor.
45	EDEADLK	Deadlock situation detected/avoided	The **read** system call would have gone to sleep generating a deadlock situation.
46	ENOLCK	No record locks available	System lock table is full.
67	ENOLINK	The link has been severed	The `path` value references a remote system that is no longer active.
77	EBADMSG	Not a data message	Message to be **read** is not a data message.

will block (by default) until data is written to the pipe or the pipe is closed.

☞ If the pipe is **open** for writing by another process, but the pipe is empty, then a **read** (in combination with the flags O_NDELAY and O_NONBLOCK) will return the values:

O_NONBLOCK	O_NDELAY	Value Returned
set	clear	-1
clear	set	0

☞ If the pipe is not opened for writing by another process, **read** will return a 0 (indicating the end-of-file condition). Note that this is the same value that is returned when the O_NDELAY flag has been set and the pipe is open but empty.

Pipes can be divided into two categories, **unnamed** pipes and **named** pipes. Unnamed pipes can only be used with related processes (e.g., parent/child or child/

child) and exist only as long as the processes using them. Since named pipes actually exist as directory entries that have file access permissions they can be used with unrelated processes.

5.2 UNNAMED PIPES

An unnamed pipe is constructed with the **pipe** system call (see Table 5.5).

Table 5.5 Summary of the **pipe** system call.

Include File(s)	<unistd.h>		Manual Section	2
Summary	int pipe(int filedes[2]);			
Return	Success	Failure	Sets errno	
	0	-1	Yes	

If successful, the **pipe** system call will return two integer file descriptors, filedes[0] and filedes[1]. The file descriptors reference two data streams. Historically pipes were always non-duplex (unidirectional) and data flowed in one direction only. If two-way communication was needed two pipes were opened, one for reading and another for writing. In current versions of UNIX the file descriptors returned by **pipe** are full duplex (bi-directional) and are both opened for reading/writing. Pictorially we can think of this relationship as is illustrated in Figure 5.2.

In a full duplex setting if the process writes to filedes[0] then filedes[1] is used for reading, otherwise the process writes to filedes[1] and filedes[0] is used for reading. In a half duplex setting filedes[1] is *always* used for writing and filedes[0] for reading—an attempt to **write** to fildes[0] will produce an error (i.e., bad file descriptor).

If the **pipe** system call fails it will return a -1 and set **errno** (Table 5.6).

As previously noted, data in a pipe is read on a first-in-first-out basis. Program 5.1 shows a pair of processes (parent/child) that use a pipe to send the first argument passed on the command line to the parent as a *message* to the child. Notice that the pipe is generated prior to forking the child process.

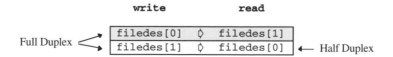

Fig. 5.2 Writing/reading from a pipe.

Table 5.6 `pipe` error messages.

#	Constant	perror **Message**	Explanation
23	ENFILE	File table overflow	System file table is full.
24	EMFILE	Too many open files	Process has exceeded the limit for number of open files.

Program 5.1 Parent/child processes communicating via a pipe.

```
/*
 *Using a pipe to send data from a parent to a child process  */
 */
#include <stdio.h>
#include <unistd.h>
#include <stdlib.h>
#include <string.h>
main(int argc, char *argv[ ]) {
  int           f_des[2];
  static char   message[BUFSIZ];
  if (argc != 2) {
    fprintf(stderr, "Usage: %s message\n", *argv);
    exit(1);
  }
  if (pipe(f_des) == -1) {                   /* generate the pipe   */
    perror("Pipe");     exit(2);
  }
  switch (fork( )) {
  case -1:
    perror("Fork");     exit(3);
  case 0:                                    /* In the child   */
    close(f_des[1]);
    if (read(f_des[0], message, BUFSIZ) != -1) {
      printf("Message received by child: [%s]\n", message);
      fflush(stdout);
    } else {
      perror("Read");     exit(4);
    }
    break;
  default:                                   /* In the Parent  */
    close(f_des[0]);
    if (write(f_des[1], argv[1], strlen(argv[1])) != -1) {
      printf("Message sent by parent   : [%s]\n", argv[1]);
      fflush(stdout);
    } else {
      perror("Write");     exit(5);
    }
  }
  exit(0);
}
```

In the parent process, the pipe file descriptor `f_des[0]` is closed and the message (the string referenced by `argv[1]`) is written to the pipe file descriptor `f_des[1]`. In the child process, the pipe file descriptor `f_des[1]` is closed and pipe file descriptor `f_des[0]` is **read** to obtain the message. While the closing of the unused pipe file descriptors is not required, it is a good practice. Remember that for **read** to be successful the number of bytes of data requested must be present in the pipe or all the **write** file descriptors for the pipe must be closed so that an end-of-file can be returned. The pipe file descriptors `f_des[0]` in the child and `f_des[1]` in the parent will be closed when each process exits. The output of Program 5.1 is:

Fig. 5.3 Output of Program 5.1.

```
% a.out this_is_a_message
Message sent by parent    : [this_is_a_message]
Message received by child: [this_is_a_message]
```

E X E R C I S E   5 – 1

Modify Program 5.1 so the child, upon receipt of the message, changes its case and returns the message (via a pipe) to the parent where it is then displayed. *If your system does not support duplex pipes, you will need to generate two pipes prior to forking the child process.*

On the command line we often use pipes to connect programs so that standard output of one program becomes the standard input of the next. For example, the command:

```
% last | sort
```

will execute the **last** command (which displays login and logout information about users) and pipe its output to the **sort** command. The redirection of the output of the **last** command to be the input to the **sort** command is accomplished with the inclusion of the command line specification of a pipe symbolized by "|". To accomplish a similar task with our parent/child pair, we will need a way to associate standard input and standard output with the pipe we have created. There are two ways in which this can be accomplished—by using the **dup** system call or the **dup2** library function (Tables 5.7 and 5.8).

The **dup2** library call supersedes the **dup** system call but both bear discussion. The **dup** system call duplicates an original open file descriptor. The *new* descriptor, `fildes`, references the system file table entry for the next available non-negative file descriptor. The *new* descriptor will share the same file pointer (offset), have the same

Table 5.7 Summary of the **dup** system call.

Include File(s)	<unistd.h>		Manual Section	**2**
Summary	`int dup( int fildes );`			
Return	Success		Failure	Sets errno
	Next available non-negative file descriptor		-1	Yes

Table 5.8 Summary of the **dup2** library function.

Include File(s)	<unistd.h>		Manual Section	**3c**
Summary	`int dup2( int fildes,` `          int fildes2 );`			
Return	Success	Failure	Sets errno	
	Next available non-negative file descriptor	-1	Yes	

access mode as the original and will be set to remain open across an **exec** call. A key point to consider is that when called, **dup** will *always* return the next lowest available file descriptor.

A code sequence of:

```
int f_des[2];
pipe(f_des);
close( fileno(stdout) );
dup(f_des[1]);
   .
   .
   .
```

declares and generates a pipe. The file descriptor for standard output (say, file descriptor 1) is closed. The following **dup** system call would return the next lowest available file descriptor, which in this case should be the previously closed standard output file descriptor (i.e., 1). Thus, any data written to standard output in following statements would now be written to the pipe. As there are two steps to this process, closing the descriptor and then **dup**-ing it, there is an outside chance that the sequence will be interrupted and the descriptor returned by **dup** will not be the one that was just closed (such as when a signal catching routine closes files upon receipt of a caught signal).

Enter the **dup2** library function. The **dup2** library function will close and duplicate the file descriptor as a single *atomic* action. When **dup2** is called, the file descriptor referenced by fildes will be a duplicate of the file descriptor referenced by fildes2. If the file referenced by fildes2 is open, it will be closed before the duplication is performed. Both the **dup** and **dup2** calls can also be implemented with the **fcntl** system call.

A short program that mimics the last | sort command is shown in Program 5.2.

Once Program 5.2 executes the **fork** system call, the process table entries for the files/pipes for the two processes are shown in Figure 5.4.

Assuming a fairly standard setting (i.e., stdin = 0, stdout = 1, stderr = 2) with both stdout and stderr mapped to the same device (most likely the terminal), initially both the parent and child processes reference the same entries in the system file table. After the child process is generated, we use the **dup2** library function to close standard output and duplicate it. The system returns the previous reference for standard output, which is now associated with the system file table entry for `f_des[1]`. Once this association has been made the file descriptors `f_des[0]` and `f_des[1]` are closed as they are not needed by the child process.

Program 5.2 A `last` | `sort` pipeline.

```
/*
 *   A home grown last | sort command pipeline
 */
#include <stdio.h>
#include <unistd.h>
#include <stdlib.h>
main(void) {
  int           f_des[2];
  if (pipe(f_des) == -1) {
    perror("Pipe");
    exit(1);
  }
  switch (fork()) {
  case -1:
    perror("Fork");
    exit(2);
  case 0:                    /* In the child        */
    dup2(f_des[1], fileno(stdout));
    close(f_des[0]);
    close(f_des[1]);
    execl("/usr/bin/last", "last", (char *) 0);
    exit(3);

  default:                   /* In the parent       */
    dup2(f_des[0], fileno(stdin));
    close(f_des[0]);
    close(f_des[1]);
    execl("/bin/sort", "sort", (char *) 0);
    exit(4);
  }
}
```

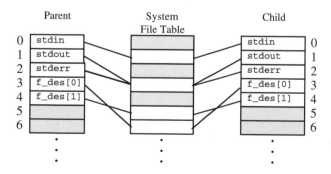

Fig. 5.4 Initial process table entries for files/pipes.

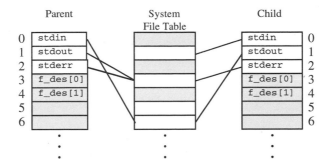

Fig. 5.5 End process table entries for files/pipes.

In the parent process, the **dup2** library function closes standard input and duplicates it as the reference f_des[0]. The process table entries for the files would now look like those shown in Figure 5.5.

When running Program 5.2, the two processes (parent and the child) are running concurrently (at the same time). There is no guarantee as to the sequence in which these processes will be executed. For the processes involved, this is not a concern as the pipe allows both processes to write/read at the same time.

We can summarize the steps involved for communication via unnamed pipes as:

1. Create the pipe(s) needed.
2. Generate the child process(es).
3. Close/duplicate file descriptors to properly associate the *ends* of the pipe.
4. Close the unneeded ends of the pipe.
5. Perform the communication activities.
6. Close any remaining open file descriptors.
7. If appropriate, wait for child processes to terminate.

If either **dup** or **dup2** fail they will return a -1 and set **errno**. The error codes for **dup** and **dup2** are shown in Table 5.9.

Table 5.9 dup/dup2 error messages.

#	Constant	perror **Message**	**Explanation**
4	EINTR	Interrupted system call	Signal was caught during the system call.
9	EBADF	Bad file number	The value in fildes is not a valid open file descriptor.
24	EMFILE	Too many open files	Process has exceeded the limit for number of open files.
67	ENOLINK	The link has been severed	The path value references a remote system that is no longer active.

E X E R C I S E   5 – 2

Most UNIX systems include a utility program called **tee** that copies standard input to standard output and to the file descriptor passed on the command line. Thus the command sequence:

```
% cat x.c | tee /dev/console | wc
```

would **cat** the contents of the file x.c and pipe the standard output to **tee**. The **tee** program would copy its standard input (from the **cat** command) to the file /dev/console and copy standard input to its standard output where it would be piped to the **wc** (word count) program. Using unnamed pipes, write your own version of **tee**. *Hint:* On most systems the command **who** will display the terminal you are on—be sure to include the prefix path indicating the device directory (i.e., /dev).

E X E R C I S E   5 – 3

Modify Program 5.2 so a variable number of commands can be passed to the program. Each command passed to the program should be *connected* to the next command via a pipe. When using this new program a three-command sequence such as:

```
% last | sort | more
```

would be indicated as:

```
% a.out  last  sort  more
```

E X E R C I S E   5 – 4

Rework the program written for Exercise 4.2 (the producer/consumer problem) so the producer and consumer now use a pipe to communicate with one another.

Since the sequence of generating a pipe, forking a child process, duplicating file descriptors, and passing command execution information from one process to another via the pipe is relatively common, a set of standard I/O functions is available to simplify this task. The I/O functions that are used are **popen** and **pclose**. See Tables 5.10 and 5.11.

Table 5.10 Summary of the **popen** I/O function.

Include File(s)	`<stdio.h>`		Manual Section	**3s**
Summary	`FILE *popen( const char *command,` `                  const char *type );`			
Return	Success	Failure	Sets errno	
	Pointer to a FILE	NULL pointer		

Table 5.11 Summary of the `pclose` I/O function.

Include File(s)	<stdio.h>		Manual Section	**3s**
Summary	int pclose(FILE *stream);			
Return	Success	Failure	Sets errno	
	Exit status of command	-1		

When successful, the **popen** call returns a pointer to a file (not an integer file descriptor). The arguments for **popen** are a pointer to the *shell* command[2] that will be executed and an I/O mode `type`. The I/O mode `type` determines how the process will handle the file pointer returned by the **popen** call.

When invoked, the **popen** call automatically generates a child process. The child process **exec**'s a Bourne shell, which will execute the shell command passed to it. Input to, and output from, the child process is accomplished via a pipe. If the I/O mode `type` for **popen** is specified as "w" the parent process can **write** to the standard input of the shell command. In other terms, writing to the file pointer reference generated by the **popen** in the parent process will enable the child process running the shell command to **read** the data as its standard input. Conversely, if the I/O type is "r", using the popen file pointer, the parent process can **read** from the standard output of the shell command (run by the child process).

The **pclose** call is used to close a data stream opened with a **popen** call. If the data stream being closed is associated with a **popen**, **pclose** will return the exit status of the shell command referenced by the **popen**. If the data stream is not associated with a **popen** call, the **pclose** call will return a value of -1.

Program 5.3 shows one way the **popen** and **pclose** calls can be used to pipe the output of one shell command to the input of another.

Program 5.3 Using **popen** and **pclose**.

```
/*
 *  Using the popen and pclose I/O commands
 */
#include <stdio.h>
#include <unistd.h>
#include <stdlib.h>
#include <limits.h>
int
main(int argc, char *argv[ ]) {
   FILE            *fin, *fout;
   char             buffer[PIPE_BUF];
```

---

2. This can be any valid shell command, including those with I/O redirection.

```
int              n;
if (argc < 3) {
  fprintf(stderr, "Usage %s cmd1 cmd2\n", argv[0]);
  exit(1);
}
fin  = popen(argv[1], "r");
fout = popen(argv[2], "w");

while ((n = read(fileno(fin), buffer, PIPE_BUF)) > 0)
  write(fileno(fout), buffer, n);

pclose(fin);
pclose(fout);
exit(0);
}
```

As written, Program 5.3 requires two command line arguments. These two arguments are two shell commands whose standard output/input will be *redirected* via pipes generated when using the **popen** call. The first **popen** call, with the I/O option of "r", directs the system to **fork** a child process that will execute the shell command. The output of the command will be redirected so it can be **read** by the parent process when using the file pointer reference, fin. In a similar manner, the second **popen** with the I/O option of "w" directs the system to **fork** a second child process. As this child process executes its shell command, its standard input will be the data written to the pipe by the parent process. The parent process writes data to the second pipe using the file pointer reference fout and reads data from the first pipe using the file pointer reference fin. The **while** loop in the program is used to copy the data from the output end of one pipe to the input end of the other.

EXERCISE   5 – 5

When using *just* the **popen** call to generate pipes, can we create a pipeline consisting of *three* separate shell commands? (e.g., a program that when passed three shell commands on the command line, would *pipe* the commands together in the manner: cmd1 | cmd2 | cmd3) If yes, write a program that shows how this can be done. If no, give the reason(s) why.

5.3 NAMED PIPES

UNIX provides for a second type of pipe called a named pipe or FIFO (we will use the terms interchangeably). Named pipes are similar in spirit to unnamed pipes but have additional benefits. When generated, named pipes have a directory entry. With the directory entry are file access permissions and the capability for unrelated processes to use the pipe file. Named pipes can be created at the shell level (on the command line) or within a program. It is instructive to look at the generation of a named pipe at the shell level before addressing its use in a program.

At the shell level the command used to make a named pipe is **mknod**. Officially **mknod** is a utility command designed to generate special files. It is most commonly used by the superuser to generate special device files (e.g., the block, character device files found in the /dev directory). For non-privileged users, **mknod** can only be used to generate a named pipe. The syntax for the **mknod** command is:

```
% mknod PIPE p
```

The first argument to the **mknod** command is the file name for the FIFO (this can be any valid UNIX file name, however it is common to use an uppercase file name to alert the user to the *special* nature of the file). The second argument is a lowercase "p", which notifies **mknod** that a FIFO file is to be created. If we issue the command shown above and check the directory entry for the file that it has created, we will find a listing similar to that shown below:

```
% ls -l PIPE
prw-r--r--   1 gray     other      0 Mar 10 15:36 PIPE
```

The lowercase letter "p" at the start of the permission string indicates the file called PIPE is a FIFO. The default file permissions for a FIFO are assigned using the standard **umask** arrangement discussed previously. The number of bytes in the FIFO is listed as 0. As soon as all the processes that are using a named pipe are done with it, any remaining data in the pipe is released by the system and the byte count for the file reverts to 0. If we wish to, we can, on the command line, redirect the output from a shell command to a named pipe. If we do this, we should place the command sequence in the background to prevent it from hanging. We could then redirect the output of the same FIFO to be the input of another command.

For example, the command:

```
% cat test_file.c > PIPE &
[1] 19472
```

will cause the display of the contents of file test_file.c to be redirected to the named pipe PIPE. If this command is followed by:

```
% cat < PIPE
```

the second **cat** command will read its input from the named pipe PIPE and display its output to the screen.

E X E R C I S E   5 – 6

As long as there is one active reader and/or writer for a FIFO, the system will maintain its contents. Produce a command sequence that proves this is so. *Hint*: Use the **ls -l** command to show the pipe actually has contents.

While the previous discussion is instructive, it is of limited practical use. Under most circumstances, FIFOs are created in a programming environment, not on the command line. The system call to generate a FIFO in a program has the same name as the system command equivalent, i.e., **mknod** (Table 5.12).

Table 5.12 Summary of the **mknod** system call.

Include File(s)	`<sys/types.h>` `<sys/stat.h>`	Manual Section	**2**

Summary	`int mknod( const char *path,`
	`            mode_t mode,`
	`            dev_t dev );`		

Return	**Success**	**Failure**	**Sets errno**
	0	-1	Yes

The **mknod** system call will create the file referenced by path. The type of the file created (FIFO, character or block special, directory or plain) and its access permissions are determined by the mode value. Most often the mode for the file is created by OR-ing a symbolic constant indicating file type with the file access permissions (see the section on **umask** for a more detailed discussion). Permissible file types are:

Table 5.13 File type specification constants for **mknod**.

Symbolic Constant	File Type
S_IFIFO	FIFO special
S_IFCHR	character special
S_IFDIR	directory
S_IFBLK	block special
S_IFREG	ordinary file

The dev argument for **mknod** is used only when a character or block special file is specified. For non-privileged users, the **mknod** system call can only be used to generate a FIFO. When generating a FIFO, the dev argument should be left as 0. If **mknod** is successful, it returns a value of 0. Otherwise **errno** is set to indicate the error and a value of -1 is returned.

In many versions of UNIX, there is a C library function called **mkfifo** that simplifies the generation of a FIFO. The **mkfifo** library function uses the **mknod** system call to generate the FIFO. Most often, unlike **mknod**, **mkfifo** does not require the user have superuser privileges.

If **mkfifo** is used in place of **mknod**, the mode argument for **mkfifo** refers only to the file access permission for the FIFO, as the file type, by default, is set to S_IFIFO. If the **mkfifo** call fails it will return a -1 and set the value in **errno**. When generating a FIFO the errors that may be encountered with **mkfifo** are similar to those previously listed for the **mknod** system call (Table 5.14). In our examples, we will use the more universal **mknod** system call when generating a FIFO.

Table 5.14 **mknod** error messages.

#	Constant	perror **Message**	**Explanation**
1	EPERM	Not owner	The effective ID of the calling process is not that of the superuser.
2	ENOENT	No such file or directory	One or more parts of the path to the file to process does not exist (or is NULL).
4	EINTR	Interrupted system call	Signal was caught during the system call.
14	EFAULT	Bad address	path references an illegal address.
20	ENOTDIR	Not a directory	Part of the specified path is not a directory.
22	EINVAL	Invalid argument	Invalid dev specified.
28	ENOSPC	No space left on device	File system has no inodes left for file generation.
30	EROFS	Read-only file system	Referenced file is (or would be) on a read-only file system.
67	ENOLINK	The link has been severed	The path value references a remote system that is no longer active.
74	EMULTIHOP	Multihop attempted	The path value requires multiple hops to remote systems but file system does not allow it.
78	ENAMETOOLONG	File name too long	The path value exceeds system path/file name length.
90	ELOOP	Number of symbolic links encountered during path name traversal exceeds MAXSYMLINKS	The **perror** message says it all.

Our next example is somewhat more grand in scope than some of the past examples. We will combine the use of unnamed and named pipes to produce a **client-server** relationship. Both the client and server processes will run on the same platform. The single server process will be run first and placed in the background. Client processes, run subsequently, will be in the foreground. The client processes will accept a shell command from the user. The command will be sent to the server, via a *public* FIFO (known to all clients) for processing. Once received, the server will execute the command using the **popen–pclose** sequence (which generates an unnamed pipe in the process). The server process will return the output of the command to the

Table 5.15 Summary of the `mkfifo` library function.

Include File(s)	`<sys/types.h>` `<sys/stat.h>`		Manual Section	**3c**
Summary	`int mkfifo( const char *path,` `                mode_t mode );`			
Return	Success	Failure	Sets `errno`	
	0	-1	Yes	

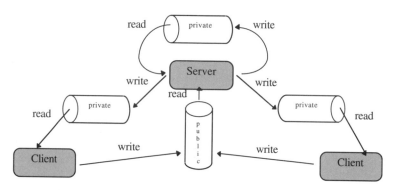

Fig. 5.6 Client-server process relationships.

client over the *private* FIFO where the client displays it to the screen. Figure 5.6 shows the process and pipe relationships.

More succinctly, the steps taken by the processes involved will be:

☞ Server generates the *public* FIFO (available to all participating client processes).

☞ Client process generates its own *private* FIFO.

☞ Client prompts for, and receives, a shell command.

☞ Client writes the name of its *private* FIFO and the shell command to the *public* FIFO.

☞ Server reads the *public* FIFO, obtains the *private* FIFO name and the shell command.

☞ Server uses a **popen–pclose** sequence to execute the shell command. The output of the shell command is sent back to the client via the *private* FIFO.

☞ Client displays the output of the command.

To ensure that both server and client processes will use the same *public* FIFO name, and have the same message format, a local header file is used. This header file is shown in Figure 5.7.

Fig. 5.7 Header file for client-server example.

```
/*
 *  local header file for pipe client-server
 */

#include <stdio.h>
#include <sys/types.h>
#include <sys/stat.h>
#include <fcntl.h>
#include <unistd.h>
#include <string.h>
#include <limits.h>
#include <stdlib.h>

#define PUBLIC "/tmp/PUBLIC"
#define B_SIZ (PIPE_BUF / 2)

struct message {
  char            fifo_name[B_SIZ];
  char            cmd_line[B_SIZ];
};
```

In this file, a #define is used to define the name for the *public* FIFO as /tmp/PUBLIC. The format of the message that will be sent over the *public* FIFO is declared with the **struct** statement. The message structure consists of two character array members. The first member, called fifo_name, contains the name of the *private* FIFO. The second structure member, cmd_line, contains the command to be executed by the server.

Program 5.4 shows the code for the client process:

Program 5.4 The client process.

```
/*
 *The client process
 */
#include "local.h"
void
main( void ){
  int            n, privatefifo, publicfifo;
  static char    buffer[PIPE_BUF];
  struct message msg;

  /* Make the name for the private FIFO  */
  sprintf(msg.fifo_name, "/tmp/fifo%d", getpid( ));

  /* Generate the private FIFO  */
  if (mknod(msg.fifo_name, S_IFIFO | 0666, 0) < 0) {
    perror(msg.fifo_name);
    exit(1);
  }
  /* OPEN the public FIFO for writing  */
  if ((publicfifo = open(PUBLIC, O_WRONLY)) == -1) {
    perror(PUBLIC);
    exit(2);
  }
  while ( 1 ) {                              /* FOREVER      */
    write(fileno(stdout), "\ncmd>", 6);      /* prompt       */
```

```
    memset(msg.cmd_line, 0x0, B_SIZ);           /* clear first  */
    n = read(fileno(stdin), msg.cmd_line, B_SIZ); /* Get cmd */
    if (!strncmp("quit", msg.cmd_line, n - 1))    /* EXIT ?  */
      break;
    write(publicfifo, (char *) &msg, sizeof(msg));/* to PUBLIC*/

    /* OPEN private FIFO to read returned command output    */

    if ((privatefifo = open(msg.fifo_name, O_RDONLY)) == -1) {
      perror(msg.fifo_name);
      exit(3);
    }
    /* READ private FIFO and display on standard error  */

    while ((n = read(privatefifo, buffer, PIPE_BUF)) > 0) {
      write(fileno(stderr), buffer, n);
    }
    close(privatefifo);
  }
  close(publicfifo);
  unlink(msg.fifo_name);                         /* REMOVE   */
}
```

Using the **sprintf** function, the client creates a unique name for its *private* FIFO by incorporating the value returned by the **getpid** system call. The **mknod** system call is used next to create the *private* FIFO with read and write permissions for all. The following **open** statement opens the *public* FIFO for writing. If for some reason the *public* FIFO has not been previously generated by the server, the **open** will fail. In this case the **perror** call will produce an error message and the client process will exit. If the **open** is successful, the client process then enters an endless loop. The client first prompts the user for a command[3]. Prior to obtaining the command, the structure member where the command will be stored is set to all NULLs using the C library function **memset**. This action assures that no extraneous characters will be left at this storage location. The following **read** statement obtains the user's input from standard input and stores it in msg.cmd_line. The input is checked to determine if the user would like to quit the program. The check is accomplished by comparing the input to the character string quit. We use n-1 as the number of characters for comparison to avoid including the \n found at the end of the user's input. If quit was entered, the **while** loop is exited via the **break** statement, the *private* FIFO is removed, and the client process terminates. If the user does not want to quit, the entire message structure, consisting of the *private* FIFO name and the command the user entered, is written to the *public* FIFO. The client process then attempts to **read** its *private* FIFO to obtain the output that will be sent to it from the server. At this juncture, if the server has not finished with its execution of the client's command, the client process will block (which is the default for **read**). Once data is available from the *private* FIFO, the **while** loop in the client will **read** and **write** its contents to standard error.

---

3. Notice that all the I/O in the program is done with **read/write** to avoid buffer flushing problems associated with standard I/O library calls.

The code for the server process is shown in Program 5.5:

Program 5.5 The server process.

```
/*
 *   The server process
 */
#include "local.h"
main( void ){
    int             n, done, dummyfifo, publicfifo, privatefifo;
    struct message  msg;
    FILE            *fin;
    static char     buffer[PIPE_BUF];

    /* Generate the public FIFO    */
    mknod(PUBLIC, S_IFIFO | 0666, 0);

    /*  OPEN public FIFO for reading and writing */
    if ((publicfifo = open(PUBLIC, O_RDONLY)) == -1 ||
        (dummyfifo  = open(PUBLIC, O_WRONLY | O_NDELAY)) == -1 ) {
        perror(PUBLIC);
        exit(1);
    }
    /*  message can be read from the PUBLIC pipe        */

    while (read(publicfifo, (char *) &msg, sizeof(msg)) > 0) {
        n = done = 0;                    /* clear counters / flags   */
        do {                             /* try OPEN of private FIFO */
            if ((privatefifo=open(msg.fifo_name,
                             O_WRONLY|O_NDELAY)) == -1)
              sleep(3);                  /* sleep a while            */
            else {                       /* OPEN successful          */
              fin = popen(msg.cmd_line, "r"); /* execute the cmd     */
              write(privatefifo, "\n", 1);   /* keep output pretty */
              while ((n = read(fileno(fin), buffer, PIPE_BUF)) > 0) {
                 write(privatefifo, buffer, n);/* to private FIFO    */
                 memset(buffer, 0x0, PIPE_BUF);/* clear it out       */
              }
              pclose(fin);
              close(privatefifo);
              done = 1;                  /* record success          */
            }
        } while (++n < 5 && !done);
        if (!done)                       /* Indicate failure        */
          write(fileno(stderr),
          "\nNOTE: SERVER ** NEVER ** accessed private FIFO\n", 48);
    }
}
```

The server process is responsible for creating the *public* FIFO. Once created, the *public* FIFO is opened for both reading and writing. This may appear to be a little odd as the server process only needs to **read** from the *public* FIFO. By opening the *public* FIFO for writing as well, the *public* FIFO always has at least one writing process associated with it. Therefore, the server process will never receive an end-of-file on the *public* FIFO. The server process will block on an empty *public* FIFO waiting for additional messages to be written. This technique will save us from having to close and reopen the *public* FIFO every time a client process finishes its activities.

Once the *public* FIFO is established, the server will attempt to **read** a message from the *public* FIFO. When a message is **read** (consisting of a private FIFO name and a command to execute) the server will try to **open** the indicated *private* FIFO for writing. The attempt to **open** the *private* FIFO is done within a **do-while** loop. The O_NDELAY flag is used to keep the **open** from generating a deadlock situation. Should the client, for some reason, not open its end of the private FIFO for reading, the server would, without the O_NDELAY flag specification, block at the **open** of the *private* FIFO for writing. If the attempt to open the *private* FIFO fails, the server sleeps three seconds and tries again. After five unsuccessful attempts, the server will display an informational message to standard output and continue with its processing. If the *private* FIFO is successfully opened, a **popen** is used to execute the command that was passed in the message structure. The output of the command (which is obtained from the unnamed pipe) is written to the *private* FIFO using a **while** loop. When all of the output of the command has been written to the unnamed pipe, the unnamed pipe and *private* FIFO are closed.

A sample run of the client-server programs follows:

Fig. 5.8 Typical client-server output.

```
% server &
[1] 3101
% client

cmd>ps

      PID TTY           TIME COMD
     3104 term/2       0:00 ps
     1001 term/2       0:02 csh
     3102 term/2       0:00 client
     3103 term/2       0:00 sh
     3101 term/2       0:00 server

cmd>who

rlopes      pts/2         Mar 14 12:56      (backroom)
root        pts/1         Mar 14 11:18
lindh       term/0        Mar 14 14:16
gray        term/2        Mar 14 13:36

cmd>quit
% kill -9 3101
```

The server process is placed in the background. The client process is then run and shell commands (**ps** and **who**) are entered in response to the cmd> prompt. The output of each command (after being executed by the server process and its output sent back to the client) is shown. The client process is terminated by the entry of the word "quit". The server process, which remains in the background, even after the client has been removed, is terminated by using the **kill** command.

EXERCISE   5 – 7

There are a number of additions that can be made to the client program to make it more
robust. For example, if the client exits due to the receipt of an interrupt signal
(CTRL+"C"), the *private* FIFO is not removed. Use a signal catching routine to correct this
oversight. When the client process is initiated, it will fail if the server process is not available. Correct this by having the client start the server process if it is not active.

EXERCISE   5 – 8

As written, the server program will process each command request in turn. Should one of
these requests require a long time to execute, all other client processes must wait to be
serviced. Rewrite the server program so that when the server process receives a message,
it **fork**s a child process to carry out the task of executing the command and returning the
output of the command to the client process.

5.4 SUMMARY

Pipes provide the user with a more reliable, synchronized means of interprocess communication. Unnamed pipes can only be used with related processes. The **popen** system call provides the user with an easy way to generate an unnamed pipe to execute a
shell command. Named pipes (FIFOs), which exist as actual directory entries, can be
shared by unrelated processes. The amount of data a pipe can contain is limited by the
system. When a pipe is no longer associated with any processes, its contents are
flushed by the system. The **read** and **write** system calls, which can be used with pipes,
provide the user with an easy means of coordinating the flow of data in a pipe. Care
must be taken when using pipes to prevent deadlock situations. Deadlock can occur
when one process opens one end of a pipe for writing and another process opens the
other end of the same pipe for writing. Each process, in turn, is waiting for the other to
complete its action[4]. Pipes can only be used by processes that are running on the same
platform. Unfortunately pipes provide no easy way for a reading process to determine
who the writing process was. All processes involved with using pipes must have fore-
hand knowledge of their existence.

---

4. As the unnamed pipe generated by **popen** is done without the user's direct use of the **open** system call, should the O_NDELAY or O_NBLOCK flags need to be set, the **fcntl** system call must be
used.

CHAPTER 6

Message Queues

6.1 INTRODUCTION

The designers of UNIX found the types of interprocess communications that could be implemented using signals and pipes to be restrictive. To increase the flexibility and range of interprocess communication, supplementary communication facilities were added. These facilities, added with the release of System V and grouped under the heading IPCs, are:

☞ **Message queues**—Information to be communicated is placed in a predefined message structure. The process generating the message specifies its type and places the message in a system-maintained message queue. Processes accessing the message queue can use the message type to *selectively* read messages of specific types in a first-in-first-out manner. Message queues provide the user with a means of multiplexing data from multiple producers.

☞ **Semaphores**—System-implemented data structures used to communicate small amounts of data between processes. Most often, semaphores are used for process synchronization.

☞ **Shared memory**—Information is communicated by accessing shared process data space. This is the fastest method of interprocess communication. Shared memory allows participating processes to randomly access the shared memory segment. Semaphores are often used to synchronize the access to the shared memory segments.

143

Like a file, an IPC facility must be generated before it can be used. Each IPC facility has a creator, owner and access permissions. These attributes, established when the IPC is created, can be modified using the proper system calls. At a system level, information on IPCs can be obtained with the **ipcs** command. For example, on our system the **ipcs** command with the **-b** option produces the following output:

Fig. 6.1 Some **ipcs** output.

```
% ipcs -b

IPC status from <running system> as of Tue Mar 29 11:41:09 1994
T     ID     KEY          MODE        OWNER     GROUP QBYTES
Message Queues:
q     50 0x67028a01 -Rrw-rw----      gray      other   4096
Shared Memory facility not in system.
T     ID     KEY          MODE        OWNER     GROUP NSEMS
Semaphores:
s      0 0x000187cf --ra-ra-ra-      root      root    2
s      1 0x000187ce --ra-ra-ra-      root      root    1
```

The **-b** option causes **ipcs** to display the maximum number of bytes for a message queue message, the maximum size of a shared memory segment, and the maximum number of semaphores in a set of semaphores. The message Shared Memory facility not in system. does not indicate the shared memory facility is unavailable, only that it is not currently in use. The mode for an IPC contains an extra two leading characters that denote the IPC's current state. The meaning of these special characters is given in Table 6.1.

IPCs exist and maintain their contents even after the process that created them has terminated. An IPC facility can be removed by its owner by using the appropriate system call within a program, or by using the system level command, **ipcrm**. The message queue, shown in the output of the previous **ipcs** command, could be removed by its owner by issuing the command:

```
% ipcrm -q 50
```

Table 6.1 **ipcs** mode indicators.

Letter	Interpretation
R	waiting on an **msgrcv**
S	waiting on an **msgsnd**
D	shared memory segment has been removed. Will disappear when last process detaches it.
C	shared memory segment will be cleared when first attached
-	Flag not set

The **-q** option tells **ipcrm** that a message queue is to be removed, and the argument 50 is the ID number of the queue[1]. As there are per-user and system-wide limits to the number of IPC facilities available, users should make a conscientious effort to remove unneeded IPCs. Under Solaris, the command **sysdef -i** can be used to display the current limits for tunable kernel parameters which include the IPC constructs.

6.2 IPC System Calls—A Synopsis

A set of similar system calls are used to create an IPC facility and manipulate IPC information. Due to their flexibility, the syntax for these calls is somewhat arcane (the calls appear, like the camel, to have been designed by a committee). The System V IPC calls are summarized in Table 6.2.

Table 6.2 Summary of the System V IPC calls.

Functionality	Message Queue	System Call Semaphore	Shared Memory
Allocate an IPC, gain access to an IPC.	msgget	semget	shmget
Control an IPC, obtain/modify status information, remove an IPC.	msgctl	semctl	shmctl
IPC operations: send/receive messages, perform semaphore operations, attach/free a shared memory segment.	msgsnd msgrcv	semop	shmat shmdt

The *get* system calls[2] (**msgget**, **semget**, and **shmget**) are used either to allocate a new IPC facility (which generates its associated system IPC structure), or gain access to an existing IPC. Each IPC has an owner and a creator which, under most circumstances, are usually one and the same. When a new facility is allocated, the user must specify the access permissions for the IPC. Like the **open** system call, the *get* system calls return an integer value, called an IPC identifier, which is analogous to a file descriptor. The IPC identifier is used to reference the IPC. From a system standpoint, the IPC identifier is an index into a system table containing IPC permission structure information. The IPC permission structure is defined in the header file <sys/ipc.h> as:

```
struct ipc_perm {
        uid_t    uid;     /* owner's user ID */
```

---

1. For the masochist, there is a **-Q** option for **ipcrm** for which the user must enter in the hexadecimal key as the argument to indicate which message queue to remove.

2. The term *get* (in *italics*) will be used to reference the group of system calls. Do not confuse this *get* with the command **get** which returns the version of an SCCS file.

```
        gid_t   gid;     /* owner's group ID */
        uid_t   cuid;    /* creator's user ID */
        gid_t   cgid;    /* creator's group ID */
        mode_t  mode;    /* access modes */
        ulong   seq;     /* slot usage sequence number */
        key_t   key;     /* key */
        long    pad[4];  /* reserve area */
};
```

The type definitions for uid_t, qid_t, etc. can be found in the header file <sys/types.h>. In general, all programs that make use of the IPC facilities should include the <sys/types.h> and <sys/ipc.h> files. As will be discussed in the section on *ctl* system calls, some members of this structure can be modified by the user.

There are two arguments common to each of the three *get* system calls. Each *get* system call takes an argument of defined type key_t (of base type long integer). This argument, known as the key value, is used by the *get* system call to generate the IPC identifier. There is a direct, one-to-one, relationship between the IPC identifier returned by the *get* system call and the key value. While the key can be generated in an arbitrary manner, there is a C library function called **ftok** that is often used to standardize key production[3].

By calling **ftok** with the same arguments, unrelated processes can be assured of producing the same **key** value and thus reference the same IPC facility. The **ftok** function is defined as:

Table 6.3 Summary of the **ftok** library function.

Include File(s)	<sys/types.h> <sys/ipc.h>		Manual Section	**3c**
Summary	`key_t ftok( const char *path,` `              int id );`			
Return	Success	Failure	Sets errno	
	key value for an IPC *get* system call	-1		

The **ftok** function requires two arguments. The first, path, is a reference to an existing accessible file. Often the value "." is used for this argument, as in most situations the self-referential directory entry "." is always present, accessible and not likely to be subsequently deleted. The second argument for **ftok,** id, is an integer value most commonly represented by a single character. The value returned by a successful call to **ftok** is of defined type key_t. As demonstrated in Program 6.1, the most signif-

---

3. In all honesty, the **ftok** library function is superfluous, but is presented for historical and continuity reasons. As long as processes that wish to access a *common* IPC have a method to communicate the key value for the IPC (such as in a common header file), **ftok** can be avoided.

icant byte of the value returned by **ftok** is the character id value which is passed as the second argument.

Program 6.1 Generating some key values with **ftok**.

```
/*
 *Using ftok to generate key values */
 */
#include <stdio.h>
#include <sys/types.h>
#include <stdlib.h>
#include <sys/ipc.h>
main(void){
  key_t            key;
  char             i;
  for (i = 'a'; i <= 'd'; ++i) {
    key = ftok(".", i);
    printf(" id = %c key = [%08X] MSB = %c\n", i, key, key >> 24);
  }
exit( 0 );
}
```

When run on a local 32-bit system the output of Program 6.1 was:

Fig. 6.2 Output of Program 6.1.

```
% a.out
 id = a key = [61028A5D] MSB = a
 id = b key = [62028A5D] MSB = b
 id = c key = [63028A5D] MSB = c
 id = d key = [64028A5D] MSB = d
```

E X E R C I S E   6 – 1

The most significant byte of **ftok**'s returned key value is the character id. What part of the returned key value is taken from the file reference argument to **ftok**? Write a short program that supports your answer.

The key value for the *get* system calls may also be set to the defined constant, IPC_PRIVATE. Beneath the covers, IPC_PRIVATE is defined as having a value of 0. Note, regardless of its argument values, the **ftok** library function will *not* return a value of 0. Specifying IPC_PRIVATE instructs the *get* system call to create an IPC facility with a unique IPC identifier. Thus, no other process creating or attempting to gain access to an IPC facility will receive this same IPC identifier. An IPC facility created with IPC_PRIVATE is normally shared between related processes (such as parent/child or child/child) or in client-server settings. In the related process settings, the parent process creates the IPC facility. When performing an **exec** the associated IPC identifier is passed to the child process by way of the environment, or as a command line parameter. In client-server relationships, the server process usually creates the

IPC using IPC_PRIVATE. The IPC identifier is then made available to the client via a file. Note that, in either scenario, the child/client process would not specify IPC_PRIVATE when issuing its *get* system call.

The second argument common to all of the IPC *get* system calls is the message flag. The message flag, an integer value, is used to set the access permissions when the IPC facility is created. Table 6.4 summarizes the subsequent types of permissions required for each of the IPC system calls[4] to perform their functions. The execute bit is not relevant for IPC facilities.

In addition to setting access modes, there are two defined constants, found in <sys/ipc.h>, that can be **OR**ed with the access permission value(s) to modify the actions taken when the IPC is created. The constant, IPC_CREAT, directs the *get* system call to create an IPC facility if one does not presently exist. When specifying IPC_CREAT, if the facility is already present, and it was not created using IPC_PRIVATE, its IPC identifier is returned. In conjunction with IPC_CREAT, the creator may also specify IPC_EXCL. Using these two constants together (i.e., IPC_CREAT | IPC_EXCL) causes the *get* system call to act in a *no clobber* manner. That is, should there already be an IPC present for the specified key value, the *get* system call will fail; otherwise, the facility is created. Using this technique, a process can be assured that it is the creator of the IPC facility and is not gaining access to a previously created IPC. In this context, specifying IPC_EXCL by itself has no meaning.

Table 6.4 Required permissions for IPC system calls.

Permissions Required	Message Queues	Semaphores	Shared Memory
write (alter)	**msgsnd**—place message in the queue	**semop**—increase or decrease a semaphore value	**shmat**—to write to the shared memory segment
	msgctl—write out modified IPC status information	**semctl**—set the value of one semaphore or a whole set, write out modified IPC status information	**shmctl**—write out modified IPC status information
read	**msgrcv**—obtain message from queue	**semop**—block until a semaphore becomes 0	**shmat**—read from the shared memory segment
	msgctl—to retrieve IPC status information	**semctl**—to retrieve IPC status information	**shmctl**—to retrieve IPC status information

---

4. The header files for each of the IPC facilities (i.e., <sys/msg.h>, <sys/sem.h> and <sys/shm.h>) contain defined constants for read/write (access) permissions for the facility. As noted previously, using defined constants does increase the portability of code. However, there is no free lunch, as the programmer must often take the time to look up the correct *spelling* of infrequently used defined constants.

The *ctl* system calls (**msgctl**, **semctl** and **shmctl**) act upon the information in the system IPC permission structure described previously. All of these system calls require an IPC identifier and an integer command value to stipulate their action. The values the command may take are represented by the following defined constants (found in the header file <sys/ipc.h>):

☞ **IPC_STAT**—Return the referenced IPC facility status information. When specifying IPC_STAT, the *ctl* system call must pass a pointer to an allocated structure of the appropriate type to store the returned information.

☞ **IPC_SET**—Change the owner, group or mode for the IPC facility. In addition, as with IPC_STAT, a pointer to a structure of the appropriate type (with the changed member information) must be passed.

☞ **IPC_RMID**—Destroy the contents of the IPC facility and remove it from the system.

A process can only specify IPC_SET or IPC_RMID if it is the owner or creator of the IPC (or if it has superuser privileges). Some of the *ctl* system calls have additional functionality which will be presented in future sections.

The remaining IPC system calls are used for IPC *operations*. The **msgsnd** and **msgrcv** calls are used to send and receive a message from a message queue. By default, the system will block on an **msgsnd** if a message queue is full, or on an **msgrcv** if the message queue is empty. The process will remain blocked until the indicated operation is successful, a signal is received, or the IPC facility is removed. A process can specify to not block by ORing in the IPC_NOWAIT flag with the specified operation flag. The **semop** system call performs a variety of operations on semaphores (such as setting, testing, etc.). Again, the default is to block when attempting to decrement a semaphore that is currently at 0, or if the process is waiting for a semaphore to become 0. The **shmat** and **shmdt** system calls are used with shared memory to map/attach and unmap/detach shared memory segments. These calls do not block.

For some reason, known only to those who authored the documentation, the **msgsnd** and **msgrcv** manual pages (found in section two) contain a reference to **msgop**. However, there is no system call **msgop**. Likewise, the **shmat** and **shmdt** manual pages make reference to **shmop,** which also is not a system call. The manual page for **semop** only makes reference to **semop** (which is indeed a system call). One must only conclude that initial intent was to group all of these calls under the general heading of IPC operations.

We will address each set of IPC system calls in detail as we cover message queues, semaphores and shared memory.

6.3 CREATING A MESSAGE QUEUE

A message queue is created using the **msgget** system call (Table 6.5). If the **msgget** system call is successful, a non-negative integer is returned. This value is the message queue identifier and can be used in subsequent calls to reference the message queue.

Table 6.5 Summary of the `msgget` system call.

Include File(s)	`<sys/types.h>` `<sys/ipc.h>` `<sys/msg.h>`	Manual Section	**2**
Summary	`int msgget( key_t key,` `                int msgflg );`		

Return	Success	Failure	Sets errno
	Non-negative message queue identifier associated with key	-1	Yes

If the `msgget` system call fails, the value -1 is returned and the global variable **errno** is set appropriately to indicate the error (see Table 6.6). The value for the argument key can be specified directly by the user or generated using the **ftok** library function (see previous discussion). The value assigned to key is used by the system to produce a unique message queue identifier. The low-order bits of the msgflg argument are used to determine the access permissions for the message queue. Additional flags (e.g., IPC_CREAT, IPC_EXCL) may be ORed with the permission value to indicate special creation conditions.

Table 6.6 `msgget` error messages.

#	Constant	`perror` **Message**	**Explanation**
2	EOENT	No such file or directory	Message queue identifier does not exist for this key and IPC_CREAT was not set.
13	EACCES	Permission denied	Message queue identifier exists for this key but requested operation is forbidden by current access permissions.
17	EEXIST	File exists	Message queue identifier exists for this key but IPC_CREAT and IPC_EXCL are both set.
28	ENOSPC	No space left on device	System imposed limit for the number of message queues has been reached.

A new message queue is created if the defined constant IPC_PRIVATE is used as the key argument, or if the IPC_CREAT flag is ORed with the access permissions and no previously existing message queue is associated with the key value. If IPC_CREAT is specified (without IPC_EXCL) and the message queue already exists, **msgget** will *not* fail but will return the message queue identifier associated with the key value (Table 6.6).

Program 6.2 generates five message queues with read/write access, uses the **ipcs** command (via a pipe) to display message queue status and then removes the message queues.

Program 6.2 Generating message queues.

```c
/*
 *Message queue generation
 */
#include <stdio.h>
#include <unistd.h>
#include <stdlib.h>
#include <limits.h>
#include <sys/types.h>
#include <sys/ipc.h>
#include <sys/msg.h>
#define MAX   5
main(void){
  FILE            *fin;
  char            buffer[PIPE_BUF], u_char = 'A';
  int             i, n, mid[MAX];
  key_t           key;
  for (i = 0; i < MAX; ++i, ++u_char) {
    key = ftok(".", u_char);
    if ((mid[i] = msgget(key, IPC_CREAT | 0660)) == -1) {
      perror("Queue create");
      exit(1);
    }
  }
  fin = popen("ipcs", "r");                /* run the ipcs command */

  while ((n = read(fileno(fin), buffer, PIPE_BUF)) > 0)
    write(fileno(stdout), buffer, n);    /* display ipcs output  */
  pclose(fin);

  for (i = 0; i < MAX; ++i )
    msgctl(mid[i], IPC_RMID, (struct msqid_ds *) 0); /* remove    */
  exit(0);
}
```

When run on our system, this program produces the following output indicating that five message queues have been generated:

Fig. 6.3 Output of Program 6.2.

```
% a.out
IPC status from <running system> as of Mon Apr  4 10:10:20 1994
T    ID    KEY         MODE        OWNER     GROUP
Message Queues:
q    800 0x41028a01 --rw-rw----   gray     other
q    651 0x42028a01 --rw-rw----   gray     other
q    652 0x43028a01 --rw-rw----   gray     other
q    653 0x44028a01 --rw-rw----   gray     other
q    654 0x45028a01 --rw-rw----   gray     other
Shared Memory facility not in system.
Semaphores:
s      0 0x000187cf --ra-ra-ra-   root     root
s      1 0x000187ce --ra-ra-ra-   root     root
```

EXERCISE   6 - 2

Run Program 6.2 several times in rapid succession. Look at the message queue identifiers
that are produced. What appears to be the numbering scheme the system is using? *Hint:*
Look in the header file <sys/msg.h>. Can you find any rationale for this approach? Now
add the statement sleep(5); after the statement pclose(fin);. Recompile the program and invoke the program twice, placing it in background each time. Assuming the
program is a.out this can be accomplished by:

```
% a.out &; a.out &
```

Count the number of message queues generated and explain why there are not ten
present.

When a message queue is created, a system message queue data structure called
msqid_ds is generated. This structure, maintained by the system, is defined in the
header file <sys/msg.h> as:

```
struct msqid_ds {
    struct ipc_perm msg_perm;   /* operation permission struct */
    struct msg      *msg_first; /* ptr to first message on q */
    struct msg      *msg_last;  /* ptr to last message on q */
    ulong           msg_cbytes; /* current # bytes on q */
    ulong           msg_qnum;   /* # of messages on q */
    ulong           msg_qbytes; /* max # of bytes on q */
    pid_t           msg_lspid;  /* pid of last msgsnd */
    pid_t           msg_lrpid;  /* pid of last msgrcv */
    time_t          msg_stime;  /* last msgsnd time */
    long            msg_pad1;   /* reserved for time_t expansion */
    time_t          msg_rtime;  /* last msgrcv time */
    long            msg_pad2;   /* time_t expansion */
    time_t          msg_ctime;  /* last change time */
    long            msg_pad3;   /* time_t expansion */
    short           msg_cv;
    short           msg_qnum_cv;
    long            msg_pad4[3];/* reserve area */
};
```

The first member of this structure is the IPC permission structure discussed earlier. The system will set, respectively, the msg_perm.cuid, msg_perm.uid,
msg_perm.cgid, and msg_perm.gid members to the effective user and group ID of the
invoking process. The low-order nine bits of msgflg (taken from the **msgget** call) will
be used to set the value in msg_perm.mode.

Next in msqid_ds structure are two pointers to the first and last messages in the
queue. From the system's standpoint, the individual messages in the queue are structures of type msg. The msg structure is defined in the header file <sys/msg.h> as:

```
struct msg {
    struct msg      *msg_next;  /* ptr to next message on q */
    long            msg_type;   /* message type */
    ushort          msg_ts;     /* message text size */
    short           msg_spot;   /* message text map address */
};
```

Individual messages are placed in a linked list form by the system. Each `msg` structure contains a reference to the next `msg` in the list, a long integer value denoting the message type, a short integer value indicating the size in bytes of the message, and a reference, `msg_spot`, to the actual message.

When the message queue is created the system will set the `msqid_ds` members `msg_qnum`, `msg_lspid`, `msg_lrpid`, `msg_stime`, and `msg_rtime` to 0. The member, `msg_ctime`, will be set to the current time and `msg_qbytes` will be set to the system limit.

Thus, *conceptually* we can envision a message queue with N items as being similar to Figure 6.4.

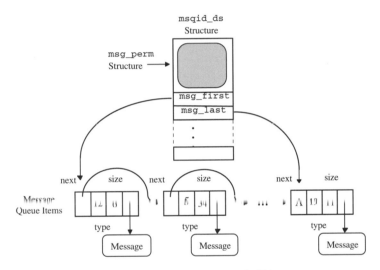

Fig. 6.4 A message queue with N items.

6.4 Message Queue Control

The ownership and access permissions, established when the message queue was created, can be examined and modified using the **msgctl** system call (see Table 6.7).

The **msgctl** system call will reference the message queue indicated by the `msqid` argument. The value of the `cmd` argument is used to indicate the action that **msgctl** should take. The following defined constants/actions can be specified:

☞ IPC_STAT—return the current values for each member of the `msqid_ds` data structure (remember that this also contains the permission structure). When using the IPC_STAT flag, the user *must* provide a location to store the returned information. The address of the storage location for the information is passed as the third argument to the **msgctl** system call.

☞ IPC_SET—with this flag, the user can modify a limited number of `msqid_ds` structure member values. The following members can be modified:

   `msg_perm.uid, msg_perm.gid, msg_perm.mode and msg_qbytes`

Table 6.7 Summary of the **msgctl** system call.

Include File(s)	`<sys/types.h>`
	`<sys/ipc.h>`
	`<sys/msg.h>`
			Manual
			Section
				2

Summary	`int msgctl( int msqid,`
	`            int cmd,`
	`            /****`
	`            struct msqid_ds *buf`
	`            ****/ ... †);`			

Return	Success	Failure	Sets errno	
	0	-1	Yes	

†The ellipses (...) in the function prototype indicate a variable number of arguments.

Similar to IPC_STAT, the user must first generate a structure of type msqid_ds, modify the appropriate structure members and then call **msgctl** with the IPC_SET flag and the address of the modified structure.

☞ IPC_RMID—removes all associated message queue structures. When specifying IPC_RMID, the third argument to **msgctl** is not considered and thus may be left out. However, wanting to leave nothing to chance, many programmers enter the third argument as a NULL value cast to be a pointer to an msqid_ds structure.

If the **msgctl** system call fails it will return a -1 and set **errno**; otherwise it will return a 0 indicating success. The value that **errno** may be assigned when **msgctl** fails is given in Table 6.8.

Table 6.8 msgctl error messages.

#	Constant	perror **Message**	Explanation
1	EPERM	Not superuser	• cmd is IPC_RMID and the calling process is not the owner or superuser. • cmd is IPC_SET and non-superuser process is attempting to increase msg_qbytes beyond the system limit.
13	EACCES	Permission denied	cmd is IPC_STAT but operation is forbidden by the current access permissions.
14	EFAULT	Bad address	buf references a bad address.
22	EINVAL	Invalid argument	• Message queue identifier is invalid. • cmd is invalid. • cmd is IPC_SET but msg_perm.uid or msg_perm.gid value is invalid.
79	EOVERFLOW	Value too large for defined data type	cmd is IPC_STAT and location referenced by buf is too small to hold the uid or gid values.

Program 6.3 creates a message queue, uses the **msgctl** system call to obtain the message queue structure information, and displays pertinent data to the screen.

Program 6.3 Using **msgctl**.

```
/*
 *  Displaying message queue status information
 */
#include <stdio.h>
#include <unistd.h>
#include <stdlib.h>
#include <sys/types.h>
#include <sys/ipc.h>
#include <sys/msg.h>

main(void){
  int             mid;
  key_t           key;
  struct msqid_ds buf;
  key = ftok(".", 'z');
  if ((mid = msgget(key, IPC_CREAT | 0660)) == -1) {
    perror("Queue create");
    exit(1);
  }

  msgctl(mid, IPC_STAT, &buf);

  printf("Message Queue *Permission* Structure Information\n");
  printf("Owner's user ID   \t%d\n", buf.msg_perm.uid);
  printf("Owner's group ID  \t%d\n", buf.msg_perm.gid);
  printf("Creator's user ID \t%d\n", buf.msg_perm.cuid);
  printf("Creator's group ID\t%d\n", buf.msg_perm.cgid);
  printf("Access mode in HEX \t%06X\n", buf.msg_perm.mode);
  printf("\n\nAdditional Selected Message Queue Structure Information\n");
  printf("Current # of bytes on queue\t %d\n", buf.msg_cbytes);
  printf("Current # of messages on queue\t %d\n", buf.msg_qnum);
  printf("Maximum # of bytes on queue\t %d\n", buf.msg_qbytes);
  msgctl(mid, IPC_RMID, (struct msqid_ds *) 0 );
  exit(0);
}
```

Run locally, Program 6.3 produces the following output:

Fig. 6.5 Output of Program 6.3.

```
% a.out
Message Queue *Permission* Structure Information
Owner's user ID         107
Owner's group ID        1
Creator's user ID       107
Creator's group ID      1
Access mode in HEX      0081B0

Additional Selected Message Queue Structure Information
Current # of bytes on queue       0
Current # of messages on queue    0
Maximum # of bytes on queue       4096
```

As shown, when first generated, the creator of the message queue and the owner are the same. If we convert the displayed hexadecimal access mode value to binary:

$$0081B0_{16} \equiv 1000000 \; |110| \; |110| \; |000|_2$$

and examine the lower nine bits of the binary number we see the access permissions are indeed 0660 as we specified. The value for the maximum number of bytes on the message queue, shown here as 4096, is one of several system imposed message queue limits. Additional message queue limit information can be found in the header file <sys/msg.h>.

E X E R C I S E   6 – 3

Using the **msgctl** system call with the IPC_SET flag, modify Program 6.3 to change the value for msg_qbytes to one greater than the current system maximum. What is the error message that is returned by **perror** when the **msgctl** system call fails? Is the message misleading? Why? Why not?

6.5 MESSAGE QUEUE OPERATIONS

Message queues are used to send and receive messages. An actual message, from the system's standpoint, is defined by the msgbuf structure found in the header file <sys/msg.h> as:

```
struct msgbuf {
        long    mtype;              /* message type */
        char    mtext[1];          /* message text */
};
```

This structure is used as a *template* for the messages to be sent to, and received from, the message queue.

The first member of the msgbuf structure is the message type. The message type, mtype, is a long integer value normally greater than 0. The message type, generated by the process that originates the message, is used to indicate the kind of (category for the) message. The type value will be used by the **msgrcv** system call to selectively retrieve messages falling within certain boundary conditions. Messages are placed in the message queue in the order they are sent and *not* grouped by their message type.

Following mtype is the reference to the body of the message. As shown, this appears as a character array with one element, i.e., mtext[1]. In actuality, any valid structure member(s), character arrays or otherwise, that make up a message can be placed after the requisite mtype entry. The system assumes a valid message always consists of a long integer followed by a series of 0 or more bytes. It is the address of the first structure member after mtype that the system uses as its reference when assigning values to the msg structure (discussed in the section **Creating a Message Queue**). Therefore, users can generate their own message structures to be placed in the message queue so long as the first member (on most systems this is the first four bytes) is occupied by a long integer.

Messages are placed in the message queue (sent) using the system call **msgsnd** (Table 6.9).

Table 6.9 Summary of the **msgsnd** system call.

Include File(s)	<sys/types.h> <sys/ipc.h> <sys/msg.h>		Manual Section	**2**

Summary	int msgsnd(int msqid,
	        const void *msgp,
	        size_t msgsz,
	        int msgflg);			

Return	Success	Failure	Sets errno	
	0	-1	Yes	

The **msgsnd** system call requires four arguments. The first argument, msqid, is a valid message queue identifier returned from a prior **msgget** system call. The second argument, msgp, is a pointer to the message to be sent. As noted, the message is a structure with the first member being of the type long integer. The message structure must be allocated (and hopefully initialized) prior to its being sent. The third argument, msgsz, is the size (number of bytes) of the message to be sent. The size of the message can be from 0 to the system-imposed limit. The fourth argument to **msgsnd**, msgflg, is used to indicate what action should be taken if system limits for the message queue (e.g., the limit for the number of bytes in a message queue) have been reached. The msgflg can be set to IPC_NOWAIT or to 0. If set to IPC_NOWAIT and a system limit has been reached, **msgsnd** will not send the message and will return to the calling process immediately with **errno** set to EAGAIN. If msgflg is set to 0, **msgsnd** will block until the limit is no longer at system maximum (at which time the message is sent), the message queue is removed, or the calling process catches a signal. The system will use the msgsz argument to **msgsnd** as its msg.msg_ts value, the msgbuf.mtype value as its msg.msg_type and the msgbuf.mtext reference as msg.msg_spot.

If **msgsnd** is successful, it returns a value of 0, otherwise it will return a value of -1 and set **errno** to indicate the nature of the error. See Table 6.10.

Messages are retrieved from the message queue using the system call **msgrcv** as shown in Table 6.11.

The **msgrcv** system call requires five arguments. The first, like the **msgsnd** system call, is the message queue identifier. The second, msgp, is a pointer to the location (structure) where the received message will be placed. The receiving location should have as its first field a long integer to accommodate the message type information. The third argument, msgsz, is the maximum size of the message in bytes. This value should be equal to the longest message to be received. Truncation of the message will occur if the size value is incorrectly specified, and depending upon the value for msgflg (see following section), an error may be generated. The fourth argument, msgtyp, is the type of the message to be retrieved. The message type information is interpreted by the **msgrcv** system call as shown in Table 6.12.

Table 6.10 **msgsnd** error messages

#	Constant	perror **Message**	Explanation
13	EACCES	Permission denied	Attempt made to access message queue in a forbidden way.
11	EAGAIN	No more processes	Message cannot be sent and IPC_NOWAIT was specified.
14	EFAULT	Bad address	msgp references a bad address.
22	EINVAL	Invalid argument	• Message queue identifier is invalid. • mtype is less than 1. • msgsz is less than 0 or greater than system limit.

Table 6.11 Summary of the **msgrcv** system call.

Include File(s)	`<sys/types.h>`
	`<sys/ipc.h>`
	`<sys/msg.h>`
			Manual Section	**2**

Summary	`int msgrcv( int msqid,`
	`            void *msgp,`
	`            size_t msgsz,`
	`            long msgtyp,`
	`            int msgflg );`			

Return	Success	Failure	Sets errno	
	Number of bytes actually received	-1	Yes	

Table 6.12 Actions for **msgrcv** as indicated by msgtyp values.

When **msgtyp** value is:	msgrcv **takes this action**
0	retrieve the first message of **any** msgtyp
> 0	retrieve the first message **equal** to msgtyp
< 0	retrieve the first message of the **lowest** type <= to absolute value of msgtyp

Using the type argument judiciously a user can, with minimal effort, implement a priority-based messaging arrangement.

The fifth and final argument, `msgflg`, is used to indicate what actions should be taken if a given message type is not in the message queue, or if the message to be retrieved is larger in size than the number of bytes indicated by `msgsz`. There are two predefined values that `msgflg` can take. IPC_NOWAIT is used to indicate to the **msgrcv** system call that it should not block if the requested message type is not in the message queue. MSG_NOERROR directs **msgrcv** to silently truncate messages to `msgsz` bytes if they are found to be too long. If MSG_NOERROR is not specified and **msgrcv** receives a message that is too long, it will return a -1 and set the value in **errno** to E2BIG to indicate the error. In don't-care situations, the value for `msgflg` can be set to 0. When **msgrcv** is successful, it returns the number of bytes actually retrieved. See Table 6.13.

Table 6.13 `msgrcv` error messages.

#	Constant	`perror` Message	Explanation
7	E2BIG	Argument list too long	`mtext` is greater than `msgsz` and MSG_NOERROR is not set.
13	EACCES	Permission denied	Attempt made to access message queue in a forbidden way.
14	EFAULT	Bad address	`msgp` references a bad address.
22	EINVAL	Invalid argument	• Message queue identifier is invalid. • `msgsz` is less than 0.
35	ENOMSG	No message of desired type	Message queue does not have a message of type `msgtyp` and IPC_NOWAIT is set.

6.6 A CLIENT-SERVER MESSAGE QUEUE EXAMPLE

At this point we can use our knowledge of message queues to write a pair of programs that establish a client-server relationship and use message queues for bi-directional interprocess communication. The client process will obtain input from the keyboard and send it, via a message queue, to the server. The server will read the message from the queue, *process* the message by converting all alphabetic text in the message to uppercase and place the message back in the queue for the client to read. By mutual agreement, the client process will identify messages designated for the server by placing the value 1 in the message type member of the message structure[5]. In addition, the client will include its process ID number in the message. The server will use the

---

5. This works nicely, as in multiple client situations, not every client has initial access to the process ID of the server.

process ID number of the client to identify messages it has processed and placed back in the queue. Labeling the processed messages in this manner allows the server to handle messages from multiple clients.

For example, if the client process had a process ID of 17, and had placed two messages consisting of the words happy and joy in the message queue, Figure 6.6 would depict the current state of the message queue. As shown, both messages, placed in the queue by the client (process ID 17), are labeled as being a message type of 1 (for the server).

When the server reads the queue, it will obtain the first message of type 1. In our example this will be the message containing the word happy. The server will *process* the message, change the message type to that of the client, and put the message back on the queue. This will leave the message queue in the state shown in Figure 6.7.

To accomplish their task, both the client and server programs will need to access common include files and data structures. These items are placed in a local header file called local.h, whose contents are shown in Figure 6.8. An examination of this file will reveal that the messages that will be placed in the queue consist of a structure with three members. The first member (which must be of type long if things are to work correctly) will act as the message type (mtype) member. Here we have called this member msg_to as it will contain a value that indicates the process to whom we are addressing the message. We will use the value of 1 to designate a message for the server process and other positive process ID values to indicate a message for a client. The second member of the message structure, called msg_fm, will contain the ID of the process that is sending the message. If the message is sent by a client, this value will

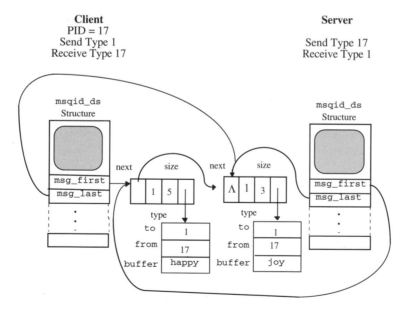

Fig. 6.6 Conceptual view of message queue after
the client has sent two messages.

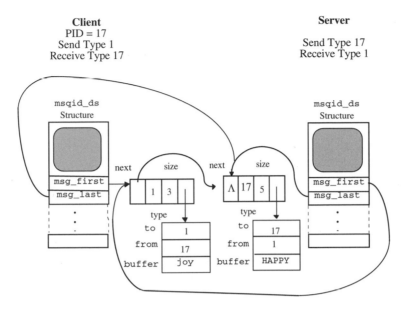

Fig. 6.7 Conceptual view of message queue after
the first client message has been processed.

be the client process ID. If the message is sent by the server, this value will be set to 1.
The third member of the message structure will contain the text of the actual message.

Fig. 6.8 Local header file for message queue example.

```
/*
 *Common header file for Message Queue Example   */
 */
#include <stdio.h>
#include <sys/types.h>
#include <sys/ipc.h>
#include <sys/msg.h>
#include <string.h>
#include <ctype.h>
#include <unistd.h>
#include <stdlib.h>
#include <errno.h>

#define SEED   'g'           /* seed for ftok          */
#define SERVER 1L            /* message for the server */

typedef struct {
  long          msg_to;   /* Placed in the queue for */
  long          msg_fm;   /* Placed in the queue by  */
  char          buffer[BUFSIZ];
}MESSAGE;
```

The client program, shown in Program 6.4, begins by obtaining its process ID. This value will be used later to "tag" messages sent to the server, identifying them as coming from a particular client process. The **ftok** library function is used to produce a key. When the client process is invoked, we want it to create the message queue, if one does not already exist. Further, if the server process is not present, we want the client to start it. We will assume that if the message queue is not present, the server process is not present as well. To accomplish this the initial call to **msgget**, i.e., mid=msgget(key, 0), is tested to determine if the call has failed. If the message queue is not found (the call fails), the message queue is created by the second call to **msgget**. If this occurs, the client process then **fork**s a child process and overlays it with a call to **exec** to run the server process. The server is passed the message queue identifier via the command line. As all command line arguments are strings, the **sprintf** string function is used to put the message queue identifier in the correct format.

Once the message queue is created, the client program enters an endless loop, prompting for user input, placing the input in the message queue for the server to process, retrieving the processed input and displaying the results to standard output. If the user enters a message of 0 bytes (i.e., CTRL+"D" from the keyboard), the client exits its loop and sends the server a special 0 byte length message indicating it is done.

Program 6.4 The client.

```
/*
 *CLIENT ... sends messages to the server   */
 */
#include "local.h"
main(void){
    key_t           key;            /* Key value for ftok */
    pid_t           cli_pid;        /* Process ID */
    int             mid, n;         /* Message queue ID */
    MESSAGE msg;                    /* Message structure */
    static char     m_key[10];      /* For string version of mid */
    cli_pid = getpid();

    if ((key = ftok(".", SEED)) == -1) {   /* generate the key */
      perror("Client: key generation");
      exit(1);
    }
    /*      Create and gain access to message queue        */
    if ((mid=msgget(key, 0 )) == -1 ) {
      mid = msgget(key,IPC_CREAT | 0660);
      switch (fork()) {
      case -1:
        perror("Client: fork");
        exit(3);
      case 0:
        sprintf(m_key, "%d", mid);        /* turn into string */
        execlp("server", "server", m_key, "&", 0);
        perror("Client: exec");
        exit(4);
      }
```

```
  }
  while (1) {
    msg.msg_to = SERVER;                  /* Message type */
    msg.msg_fm = cli_pid;                 /* Tag with client PID */
    write(fileno(stdout), "cmd>", 6);     /* Prompt */
    memset(msg.buffer, 0x0, BUFSIZ);      /* Clear buffer */
    n = read(fileno(stdin), msg.buffer, BUFSIZ);
    if (n == 0 )                          /* EOF ? */
      break;
    if (msgsnd(mid, &msg, sizeof(msg), 0) == -1 ) {
      perror("Client: msgsend");
      exit(5);
    }                                     /* Display */
    if( (n=msgrcv(mid, &msg, sizeof(msg), cli_pid, 0)) != -1 )
      write(fileno(stdout), msg.buffer, strlen(msg.buffer));
  }
  msgsnd(mid, &msg, 0, 0);
  exit(0);
}
```

The server process (shown in Program 6.5) starts by checking the number of command line arguments. If three command line arguments are not found, an error message is generated and the server program exits. Otherwise, the contents of argv[1] are converted to an integer value to be used as the message queue identifier. The server then enters into a loop. It first attempts to receive a message of type SERVER (1) from the queue. If the number of bytes returned by **msgrcv** is 0, the server assumes that the client process is done. In this case, the loop is exited and the server removes the message queue with a **msgctl** system call and exits. However, if a message is successfully retrieved from the message queue, it is *processed* (in the function process_msg) and placed back on the queue so the client process can retrieve it.

Program 6.5 The server.

```
/*
 * SERVER - receives messages from clients
 */
#include "local.h"

main(int argc, char *argv[ ]) {

  int              mid, n;
  MESSAGE          msg;
  void             process_msg(char *, int);

  if (argc != 3) {
    fprintf(stderr, "Usage: %s msq_id &\n", argv[0]);
    exit(1);
  }
  mid = atoi(argv[1]);              /* message queue ID via cmd line */
  while (1) {
    if ((n=msgrcv(mid, &msg, sizeof(msg), SERVER, 0)) == -1 ) {
      perror("Server: msgrcv");
      exit(2);
    } else if (n == 0)             /* client is done */
      break;
```

```
    else {                          /* process the message */
      process_msg(msg.buffer, strlen(msg.buffer));
      msg.msg_to = msg.msg_fm;      /* swap to <-> from info */
      msg.msg_fm = SERVER;
      if (msgsnd(mid, &msg, sizeof(msg), 0) == -1 ) {
        perror("Server: msgsnd");
        exit(3);
      }
    }
  }                                 /* remove the message queue */
  msgctl(mid, IPC_RMID, (struct msqid_ds *) 0 );
  exit(0);
}
/*
 Convert lower case alphabetics to upper case
*/
void
process_msg(char *b, int len){
  int         i;
  for (i = 0; i < len; ++i)
    if (isalpha(*(b + i)))
      *(b + i) = toupper(*(b + i));
}
```

The program is run by entering the name of the client program on the command line. The client will create the message queue and invoke the server process (which must reside locally). A prompt will be placed on the screen requesting input. Each time the user enters a string of characters and presses return the client will place the input in the message queue for processing. After the message has been processed, the client retrieves the message from the message queue and displays it to the screen. From the keyboard the client process is terminated by entering the key sequence CTRL+"D". As implemented, multiple copies of the client process can run/communicate with the server at the same time. One way to give this a try is to place the executable version of the client and server programs in /tmp (be sure to change the permissions so that all users have access to them). Then **cd** to /tmp and run the client program. Ask another user to do the same (remember this is all done on the same machine). Each of you should be able to run the client program and receive processing service. Just one message queue will be generated.

E X E R C I S E   6 – 4

As written the server program removes the message queue when any client sends a message of length 0. Modify the server program so that it only removes the message queue after *all* client processes are done with it.

E X E R C I S E   6 – 5

Modify the client-server programs to implement a *rudimentary chat* program that allows users to interactively talk to one another (a poor man's **talk**). One way to do this is to have the server examine the first character of the text portion of a SERVER message. If the character is, say, a ".", then the message is assumed to be a command the server should act on. If the sequence is ". lo", then the server records the process ID of the client as "logged in". If the sequence is ". who", the server returns the list of the process IDs of all logged-in (attached) clients. The process ID information can then be used to *connect* the two processes so that interactive communication can occur.

6.7 SUMMARY

Message queues are one of three interprocess communication facilities added to UNIX with the release of System V. Once created, a message queue is maintained by the system. Non-related processes, executing at different times, can use a message queue to pass information. Each message has an associated type that can be used to implement a rudimentary form of data multiplexing when multiple producers are involved. Message queues are created and accessed using the **msgget** system call. Messages are placed in the message queue with the **msgsnd** system call and retrieved from the queue with the **msgrcv** system call. Additional message queue manipulations are carried out with the **msgctl** system call. The **msgctl** system call will return information about the message queue, permit modification of access permissions and allow the owner to remove the message queue facility.

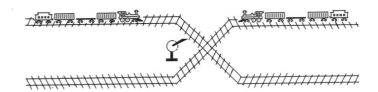

Semaphores

7.1 INTRODUCTION

Conceptually, a semaphore is a data structure that is shared by several processes. Semaphores are most often used to synchronize operations when multiple processes access a common, non-shareable resource. By using semaphores we attempt to avoid **starvation** (which occurs when a process is continually denied access to a resource it needs) and **deadlock** (which occurs when two or more processes each hold a resource that the other needs while waiting for the other process to release its resource). When used to synchronize the access to a resource, a semaphore is initially set to the number of available resources. Each time a process wants to obtain the resource, the associated semaphore is tested. A positive, non-zero semaphore value indicates the resource is available. To indicate it has gained access to the resource the process decrements the semaphore. For events to progress correctly, the test and decrement operation on the semaphore must be **atomic** (i.e., non-interruptible/indivisible). If the tested semaphore is zero, indicating the resource is not available, the requesting process must wait. When a process is finished with a semaphore-associated resource, the process indicates the return of the resource by incrementing the semaphore. Once a resource is returned, other processes that have been waiting for the resource are notified by the system. Semaphores that control access to a single resource, taking the value of 0 (resource is in use) or 1 (resource is available), are often called **binary** semaphores. Semaphores controlling access to multiple resources, thus assuming a range of non-negative values, are frequently called **counting** semaphores.

167

E.W. Dijkstra [1965] did much of the early work describing the use of semaphores to coordinate access to shared resources. Most college level operating systems text books, for example, Silberschatz and Peterson [1989] or Deitel [1990], contain excellent discussions on the theory and use of semaphores for process synchronization.

Implementation-wise, a semaphore is a non-negative integer that is stored in the kernel. Access to the semaphore is provided by a series of semaphore system calls. The semaphore system calls assure the user the test and decrement operations on the semaphore will be atomic. Likewise, the semaphore system calls will, by default, cause the invoking process to block if the semaphore value indicates the resource is not available (i.e., the semaphore is a zero). When the resource becomes available, the semaphore becomes non-zero, the system will notify the queued, waiting, processes of this event. To increase their flexibility, in UNIX semaphores are generated as sets consisting of one or more semaphores. Operations acting upon individual semaphores within the set or upon the entire semaphore set are provided.

7.2 CREATING AND ACCESSING SEMAPHORE SETS

Before a semaphore set can be used, it must be created. The creation of the semaphore set generates a unique data structure that the system uses to identify and manipulate the semaphores. The semaphore data structure used by the system is found in the include file <sys/sem.h>. Similar to the system message queue structure, the system semaphore data structure, semid_ds, contains a permission structure of type ipc_perm, which is used to specify the access permissions for the semaphore set:

```
struct semid_ds {
    struct ipc_perm sem_perm;     /* operation permission struct */
    struct sem      *sem_base;    /* ptr to first semaphore in set */
    ushort_t        sem_nsems;    /* # of semaphores in set */
    time_t          sem_otime;    /* last semop time */
    long            sem_pad1;     /* reserved for time_t expansion */
    time_t          sem_ctime;    /* last change time */
    long            sem_pad2;     /* time_t expansion */
    long            sem_pad3[4];  /* reserve area */
};
```

Following the access permission structure, the system semaphore data structure contains a reference, sem_base, to an array (set) of structures of type sem. The sem structure, also found in the <sys/sem.h> file, contains the semaphore value, the ID of the last process to operate on the semaphore and two counters indicating the number of processes waiting for the semaphore to increase and go to zero respectively. Each semaphore in the set has a sem structure associated with it:

```
struct sem {
        ushort  semval;       /* semaphore value */
        pid_t   sempid;       /* pid of last operation */
        ushort  semncnt;      /* # awaiting semval > cval */
        ushort  semzcnt;      /* # awaiting semval = 0 */
};
```

The system semaphore data structure also keeps track of the number of semaphores in the set (sem_nsems), the time of the last operation on the set (sem_otime) and the time of the last modification to the set (sem_ctime). The semid_ds also contains other members that, at present, are reserved for future use.

A conceptual arrangement of structures for a set of three semaphores is shown in Figure 7.1.

To create a semaphore, or gain access to one that exists, the **semget** system call, shown in Table 7.1, is used.

Table 7.1 Summary of the **semget** system call.

Include File(s)	<sys/types.h> <sys/ipc.h> <sys/sem.h>		Manual Section	**2**

Summary	`int semget( key_t key,`
	`              int nsems,`
	`              int semflg );`			

Return	Success	Failure	Sets errno	
	The semaphore identifier	-1	Yes	

The **semget** system call requires three arguments. The first argument, key, is used by the system to generate a unique semaphore identifier. The second argument, nsems, is the number of semaphores in the set. The system will use the nsems value when allocating the array of sem structures. As with all arrays in C, the array of sem structures that represents the set of semaphores is indexed starting at 0. The third argument, semflg, is used to specify access permission and/or special creation conditions. The low-order bits of the semflg value are used to specify the access permissions. The flags IPC_CREAT and IPC_EXCL may be ORed with the permission value.

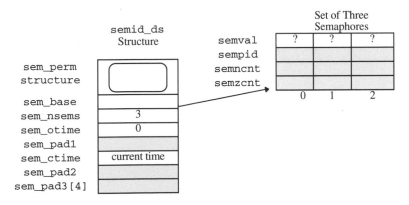

Fig. 7.1 Data structures for a set of three semaphores.

If the **semget** system call is successful, a non-negative integer, the semaphore identifier, is returned. If the value for key is IPC_PRIVATE, or the value for key does not have a semaphore identifier associated with it, and IPC_CREAT has been specified, a new set of semaphores is created. When created, the semaphore set represented by the array of sem structures is not initialized. If IPC_CREAT is specified (but not IPC_EXCL) and the semaphore set for the indicated key value already exists, the **semget** system call will return the associated semaphore identifier. When using **semget** to access an established semaphore set (such as in a client process) the value of nsems can be set to 0 (a don't-care value).

If the **semget** system call fails, it will return a -1 and set the value stored in **errno.** Error messages for **semget** are shown in Table 7.2.

Table 7.2 semget error messages.

#	Constant	perror Message	Explanation
2	EOENT	No such file or directory	Semaphore identifier does not exist for this key and IPC_CREAT was not set.
13	EACCES	Permission denied	Semaphore identifier exists for this key but the requested operation is forbidden by current access permissions.
17	EEXIST	File exists	Semaphore identifier exists for this key but IPC_CREAT and IPC_EXCL are both set.
22	EINVAL	Invalid argument	• Value for nsems is less than 0 or greater than the system limit. • Semaphore identifier exists but there are fewer semaphores in the set than specified by nsems.
28	ENOSPC	No space left on device	System imposed limit for number of semaphores or semaphore identifiers has been reached.

Program 7.1 attempts to create several semaphore sets, each containing three semaphores.

Program 7.1 Creating semaphore sets.

```
/*
 *Creating sets of semaphores    */
 */
#include <stdio.h>
#include <sys/types.h>
#include <sys/ipc.h>
#include <sys/sem.h>
#include <unistd.h>

main(void){
  int            sem1, sem2, sem3;
  key_t          ipc_key;
```

```
  ipc_key = ftok(".", 'S');
  if ((sem1 = semget(ipc_key, 3, IPC_CREAT | 0666)) == -1) {
    perror("semget: IPC_CREAT | 0666");
  }
  printf("sem1 identifier %d\n", sem1);
  if ((sem2=semget(ipc_key, 3, IPC_CREAT|IPC_EXCL|0666)) == -1) {
    perror("semget: IPC_CREAT | IPC_EXCL | 0666");
  }
  printf("sem2 identifier %d\n", sem2);
  if ((sem3 = semget(IPC_PRIVATE, 3, 0600)) == -1) {
    perror("semget: IPC_PRIVATE");
  }
  printf("sem3 identifier %d\n", sem3);
}
```

The first call to **semget** will, provided the system limits have not been reached, create a set of three semaphores. The permissions for the set will be **read** and **alter** (write) for the owner, group and others (world). The value of the semaphore identifier will be tied to the key value that is produced by the call to **ftok**. The second call to **semget** attempts to create a second set of three semaphores. The call uses the same key value as the first but includes the specification IPC_EXCL. With the IPC_EXCL flag set and the previous successful creation of the semaphore set using the same key value, this invocation of **semget** will fail. The third call to **semget** creates a three-semaphore set used by specifying IPC_PRIVATE instead of using the **ftok** key value. The semaphore identifier generated for this set will be *private* to this process.

When the program is run twice consecutively, the output generated will be similar to that shown in Figure 7.2.

Fig. 7.2 Two consecutive runs of Program 7.1.

```
% a.out
sem1 identifier 346
semget: IPC_CREAT | IPC_EXCL | 0666: File exists
sem2 identifier -1
sem3 identifier 217

% a.out
sem1 identifier 346
semget: IPC_CREAT | IPC_EXCL | 0666: File exists
sem2 identifier -1
sem3 identifier 98
```

Notice that when the program is run the second time, the same semaphore identifier (346) is returned from the initial call to **semget**. Without the IPC_EXCL flag, the **semget** system call will not fail if the semaphore set has already been created, but will instead return the associated semaphore identifier. The creation of a second *private* semaphore set by the second invocation of the program produces another unique semaphore identifier (98) which is different from the first private semaphore identifier (217). The output of the **ipcs** command, shown in Figure 7.3, verifies the presence and permissions of the three semaphore sets that were created by the user gray.

Fig. 7.3 `ipcs` output.

```
% ipcs
IPC status from <running system> as of Thu Apr 28 08:40:23 1994
Message Queue facility not in system.
Shared Memory facility not in system.
Semaphores:
s       0 0x000187cf    --ra-ra-ra-      root     root
s       1 0x000187ce    --ra-ra-ra-      root     root
s     346 0x53028109    --ra-ra-ra-      gray     other
s     217 0x0x00000000  --ra-------      gray     other
s      98 0x0x00000000  --ra-------      gray     other
```

As written, Program 7.1 does not remove the semaphore sets it creates. Semaphores, like message queues, are a limited resource. In a programming setting, semaphores can be removed with the **semctl** system call (see the following section). Semaphores may also be removed at the command line level using the **ipcrm** command (as discussed in section 6.1). If there are several semaphores to remove, a shell script, such as that shown in Program 7.2, can be used to automate the removal process.

Program 7.2 A C shell script to remove all semaphores for a user.

```
#!/bin/csh -f
#
# C Shell script to remove all existing semaphores for a user
#
set l = `ipcs -s | grep "$user" | cut -c2-9`
foreach s ( $l )
 ipcrm -s $s >& /dev/null
end
if ( $#l != 0  ) echo $#l semaphore\(s\) for $user removed
```

E X E R C I S E   7 – 1

Rewrite the C shell script, shown as Program 7.2, to permit the user to specify four command line options: **-q** to remove their message queues, **-s** to remove their semaphores, **-m** to remove their shared memory segments and **-a** to remove all their IPC facilities.

E X E R C I S E   7 – 2

Write a program that determines the maximum number of semaphores, semaphores per semaphore set and semaphore sets. You may find the **ipcs** with the **-a** option helpful to determine if other semaphores are present that you have not generated.

7.3 SEMAPHORE CONTROL

As shown, the **semget** system call is used to create or gain access to a set of semaphores. The **semctl** system call allows the user to perform a variety of generalized control operations on the system semaphore structure, on the semaphores as a set and on individual semaphores. Additional manipulative operations on specific semaphores within a set are covered in the following section on semaphore operations (section 7.4).

Table 7.3 Summary of the **semctl** system call.

Include File(s)	<sys/types.h> <sys/ipc.h> <sys/sem.h>		Manual Section	**2**

Summary	`int semctl( int semid,`
	`            int semnum,`
	`            int cmd,`
	`            /* union semun arg */`
	`            ... );`			

Return	Success		Failure	Sets errno
	0 or the value requested by cmd		-1	Yes

The **semctl** system call accepts four arguments. The first argument, semid, is a valid semaphore identifier that was returned by a previous **semget** system call. The second argument, semnum, is the number of semaphores in the semaphore set. In most cases, this value is greater than zero but less than the system limit. We will see occasions when the value for semnum will be set to 0. These occasions arise when we ask **semctl** to perform an operation for which the number of semaphores in the set is not important. The third argument to **semctl**, cmd, is an integer command value (usually expressed as one of the symbolic constants found in the header files <sys/ipc.h> or <sys/sem.h>). As discussed in detail in a following section, the cmd value will direct **semctl** to take one of several control actions. Each action requires specific access permissions to the semaphore control structure (i.e., **read** or **alter**). The fourth argument to **semctl**, arg, is a union of type semun. The manual page entry for **semctl** often shows this argument, referenced as arg, placed in comments. This argument is what I refer to as a *neither-fish-nor-fowl* argument. Depending upon the action specified by the preceding cmd argument, the value in arg is either an integer, a reference to a semid_ds structure or the base address of an array of short integers. In most versions of UNIX, the declaration for the union semun is found in the header file, <sys/sem.h>. Nonetheless, in some versions of UNIX (most notably the current versions of Solaris), this declaration has been omitted. This omission will cause the **semctl** system call to fail, returning the value EFAULT (bad address), when the arg value is a reference to a semid_ds structure or the base address of the ushort array. This *oversight* can be cor-

rected by including the following code in programs that will make use of the **semctl**
system call. This segment of code will properly define the semun union and declare arg
to be of type semun in the process:

```
union semun {
        int val;
        struct semid_ds *buf;
        ushort *array;
    };
union semun arg;
```

When specifying arg as the fourth argument to **semctl,** arg should be explicitly
assigned, e.g., arg.array = my_array, or arg.buf = ptr_to_my_structure. This
assignment must be done prior to the calling of **semctl** (see Program 7.3).

7.3.1 Semaphore Control Details

The following cmd values will cause **semctl** to act upon the system semaphore
structure (semid_ds):

- ☞ **IPC_STAT**—Return the current values of the semid_ds structure for the indicated semaphore identifier. The returned information is stored in a user-generated structure referenced by the fourth argument to **semctl**. To specify
IPC_STAT the process must have **read** permission for the semaphore set associated with the semaphore identifier.

- ☞ **IPC_SET**—Modify a restricted number of members in the semid_ds structure.
The members sem_perm.uid, sem_perm.gid and sem_perm.mode (in the permissions structure within semid_ds) can be changed if the effective ID of the
accessing process is that of the superuser, or is the same as the ID value stored
in sem_perm.cuid or sem_perm.uid. To make these changes, a structure of the
type semid_ds must be allocated. The appropriate members' values are then
assigned and a reference to the modified structure is passed as the fourth argument to the **semctl** system call.

- ☞ **IPC_RMID**—Remove the semaphore set associated with the semaphore identifier.

When specifying IPC_STAT, IPC_SET or IPC_RMID, the value for semnum (the
number of semaphores in the set) is not considered and can be set to 0.

The following cmd values will cause **semctl** to act upon the entire set of semaphores:

- ☞ **GETALL**—return the current values of the semaphore set. The values are
returned via the array reference passed as the fourth argument to **semctl**. The
user is responsible for allocating the array of the proper size and type prior to
passing its address to **semctl**. **Read** permission for the semaphore is required to
specify GETALL.

- ☞ **SETALL**—Initialize all semaphores in a set to the values stored in the array referenced by the fourth argument to **semctl**. Again, the user must allocate the ini-

tializing array and assign values prior to passing the address of the array to **semctl**. The process must have **alter** access for the semaphore set to use SET-ALL.

The last set of **semctl** cmd values acts upon individual semaphores or upon specific members in the semid_ds structure. All of these commands require **read** permission, except for SETVAL that requires **alter** permission:

☞ **GETVAL**—Return the current value of the individual semaphore referenced by the value of the semnum argument (remember, arrays in C are zero-based, thus the first semaphore of a set is at index 0).

☞ **SETVAL**—Set the value of the individual semaphore referenced by the semnum argument to the value specified by the fourth argument to **semctl** (e.g., the value stored in arg.val).

☞ **GETPID**—Return the process ID from the sem_perm structure within the semid_ds structure.

☞ **GETNCNT**—Return the number of processes waiting for the semaphore referenced by the semnum argument to increase in value.

☞ **GETZCNT**—Return the number of processes waiting for the semaphore referenced by the semnum argument to become zero.

If **semctl** is successful issuing any of these commands, the requested integer value will be returned. If **semctl** fails, it will return a value of -1 and set **errno** to indicate the specific error. The errors returned by **semctl** with an explanation of their meaning are shown in Table 7.4.

Table 7.4 semctl error messages.

#	Constant	perror **Message**	**Explanation**
1	EPERM	Not superuser	Value for cmd is IPC_RMID or IPC_SET and the calling process in not the owner or superuser.
13	EACCES	Permission denied	The requested operation is forbidden by the current access permissions.
14	EFAULT	Bad address	The fourth argument to semctl contains a reference to an illegal address. The union semun may not have been declared.
22	EINVAL	Invalid argument	• The semaphore identifier is invalid. • The number of semaphores specified is < 0 or greater than the number in the semaphore set. • The value for cmd is invalid. • The value for cmd is IPC_SET but the value for sem_perm.uid or sem_perm.gid is invalid.

Table 7.4 `semctl` error messages. (Continued)

#	Constant	perror **Message**	**Explanation**
34	ERANGE	Result too large	The value for cmd is SETVAL or SETALL and the value to be assigned is greater than the system maximum.
79	EOVERFLOW	Value too large to be stored in data type	The value for cmd is IPC_STAT but the value for the user or group ID is too large.

Program 7.3 uses the `semctl` system call to perform a number of semaphore control operations.

Program 7.3 Using `semctl`.

```
/*
 * The semctl system call
 */
#include <stdio.h>
#include <sys/types.h>
#include <sys/ipc.h>
#include <sys/sem.h>
#include <unistd.h>
#include <stdlib.h>
#define  NS     3

/* This declaration is *MISSING* in many Solaris environments.
 * It should be in the <sys/sem.h> file but often is not!  If you
 * receive a duplicate definition error for semun then comment out
 * the union definition.
 */
union semun {
  int             val;
  struct semid_ds *buf;
  ushort          *array;
};
main(void){
  int             sem_id, sem_value, i;
  key_t           ipc_key;
  struct semid_ds sem_buf;
  static ushort   sem_array[NS] = {3, 1, 4};
  union semun     arg;
  ipc_key = ftok(".", 'S');
  /*
   * Create the semaphore
   */
  if ((sem_id = semget(ipc_key, NS, IPC_CREAT | 0666)) == -1) {
    perror("semget: IPC_CREAT | 0666");
    exit(1);
  }
```

```
  printf("Semaphore identifier %d\n", sem_id);
  /*
   * Set arg (the union) to the addr of the storage location for
   * returned semid_ds values.
   */
  arg.buf = &sem_buf;
  if (semctl(sem_id, 0, IPC_STAT, arg) == -1) { /* obtain info  */
    perror("semctl: IPC_STAT");
    exit(2);
  }
  printf("Created %s", ctime(&sem_buf.sem_ctime));
  /*
   * Set arg (the union) to the addr of the initializing vector
   */
  arg.array = sem_array;
  if (semctl(sem_id, 0, SETALL, arg) == -1) {
    perror("semctl: SETALL");
    exit(3);
  }
  for (i = 0; i < NS; ++i) {           /* display contents */
    if ((sem_value = semctl(sem_id, i, GETVAL, 0)) == -1) {
      perror("semctl: GETVAL");
      exit(4);
    }
    printf("Semaphore %d has value of %d\n", i, sem_value);
  }
  if (semctl(sem_id, 0, IPC_RMID, 0) == -1) {
    perror("semctl: IPC_RMID"),        /* remove semaphore */
    exit(5);
  }
}
```

Program 7.3 creates a set of three semaphores. The semaphore identifier for the set is printed. Then, by specifying IPC_STAT and passing the address of a semid_ds structure[1], **semctl** is used to obtain the current values of the system semaphore structure. The date and time the semaphore was created are displayed using the library function **ctime**. Using similar syntax, other members of the semid_ds structure could be displayed. However, there is another easy way to obtain the entire contents of the semid_ds structure (albeit on a temporary basis). To do this, compile Program 7.3 with the **-g** option and then use the debugger, **dbx**, to examine the semid_ds structure. This can be accomplished by invoking **dbx** with the executable program name, e.g., % dbx a.out. When in **dbx**, tell **dbx** to stop at the correct line (say, stop at 46). The program is then run and when **dbx** stops at line 46, it is asked to print the contents of the structure: print sem_buf. The output of such a sequence will display the contents of the entire sem_buf structure. On our system, Program 7.3 run in **dbx** produces the output shown in Figure 7.4:

---

1. We declared sem_buf to be a semid_ds. The address of sem_buf is assigned to arg (of type union semun). Arg is then passed as the fourth argument to **semctl**.

Fig. 7.4 **dbx** output of Program 7.3.

```
(dbx) stop at 46
(2) stop at "p73.c":46
(dbx) run
Running: a.out
Semaphore identifier 43
stopped in main at line 46 in file "p73.c"
   46      printf("Created %s", ctime(&sem_buf.sem_ctime));
(dbx) print sem_buf
sem_buf = {
    sem_perm  = {
        uid   = 107
        gid   = 1
        cuid  = 107
        cgid  = 1
        mode  = 33206
        seq   = 4
        key   = 1392673033
        pad   = (0, 0, 0, 0)
    }
    sem_base  = 0xfc17cc40
    sem_nsems = 3
    sem_otime = 0
    sem_pad1  = 0
    sem_ctime = 767889997
    sem_pad2  = 0
    sem_pad3  = (0, 0, 0, 0)
}
```

Notice that the number of semaphores in the set, three, has been stored in the sem_nsems member. The reference (address) of the array of sem structures that holds individual semaphore information is also displayed (as the member sem_base).

Program 7.3 uses the **semctl** system call to initialize the three-semaphore set to the values stored in the array sem_array. Once these values are assigned, the program uses a loop to display to the screen the value stored in each semaphore. The last action of Program 7.3 is to use the **semctl** system call with the IPC_RMID flag to remove the semaphore set.

When run outside of **dbx**, the output of Program 7.3 should be similar to that shown in Figure 7.5.

Fig. 7.5 Output of Program 7.3.

```
% a.out
Semaphore identifier 33
Created Mon May  2 10:03:13 1994
Semaphore 0 has value of 3
Semaphore 1 has value of 1
Semaphore 2 has value of 4
```

After generating a set of, say, three semaphores, can **semctl** be used to alter the values of
sem_nsems to indicate an increase or decrease in the number of semaphores in a set? Provide a program segment that supports your answer.

Are the GETVAL, GETNCNT and GETZCNT options for **semctl** superfluous? Can the
values stored in the array of sem structures referenced by sem_base be accessed directly?
If yes, show how this can be done; if no, explain why not.

7.4 SEMAPHORE OPERATIONS

Additional operations on individual semaphores are accomplished by using the **semop**
system call, shown in Table 7.5.

Table 7.5 Summary of the **semop** system call.

Include File(s)	`<sys/types.h>` `<sys/ipc.h>` `<sys/sem.h>`		Manual Section	**2**
Summary	`int semop( int semid,` `        struct sembuf *sops,` `        size_t nsops );`			
Return	Success	Failure	Sets errno	
	0	-1	Yes	

The **semop** system call requires three arguments and returns an integer value. If
successful, **semop** returns a zero; otherwise it returns a -1 and sets **errno** to indicate
the source of the error (see Table 7.9 for details). The first argument for **semop**, semid,
is the semaphore identifier returned by a previous successful call to **semget**. The second argument, sops, is a reference to the base address of an array of semaphore operations that will be performed on the semaphore set denoted by the semid value. The
semop system call will attempt to perform, in an all-or-nothing manner, all of the
semaphore operations indicated by sops. The third argument, nsops, is the number of
elements in the array of semaphore operations.

Each element of the semaphore operation array is a structure of type sembuf.
The declaration of sembuf, which can be found in the include file, `<sys/sem.h>`, is:

```
/*
 * User semaphore template for semop system calls.
 */

struct sembuf {
        ushort   sem_num;         /* semaphore # */
        short    sem_op;          /* semaphore operation */
        short    sem_flg;         /* operation flags */
};
```

The first member of the `sembuf` structure, `sem_num`, is the semaphore number (i.e., the index into the array of `sem` structures referenced by the `sem_base` member of the `semid_ds` structure). The second member of `sembuf`, `sem_op`, is the operation to be performed on the semaphore. A positive integer value means to increment the semaphore (in general, indicating a release or return of a resource), a negative value for `sem_op` means to decrement the semaphore (an attempt to acquire or obtain a resource) and a value of zero means to test if the semaphore is currently at 0 (in use—all resource(s) allocated). Additional details on semaphore operations will be provided in a subsequent section. The third member of `sembuf` is an operation flag. These flags are:

☞ **IPC_NOWAIT**—if the semaphore operation cannot be performed (such as when attempting to decrement a semaphore or test if it is equal to zero), the call will return immediately. No other semaphores in the set will be modified if one of the specified semaphore operations fails with the IPC_NOWAIT flag.

☞ **SEM_UNDO**—if IPC_NOWAIT has not been indicated, the SEM_UNDO flag allows an operation to be undone if a blocked operation (one waiting for a specific condition) subsequently fails. The system will keep track of the adjustment values needed for each semaphore set. The adjustment values are kept on a per-process basis and actually indicate how many "resources" are being held while the system-wide semaphore value indicates how many "resources" are currently free.

Figure 7.6 shows a relationship of an arbitrary three-element semaphore operation array to an N element set of semaphores.

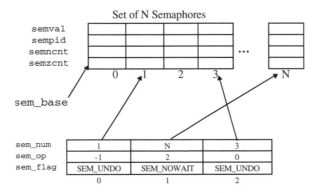

Fig. 7.6 Three-semaphore operations for an N
element set of semaphores.

7.4.1 Semaphore Operation Details

When the sem_op value is *negative*, the process specifying the operation is attempting to decrement the semaphore. The decrement of the semaphore is used to record the acquisition of the resource affiliated with the semaphore. When a semaphore value is to be modified, the accessing process must have **alter** permission for the semaphore set. The actions taken by the **semop** system call when the value for sem_op is negative are summarized in Table 7.6.

Table 7.6 Actions taken by **semop** when the value for sem_op is negative.

Condition	Flag Set	Action Taken by semop
semval >= abs(semop)		Subtract abs(sem_op) from semval.
semval >= abs(semop)	SEM_UNDO	Subtract abs(sem_op) from semval and add abs(sem_op) to semadj value.
semval < abs(semop)		Increment semncnt for the semaphore and wait (block) until: • semval >= abs(semop) then adjust semncnt and subtract as noted in the previous two rows of table. • semid is removed then return -1 and set **errno** to EIDRM. • A signal is caught, then adjust semncnt and set errno to EINTR.
semval < abs(semop)	IPC_NOWAIT	Return -1 immediately and set **errno** to EAGAIN.

When the sem_op value is *positive*, the process is adding to the semaphore value. The addition is used to record the return (release) of the resource affiliated with the semaphore. Again, when a semaphore value is to be modified, the accessing process must have **alter** permission for the semaphore set. The actions taken by the **semop** system call when the value for sem_op is positive are summarized in Table 7.7.

Table 7.7 Actions taken by **semop** when the value for sem_op is positive.

Condition	Flag Set	Action Taken by semop
		Add sem_op to semval.
	SEM_UNDO	Add sem_op to semval and subtract sem_op from semadj value.

When the sem_op value is *zero*, the process is testing the semaphore to determine if it is at zero. When a semaphore is at zero the testing process can assume that all the resources affiliated with the semaphore are currently allocated (in use). For a semaphore value to be tested, the accessing process must have **read** permission for the semaphore set. The actions taken by the **semop** system call when the value for sem_op is zero are summarized in Table 7.8.

The errors returned by **semop,** with an explanation of their meaning, are shown in Table 7.9.

Table 7.8 Actions taken by **semop** when the value for sem_op is zero.

Condition	Flag Set	Action Taken by semop
semval == 0		Return immediately.
semval != 0	IPC_NOWAIT	Return -1 immediately and set **errno** to EAGAIN.
semval != 0		Increment semzcnt for the semaphore and wait (block) until: • semval == 0 then adjust semzcnt and return. • semid is removed then return -1 and set **errno** to EIDRM. • A signal is caught then adjust semzcnt and set **errno** to EINTR.

Table 7.9 **semop** error messages.

#	Constant	perror **Message**	Explanation
4	EINTR	Interrupted system call	A signal was received by the calling process.
7	E2BIG	Arg list too long	The value for semops is greater than the system limit.
11	EAGAIN	Resource temporarily unavailable	The requested operation would cause the calling process to block but IPC_NOWAIT was specified.
13	EACCES	Permission denied	The requested operation is forbidden by the current access permissions.
14	EFAULT	Bad address	The value for sops references an illegal address.
22	EINVAL	Invalid argument	• The semaphore identifier is invalid. • The number of semaphores requesting SEM_UNDO is greater than the system limit.
27	EFBIG	File too large	The value for sem_num is < 0 or >= to the number of semaphores in the set.
28	ENOSPC	No space left on the device	The limit for number of processes requesting SEM_UNDO has been exceeded.
34	ERANGE	Result too large	The requested operation would cause the system semaphore adjustment value to exceed its limit.
36	EIDRM	Identifier removed	The semaphore set associated with semid value has been removed.

If **semop** is successful, for each of the semaphores modified/referenced, **semop** will set the value of sempid to that of the calling process.

Program 7.4 demonstrates the use of the **semop** system call. Two semaphores are used to coordinate concurrent producer and consumer processes. The producer process generates (at its own pace) an integer value. The value is stored in a non-shareable resource (in this case a file in the *local* directory). The consumer process, once a new value has been generated, retrieves the value from the same file and displays the value to the screen. Two semaphores are used by the producer process to prevent it from overwriting a previously stored integer value before the consumer process has retrieved it (should the producer process be speedier than the consumer process). The consumer process uses the two semaphores to prevent it from retrieving the same value multiple times should the producer process be slow in generating new values. The semaphores, which we will call READ and MADE, will be treated in a binary manner. By convention, the MADE semaphore will be set to 1 by the producer process once the producer has stored its newly created integer value in the file. The READ semaphore will be set to 1 by the consumer process once the consumer has read the value stored in the file by the producer. If the number has yet to be made by the producer, or the number has not been read by the consumer, the corresponding semaphore value will be 0. The producer will only gain access to the file to store the generated number if the number currently in the file has been consumed. Likewise, the consumer can only gain access to the file to read the stored number if a new value has been made. Figure 7.7 shows the contents of the two semaphores in the producer and consumer processes and their relationship to one another. Initially we indicate that the current stored number has been read (i.e., we set READ to 1) and that a new number has not been generated (i.e., we set MADE to 0).

A high level algorithm for the producer and consumer processes would be:

Producer

```
While 10 new numbers not generated
```
☞ Generate a new number
☞ If the current stored number has not been read then wait
☞ Store the new number in the file
☞ Indicate that a new number has been made

Consumer

```
Forever
```
☞ If a new number has not been made then wait
☞ Retrieve the new number from the file
☞ Indicate new number has been read
☞ Display the retrieved number

For discussion purposes, the program has been divided into three sections which are shown in Programs 7.4A, B and C. The first part of the program, which establishes the operations that will be performed on the semaphores, creates the set of two semaphores and initializes them, is shown in Program 7.4A.

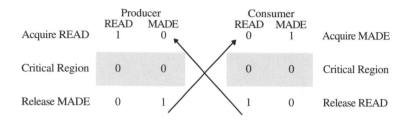

Fig. 7.7 Semaphore values in the producer and consumer processes.

Program 7.4A The first section of the producer/consumer problem.

```
/*
 *First section -- producer/consumer problem   */
 */
#include <stdio.h>
#include <unistd.h>
#include <stdlib.h>
#include <sys/types.h>
#include <sys/ipc.h>
#include <sys/sem.h>
#define BUFFER "./buffer"

/* This declaration is *MISSING* in many Solaris environments.
   It should be in the <sys/sem.h> file but often is not!  If you
   receive a duplicate definition error message for semun then
   comment out the union declaration.
*/
union semun {
  int            val;
  struct semid_ds *buf;
  ushort          *array;
};
main(int argc, char *argv[ ]) {
  FILE           *fptr;
  static struct sembuf acquire = {0, -1, SEM_UNDO},
                       release = {0,  1, SEM_UNDO};
  pid_t          c_pid;
  key_t          ipc_key;
  static ushort  start_val[2] = {1, 0};
  int            semid, producer = 0, i, n, p_sleep, c_sleep;
  union semun    arg;
  enum { READ, MADE };
  if (argc != 2) {
    fprintf(stderr, "%s sleep_time \n", argv[0]);
    exit(-1);
  }
  ipc_key = ftok(".", 'S');
  if ((semid=semget(ipc_key, 2, IPC_CREAT|IPC_EXCL|0666)) != -1) {
    producer = 1;
    arg.array = start_val;
    if (semctl(semid, 0, SETALL, arg) == -1) {
      perror("semctl -- producer -- initialization");
      exit(1);
    }
```

```
    } else if ((semid = semget(ipc_key, 2, 0)) == -1) {
        perror("semget -- consumer -- obtaining semaphore");
        exit(2);
    }
```

The program uses the symbolic constant BUFFER to reference a local file named ./buffer. This file will act as the non-shareable resource to be accessed by the producer and consumer processes. Following this definition is the declaration of the union semun. An argument of type semun is required for the **semctl** system call. As noted earlier, some versions of UNIX do not contain this declaration in their header files. If the declaration is missing, it must be included by the program author. When included, if upon compilation of the program an error message indicating that semun has a duplicate definition is generated, this section of code should be removed or placed in comments.

Using the sembuf structure as a template, the program defines two operations—acquire, and release—that can be used with either of the semaphores. For both operations the value for the member sem_num has been set to 0. This value acts as a place holder and will be changed dynamically to indicate which of the two semaphores we are referencing. The sem_op member of each is set to -1 and 1 for acquire and release respectively. The value of -1 will be used when we want to acquire a resource that is associated with a semaphore (indicated by decrementing the semaphore). The value 1 will be used when we want to indicate the return of the resource (thus incrementing the associated semaphore). In either case, we will set the value for sem_flg to SEM_UNDO to allow rollback. The variable, arg, of type union semun, is declared and will be used as the fourth argument to the **semctl** system call. The values in the array start_val (1, 0) will be used to set the initial values for the two semaphores. The enumerated constants READ and MADE will act as indices to reference which of the two semaphores we are using.

The program begins by checking the command line to determine if an argument has been passed. The program expects a small integer value will be passed. This value will be used to indicate the number of seconds the process should **sleep** in its processing cycle. The inclusion of **sleep** will allow the producer and consumer process to progress at different rates, thus providing the user with an easy way to check the integrity of the semaphore arrangement.

The **semget** system call is used to create/gain access to the semaphore set. The flag combination IPC_CREAT | IPC_EXCL insures that the first time the program is run it will create the two-semaphore set. As written, the first invocation of the program is considered to be the producer (the process that will generate the integer values). The variable producer is set to 1 in the producer process to indicate this. Once the semaphore set is successfully created the program uses the **semctl** system call to initialize the semaphore set to the values stored in start_val[2]. When the program is run a second time, the resulting process is considered to be a consumer (a process that

---

2. Notice that the union member arg.array is assigned the base address of the array start_val prior to invoking **semctl**.

will obtain the stored integer value). In the second program invocation, the initial **semget** system call, which is within the **if** statement, will fail as the semaphore set has already been generated by the producer. The **else-if** branch of the same **if** statement will invoke **semget** a second time without any flags set. This second invocation of **semget** will allow the consumer process to gain access to the previously generated semaphore set.

The second section of the program, which contains the logic executed by the producer, is shown in Program 7.4B.

Program 7.4B The second section of the producer/consumer problem—the *producer* logic.

```
/*
 *Second section of the producer/consumer problem
 */
switch (producer) {
  case 1:                        /* the PRODUCER */
    p_sleep = atoi(argv[1]);
    srand((unsigned) getpid());
    for (i = 0; i < 10; i++) {
      sleep(p_sleep);
      n = rand() % 99 + 1;
      printf("A. The number [%2d] generated by producer\n", n);
      acquire.sem_num = READ;
      if (semop(semid, &acquire, 1) == -1) {
        perror("semop -- producer -- waiting for consumer to read number");
        exit(3);
      }
      if ( (fptr = fopen(BUFFER, "w")) == NULL ){
       perror(BUFFER);
       exit(4);
      }
      fprintf(fptr, "%d\n", n);
      fclose(fptr);
      release.sem_num = MADE;
      printf("B. The number [%2d] deposited by producer\n", n);
      if (semop(semid, &release, 1) == -1) {
        perror("semop -- producer -- indicating new number has been made");
        exit(5);
      }
    }
    sleep(5);
    if (semctl(semid, 0, IPC_RMID, 0) == -1) {
      perror("semctl -- producer");
      exit(6);
    }
    printf("Semaphore removed\n");
    break;
```

As noted the first time, when the program is run, the value of the variable, producer, will be set to 1. When producer contains a 1 the case 1: section of program code, the *producer* logic, will be executed. The small integer value passed on the command line, to indicate the number of seconds the process should sleep, is converted by the library function **atoi** and stored for future reference in the variable p_sleep. Following this, the random number generator is initialized using the value of the current process ID. A **for** loop, that produces ten random integer values in the range 1-99, is entered. After sleeping for `p_sleep` seconds, a random number is generated and displayed to the screen (this allows the user to verify the activity of the program). Following this, the `sem_num` member of the `acquire` operation is set to the value READ. This will direct the ensuing **semop** system call to reference the READ semaphore, which is the first semaphore of the set. We are using the presence of a value of 1 for the READ semaphore to indicate the current stored number has been read (consumed) and a value of 0 to indicate the number has *not* been read. As the initial value for the READ semaphore is 1, the very first time the producer tests the READ semaphore with the **semop** system call, the producer will be able to acquire the semaphore. Once this occurs, the producer continues on to the next section of code where it opens the file, stores the generated value and closes the file. In later passes through this code, the producer may or may not find the READ semaphore at 1. If the semaphore is at 0 (indicating the consumer has not read the value), the producer will, by default, block (wait) for this event to occur. Once the produced value has been written to the file, the producer process, using the `release` operation, increments the MADE semaphore. By incrementing the MADE semaphore, the producer indicates a new number is now available for the consumer. When all ten numbers have been generated, the producer exits the **for** loop and, after sleeping five seconds to allow for the consumption of the last produced value, it removes the semaphore set with the **semctl** system command. If needed the **unlink** call could be used to remove the temporary file.

The logic for the *consumer* is shown in Program 7.4C:

Program 7.4C The third section of the producer/consumer problem—the *consumer* logic.

```
case 0:                            /* the CONSUMER */
    c_sleep = atoi(argv[1]);
    c_pid = getpid();
    while (1) {
      sleep(c_sleep);
      acquire.sem_num = MADE;
      if (semop(semid, &acquire, 1) == -1) {
       perror("semop -- consumer -- waiting for new number to be made");
       exit(7);
      }
      if ( (fptr = fopen(BUFFER, "r")) == NULL ){
       perror(BUFFER);
       exit(8);
      }
      fptr = fopen(BUFFER, "r");
      fscanf(fptr, "%d", &n);
      fclose(fptr);
      release.sem_num = READ;
      if (semop(semid, &release, 1) == -1) {
        perror("semop -- consumer -- indicating number has been read");
        exit(9);
      }
     printf("C. The number [%2d] obtained  by consumer %6d\n", n,
            c_pid);
    }
  }
exit(0);
}
```

The consumer process, like the producer, converts the value passed on the command line into an integer value by using the library function **atoi**. The consumer then obtains its process ID using the **getpid** system call. The process ID will be used to identify individual consumer processes when more than one consumer process is present. The consumer then enters an endless loop. It sleeps c_sleep seconds and then goes on to test the MADE semaphore. To accomplish this, the sem_num member of the acquire operation structure is set to MADE. The call to **semop**, which is passed the reference to acquire, will cause the consumer to block (wait) if the semaphore is at 0. Once the MADE semaphore becomes 1, the consumer will open the file where the number was written, read the number and close the file. The consumer then indicates that it has read the number. The release structure member, sem_num, is set to READ to reference the second semaphore of the set. The following **semop** system call will cause the contents of the READ semaphore to be incremented. The consumer then displays a short message to the screen indicating the value retrieved and its process ID value. The consumer will continue to *consume* values until the call to **semop** fails due to the removal of the semaphore set by the producer.

We can run the program to simulate a number of conditions. We begin by making the producer process slower than a single consumer process. The output shown in Figure 7.8 shows how this is accomplished.

Fig. 7.8 A single *slow* producer with a single consumer.

```
% p74 2 & ; p74 0
[1] 7387
A. The number [13] generated by producer
B. The number [13] deposited by producer
C. The number [13] obtained  by consumer    7388
A. The number [19] generated by producer
B. The number [19] deposited by producer
C. The number [19] obtained  by consumer    7388
                .
                .
                .
C. The number [25] obtained  by consumer    7388
A. The number [38] generated by producer
B. The number [38] deposited by producer
C. The number [38] obtained  by consumer    7388
semop -- consumer -- waiting for new number to be made: Identifier removed
[1]    Done                   p74 2
```

In this example the program, p74, is run twice on the command line. The first invocation of the program, which will be the producer[3], is passed the value 2. This directs the producer process to sleep two seconds each time it cycles through the **for**

---

3. This may be an invalid assumption on some systems as process scheduling may allow the program invoked second to be run first and thus become the producer. If your output indicates this is happening, enter the two commands on separate lines—do not forget to add the "&" after the first command to place it in the background.

loop. The producer process is placed in background by specifying "&" after the command line sleep value. In the second invocation of the program, the consumer is passed the value 0 as the sleep value. The system responds to the command sequence by displaying the process ID of the commands that were placed in background. The display of:

```
[1] 7387
```

means that, for this invocation, the producer process ID is 7387. As the two processes execute, we can clearly see from the output that the producer must first generate and deposit the value in the file before the consumer can obtain it. As the producing process is slower than the consuming process, the consumer process will spend a portion of its time waiting for the producer to deposit a number. When all of the numbers have been produced, the producer process removes the semaphore set. When this happens, the consumer process exits. If we run this command sequence several times, we should find it behaves in a consistent manner. Even though the consumer process is faster than the producer process, the consumer should never read the same value twice from the file (unless, by chance, the same number was generated twice by the producer).

We can reverse the conditions and make the producer process faster than the consumer process. The output shown in Figure 7.9 shows how this can be accomplished.

Fig. 7.9 A producer with a single *slow* consumer.

```
% p74 0 & ; p74 2
[1] 7391
A. The number [48] generated by producer
B. The number [48] deposited by producer
A. The number [45] generated by producer
C. The number [48] obtained  by consumer    7392
B. The number [45] deposited by producer
A. The number [28] generated by producer
C. The number [45] obtained  by consumer    7392
B. The number [28] deposited by producer
      .
      .

      .
      .
C. The number [51] obtained  by consumer    7392
B. The number [68] deposited by producer
C. The number [68] obtained  by consumer    7392
semop -- consumer -- waiting for new number to be made: Identifier removed
[1]    Done                    p74
```

This output sequence is slightly different from the previous one. Notice, as before, the producer generates and deposits the number. The producer, being faster than the consumer, then goes on to generate another number. However, this number is not deposited until the slower consumer process has read the existing stored value. If we run this command sequence several times, we should again be able to confirm that the producer process never overwrites the existing stored value until the consumer process has read it.

E X E R C I S E   7 – 5

What if there are several competing consumer processes? Will the current set of semaphores handle things correctly? Will competing consumer processes alternate their access
to the produced values? Will some consumer processes starve? Try the following command
sequences (several times each) and explain *what happens* and *why* for each.

A) % p74 2 &; p74 1 &; p74 0

B) % p74 0 & ; p74 1 & ; p74 1 & ; p74 1

C) % p74 2 & ; p74 1 & ; p74 1 & ; p74 1

E X E R C I S E   7 – 6

As shown by the code listed below we can add another operation for **semop** (called `zero`)
that can be used to determine if a specified semaphore is at 0 (see Table 7.8 for the actions
taken by **semop** when the value for sem_op is zero).

```
static struct sembuf

        acquire = {0, -1, SEM_UNDO},

        release = {0,  1, SEM_UNDO},

        zero    = {0,  0, SEM_UNDO};
```

Modify Program 7.4, incorporating the `zero` operation, so the producer can use this operation on the appropriate semaphore to determine if it should continue its processing. To
verify that your solution is not rapdily passing through the producer loop, comment out
the producer's call to sleep. Once you are positive your implementation is solid, uncom-
ment call to sleep. Generate sufficient output to assure the user the producer process
never overwrites a value that has not been consumed and that a consumer process never
consumes the same value twice.

E X E R C I S E   7 – 7

Many operating systems use buffer swapping to speed up the transfer of information when
producing and consuming processes operate at different speeds. To accomplish this, two
(or more) buffers are used. When the producing process has filled the first buffer, it moves
to the second buffer, releasing the first buffer for consumption. The producer then continues to fill the second buffer while the consumer gains accesses to the first buffer. Once the
second buffer is filled the producer returns to the first buffer (which hopefully the consumer is finished with), etc. Using semaphores, write a producer/consumer pair that uses
three files as its buffers. Each file should hold a *maximum* of five integer values.

E X E R C I S E   7 – 8

Modify Program 7.4 to support multiple producers and consumers accessing a single non-
shareable resource. *Hint:* You may need additional semaphores to coordinate activities.

7.5 SUMMARY

Semaphores are specialized data structures used to coordinate access to a non-share-able resource (section of code). Cooperating (or possibly competing) processes use the semaphore(s) to determine if a specific resource is available. If the resource is unavailable, by default, the system will place the requesting process in an associated queue. The system will notify the waiting process when the resource is available. This alleviates the process from using polling to determine the availability of the resource.

The actions needed to manipulate semaphores are provided by a series of system calls. The **semget** system call is used to generate a new semaphore/semaphore set (array), or gain access to an existing semaphore. The **semctl** system call allows the user to set initial semaphore values, obtain their current value and remove the semaphore. Operations on semaphores are performed with the **semop** system call. These operations (which are atomic) are used to decrement (obtain), increment (release), and test for zero specific semaphores. Sets of operations can be specified if several semaphores are needed to coordinate access to a specific resource. The sets of operations may also be marked as being atomic.

While the syntax for using semaphores is somewhat complex they do provide a standardized way of implementing classic primitive semaphore operations referenced in most operating system texts. As with many of the previous communication techniques, controlling access to a resource by using semaphores implies all involved processes will follow the rules. Semaphores cannot prevent processes from accessing a controlled resource.

Shared Memory

8.1 INTRODUCTION

Shared memory allows multiple processes to share virtual memory space. This is the fastest, but not necessarily the easiest (coordination-wise), way for processes to communicate with one another. In general, one process creates/allocates the shared memory segment. The size and access permissions for the segment are set when it is created. The process then attaches the shared segment, causing it to be mapped[1] into its current data space. If needed, the creating process then initializes the shared memory. Once created, and if permissions permit, other processes can gain access to the shared memory segment and map it into their data space. Each process accesses the shared memory relative to its attachment address. While the data that these processes are referencing is in *common*, each process will use different attachment address values. Ordinarily, semaphores are used to coordinate access to a shared memory segment. When a process is finished with the shared memory segment, it can detach from it. The creator of the segment may grant ownership of the segment to another process. When all processes are finished with the shared memory segment, the process that created the segment is usually responsible for removing it.

---

1. The actual mapping of the segment to virtual address space is dependent upon the memory management hardware (MMU) for the system.

8.2 CREATING A SHARED MEMORY SEGMENT

The **shmget** system call is used to create the shared memory segment and generate
the associated system data structure, or to gain access to an existing segment. The
shared memory segment and the system data structure are identified by a unique
shared memory identifier that the **shmget** system call returns (see Table 8.1).

Table 8.1 Summary of the **shmget** system call.

Include File(s)	`<sys/types.h>` `<sys/ipc.h>` `<sys/shm.h>`		Manual Section	**2**
Summary	`int shmget( key_t key,` `            int size,` `            int shmflg );`			
Return	Success	Failure	Sets `errno`	
	Shared memory identifier	-1	Yes	

Providing no system parameters are exceeded, the **shmget** system call will create
a *new* shared memory segment if:

☞ The value for its first argument, key, is the symbolic constant IPC_PRIVATE,

☞ or the value key is *not* associated with an existing shared memory identifier and
the IPC_CREAT flag is set as part of the shmflg argument (otherwise, the existing shared memory identifier associated with the key value is returned),

☞ or the value key is *not* associated with an existing shared memory identifier and
the IPC_CREAT along with the IPC_EXCL flag have been set as part of the shmflg argument. With IPC_CREAT and IPC_EXCL set, the user can be assured of
creating a unique shared memory segment without gaining access to a pre-exist-
ing segment.

As with previous IPC system calls for message queues and semaphores, the **ftok**
library function can be used to generate a key value.

The argument, size, will determine the size in bytes of the shared memory segment. If we are using **shmget** to access an existing shared memory segment, size can
be set to 0 as the segment size is set by the creating process. Common overall default
system maximums, as related to shared memory, are shown in Table 8.2.

The last argument for **shmget**, shmflg, is used to specify segment creation conditions (e.g., IPC_CREAT, IPC_EXCL) and access permissions (stored in the low order 9
bits of shmflg). To specify creation conditions along with access permissions, the indi-
vidual items are bit-wise ORed (e.g., 0666 | IPC_CREAT).

The **shmget** system call does not allow the creating process to actually use the
allocated memory, it merely reserves the requested memory. To be used by the process,

Table 8.2 Shared memory limits.

Shared Memory Segment Defaults	Value
Maximum segment size	1,048,576 bytes
Minimum segment size	1 byte
System wide maximum number of segments	100
Maximum number of segments per process that can be attached	6

the allocated memory must be attached to the process using a separate system call. The technique for accomplishing this is discussed in the section **Shared Memory Operations**.

If **shmget** is successful in allocating a shared memory segment it returns an integer shared memory identifier. At creation time, the system data structure, shmid_ds, defined in the <sys/shm.h> header file, is generated and initialized:

```
struct shmid_ds {
  struct ipc_perm shm_perm;    /* operation permission struct */
  int             shm_segsz;   /* size of segment in bytes */
  struct anon_map *shm_amp;    /* segment anon_map pointer */
  ushort          shm_lkcnt;   /* number of times it is locked */
  pid_t           shm_lpid;    /* pid of last shmop */
  pid_t           shm_cpid;    /* pid of creator */
  ulong           shm_nattch;  /* used only for shminfo */
  ulong           shm_cnattch; /* used only for shminfo */
  time_t          shm_atime;   /* last shmat time */
  long            shm_pad1;    /* reserved for time_t expansion */
  time_t          shm_dtime;   /* last shmdt time */
  long            shm_pad2;    /* reserved for time_t expansion */
  time_t          shm_ctime;   /* last change time */
  long            shm_pad3;    /* reserved for time_t expansion */
  long            shm_pad4[4]; /* reserve area   */
};
```

The shmd_ds structure contains an ipc_perm permission structure called shm_perm. When created the shm_perm.cuid and shm_perm.uid members are assigned the effective user ID of the calling process, and the shm_perm.cgid, and shm_perm.gid members are set to group ID of the calling process. The access permission bits, stored in the shm_perm.mode member, are set according to the value specified by the shmflg value. The shm_segsz member is set to the specified size from the **shmget** system call. The shm_lpid, shm_nattch, shm_atime and shm_dtime members are each set to 0, while the shm_ctime member is set to the current time.

If **shmget** fails, it returns a value of -1 and sets the value in **errno** to indicate the specific error condition. The values that **errno** may be assigned and their interpretation are shown in Table 8.3.

Program 8.1 attempts to create two shared memory segments of differing sizes.

Table 8.3 `shmget` error messages.

#	Constant	perror **Message**	Explanation
2	EOENT	No such file or directory	The shared memory identifier does not exist for this key and IPC_CREAT was not set.
3	EACCES	Permission denied	The shared memory identifier exists for this key but the requested operation is forbidden by the current access permissions.
12	ENOMEM	Not enough space	When creating a shared memory segment, insufficient memory available.
17	EEXIST	File exists	Shared memory identifier exists for this key but IPC_CREAT and IPC_EXCL are both set.
22	EINVAL	Invalid argument	• The value of size is less than system minimum or greater than system maximum. • The shared memory identifier exists but the requested size is too large.
28	ENOSPC	No space left on device	System imposed limit for number of shared memory segments has been reached.

Program 8.1 Creating shared memory segments.

```
/*
 *  Allocating a shared memory segment
 */
#include <stdio.h>
#include <unistd.h>
#include <sys/types.h>
#include <stdlib.h>
#include <sys/ipc.h>
#include <sys/shm.h>

main(void) {

  key_t          key = 15;
  int            shmid_1, shmid_2;

  if ((shmid_1=shmget(key, 1000, 0644|IPC_CREAT)) == -1){
    perror("shmget shmid_1");
    exit(1);
  }
  printf("First shared memory identifier is  %d \n", shmid_1);

  if ((shmid_2=shmget(IPC_PRIVATE, 20, 0644)) == -1){
    perror("shmget shmid_2");
    exit(2);
  }
  printf("Second shared memory identifier is %d \n", shmid_2);

  exit(0);
}
```

When invoked twice in succession, the output of Program 8.1 was:

Fig. 8.1 Output of Program 8.1.

```
% p81
First shared memory identifier is  400
Second shared memory identifier is 501

% ipcs
IPC status from <running system> as of Fri May 27 10:18:05 1994
Message Queue facility not in system.
Shared Memory:
m    400 0x0000000f   --rw-r--r--      gray     other
m    501 0x0x00000000 --rw-r--r--      gray     other
Semaphores:
s      0 0x000187cf   --ra-ra-ra-      root     root

% p81
First shared memory identifier is  400
Second shared memory identifier is 502
% ipcs
IPC status from <running system> as of Fri May 27 10:18:13 1994
Message Queue facility not in system.
Shared Memory:
m    400 0x0000000f   --rw-r--r--      gray     other
m    501 0x0x00000000 --rw-r--r--      gray     other
m    502 0x0x00000000 --rw-r--r--      gray     other
Semaphores:
s      0 0x000187cf   --ra-ra-ra-      root     root
```

Examination of the output shows the first invocation created two shared memory segments with the identifier values of 400 and 501. The first segment, with the shared memory identification value of 400, was created by the first call to **shmget**, as the key value (15) coded in the program was not associated with any other previously allocated memory segment. The second segment, identified by the 501, was created by **shmget** as the IPC_PRIVATE key was specified. However, when the program was invoked the second time, the results were slightly different. The first call to **shmget** returned the shared memory identifier from the first invocation of the program, as the shared memory segment already existed for the key value of 15. The second call to **shmget**, as it uses the IPC_PRIVATE key, still produced another unique shared memory segment. Notice that the output for the **ipcs** command shows that the key value entries for both of the unique shared memory segments generated with the IPC_PRIVATE are set to zero.

EXERCISE   8 − 1

Write a program that determines if the maximum shared memory segment size is or is not the 1,048,576 bytes noted. If the maximum is not this value, what is the maximum (to the nearest 1K)? Note: Please be sure to *remove* all shared memory segments you generate for this exercise. You may want to look ahead to the section **Shared Memory Control**, to obtain the proper syntax to accomplish the removal of the shared memory segment within your program versus using the **ipcrm** command on the command line.

8.3 SHARED MEMORY CONTROL

The **shmctl** system call permits the user to perform a number of generalized control operations on an existing shared memory segment, and on the system shared memory data structure (see Table 8.4).

Table 8.4 Summary of the **shmctl** system call.

Include File(s)	`<sys/types.h>`
	`<sys/ipc.h>`
	`<sys/shm.h>`
			Manual Section	**2**

Summary	`int shmctl( int shmid,`
	`              int cmd,`
	`              struct shmid_ds *buf );`			

Return	Success	Failure	Sets errno	
	0	-1	Yes	

There are three arguments for the **shmctl** system call. The first, shmid, is a valid shared memory segment identifier generated by a prior **shmget** system call. The second argument, cmd, specifies the operation **shmctl** is to perform. The third argument, buf, is a reference to a structure of the type shmid_ds.

The operations that **shmctl** will perform, which are specified by the following defined constants, consist of:

☞ **IPC_STAT**—Return the current values of the shmid_ds structure for the memory segment indicated by the shmid value. The returned information is stored in a user-generated structure which is passed by reference as the third argument to **shmctl**. To specify IPC_STAT the process must have **read** permission for the shared memory segment.

☞ **IPC_SET**—Modify a limited number of members in the permission structure found within the shmid_ds structure. The permission structure members that can be modified are shm_perm.uid, shm_perm.gid and shm_perm.mode. The accessing process must have the effective ID of the superuser or have an ID that is equivalent to either the shm_perm.cuid or shm_perm.uid value. To modify structure members, the following steps are usually taken. A structure of the type shmid_ds is allocated. The structure is initialized to the current system settings by calling **shmctl** with the IPC_STAT flag set and passing the reference to the *new* shmd_ds structure. The appropriate members of the structure are then assigned their *new* values. Finally, with the cmd argument set to IPC_SET, the **shmctl** system call is invoked a second time and passed the reference to the *modified* structure. To carry out this modification sequence, the accessing process must have **read** and **write** permissions for the shared memory segment.

☞ **IPC_RMID**—Remove the system data structure for the referenced shared memory identifier (shmid). When specifying IPC_RMID, an address value of 0 is used for `buf`. The 0 address value is cast to the proper type, with (`shmid_ds *`). Once all references to the shared memory segment are eliminated, i.e., `shm_nattch` equals 0, the system will remove the actual segment. If a **shmctl** system call, specifying IPC_RMID, is not done, the memory segment will remain active and associated with its `key` value.

☞ **SHM_LOCK**—Lock, in memory, the shared memory segment referenced by the `semid` argument. This can only be specified by processes that have an effective ID equal to that of the superuser.

☞ **SHM_UNLOCK**—Unlock the shared memory segment referenced by the `semid` argument. Again, this can only be specified by processes that have an effective ID equal to that of the superuser.

If **shmget** is successful, it returns a value of 0; otherwise it returns a value of -1 and sets the value in **errno** to indicate the specific error condition. The values that **errno** may be assigned and their interpretation are shown in Table 8.5.

E X E R C I S E   8 – 2
_____

The shared memory structure, shmid_ds, contains a reference to the structure anon_map. What is the definition of this structure? Where does this definition become # *included* in the compilation process? (*Hint*: Look in the /usr/include subdirectories— such as: sys, vm, etc.)
_____

Table 8.5 `shmctl` error messages.

#	Constant	`perror` **Message**	**Explanation**
1	EPERM	Not superuser	• The value for `cmd` is IPC_RMID or IPC_SET and the calling process is not the owner or superuser. • The value for `cmd` is SHM_LOCK or SHM_UNLOCK and the calling process is not the superuser.
3	EACCES	Permission denied	The requested operation is forbidden by current access permissions.
12	ENOMEM	Not enough space	The `cmd` is SHM_LOCK but there is insufficient memory available.
14	EFAULT	Bad address	The third argument to **shmctl,** buf, contains a reference to an illegal address.
22	EINVAL	Invalid argument	• The shared memory identifier is invalid. • The value for `cmd` is invalid. • The value for `cmd` is IPC_SET but the value for shm_perm.uid or shm_perm.gid is invalid.
79	EOVERFLOW	Value too large to be stored in data type	The value for `cmd` is IPC_SET but the value for the user or group ID is too large.

8.4 SHARED MEMORY OPERATIONS

There are two shared memory operation system calls. The first, **shmat**, is used to attach (map) the referenced shared memory segment into the calling process's data segment. See Table 8.6.

Table 8.6 Summary of the **shmat** system call.

Include File(s)	`<sys/types.h>` `<sys/ipc.h>` `<sys/shm.h>`		Manual Section	**2**
Summary	`void *shmat( int shmid,` `            void *shmaddr,` `            int shmflg );`			
Return	Success	Failure	Sets errno	
	Reference to the data segment address of where shared memory is attached	-1	Yes	

The first argument to **shmat**, shmid, is a valid shared memory identifier. The second argument, shmaddr, allows the calling process *some* flexibility in assigning the location of the shared memory segment. If a non-zero value is given, **shmat** will use this as the attachment address for the shared memory segment. If shmaddr is 0, the system will pick the attachment address. In most situations it is advisable to use a value of 0 and have the system pick the address. The third argument, shmflg, is used to specify the access permissions for the shared memory segment and to request special attachment conditions, such as an aligned address or a read-only segment. The value of shmaddr, with that of shmflg, are used by the system to determine the attachment address using the algorithm shown in Figure 8.2.

By default, attached segments are accessible for reading and writing. If needed, the SHM_RDONLY flag can be bitwise ORed with the shmflg value to indicate a read-only segment. When the SHM_SHARE_MMU flag is set, the access permissions speci-

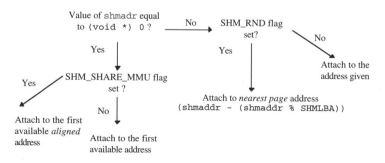

Fig. 8.2 Determining the attachment address.

fied with the **shmget** call that created the segment determines the access permissions for the attached shared memory segment. With SHM_SHARE_MMU set the attachment will be the first available aligned address. The SHM_RND flag is used to specify whether or not the attachment address should be aligned on a page boundary. The value in the defined constant SHMLBA is used by the system as the page size.

When **shmat** is successful it will return the address of the actual attachment. If **shmat** fails, it will return a value of -1 and set **errno** to indicate the source of the error. Table 8.7 lists the error codes generated and their interpretation when the **shmat** system call fails.

Table 8.7 **shmat** error messages.

#	Constant	perror **Message**	Explanation
3	EACCES	Permission denied	The requested operation is forbidden by current access permissions.
12	ENOMEM	Not enough space	There is insufficient memory available to accommodate the shared memory segment.
22	EINVAL	Invalid argument	• The shared memory identifier is invalid. • Illegal address. • SHM_SHARE_MMU requested but is not supported.
24	EMFILE	Too many open files	Number of attached memory segments has exceeded system limits.

E X E R C I S E   8 – 3

Create three, 1023-byte, shared memory segments. Specify a shmaddr of 0 when attaching the segments. Does the system place the segments at contiguous locations? Why? Will the system allow reference to/modification of the 1024th byte of *any* of these segments? Why? Are the results the same when the SHM_SHARE_MMU is set? Why?

The second shared memory operation, **shmdt,** is used to detach the calling process's data segment from the shared memory segment. See Table 8.8.

The **shmdt** system call has one argument, shmaddr, which is a reference to an attached memory segment. If **shmdt** is successful in detaching the memory segment, it will return a value of 0; otherwise, it will return a value of -1 and set **errno**. Table 8.9 gives the error code that is generated when **shmdt** fails.

In Program 8.2, a private shared memory segment, 30 bytes in length, is created at line 21. The shared memory segment is mapped to the process's data space (line 25) using the first available address (as picked by the system). The actual attachment address along with the addresses for **etext**, **edata** and **end** are displayed for reference. A character pointer is set to reference the shared memory segment and then a sequence of uppercase alphabetic characters is written to the referenced location

Table 8.8 Summary of the **shmdt** system call.

Include File(s)	`<sys/types.h>` `<sys/ipc.h>` `<sys/shm.h>`		Manual Section	**2**
Summary	`int shmdt( void *shmaddr );`			
Return	Success	Failure	Sets errno	
	0	-1	Yes	

Table 8.9 **shmdt** error message.

#	Constant	perror **Message**	**Explanation**
22	EINVAL	Invalid argument	The value in shmaddr does not reference a valid shared memory segment.

(lines 33–35). A **fork** system call is used to generate a child process. The child process redisplays the contents of the shared memory segment. The child process then modifies the contents of the shared memory by converting the uppercase alphabetics to lowercase. After it converts the alphabetics, the child process detaches the shared memory segment and exits. The parent process, after sleeping five seconds, redisplays the contents of shared memory (which now is in lowercase), detaches the shared memory segment and removes it.

Program 8.2 Creating, attaching and manipulating shared memory.

```
 1 /*  Using shared memory
 2 */
 3 #include <stdlib.h>
 4 #include <sys/types.h>
 5 #include <sys/ipc.h>
 6 #include <sys/shm.h>
 7 #include <stdio.h>
 8 #include <unistd.h>
 9 #include <string.h>
10
11 #define SHM_SIZE 30
12
13 extern etext, edata, end;
14
15 main(void) {
16    pid_t          pid;
17    int            shmid;
18    char           c, *shm, *s;
19
20
21    if ((shmid=shmget(IPC_PRIVATE,SHM_SIZE,IPC_CREAT|0666))< 0) {
```

```
22      perror("shmget fail");
23      exit(1);
24    }
25    if ((shm = (char *) shmat(shmid, 0, 0)) == (char *) -1) {
26      perror("shmat : parent ");
27      exit(2);
28    }
29    printf("Addresses in parent\n\n");
30    printf("shared mem: %X etext: %X edata: %X end: %X\n\n",
31            shm, &etext, &edata, &end);
32    s = shm;                        /* s now references shared mem */
33    for (c = 'A'; c <= 'Z'; ++c)  /* put some info there         */
34      *s++ = c;
35    *s = NULL;                      /* terminate the sequence      */
36    printf("In parent before fork, memory is : %s \n", shm);
37    pid = fork();
38    switch (pid) {
39    case -1:
40      perror("fork ");
41      exit(3);
42    default:
43      sleep(5);                          /* let the child finish    */
44      printf("\nIn parent after fork, memory is  : %s\n", shm);
45      printf("Parent removing shared memory\n");
46      shmdt(shm);
47      shmctl(shmid, IPC_RMID, (struct shmid_ds *) 0 );
48      exit(0);
49    case 0:
50      printf("In child after fork, memory is   : %s \n", shm);
51      for (; *shm; ++shm)            /* modify shared memory     */
52        *shm += 32;               \
53      shmdt( shm );
54      exit(0);
55    }
56  }
```

When Program 8.2 is run (output shown below), we find that the address the system picks for the shared memory segment is not in the text or data segment address space for the process. In addition, the child process, via the **fork** system call, obtains access to the shared memory segment without having to make its own calls to **shmget** and **shmat**. As shown, the modifications to the shared memory segment made by the child process are *seen* by the parent even after the child process has detached its reference to the shared memory segment and terminated.

Fig. 8.3 Output of Program 8.2.

```
% p82
Addresses in parent
shared mem: EF7F0000 etext: 10B50 edata: 20CAC end: 20CD0
In parent before fork, memory is : ABCDEFGHIJKLMNOPQRSTUVWXYZ
In child after fork, memory is    : ABCDEFGHIJKLMNOPQRSTUVWXYZ
%
In parent after fork, memory is   : abcdefghijklmnopqrstuvwxyz
Parent removing shared memory
```

Run Program 8.2 on your system and record the addresses it displays. Modify the program by adding a variety of static and automatic variable declarations. Does the first free address the system picks for the shared memory segment always remain the same? If not, is there a consistent set distance the system uses as an offset from the **etext**, **edata** or **end** values? Why might this be? If the shared memory segment is not in the text or data segment of the process, is it actually found in the stack segment of the process?

Using our previous producer/consumer example from the chapter on semaphores as a base, we can implement a producer/consumer relationship that uses shared memory in place of a file to convey information from one process to another. In our example, the producing process will generate a series of random messages that will be stored in a shared memory segment for the consumer process to read. To facilitate communication between the two processes, which may operate at differing rates, an array with six message buffers (slots) will be used. The message buffer array will be treated as a queue, whereby new messages will be added to the tail of the list and messages to be processed will be removed from the head of the list. The two integer indices, referencing the head and tail of the list respectively, will also be kept in the shared memory segment. The basic configuration of the shared memory segment is shown in Figure 8.4.

We will use two semaphores to coordinate access to the shared memory segment. The first semaphore, treated as a *counting* semaphore, will contain the number of available slots that can be written to. As long as this semaphore is non-zero, the producing process can continue to write its messages to the shared memory segment. Initially, this semaphore will be set to indicate that six slots are available. The second semaphore, also treated as a *counting* semaphore, will indicate the number of slots available for consumption (reading). Both the producer and consumer processes will execute concurrently and reference the same shared memory segment. The activities of the processes are shown in Figure 8.5 with the areas within the boxes indicating access to the shared memory segment.

To reduce the amount of coding and to provide programming consistency, a common local header file, called `local.h`, is generated. The `local.h` file will contain the

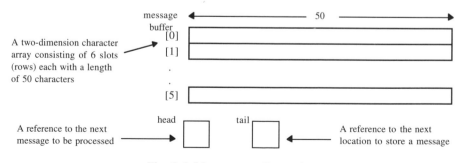

Fig. 8.4 Memory configuration.

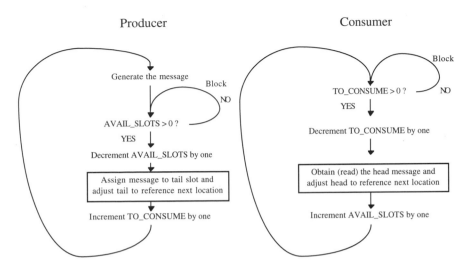

Fig. 8.5 Producer and consumer activities.

include statements and variable declarations needed by each of the programs that make up this example. Each program will reference this file in its first lines of program code via the preprocessor statement #include "local.h". The contents of the local.h file are shown in Figure 8.6. Lines 34–37 define the makeup of the shared memory segment.

Fig. 8.6 The local.h file.

```
 1 /*
 2  local.h - common header file: parent, producer and consumer
 3
 4 */
 5 #include <stdio.h>
 6 #include <unistd.h>
 7 #include <stdlib.h>
 8 #include <string.h>
 9 #include <sys/types.h>
10 #include <sys/ipc.h>
11 #include <sys/sem.h>
12 #include <sys/shm.h>
13 #include <wait.h>
14 #include <signal.h>
15
16 #define ROWS 5
17 #define COLS 3
18
19 #define SLOT_LEN 50
20 #define N_SLOTS  6
21
22 /*
23  This declaration is *MISSING* in many Solaris environments.
24  It should be in the <sys/sem.h> file but often is not!  If you
```

```
25  receive a duplicate definition error message for semun then
26  comment out the union declaration.
27  */
28  union semun {
29    int             val;
30    struct semid_ds *buf;
31    ushort          *array;
32  };
33
34  struct MEMORY {
35    char buffer[N_SLOTS][SLOT_LEN];
36    int  head, tail;
37  };
38
39  struct sembuf acquire = { 0, -1, SEM_UNDO},
40                release = { 0,  1, SEM_UNDO};
41
42  enum {AVAIL_SLOTS, TO_CONSUME};
```

In this example, a parent process will be responsible for creating and initializing the shared memory segment and the two semaphores which control access to it. Once this has been done, the parent process will **fork** two child processes. The first process will be the producing process and the second, the consuming process. The code for the parent process is shown in Program 8.3.

Program 8.3 The parent process.

```
1   #include "local.h"
2   /*
3    *The PARENT
4    */
5   main(int argc, char *argv[ ]) {
6
7     static
8     struct MEMORY    memory;
9     static ushort    start_val[2] = {N_SLOTS, 0};
10    int              semid, shmid, croaker;
11    char             *shmptr;
12    pid_t            p_id, c_id, pid = getpid( );
13    union semun      arg;
14
15    memory.head = memory.tail = 0;
16
17    if ( argc != 3 ) {
18      fprintf(stderr, "%s producer_time  consumer_time\n",
                            argv[0]);
19      exit(-1);
20    }
21    /*
22    Create, attach, and initialize the memory segment
23    */
24    if ((shmid=shmget((int)pid, sizeof(memory),
                          IPC_CREAT | 0600 )) != -1){
25      if ((shmptr=(char *)shmat(shmid, 0, 0)) == (char *) -1){
26        perror("shmptr -- parent -- attach ");
27        exit(1);
```

```
28      }
29         memcpy(shmptr, (char *)&memory, sizeof(memory));
30      } else {
31         perror("shmid -- parent -- creation ");
32         exit(2);
33      }
34      /*
35      Create and initialize the semaphores
36      */
37      if ((semid=semget((int)pid, 2, IPC_CREAT | 0666)) != -1) {
38         arg.array = start_val;
39         if (semctl(semid, 0, SETALL, arg) == -1) {
40            perror("semctl -- parent -- initialization");
41            exit(3);
42         }
43      } else {
44         perror("semget -- parent -- creation ");
45         exit(4);
46      }
47      /*
48      Fork the producer process
49      */
50      if ( (p_id=fork( )) == -1) {
51         perror("fork -- producer ");
52         exit(5);
53      } else if ( p_id == 0 ) {
54         execl( "producer", "producer", argv[1], (char *) 0);
55         perror("execl -- producer ");
56         exit(6);
57      }
58      /*
59      Fork the consumer process
60      */
61      if ( (c_id =fork( )) == -1) {
62         perror("fork -- consumer ");
63         exit(7);
64      } else if ( c_id == 0 ) {
65         execl( "consumer", "consumer", argv[2], (char *) 0);
66         perror("execl -- consumer ");
67         exit(8);
68      }
69      croaker = (int) wait( (int *) 0 );   /* wait for 1 to die  */
70      kill( (croaker == p_id ) ? c_id : p_id, SIGKILL);
                                              /* kill other    */
71      shmdt( shmptr );                      /* detach        */
72      shmctl(shmid,IPC_RMID,(struct shmid_ds *)0);          /*remove*/
73      semctl( semid, 0, IPC_RMID, 0);
74      exit(0);
75  }
```

The parent process expects two integer values to be passed via the command line (program lines 17–20). These values indicate a maximum time, in seconds, for a process to sleep during its execution cycle. The first value is passed to the producing process and the second to the consuming process. By specifying differing values on the command line, we can easily simulate producer/consumer relationships that operate at different speeds. In lines 24–28, we create and attach the shared memory segment. Once this is done, we copy the contents of our memory structure (which has been set to its initial values) to the shared memory segment using the library function **memcpy**. The **memcpy** function is one of a group of functions that work with sequences of bytes bounded by a byte count value, versus a terminating NULL character. See Table 8.10.

Table 8.10 Summary of the **memcpy** library function.

Include File(s)	<string.h>	Manual Section	**3c**

Summary	`void *memcpy( void *s1,`
	`            const void *s2,`
	`            size_t n );`		

Return	Success	Failure	Sets errno
	A pointer to s1		

The **memcpy** function will copy n number of bytes from the location referenced by s2 to the location referenced by s1. Upon completion, a pointer to the s1 location will be returned. The **memcpy** function does not check for overflow.

In lines 37–42 of the parent program, the two semaphores that will control access to the shared memory segment are created and set to their initial values. The AVAIL_SLOTS semaphore is set to 6 to reflect the six available slots, and the TO_CONSUME semaphore is set to 0. A child process is then forked and overlaid with the producer process code. The producing process is passed a single integer argument to be used as its sleep time. Following this, the parent process forks a second child process which it then overlays with the consumer process code. The consumer process is also passed an integer sleep value as its first argument. Once this is done, the parent process waits for one of its child processes (either the producer or consumer) to terminate. When this occurs, the process ID is returned and stored in the program variable croaker. The parent process then checks the contents of this variable to determine which child process is remaining. The remaining process is removed with a call to **kill** and the shared memory segment is detached and removed.

The code for the producing process is shown in Program 8.4.

Program 8.4 The producer process.

```
1   #include "local.h"
2   /*
3    *The PRODUCER ...
4    */
5   main(int argc, char *argv[]) {
6
7     static char    *source[ROWS][COLS] = {
8           {"A", "The", "One"},
9           {" red", " polka-dot", " yellow"},
10          {" spider", " dump truck", " tree"},
11          {" broke", " ran", " fell"},
12          {" down", " away", " out"}
```

```
13        };
14     static char      local_buffer[SLOT_LEN];
15     int              i, r, c, sleep_limit, semid, shmid;
16     pid_t            ppid = getppid( );
17     char             *shmptr;
18     struct MEMORY    *memptr;
19
20     if ( argc != 2 ) {
21       fprintf(stderr, "%s sleep_time", argv[0]);
22       exit(-1);
23     }
24     /*
25      *Access, attach and reference the shared memory
26      */
27     if ((shmid=shmget((int) ppid, 0, 0)) != -1 ){
28       if ((shmptr=(char *)shmat(shmid,(char *)0,0))==(char *)-1){
29         perror("shmat -- producer -- attach ");
30         exit(1);
31       }
32       memptr = (struct MEMORY *) shmptr;
33     } else {
34       perror("shmget -- producer -- access ");
35       exit(2);
36     }
37     /*
38      *Access the semaphore set
39      */
40     if ( (semid=semget((int) ppid, 2, 0)) == -1 ) {
41       perror("semget -- producer -- access ");
42          exit(3);
43     }
44     sleep_limit = atoi(argv[1]) % 20;
45     i = 20 - sleep_limit;
46     srand((unsigned)getpid());
47     while( i-- ) {
48       memset(local_buffer, '\0', sizeof(local_buffer));
49       for (r = 0; r < ROWS; ++r) {    /* Make a random string */
50         c = rand() % COLS;
51         strcat(local_buffer, source[r][c]);
52       }
53       acquire.sem_num = AVAIL_SLOTS;
54       if (semop(semid, &acquire, 1 ) == -1 ){
55         perror("semop -- producer -- acquire ");
56         exit(4);
57       }
58       strcpy(memptr->buffer[memptr->tail], local_buffer);
59       printf("P: [%d] %s.\n", memptr->tail,
                  memptr->buffer[memptr->tail]);
60       memptr->tail = (memptr->tail +1) % N_SLOTS;
61       release.sem_num = TO_CONSUME;
62       if (semop( semid, &release, 1 ) == -1 ) {
63         perror("semop -- producer -- release ");
64         exit(5);
65       }
66       sleep( rand( ) % sleep_limit + 1 );
67     }
68     exit(0);
69  }
```

The producer process allocates a two-dimensional array, source, that contains a series of strings that will be used to generate random messages to store in the shared memory segment. A storage location, local_buffer, is created that will temporarily hold the message. Next, the process ID of the parent is obtained via the **getppid** system call. The parent process ID will be used as the key value for the **shmget** system call. This enables the producer process to reference the shared memory segment that was created by the parent process. Another approach would be to pass the shared memory identifier from the parent process to the producer via the command line. If this is done, the parent process would convert the integer shared memory identifier to a character string before passing it and the producing process would convert the string back to its original integer format. In program lines 27–31, the producer process gains access to the shared memory segment and attaches it. The producer uses a local pointer, memptr, to assign the shared memory address at program line 32, in order to reference the shared memory location. The producer process then gains access to the semaphore set (again using the parent process ID as the **semget** key value). After this is done, the limit for the time to **sleep** during its processing cycle is obtained (line 44) and the maximum number of messages to be generated is calculated. The program then loops through the following steps. It clears the local_buffer by filling it with null characters. A short random message is produced and stored in the local_buffer. The producer then evaluates the AVAIL_SLOTS semaphore. Once the producer can acquire[2] the semaphore (which by definition will only occur if the semaphore is non-zero), the message in local_buffer is copied to the shared memory location using the value in the memory->tail location as an offset index. The message that is stored is displayed to the screen for reference. The memory->tail value is then incremented in a modular fashion so as to reference the next valid storage location. The TO_CONSUME semaphore is incremented next to indicate the addition of another message. The producer then sleeps a maximum of sleep_limit seconds and continues its processing loop. The producer will exit when all messages have been produced and written to the shared memory segment or when it receives a termination signal (such as from its parent process).

The code for the consumer process is shown in Program 8.5.

Program 8.5 The consumer process.

```
1   #include "local.h"
2   /*
3    *The CONSUMER
4    */
5   main(int argc, char *argv[]) {
6
7       static char     local_buffer[SLOT_LEN];
8       int             i, sleep_limit, semid, shmid;
9       pid_t           ppid = getppid( );
10      char            *shmptr;
```

---

2. The contents of the AVAIL_SLOTS semaphore is decremented when it is acquired.

```
11    struct MEMORY    *memptr;
12
13    if ( argc != 2 ) {
14      fprintf(stderr, "%s sleep_time", argv[0]);
15      exit(-1);
16    }
17    /*
18     *Access, attach and reference the shared memory
19     */
20    if ((shmid=shmget((int) ppid, 0, 0)) != -1 ){
21      if ( (shmptr=(char *)shmat(shmid,(char *)0,0)) == (char *) -1){
22        perror("shmat -- consumer -- attach ");
23        exit(1);
24      }
25      memptr = (struct MEMORY *) shmptr;
26    } else {
27      perror("shmget -- consumer -- access ");
28      exit(2);
29    }
30    /*
31     *Access the semaphore set
32     */
33    if ( (semid=semget((int) ppid, 2, 0)) == -1 ) {
34      perror("semget -- consumer -- access ");
35      exit(3);
36    }
37    sleep_limit = atoi(argv[1]) % 20;
38    i = 20 - sleep_limit;
39    srand((unsigned)getpid());
40    while( i ) {
41      acquire.sem_num = TO_CONSUME;
42      if (semop(semid, &acquire, 1 ) == -1 ){
43        perror("semop -- consumer -- acquire ");
44        exit(4);
45      }
46      memset(local_buffer, '\0', sizeof(local_buffer));
47      strcpy(local_buffer, memptr->buffer[memptr->head]);
48      printf("C: [%d] %s.\n", memptr->head,local_buffer);
49      memptr->head = (memptr->head +1) % N_SLOTS;
50      release.sem_num = AVAIL_SLOTS;
51      if (semop( semid, &release, 1 ) == -1 ) {
52        perror("semop -- consumer -- release ");
53        exit(5);
54      }
55      sleep( rand( ) % sleep_limit + 1 );
56    }
57    exit(0);
58  }
```

In most aspects, the logic for the consumer process is similar to that of the producer process. However, the consumer will be allowed access to the shared memory segment via the TO_CONSUME semaphore. If this semaphore is non-zero, it indicates there are messages available for the consumer to read. When a message is available, the consumer will copy the message to its local_buffer array from the shared memory location using the value in memory->head as an offset index. The local_buffer contents are then displayed on the screen for reference. As in the producer process, the value referenced by memory->head is incremented in a modular fashion to reference the next valid location. The AVAIL_SLOTS semaphore is incremented and the consumer continues its processing.

When viewing the output of a run of the program, note that if the parent process is passed a set of values that allow the producer process to be *faster* than the consumer process, the shared memory location will eventually become *full*. When this occurs, the producer must block and wait[3] for the consumer to read a message. Only after a message has been read by the consumer is a slot released and a new message stored by the producer.

Fig. 8.7 Output when the producer process is *faster* than the consumer process.

```
% parent 2 4
P: [0] The red spider broke away.
C: [0] The red spider broke away.
P: [1] A polka-dot dump truck fell out.
C: [1] A polka-dot dump truck fell out.
P: [2] One yellow spider fell out.                          The producer is working
P: [3] The red tree fell out.                               faster than the consumer
P: [4] One polka-dot dump truck fell down.
C: [2] One yellow spider fell out.
P: [5] One red spider ran away.
C: [3] The red tree fell out.
P: [0] A polka-dot spider fell away.
P: [1] One red dump truck ran out.
P: [2] One polka-dot tree ran out .
C: [4] One polka-dot dump truck fell down.
P: [3] One red spider broke down.
C: [5] One red spider ran away.
P: [4] The red dump truck ran down.                         The queue (buffer) is now
P: [5] One yellow dump truck fell out.                      getting  full.
C: [0] A polka-dot spider fell away.
P: [0] The red tree fell down.
C: [1] One red dump truck ran out.
P: [1] The yellow spider ran away.
C: [2] One polka-dot tree ran out.
P: [2] One yellow spider fell down.
C: [3] One red spider broke down.
P: [3] One yellow tree fell away.
C: [4] The red dump truck ran down.
P: [4] The polka-dot tree broke down.
C: [5] One yellow dump truck fell out.
P: [5] The polka-dot tree ran down.
C: [0] The red tree fell down.
```

If values are passed to the producer/consumer which permit them to work at similar rates, we find the six-element message array sufficient to allow both processes to continue their work without each having an inordinate amount of waiting for the other process to finish its task. However, the consumer process will still wait should no new messages be available.

---

3. The default action when attempting to acquire a zero value semaphore.

Fig. 8.8 Output when the consumer process is the *same as* the producer process.

```
% parent 2 2
P: [0] A red spider broke out.
C: [0] A red spider broke out.
P: [1] A polka-dot tree ran out.
C: [1] A polka-dot tree ran out.
P: [2] The red tree fell out.
P: [3] The red dump truck broke away. ◄────────── 4 messages produced, 2 consumed
C: [2] The red tree fell out.
P: [4] One red dump truck ran out.
C: [3] The red dump truck broke away.
P: [5] A yellow tree broke down.
P: [0] A red dump truck fell down.
C: [4] One red dump truck ran out.
C: [5] A yellow tree broke down. ◄────────── 7 messages produced, 6 consumed
P: [1] The polka-dot tree broke away.
C: [0] A red dump truck fell down.
P: [2] One yellow dump truck broke out.
C: [1] The polka-dot tree broke away.
P: [3] The polka-dot spider ran out.
C: [2] One yellow dump truck broke out.
P: [4] One yellow tree fell down.
C: [3] The polka-dot spider ran out.
P: [5] One polka-dot spider ran away.
C: [4] One yellow tree fell down.
C: [5] One polka-dot spider ran away.
P: [0] A polka-dot spider ran out.
P: [1] One red spider broke down. ◄────────── 13 messages produced, 11 consumed
C: [0] A polka-dot spider ran out.
P: [2] One polka-dot tree broke down.
C: [1] One red spider broke down.
P: [3] A polka-dot dump truck ran out.
C: [2] One polka-dot tree broke down.
P: [4] A yellow dump truck broke down.
C: [3] A polka-dot dump truck ran out.
P: [5] A red dump truck ran away.
C: [4] A yellow dump truck broke down.
C: [5] A red dump truck ran away. ◄────────── 18 messages produced, 18 consumed
```

EXERCISE 8 – 5

In this producer/consumer example, the code to display the message to the screen and the adjusting of the head/tail indices was done within the critical regions bounded by the two semaphores. Is this actually necessary? Why/why not? If both the producer and consumer *know* there are six buffer slots, are two semaphores actually needed? Why?

EXERCISE 8 – 6

Modify the producer/consumer example to support multiple consumers. Can this be done without adding another semaphore?

Modify the producer/consumer example to support multiple producers. Is yet another semaphore needed to coordinate process activity?

8.5 USING A FILE AS SHARED MEMORY

Most versions of UNIX also support the **mmap** system call which can be used to map a file to a process's virtual memory address space. In many ways **mmap** is more flexible than its shared memory system call counterpart. Once a mapping has been established standard system calls, versus specialized system calls, can be used to manipulate the shared memory object (Table 8.11). Unlike memory, the contents of files are non-volatile and will remain available even after a system has been shut down (rebooted).

Table 8.11 Summary of the **mmap** system call.

Include File(s)	`<sys/types.h>` `<sys/mman.h>`	Manual Section	**2**

Summary	`caddr_t`
	`mmap( caddr_t addr, size_t len,`
	`        int prot,      int flags,`
	`        int fildes,    off_t off );`		

Return	Success	Failure	Sets errno
	The address of the mapping	MAP_FAILED `((void *) -1)`	Yes

The **mmap** system call requires six arguments. The first, addr, is the address for attachment. As with the **shmat** system call, this argument is most often set to 0 which directs the system to choose a valid attachment address. The number of bytes to be attached is indicated by the second argument, len. While the call will allow the user to specify a number of bytes for len that will extend beyond the end of the mapped file, an actual reference to these locations will generate an error (a SIGBUS signal). The third argument, prot, is used to set the type of access (protection) for the segment. The prot argument uses the defined constants found in the include file `<sys/mman.h>`. These constants are shown in Table 8.12.

Constants can be ORed to provide different combinations of access. The manual page for **mmap** notes that on some systems PROT_WRITE is implemented as PROT_READ | PROT_WRITE and PROT_EXEC as PROT_READ | PROT_EXEC. In any case, PROT_WRITE must be set if the process is to write to the mapped segment. The fourth argument, flags, specifies the type of mapping. Mapping types are also indicated using defined constants from the `<sys/mman.h>` include file. These constants are shown in Table 8.13.

The first two constants specify whether or not **writes** to the shared memory will

Table 8.12 Defined protection constants.

Defined Constant	Access
PROT_READ	Read access to specified region.
PROT_WRITE	Write access to specified region.
PROT_EXEC	Execute access to specified region.
PROT_NONE	No access.

Table 8.13 Defined mapping type constants.

Defined Constant	Mapping Type
MAP_SHARED	Share all changes.
MAP_PRIVATE	Do not share changes.
MAP_FIXED	Interpret the value for the addr argument exactly.
MAP_NORESERVE	Do not reserve swap space for the mapping.

be shared with other processes or be private. MAP_SHARED and MAP_PRIVATE are exclusionary. When specifying MAP_PRIVATE a private copy is not generated until the first **write** to the mapped object has occurred. These specifications are retained across a fork system call but not across a call to exec. MAP_FIXED directs the system to *explicitly* use the address value in addr. When MAP_FIXED is indicated the values for adr and off should be a multiple of the system's page size. Specifying MAP_FIXED greatly reduces the portability of a program. The MAP_NORESERVE flag directs the system to not use swap space when generating a mapping. If this flag is not set, and MAP_PRIVATE is indicated, the system will attempt to use swap space for the mapping. In this setting results are dependent upon the current availability of swap space. The MAP_NORESERVE flag is inherited across a **fork** system call. The fifth argument, fildes, is a valid **open** file descriptor. The sixth argument, off, is used to set the starting position (offset) for the mapping.

If the **mmap** system call is successful it will return a reference to the mapped memory object. If the call fails it will return the defined constant MAP_FAILED (which is actually the value -1 cast to a void *). When the call fails it will set the value in **errno** to reflect the error encountered. The errors for **mmap** are shown in Table 8.14.

While the system will automatically unmap a region when a process terminates, the system call **munmap**, shown in Table 8.15, can be used to explicitly unmap pages of memory.

The **munmap** system call is passed the starting address of the memory mapping (argument addr) and the size of the mapping (argument len). If the call is successful it will return a value of 0. Future references to unmapped addresses will generate a SIGVEGV signal. If the **munmap** system call fails it will return the value -1 and set the value in **errno** to EINVAL. The interpretation of **munmap** related errors is given in Table 8.16.

Table 8.14 `mmap` error messages.

#	Constant	`perror` **Message**	**Explanation**
3	EACCES	Permission denied	• File descriptor is not open for reading. • File descriptor is not open for writing and PROT_WRITE was indicated with a mapping type of MAP_SHARED.
6	ENXIO	No such device or address	The values for `off` or `off + len` are illegal for the specified device.
9	EBADF	Bad file number	The file referenced by `fildes` is not open.
11	EAGAIN	Resource temporarily unavailable	• Insufficient swap space for the mapping. • Mapping could not be locked in memory. • Mapped file is already locked.
12	ENOMEM	Not enough space	Insufficient address space to implement the mapping.
19	ENODEV	No such device	`fildes` references an invalid device (such as a terminal).
22	EINVAL	Invalid argument	• MAP_FIXED specified and value for `addr` or `off` are not multiples of the system's page size. • Illegal `flag` value. • Argument `len` is less than 1.

Table 8.15 Summary of the **munmap** system call.

Include File(s)	`<sys/types.h>` `<sys/mman.h>`		Manual Section	**2**
Summary	`int munmap( caddr_t addr, size_t len );`			
Return	Success	Failure	Sets `errno`	
	0	-1	Yes	

Table 8.16 **munmap** error messages.

#	Constant	`perror` **Message**	**Explanation**
22	EINVAL	Invalid argument	• Argument `len` is less than 1. • Argument `addr` is not a multiple of the system page size. • Argument `addr` or `addr + len` is outside the process's address space.

The **msync** library function can be used in conjunction with **mmap** to synchronize the contents of mapped memory with physical storage (Table 8.17). A call to **msync** will cause the system to write all modified memory locations to their associated physical storage locations. If MAP_SHARED was specified with **mmap** the storage location is a file. If MAP_PRIVATE was specified then the storage location is the swap area.

The `addr` argument for **msync** specifies the address of the mapped memory, the `len` argument the size (in bytes) of the memory. The `flags` argument directs the system to take the actions shown in Table 8.18.

If **msync** fails it will return a -1 and set **errno** (Table 8.19). If the call is successful it will return a value of 0.

Table 8.17 Summary of the **msync** library function.

Include File(s)	`<sys/types.h>` `<sys/mman.h>`		Manual Section	**3c**
Summary	`int msync( caddr_t addr, size_t len,` `            int flags );`			
Return	Success	Failure	Sets errno	
	0	-1	Yes	

Table 8.18 Defined flag constants for **msync**.

Defined Constant	Action
MS_ASYNC	Return immediately once all writes have been scheduled.
MS_SYNC	Return once all writes have been performed.
MS_INVALIDATE	Invalidate cached copies of memory—system reloads memory from the associated storage location.

Table 8.19 **mmap** error messages.

#	Constant	`perror` Message	Explanation
1	EPERM	Not owner	MS_INVALIDATE indicated but some of the referenced locations are locked in memory.
5	EIO	I/O error	Read / Write error when accessing file `fildes`.
12	ENOMEM	Not enough space	Invalid address reference.
16	EBUSY	Device busy	MS_SYNC and MS_INVALIDATE specified but some of the referenced addresses are currently locked.
22	EINVAL	Invalid argument	• Argument `addr` is not a multiple of the page size. • Argument `flags` not a combination of MS_ASYNC and MS_INVALIDATE.

Program 8.6 demonstrates the use of the **mmap** system call.

Program 8.6 Using **mmap**.

```
/*
 * Using the mmap system call
 */
#include <stdio.h>
#include <sys/types.h>
#include <sys/mman.h>
#include <stdlib.h>
#include <fcntl.h>
#include <sys/stat.h>
#include <unistd.h>
#include <signal.h>
#include <string.h>
main(int argc, char *argv[]){
  int            fd, changes, i, random_spot, kids[2];
  struct stat    buf;
  char           *the_file,
                 *starting_string =
                 "Using mmap( ) can be fun\nand informative!";
  if (argc != 3) {
    fprintf(stderr, "Usage %s file_name #_of_changes\n", *argv);
    exit(1);
  }
  if ((changes = atoi(argv[2])) < 1) {
    fprintf(stderr, "# of changes < 1 \n");
    exit(2);
  }
  if ((fd = open(argv[1], O_CREAT | O_RDWR, 0666)) < 0) {
    fprintf(stderr, "open error on file %s\n", *argv);
    exit(3);
  }
  write(fd, starting_string, strlen(starting_string));
/*
 *      Obtain size of file to be mapped
 */
  if (fstat(fd, &buf) < 0) {
    fprintf(stderr, "fstat error on file %s\n", *argv);
    exit(4);
  }
/*
 *      Establish the mapping
 */
  if ((the_file = mmap(0, (size_t) buf.st_size,
                       PROT_READ | PROT_WRITE,
                       MAP_SHARED, fd, 0)) == (caddr_t) - 1) {
    fprintf(stderr, "mmap failure\n");
    exit(5);
  }
for (i = 0; i < 2; ++i)
    if ((kids[i] = (int) fork()) == 0)
      while (1) {
        printf("Child %d finds:\n%s\n", getpid(), the_file);
        sleep(1);
      }
```

```
  srand((unsigned) getpid());
  for (i = 0; i < changes; ++i) {
    random_spot = (int) (rand() % buf.st_size);
    *(the_file + random_spot) = '*';
    sleep(1);
  }
  printf("Parent done with changes\n");
  for (i = 0; i < 2; ++i)
    kill(kids[i], 9);
  printf("The file now contains:\n%s\n", the_file);
  exit( 0 );
}
```

Program 8.6 uses a parent/two-child process arrangement to demonstrate the use of **mmap**. The parent process will modify the contents of a memory mapped file. Each child process will repetitively display the contents of the mapped files to allow verification of the changes. The program is passed two command line arguments. The first argument is the name of a file that it will use for mapping. The second argument will indicate the number of modifications that should be made to the file. Upon execution of the program the validity of the command line arguments is checked. If problems are encountered an appropriate error message is generated and the program exits. If the command line arguments are good the program opens, for reading and writing, the file whose name was passed as the first command line argument. As the O_CREAT flag is specified, if the file does not exist it will be created. Next, the string "Using mmap( ) can be fun and informative!" is written to the first part of the file. Following this the **fstat** call is used to determine the size of the file. In our example, if we start with an empty or non-existent file, the size of the file is actually the length of the string that is written to the file. However, this would not be true if the file contained previous data. In many cases we will want to know the full size of the file to be mapped—**fstat** will provide us with a handy way of determining the file's size (it is returned as part of the stat structure). The call to **mmap** establishes the actual mapping. We allow the system to pick the address and indicate that we want to be able to read from, and write to, the mapped memory region. We also specify the region be marked as shared, that it be associated with the open file descriptor fd and have an offset (starting position within the file) of 0. Two child processes are then generated. Each child process displays the contents of the memory mapped file using the the_file reference which was returned from the initial call to **mmap**. It is important to note that a call to **read** was not needed. The child process then **sleep**s one second and repeats the same sequence of activities until a terminating signal is received. The parent process loops for the number of times specified by the second command line argument. Within this loop the parent process randomly picks a memory mapped location and changes it to an "*". Again, this is done by direct reference to the location using the the_file reference; no **write** function is used. Between changes the parent sleeps one second to slow down the processing sequence. Once the parent process is done it displays the final contents of the memory mapped file, removes the child processes, and exits. A sample run of the program is shown in Figure 8.9.

Fig. 8.9 A sample run of Program 8.6.

```
% p8.6 test 3
Child 3679 finds:
Using mmap( ) can be fun
and informative!
Child 3680 finds:
Using mmap( ) can be fun
and informative!
Child 3679 finds:
Using mmap( ) can be fun
*nd informative!
Child 3680 finds:
Using mmap( ) can be fun
*nd informative!
• • •
Child 3679 finds:
Usi*g mmap( ) can be fun
*nd in*ormative!
Child 3680 finds:
Usi*g mmap( ) can be fun
*nd in*ormative!
Parent done with changes
The file now contains:
Usi*g mmap( ) can be fun
*nd in*ormative!
```

In this invocation the child processes, PIDs 3679 and 3680, initially find the mapped location to contain the unmodified starting string. A second check of the mapped location shows that each child now *sees* the string with a single "*" replacing the letter "a" in the word "and" in the second line. Additional passes reveal further modifications. When all of the processes have terminated we will find that the file test will contain the fully modified string.

E X E R C I S E   8 – 8

If we replace MAP_SHARED with MAP_PRIVATE will the output from Program 8.6 remain the same? Why/why not? Will the file test contain the "*" modified string or the original string? Why/why not? Why is the MAP_SHARED specification retained across a **fork** but not an **exec** system call?

E X E R C I S E   8 – 9

What if the file that we map resides on a shared file system? Can we then have unrelated processes residing on different workstations use this file as a means of communication? Support your answer with a program example.

8.6 SUMMARY

Shared memory provides the user with an efficient means of communication via the sharing of data that resides in memory. Unlike pipe-based communications, this data can be accessed in a non-serial (random) manner. To prevent inconsistencies semaphores are often used to coordinate access to shared memory segments. When using System V based shared memory techniques, shared memory segments are generated with the **shmget** system call. If a shared memory segment has already been created the **shmget** call will provide the process with access to the segment. The **shmctl** system call is used to obtain the status of a memory segment, set permissions and remove a shared memory segment. The **shmat** and **shmdt** system calls are used to attach (map the segment into the process's address space) and detach memory segments.

The **mmap** system call may also be used to map the virtual memory space of a process to a file. As files remain after a process has terminated **mmap**ed files provide a means for communicating information between processes that exist at different times. Overall, **mmap**-based techniques are less complex and somewhat more portable than their System V based counterparts.

Remote Procedure Calls

9.1 INTRODUCTION

So far, the examples we have worked with have been run on the same workstation or host. However, as we gain expertise with interprocess communication techniques, it becomes evident that there will be many occasions where we will want to communicate with processes that may reside on different workstations. These workstations might be on our own local area network or part of a larger, wide area network. In a UNIX, networked computing setting there are several ways that communications of this nature can be implemented. This chapter will examine the techniques involved with remote procedure calls (RPC)[1]. As a programming interface, remote procedure calls are designed to resemble standard, local procedure (function) calls. The *client* process (the process *making* the request) invokes a local procedure commonly known as a **client stub** that contains the network communication details and the actual remote procedure call. The *server* process (the process *performing* the request) has a similar **server stub** which contains its network communication details. Neither the client nor the server needs to be aware of the underlying network transport protocols.

---

1. The word *remote* in RPC is somewhat misleading. RPCs can also be used by processes residing on the same system (indeed this approach is often used when debugging routines that contain RPCs).

The programming stubs are usually created using a protocol compiler, such as Sun Microsystems **rpcgen**. The protocol compiler is passed a protocol definition file written in a C-like language. For **rpcgen**, the language used is called RPC (Remote Procedure Call) language. The protocol definition file contains a definition of the remote procedure, its parameters with data types, and its return data type.

When the client invokes an RPC (generates a request), the client will wait for the server to reply. Since the client must wait for a response, several coordination issues are of concern:

☞ How long should a client wait for a reply from the server (the server could be down or very busy)? In general, RPCs address this problem by using a default timeout to limit the client's wait time.

☞ If the client makes multiple, identical requests, how should the server handle it? The resolution of this problem proves to be program specific. Depending upon the type of processing (such as a read request) the requested activity may, indeed, be done several times. In other settings, such as transaction processing, the request must be done only once. In these settings, the software implements its own management routines. However, while by definition RPCs are independent of transport protocols, if an RPC runs on top of a reliable transport (such as TCP), the client can infer from receiving a *reply* from the server process that its request will be executed.

☞ How can call-by-reference (the passing of address pointers) be implemented when the processes reside in separate process spaces? Further, it is entirely possible that the client and server processes, while not being on the same system, may even be executing on different platforms (e.g., Sun, VAX, IBM, etc.). To resolve these issues, and to ensure that client and server processes can communicate using RPC, the data that is passed between the processes is converted to an architecture independent representation. The data format used by Sun is known as XDR (e**X**ternal **D**ata **R**epresentation). The client and server program stubs are responsible for translating the transmitted data to and from the XDR format (procedures known as **serialization** and **deserialization**). The high-level relationships of client and server processes using an RPC are shown in Figure 9.1.

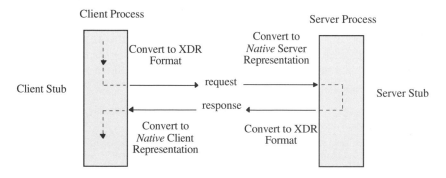

Fig. 9.1 An RPC client-server communications overview.

We will find that, while hidden from the casual user, RPC uses socket-based communication. The details of socket-based communication will be covered in Chapter 10.

At a system level, the **rpcinfo** command can be used to direct the system to display all of the currently registered RPC services. When the **-s** flag is passed to **rpcinfo**, a condensed output display format is used. If you have an older version of **rpcinfo** on your system, use the **-p** option (versus **-s**) for the condensed output display. Some versions of **rpcinfo** require the host name to be specified. If you do not know the host name, the **hostname** command will display the name of the host upon which you are working.

9.2 EXECUTING REMOTE COMMANDS AT A SYSTEM LEVEL

Before delving into the fine points of remote procedure calls from a programming standpoint, it is instructive to look at the execution of remote commands at a system level. Most UNIX systems offer several commands that allow the user to execute commands on a remote system. The most commonly supported remote execution command is **rsh** (the **r**emote **sh**ell command). The general syntax for the **rsh** command is:

```
% rsh   [options] remote_host_name   the_command
```

The **rsh** command will connect to the specified host and execute the indicated command. Standard input from the local host is copied to standard input on the remote host. The remote host's standard output and error will be copied to the local host's standard output and error respectively. For example, on our system the command sequence:

```
morpheus% rsh obiwan whodo
```

would run the **whodo** command on the remote host obiwan. The output of the command would be displayed on the local host morpheus. It is possible to redirect the output produced by the remote command. However, there are some interesting wrinkles that we should be aware of when we specify I/O redirection with the command to be remotely executed. For example, the two command sequences that follow *appear* to be very similar:

```
morpheus% rsh   obiwan whodo > /tmp/whoosie
morpheus% rsh obiwan whodo ">" /tmp/whoosie
```

The first command sequence places the output of the **whodo** command in the file whoosie in the tmp directory of the local host morpheus. The second command sequence places the output of the **whodo** command in the file whoosie in the tmp directory of the remote host obiwan! This occurs because in the second command sequence the redirection, which has been placed in quotes, is passed as part of the remote command and is not acted upon by the local host.

On occasion commands executed with **rsh** will hang mysteriously. Often the problem can be remedied by adding the **-n** flag (placed before the remote host name) which redirects the input of **rsh** to /dev/null. As would be expected, **rsh** should be used to execute remote command sequences that do not require interactive input. An interesting aside about the **rsh** command is that if it is invoked with any other name than **rsh** it will take its *new* name as the remote host name argument. Thus, if you generate a symbolic link to the **rsh** command (type **whereis rsh** to find its true resting place) with the name of a remote host, you then only need enter the host name (which is now the symbolic link to **rsh**) followed by the command to have the command executed on the remote host.

When invoking **rsh,** the **rsh** process on the local host acts as the client. The **rsh** client process communicates with the server process on the remote host. The server process for **rsh** is **rshd** (the remote shell daemon). It is the **rshd** process that executes the command on the remote host and returns the output to the client process on the local host. The execution of remote commands with **rsh** only works transparently when we are dealing with *trusted* hosts/users. If a host is *trusted* then any user with the same user name on both hosts can execute the **rsh** command without having to enter his or her password. If specified as a *trusted* user on a remote host, the user on the local host can execute the **rsh** command on the remote host even though he or she do not have an account on the remote host. While trust has its advantages, such as not requiring the entry of passwords, it also has its down side as it provides a very real opportunity for security breaches.

The file /etc/hosts.equiv contains the list of hosts (and user names) that the local host will trust. Figure 9.2 shows the contents of a typical hosts.equiv file.

Fig. 9.2 A typical hosts.equiv file.

```
% cat /etc/hosts.equiv
morpheus
thetic
stimpy
skynet
hobbes
hal
faust
faraday
obiwan
```

Entries in the hosts.equiv file can also be fully qualified, such as foozie.hartford.edu. If the host name is followed by a user name then the user on the indicated host is to be trusted. While the hosts.equiv file is used by the host system to indicate trusted hosts and users, additional trusted host and user information is stored in the .rhosts file found in each user's home directory. The .rhosts file specifies hosts and users that are permitted access by the individual user. For example, the .rhosts file on the host morpheus with the contents shown in Figure 9.3:

Fig. 9.3 A sample .rhosts file.

```
morpheus % cat .rhosts
caribou.hartford.edu bgray
misho
```

---

would indicate that the user `bgray` on the host `caribou.hartford.edu` is to be trusted. Thus, if the user `bgray` was on the host `caribou.hartford.edu` they could issue the command:

```
caribou% rsh -l gray morpheus rm important_file
```

and the host `morpheus` would accept, and execute the **rm** command (removing the file) as if the user `gray` had issued the command! The entry `misho` indicates user `gray` on the host `misho` is also to be trusted. The `.rhosts` file can also be used to *remove* access by specific hosts and users. This is done by placing a minus in front of the host or user name, e.g., `misho -bob` would disallow access by the user `bob` when on the host `misho`.

The system begins its authentication sequence by examining the `hosts.equiv` file and then goes on to the `.rhosts` file. The system stops evaluating the files once a positive match has been made. Therefore, the order of entries, especially those entries meant to disallow access, should be checked carefully. In addition, a "+" can be placed in either of these files to indicate all hosts and users are to be trusted. Needless to say most often you would *not* want your system to be compromised in this manner. Because of the potential for misuse, some system administrators do not allow users to have their own `.rhosts` file.

9.3 EXECUTING REMOTE COMMANDS IN A C PROGRAM

The network library function **rexec** can be used in a C program to execute a system level command on a remote host. In many ways we can think of the **rexec** library function as a *remote* version of the system call **system** that was discussed earlier. The syntax for **rexec** is summarized in Table 9.1.

The **rexec** library call accepts six arguments. The first is a reference to the name of the remote host. This reference will be passed by **rexec** to the **gethostbyname** net-

Table 9.1 Summary of the **rexec** library call.

Include File(s)	`<netdb.h>`		Manual Section	**3N**

Summary	`int`
	`rexec( char **ahost,`
	`        unsigned short inport,`
	`        const char *user,`
	`        const char *passwd,`
	`        const char *cmd,`
	`        int *fd2p );`			

Return	Success		Failure	Sets errno
	A stream socket file descriptor		-1	

work call for authentication (the details of the **gethostbyname** function are covered in Chapter 10). The second argument, inport, is an integer value that indicates the port to be used for the connection. Most often the port number used with **rexec** is 512 (the port associated with the execution of remote commands, which uses TCP protocol). The port argument is followed by two character string reference arguments that indicate the user's name and password respectively. If these entries are set to NULL the system will check the contents of the file .netrc that resides in the user's home directory for machine (host), login (user name) and password information. If the .netrc file does not exist, or it contains only partial information, the user will be prompted for their name and/or password. The sixth argument to **rexec** is a reference to an integer. If this value is not 0 **rexec** will assume it is a reference to a valid file descriptor and will map standard error from the execution of the remote command to the indicated file descriptor. If the **rexec** command is successful it returns a valid stream socket file descriptor that is mapped to the local host's standard input and output. If the **rexec** function fails it returns a -1.

Program 9.1 demonstrates the use of the **rexec** library call.

Program 9.1 Using **rexec** to execute a remote command.

```
/*
 * Using rexec
 */
#include <stdio.h>
#include <sys/types.h>
#include <unistd.h>
#include <stdlib.h>
#include <netinet/in.h>
#include <netdb.h>
main(int argc, char *argv[]) {
    int           fd, count;
    char          buffer[BUFSIZ], *command, *host;
    if (argc != 3) {
        fprintf(stderr, "Usage %s host command\n", argv[0]);
        exit(1);
    }
    host    = argv[1];
    command = argv[2];
    if ((fd = rexec(&host, htons(512), 0, 0, command, 0)) == -1) {
        fprintf(stderr, "rexec failed\n");
        exit(2);
    }
    while ((count = read(fd, buffer, BUFSIZ)) > 0)
        fwrite(buffer, count, 1, stdout);
}
```

In Program 9.1 the first command line argument is the host on which the remote command will be executed. The second command line argument is the command that will be passed to the remote host. The invocation of the **rexec** function uses the **htons** network call on its second argument to ensure the proper network byte ordering when specifying the port number. The prototype for **htons** resides in the include file

<netinet/in.h>. The arguments for the user name and password are set to 0. This will direct **rexec** to first check the .netrc file in the owner's home directory for user name and password information. If the .netrc file is not present or incomplete **rexec** will prompt the user for this information. If the **rexec** call completes without error, the output from the execution of the command on the remote host is read and displayed to standard output. Figure 9.4 shows a compilation (note the library inclusions) and run of Program 9.1.

Fig. 9.4 Using Program 9.1.

```
morpheus% CC p91.c  -o p91  -lsocket  -lnsl
morpheus% p91 stimpy who
Name (stimpy:gray): gray
Password (stimpy:gray):
bjeroszk    console       Apr 14 15:20
bjeroszk    pts/1         Apr 14 15:21
```

We can see from the output of Program 9.1 that the user's .netrc file did not contain an entry for the host stimpy. The user's password entry was not echoed back to the screen.

The **rexec** function communicates with **rexecd** (remote execution daemon) on the host system. While **rexec** is interesting, and does provide a fairly painless way to execute commands on a remote host, we more often want to write our own client-server pairs that will perform specific, directed tasks.

9.4 TRANSFORMING A LOCAL FUNCTION CALL INTO A REMOTE PROCEDURE

We begin our exploration of RPC programming by converting a simple C program with a single local function call into a client-server configuration with a single remote procedure call. Once generated, this RPC-based program can be run in a distributed setting, whereby the server process, which will contain the function to be executed, can reside on a workstation different from the client process. The program that we will convert (Program 9.2) is a C program that invokes a single local function, **print_hello**, which generates the message Hello, world. As written, the **print_hello** function will display its message and return to the function **main** the value returned from **printf**. This value indicates whether or not **printf** was successful in carrying out its action[2].

---

2. Many programmers are not aware that **printf** returns a value. However, a pass of any C program with a **printf** function through the **lint** utility will normally return a message indicating that the value returned by **printf** is not being used.

Program 9.2 A simple C program to display a message.

```
/*
 *   A C program with a local function
 */
#include <stdio.h>
#include <stdlib.h>
void
main(void){
  int             print_hello(void);
  if (print_hello())
    printf("Mission accomplished\n");
  else
    printf("Unable to display message");
  exit( 0 );
}
int
print_hello(void) {
  return printf("Hello, world.\n");
}
```

In its current configuration, the **print_hello** function and its invocation reside in a single source file. When compiled and run, the output of Program 9.2 is shown in Figure 9.5.

Fig. 9.5 Output of Program 9.2.

```
% p92
Hello, world.
Mission accomplished
```

The first step in converting a program with a local function call to a remote procedure call is to create a protocol definition file. This file will help the system keep track of what procedures are to be associated with the server program. The definition file will define the data type returned by the remote procedure and the data types of its arguments. When using RPC, the remote procedure is part of a remote program that runs as the server process. The RPC language is used to define the remote program and its component procedures. The RPC language is actually XDR with two extensions—the **program** and **version** types. **Appendix C** addresses the syntax of the RPC language. The 3N manual pages on **xdr_simple** and **xdr_complex** provide an additional overview of XDR data type definitions and syntax.

Figure 9.6 contains the protocol definition file for the **print_hello** function. The RPC language is a mix of C and Pascal syntax. By custom, the extension for protocol definition files is **.x**.

Fig. 9.6 Protocol definition file hello.x.

```
/*
 * This is the protocol definition file written in RPC language that
 * will be passed to protocol generator rpcgen.  Every remote procedure
 * is part of a remote program.  Each procedure has a name and number.
```

```
 * A version number is also supplied so different versions of
 * the same procedure may be generated.
 */
/* 1 */ program DISPLAY_PRG {
/* 2 */  version DISPLAY_VER {
/* 3 */    int print_hello( void ) = 1;
/* 4 */  } = 1;
/* 5 */ } = 0x20000001;
```

The keyword **program** marks the following user-defined identifier, DISPLAY_PRG, as the name of the remote procedure program[3]. The program name, like the program name in a Pascal program, does not need to be the same as the name of the executable file. The program block encloses a group of related remote procedures. Nested within the program definition block is the keyword **version** followed by a second user-generated identifier, DISPLAY_VER, which is used to identify the version of the remote procedure. It is permissible to have several versions of the same procedure, each indicated by a different integer value. The ability to have different versions of the same procedure eases the upgrade process when updating software by facilitating backward compatibility. If the number of arguments changes, the data type of an argument changes, or the data type returned by the function changes, the version number should be changed. As this is our first pass at generating a remote procedure, the version number is set to one after the closing brace for the version block. Inside the version block is the declaration for the remote procedure (line 3)[4]. The remote procedure declaration is followed by a procedure number. As there is only one procedure defined, the value is set to one. The closing brace for the program block is followed by an eight-digit hexadecimal program number. The program, version and procedure numbers form a triplet that uniquely identifies a specific remote procedure. To prevent conflicts, the numbering scheme shown in Table 9.2 should be used in assigning version numbers.

Protocol specifications can be registered with Sun by sending a request (including the protocol definition file) to rpc@sun.com. Accepted specifications will receive a unique program number from Sun (in the range 00000000-1FFFFFFF).

Table 9.2 RPC program numbers.

Numbers	Description
00000000 -1FFFFFFF	Defined by Sun
20000000 -3FFFFFFF	User defined
40000000 -5FFFFFFF	User defined for programs that dynamically allocate #'s
60000000 -FFFFFFFF	Reserved for future use

3. Most often, the identifiers placed in the protocol definition file are in capitals. Note that this is a convention, not a requirement.

4. If the procedure name is placed in capitals, the RPC compiler, **rpcgen**, will automatically convert it to lowercase during compilation.

As shown below, the name of the protocol definition file is passed to the RPC protocol compiler, **rpcgen**, on the command line:

```
% rpcgen -C hello.x
```

The **rpcgen** compiler will produce the requisite C code to implement the defined remote procedure calls. There are a number of command line options for **rpcgen**, of which we will only explore a limited subset. A summary of the command line options and syntax for **rpcgen** is given in Figure 9.7.

Fig. 9.7 Command line options for **rpcgen**.

```
usage:   rpcgen infile

rpcgen [-abCLNTM] [-Dname[=value]] [-i size] [-I [-K seconds]]
       [-Y path]  infile

rpcgen [-c | -h | -l | -m | -t | -Sc | -Ss | -Sm][-o outfile] [infile]
rpcgen [-s nettype]* [-o outfile] [infile]
rpcgen [-n netid]* [-o outfile] [infile]

options:
-a                generate all files, including samples
-b                backward compatibility mode (generates code for
                  SunOS 4.X)
-c                generate XDR routines
-C                ANSI C mode
-Dname[=value]    define a symbol (same as #define)
-h                generate header file
-i size           size at which to start generating inline code
-I                generate code for inetd support in server(for SunOS 4.X)
-K seconds        server exits after K seconds of inactivity
-l                generate client side stubs
-L                server errors will be printed to syslog
-m                generate server side stubs
-M                generate MT-safe code
-n netid          generate server code that supports named netid
-N                supports multiple arguments and call-by-value
-o outfile        name of the output file
-s nettype        generate server code that supports named nettype
-Sc               generate sample client code that uses remote
                  procedures
-Ss               generate sample server code that defines
                  remote procedures
-Sm               generate makefile template
-t                generate RPC dispatch table
-T                generate code to support RPC dispatch tables
-Y path           path where cpp is found
```

E X E R C I S E   9 – 1

Other than standard C comments, **rpcgen** will attempt to interpret all of the lines in the protocol definition file. How do you notify **rpcgen** that you would like to have a statement passed on without having it interpreted?

In our invocation, we have specified the **-c** option requesting **rpcgen** output conform to the standards for ANSI C. When processing the hello.x file, **rpcgen** will create three output files—a header file, a client stub and a server stub file. Again, by default[5] **rpcgen** will give the same name to the header file as the protocol definition file, replacing the .x extension with .h. In addition, the client stub file will be named hello_clnt.c (the **rpcgen** source file name with _clnt.c appended) and the server stub file will be named hello_svc.c. Should the default naming convention be too restrictive, the header file as well as the client and server stub files can be generated independently and their name uniquely specified. For example, to generate the header file with a uniquely specified name, **rpcgen** would be passed the following options and file names:

```
% rpcgen -h -o unique_file_name  hello.x
```

With this invocation, **rpcgen** will generate a header file called unique_file_name.h. Using a similar technique, unique names for the client and server stub files can be specified with the **-sc** and **-ss** options (see Figure 9.7 for syntax details).

The contents of the header file, hello.h, generated by **rpcgen** is shown in Figure 9.8.

Fig. 9.8 File hello.h generated by **rpcgen** from the protocol definition file hello.x.

```
/* Please do not edit this file.
 * It was generated using rpcgen.
 */

#ifndef _HELLO_H_RPCGEN
#define _HELLO_H_RPCGEN

#include <rpc/rpc.h>

#ifdef __cplusplus
extern "C" {
#endif
#define DISPLAY_PRG ((unsigned long)(0x20000001))
#define DISPLAY_VER ((unsigned long)(1))
#if defined(__STDC__) || defined(__cplusplus)
#define print_hello ((unsigned long)(1))
extern  int * print_hello_1(void *, CLIENT *);
extern  int * print_hello_1_svc(void *, struct svc_req *);
extern int display_prg_1_freeresult(SVCXPRT *, xdrproc_t, caddr_t);

#else /* K&R C */
#define print_hello ((unsigned long)(1))
extern  int * print_hello_1();
extern  int * print_hello_1_svc();
extern int display_prg_1_freeresult();
#endif /* K&R C */
```

---

5. This can be a troublesome default if, per chance, you have also generated your own local header file with the same name and extension.

```
#ifdef __cplusplus
}
#endif
#endif /* !_HELLO_H_RPCGEN */
```

The `hello.h` file created by **rpcgen** will be referenced as an include file in both the client and server stub files. The `#ifndef _HELLO_H_RPCGEN`, `#define _HELLO_H_RPCGEN` and `#endif` preprocessor directives will prevent the `hello.h` file from being included multiple times. Within the file `hello.h`, the inclusion of the file `<rpc/rpc.h>` will, as noted in the internal comments of `rpc.h`, "... *Just include[s] the billions of rpc header files necessary to do remote procedure calling...*"[6] The variable `__cplusplus` is used to determine if a C++ environment is present. In a C++ environment, the compiler will internally add a series of suffixes to a function name that encodes the data types of its parameters. These new *mangled* function names allow C++ to check functions to ensure parameters match correctly when the function is invoked. The C compiler does not provide the mangled function names that the C++ compiler needs. The C++ compiler has to be warned that standard C linking conventions and non-mangled function names are to be used. This is accomplished by the lines following the `#ifdef __cplusplus` compiler directive.

The **program** and **version** identifiers specified in the protocol definition file are found in the `hello.h` file as defined constants of the type unsigned long integer. These constants are assigned the value specified in the protocol definition file. Since we indicated, the **-c** option to **rpcgen** (standard ANSI C), the **if** branch of preprocessor directive (i.e., `#if defined (__STDC__)`) contains the statements we are interested in. If the remote procedure name in the protocol definition file was specified in uppercase, it is mapped to lowercase in the header file. The procedure name is defined as an unsigned long integer and assigned the value previously given as its procedure number. We will find this defined constant used again in a **switch** statement in the server stub to select the code to be executed when calling the remote procedure. Following this define are two **print_hello** function prototypes. The first prototype, **print_hello_1**, is used by the client stub file. The second, **print_hello_1_svc**, is used by the server stub file. Here the naming convention used by **rpcgen** is to use the name of the remote procedure as the root and append underscore (_), version number (1), for the client stub, and underscore, version number, underscore, **svc** for the server. The **else** branch of the preprocessor directive contains a similar set of statements that are used in environments that do not support standard C prototyping. If the **-c** option was not used with **rpcgen**, the resulting header file would contain a single function prototype for **print_hello**, called **print_hello_1**.

Before we explore the client and server stub files created by **rpcgen**, we should examine how to split our initial program into client and server components. Once the initial program is split, and we have run **rpcgen**, we will have the six files shown in Figure 9.9 available to us.

---

6. While this comment is somewhat tongue-in-cheek, it is not all that farfetched (check it out)!

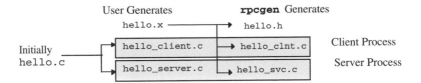

Fig. 9.9 Client-server files and relationships.

We begin with writing the client component. As in the initial program, the client will invoke the **print_hello** function. However, in our new configuration, the code for the **print_hello** function, which used to be a local function, will reside in a separate program that will be run by the server process. The code for the client component program, which has been placed in a file named hello_client.c, is shown in Program 9.3.

Program 9.3 The client program hello_client.c.

```
/*
 *    The CLIENT program:  hello_client.c
 *    This will be the client code executed by the local client process.
 */
#include <stdio.h>
#include <stdlib.h>
#include "hello.h"            /*** Generated by rpcgen from hello.x  */
void
main(int argc, char *argv[]) {
  CLIENT          *client;
  int             *return_value, filler;
  char            *server;
/*
 *  We must specify a host on which to run.  We will get the host name
 *  from the command line as argument 1.
 */
  if (argc != 2) {
    fprintf(stderr, "Usage: %s host_name\n", *argv);
    exit(1);
  }
   server = argv[1];
/*
 * Generate the client handle to call the server
 */
  if ((client = clnt_create(server, DISPLAY_PRG, DISPLAY_VER, "visible")) ==
      (CLIENT *) NULL) {
    clnt_pcreateerror(server);
    exit(2);
  }
  return_value = print_hello_1((void *) &filler, client);
  if (*return_value)
    printf("Mission accomplished\n");
  else
    printf("Unable to display message\n");
  exit( 0 );
}
```

While much of the code is similar to the original program some changes have been made to accommodate the remote procedure call. Let's examine these changes point by point. Two additional include files have been referenced. The client component will make use of the **exit** system call, thus the inclusion of the <stdlib.h> file which contains the **exit** prototype. The second include file hello.h, generated by **rpc-gen**, and whose contents were previously discussed, is also referenced. This file is assumed to reside locally.

In this example, we will be passing information from the command line to the function **main** in the client program. Therefore, the **void** parameter has been replaced with standard C syntax to reference the **argc** and **argv** parameters. In the declaration section of the client program, a pointer to the data type CLIENT is allocated. A description of the CLIENT data type is shown in Figure 9.10.

Fig. 9.10 The CLIENT data structure.

```
/* Client rpc handle.
 * Created by individual implementations.
 * Client is responsible for initializing
 */
typedef struct {
    AUTH                *cl_auth;        /* authenticator */
    struct clnt_ops {
        enum clnt_stat  (*cl_call)();    /* call remote procedure */
        void            (*cl_abort)();   /* abort a call */
        void            (*cl_geterr)();  /* get specific error code */
        bool_t          (*cl_freeres)(); /* frees results */
        void            (*cl_destroy)(); /* destroy this structure */
        bool_t          (*cl_control)(); /* the ioctl() of rpc */
    } *cl_ops;
    caddr_t             cl_private;      /* private stuff */
    char                *cl_netid;       /* network identifier */
    char                *cl_tp;          /* device name */
} CLIENT;
```

The CLIENT **typedef** is found in the include file <rpc/clnt.h>. The pointer to the CLIENT data structure will be used when the client handle is generated. Following the declarations in Program 9.3 is a section of code to obtain the host name on which the server process will be running. In the previous invocation, this was not a concern, as all code was executed locally. However, in this new configuration, the client process must know the name of the host where the server process is located. The name of the host is passed via the command line as the first argument to the **hello_client** process. As written, there is no checking to determine if a valid, reachable host name has been passed. The client handle is created next. This is done with the **clnt_create** library function. The **clnt_create** library function, which is part of a suite of remote procedure functions, is summarized in Table 9.3.

The **clnt_create** library call requires four arguments. The first, host, a character string reference, is the name of the remote host where the server process is located. The next two arguments, prognum and versnum, are, respectively, the program and version number. The nettype argument is used to specify the class of transport protocol. This argument may be set to any one of the strings shown in Table 9.4.

Table 9.3 Summary of the `clnt_create` library call.

Include File(s)	`<rpc/rpc.h>`	Manual Section	**3N**

Summary	`CLIENT *clnt_create( const char *host,`
	`                    const u_long prognum,`
	`                    const u_long versnum,`
	`                    const char *nettype );`		

Return	Success	Failure	Sets errno
	A valid client handle	NULL	Yes

Table 9.4 `nettype` specifiers.

String	Description—Action Taken
`netpath` or `NULL`	Examine the NETPATH environment variable which contains a list of network identifiers separated by colons (:). The transports (see Table 9.5) specified will be tried, one at a time from left to right, until a successful one has been found. If the NETPATH variable has not been set, or is set to NULL, the default `nettype` will be visible.
`visible`	Sequentially search the `/etc/netconfig` file choosing transports with the "v" (`visible`) flag set. Stop when a successful transport has been found.
`circuit_v`	Similar to `visible` but choose only *connection oriented* transports (`tpi_cots` or `tpi_cots_ord`).
`datagram_v`	Similar to `visible` but choose only *connectionless* transports (`tpi_clts`).
`circuit_n`	Similar to `netpath` but choose only *connection oriented datagram* transports (`tpi_cots` or `tpi_cots_ord`).
`datagram_n`	Similar to `netpath` but choose only *connectionless datagram* transports (`tpi_clts`).
`udp`	Internet UDP protocol.
`tcp`	Internet TCP protocol.

A sample `/etc/netconfig` file from a local host is shown in Table 9.5.

The overall semantics and use of the **netconfig** file are beyond the scope of this text[7]. It is sufficient to note, at this point, that the protocol family entries flagged as "v" (visible) are available. Since the file is scanned sequentially, on this host `udp` will be the protocol of *choice* if the string `visible` is passed to **clnt_create**. If a reliable protocol is desired, the string `visible` should be replaced with `tcp`.

---

7. The pages on **netconfig** in section 4 of the manual present the details of the **netconfig** file.

Table 9.5 A typical **netconfig** file.

```
#
# The "Network Configuration" File.
#
# Each entry is of the form:
#
# <network_id> <semantics> <flags> <protofamily> <protoname> <device> \
#                <nametoaddr_libs>
#
udp        tpi_clts       v    inet      udp   /dev/udp        switch.so,tcpip.so
tcp        tpi_cots_ord   v    inet      tcp   /dev/tcp        switch.so,tcpip.so
rawip      tpi_raw        -    inet      -     /dev/rawip      switch.so,tcpip.so
ticlts     tpi_clts       v    loopback  -     /dev/ticlts     straddr.so
ticotsord  tpi_cots_ord   v    loopback  -     /dev/ticotsord  straddr.so
nsp        tpi_cots_ord   -    decnet    nsp   /dev/nsp        straddr.so
ticots     tpi_cots       v    loopback  -     /dev/ticots     straddr.so
```

If the **clnt_create** library call fails, it will return a NULL value. If this occurs, as noted, the library routine **clnt_pcreateerror** can be invoked to display a message that indicates the reason for failure. See Table 9.6.

Table 9.6 Summary of the **clnt_pcreateerror** library call.

Include File(s)	`<rpc/rpc.h>`		Manual Section	**3N**
Summary	`void clnt_pcreateerror(const char *s);`			
Return	Success	Failure	Sets errno	
	Print RPC create error message to standard error			

The error message generated by **clnt_pcreateerror**, which indicates why the creation of the client handle failed, will be appended to the string passed as **clnt_pcreateerror**'s single argument (Table 9.7). The argument string and the error message will be separated with a colon and the entire message will be followed by a newline. If you want more control over the error messaging process, there is another library call, **clnt_spcreateerror**(const char *s), that will return an error message string that can be incorporated in a personalized error message. In addition, the cf_stat member of the external structure rpc_createerr may be examined directly to determine the source of the error.

In the client program, the prototype for the **print_hello** function has been eliminated. The function prototype is now in the hello.h header file. The invocation of the **print_hello** function uses its *new* name, **print_hello_1**. The function now returns a pointer to an integer (versus an integer), and has two arguments (versus none). By design, all RPCs return a pointer reference. In general, all arguments passed to the

Table 9.7 `clnt_creat` error messages.

#	Constant	clnt_pcreate error **Message**	**Explanation**
13	RPC_UNKNOWNHOST	Unknown host	Unable to find the referenced host system.
17	RPC_UNKNOWNPROTO	Unknown protocol	The protocol indicated by the `nettype` argument is not found, or is invalid.
19	RPC_UNKNOWNADDR	Remote server address unknown	Unable to resolve address of remote server.
21	RPC_NOBROADCAST	Broadcast not supported	System does not allow broadcasting of (message sending to all **rpcbind** daemons on a network).

RPC are passed by reference, not by value. As this function originally did not have any parameters, the identifier `filler` is used as a place holder. The second argument to **print_hello_1**, `client`, is the reference to the client structure returned by the **clnt_create** call.

The server component, which now resides in the file `hello_server.c`, is shown in Program 9.4.

Program 9.4 The `hello_server.c` component.

```
/*
 * The SERVER program: hello_server.c
 * This will be the server code executed by the "remote" process
 */

#include <stdio.h>
#include "hello.h"          /*** is generated by rpcgen from hello.x   */

int            *
print_hello_1_svc(void * filler, struct svc_req * req)
{
  static int      ok;
  ok = printf("Hello, world.\n");
  return (&ok);
}
```

The server component contains the **print_hello** function. Notice that to accommodate the remote procedure call, several things have been added and/or modified. First, as noted in the discussion of the client program, the **print_hello** function now returns an integer pointer, not an integer value. In this example, the address that is to be returned is associated with the identifier `ok`. This identifier is declared to be of storage class **static**. It is *imperative* that the return identifier referenced be of type **static**, as opposed to local. Local identifiers are allocated on the stack and a reference to their contents would be invalid once the function returns. The name of the function has had an additional **_1** added to it (the version number). As the **-c** option was used with **rpcgen**, the auxiliary suffix **_svc** has also been added to the function name. Do not be concerned by the apparent mismatch of function names. The mapping of the function invocation as **print_hello_1** in the client program to **print_hello_1_svc** in the server program is done by the code found in the stub file hello_svc.c produced by **rpcgen**. The argument passed to the **print_hello** function is a pointer reference. If needed, multiple items (representing multiple parameters) can be placed in a structure and the reference to the structure passed. In newer versions of **rpcgen**, the **-N** flag can be used to write multiple argument RPCs, when a parameter is to be passed by value not reference, or when a value, not a pointer reference, is to be returned by the RPC. A second argument, struct svc_req *req, is added which will contain invocation information.

The client component is compiled first. When only a few files are involved a straight command line compilation sequence is adequate. Later we will discuss how to generate a make file to automate the compilation process. The compiler is passed the names of the two client files, hello_client.c (which we wrote) and hello_clnt.c (which was generated by **rpcgen**). We specify the executable be placed in the file client. As the client source files reference functions found in the networking library, libnsl must be passed to the linker using the -lnsl option. Figure 9.11 shows details of the compilation command.

Fig. 9.11 Compiling the client component.

```
% CC hello_client.c hello_clnt.c -o client  -lnsl
hello_client.c:
hello_clnt.c:
```

When we compile the server component, we find the compiler generates a number of warning messages (see Figure 9.12). The warnings are informational (identifiers declared and not used, etc.) and do not prevent the compiler from generating the executable file. If compiled using **gcc**, which is sometimes less stringent, no warning messages will be generated.

Fig. 9.12 Compiling the server component.

```
% CC hello_server.c hello_svc.c -o server -lnsl
hello_server.c:
"hello_server.c", line 10: warning:  filler not used
"hello_server.c", line 10: warning:  req not used
hello_svc.c:
"hello_svc.c", line 70: warning:  rlim_t assigned to  int
"hello_svc.c", line 55: warning:  sig not used
"hello_svc.c", line 195: warning:  rlim_t assigned to  int
"hello_svc.c", line 32: warning:  ::_rpcpmstart defined but not used
```

EXERCISE   9 – 2

Is the `filler` variable really needed? Try commenting out the references to `filler` in the `hello_client.c` and `hello_server.c` files. Adjust the `hello.x` protocol definition file as well. Run **rpcgen** and recompile the modified components. What happens? Why?

EXERCISE   9 – 3

Modify the server component of the `hello` application so that the server will remove itself if it has not been referenced over a specified period of time (say, five minutes). Use the **signal** system call to associate the receipt of an **alarm** with a terminating function. You will need to place code in both the `hello_server.c` and `hello_svc.c` files to accomplish this task.

Initially, we will test the program by running both the client and server on the same workstation. We begin by invoking the server by typing its name on the command line. The server process is *automatically* placed in the background and no trailing "&" is needed. A check of the **ps** command will verify the server process is running (see Figure 9.13).

Fig. 9.13 Running the server program and checking for its presence with **ps**.

```
% server
% ps -ef | grep server
  ...
gray  9274 8022  5  08:40:54 term/2      0:00 grep server
gray  9267    1  26 08:40:44 ?           0:00 server
```

The **ps** command reports that the server process, in this case process ID 9267, is in memory. Its parent process ID is 1 (**init**) and its associated controlling terminal device is listed as "?", which indicates no controlling terminal device. The server process will remain in memory even after the user who initiated it has logged out. When generating and testing RPC programs, it is important the user remember to remove extraneous RPC-based server type processes before they log out.

When running the process locally the client program is invoked by name and passed the name of the current workstation. When this is done the output will be as shown in Figure 9.14.

Fig. 9.14 Running the client program.

```
morpheus % client morpheus
Mission accomplished
```

Interestingly, the client program displayed the message `Mission accomplished` but did *not* display the message `Hello, world`. The answer to this puzzle lies with the controlling terminal device associated with standard output for the server process. As we saw in Figure 9.13, the output device for the server process is listed as none, thus the output from the server is discarded (into the bit bucket it goes!). There are several ways of correcting this problem. The output from the server could be hard coded to be displayed on the console. In this scenario, the server would, upon invocation, execute an **fopen** on the /dev/console device. The FILE pointer returned by the **fopen** call could then be used with the **fprintf** function to display the output on the console. Unfortunately, there is a potential problem with this solution: the user may not have access to the console device. If this is so, the **fopen** will fail. A second approach would be to pass the console device of the client process to the server as the first parameter of the remote procedure call. This is a somewhat better solution, but will still fail when the client and server processes are on different workstations with different output devices. A third approach would be to have the server process return its message to the client and have the client display it locally.

While our client-server application still needs some polishing we can test it in a setting whereby the server runs on one workstation and the client on another. If the two workstations are homogeneous (running the same version of OS), we can accomplish our task by issuing a command sequence similar to that shown in Figure 9.15.

Fig. 9.15 Running the client-server application in a distributed setting.

```
morpheus % server
morpheus % rsh obiwan $cwd/client morpheus
Mission accomplished
```

In this example, when on the workstation morpheus, we invoke the server program. Following this, we use the **rsh** (remote shell) command to execute, on the workstation obiwan, the client program. As the current directory where the application programs reside is not part of the standard path, the current working directory (stored in the system variable **cwd**) must be passed to the remote workstation[8]. Thus, in this example, the workstation obiwan will run the client program which is passed the name of the workstation morpheus, as the host which is running the server program. As shown, the client process on obiwan successfully requests the workstation morpheus run the **print_hello** function. As in the previous example (and for the same reason), the Hello, world message is still not displayed.

We might also want to examine the two RPC stub files generated by **rpcgen**. The hello_clnt.c file is quite small (Figure 9.16). This file contains the actual call to the **print_hello_1** function.

---

8. The output of the **pwd** command could also have been used to obtain the current working directory in place of $cwd variable, i.e., "**pwd**." However, it is usually more efficient to reference variable contents than to execute commands.

The following program will use the **ttyname** library function to display the output device associated with stdout.

```
#include <stdio.h>
#include <stdlib.h>
main(void){
  char            *dev = ttyname(fileno(stdout));
  if (dev)
    printf("My standard output device is %s\n", dev);
  else
  fprintf(stderr,
          "Don't know my standard output device!\n");
}
```

Modify the client and server programs so the output device associated with stdout is determined by the client and passed to the server as the first argument to the **print_hello** function. The server will open the device for writing to display the Hello, world message. *Hint:* The output device must be stored as an array of characters by the client so that it may be passed to the server. The **void** argument in the protocol definition file must be changed to reflect the passing of the character array. However, when making this change, you cannot use the data type **char** * as it is ambiguous—it could be a reference to a single character or an array of characters. In the RPC language, the data type, **string**, is used to indicate a NULL terminated array of characters.

Fig. 9.16 The hello_clnt.c file.

```
/*
 * Please do not edit this file.
 * It was generated using rpcgen.
 */

#include <memory.h>              /* for memset */
#include "hello.h"

/* Default timeout can be changed using clnt_control() */
static struct timeval TIMEOUT = {25, 0};

int             *
print_hello_1(void *argp, CLIENT * clnt)
{
  static int      clnt_res;
  memset((char *) &clnt_res, 0, sizeof(clnt_res));
  if (clnt_call(clnt, print_hello,
                (xdrproc_t) xdr_void, (caddr_t) argp,
                (xdrproc_t) xdr_int, (caddr_t) & clnt_res,
                TIMEOUT) != RPC_SUCCESS) {
    return (NULL);
  }
  return (&clnt_res);
}
```

As we are using **rpcgen** to reduce the complexity of RPC we will not formally present the **clnt_call**. However, in passing we note that the **clnt_call** function (which actually does the remote procedure call) is passed the client handle that was generated from the previous call to **clnt_creat**. The second argument for **clnt_call** is obtained from the hello.h include file and is actually the print_hello constant therein. The third and fifth arguments are references to the XDR data encoding/decoding routines. Sandwiched between these arguments is a reference to the initial argument that will be passed to the remote procedure by the server process. The sixth argument for **clnt_creat** is a reference to the location where the return data will be stored. The seventh and final argument is the TIMEOUT value. While the cautionary comments indicate you should not edit this file, and, in general, you should not, the TIMEOUT value can be changed from the default of 25 to some other reasonable user-imposed maximum.

The code in the hello_svc.c file is much more complex and, in the interest of space, not presented here. Interested readers are encouraged to enter the protocol definition in hello.x and to generate and view the hello_svc.c file. At this juncture it is sufficient to note that the hello_svc.c file contains the code for the server process. Once invoked, the server process will remain in memory. When notified by a client process, it will execute the **print_hello_1_svc** function.

9.5 DEBUGGING RPC APPLICATIONS

Because of their distributed nature, RPC applications can be very difficult to debug. One easy way to test and debug an RPC application with, say, **dbx**, is to link the client and server programs *without* their **rpcgen** stubs. To do this, comment out the RPC reference in the client program. If the **-c** option was passed to **rpcgen**, then you must adjust the name of the function call appropriately (i.e., add the **_svc** suffix). In addition, you may need to cast the function call argument with the client reference to the correct type (i.e., svc_req *). Incorporating these changes with preprocessor directives, our hello_client.c file now would be:

Fig. 9.17 A "debug ready" version of hello_client.c.

```
#include <stdio.h>
#include <stdlib.h>
#include "hello.h"     /*** is generated by rpcgen from hello.x */
void
main(int argc, char *argv[])
{
 ...                   /* Same as before */

/*
 * Generate the client handle to call the server
 */
#ifndef DEBUG
  if ((client=clnt_create(server,DISPLAY_PRG,DISPLAY_VER,"visible")) ==
      (CLIENT *) NULL) {
```

```
      clnt_pcreateerror(server);
      exit(2);
    }
    return_value=print_hello_1( (void *) &filler, client );
#else
    return_value=print_hello_1_svc( (void *) &filler,
                                    (svc_req *) client );
#endif
    if (*return_value)
      printf("Mission accomplished\n");
    else
      printf("Unable to display message\n");
    exit( 0 );
}
```

We would compile this modified version with the command sequence shown in Figure 9.17. As none of the network libraries are referenced, the libnsl library does not need to be linked. The compiler is passed the **-g** flag (to generate the symbol table information for **dbx**) and **-DDEBUG** is specified to define the **DEBUG** constant the preprocessor will test.

Fig. 9.18 Debugging the client-server application with **dbx**.

```
% CC -DDEBUG -g hello_client.c hello_server.c ◄────────── Compile with CC. Define
hello_client.c:                                             the DEBUG constant —
"hello_client.c", line 9: warning:  client used but not set   generate symbol table
hello_server.c:                                             information
"hello_server.c", line 9: warning:  filler not used
"hello_server.c", line 9: warning:  req not used

% dbx a.out
Reading symbolic information for a.out
Reading symbolic information for rtld /usr/lib/ld.so.1
Reading symbolic information for ../../../../../../../lib/libc.so.1
Reading symbolic information for ../../../../../../../lib/libdl.so.1
(dbx) trace ◄──────────────────────────────────────────── Show each statement
(2) trace                                                   before execution.
(dbx) run morpheus
Running: a.out morpheus
entering function main
trace:     16      if (argc != 2) {
trace:     20      server = argv[1];
trace:     33      return_value = print_hello_1_svc( (void *) &filler,
                   (svc_req *) client);
entering function print_hello_1_svc ◄──────────────────── Call of the procedure that
trace:     12      ok = printf("Hello, world.\n");           will eventually be a remote
Hello, world.                                               procedure.
trace:     13      return (&ok);
trace:     14    }
leaving function print_hello_1_svc
trace:     35      if (*return_value)
trace:     36        printf("Mission accomplished\n");
Mission accomplished
trace:     39    }
leaving function main
execution completed, exit code is 2
program exited with 2
(dbx) quit
```

9.6 USING RPCGEN TO GENERATE TEMPLATES AND A MAKEFILE

The **rpcgen** command has additional functionality to assist the developer of RPC applications. If the **-a** flag (see Figure 9.7) is passed to **rpcgen,** it will generate, in addition to the client and server stub files and header file, a set of template files for the client and server and a makefile for the entire application. Unlike the **-c** flag, which will cause **rpcgen** to overwrite preexisting stub files, the **-a** flag will cause **rpcgen** to halt with a warning message if the template files (with the default names) are present in the current directory. Therefore, it is best to use the **-a** flag only when you are positive the protocol definition file is accurate; otherwise you must manually remove or rename the previously generated template files.

For example, suppose we have a program called `fact.c` (Program 9.5) that requests an integer value and returns the factorial of that value if it is within the range of values that can be stored in a long integer; otherwise, it returns a value of 0.

Program 9.5 The original factorial program, `fact.c`.

```
/*
 *   A program to calculate Factorial numbers
 */
#include <stdio.h>
void
main(void){
  long int        f_numb, calc_fact(int);
  int             number;
  printf("Factorial Calculator\n");
  printf("Enter a positive integer value ");
  scanf("%d", &number);
  if (number < 0)
    printf("Positive values only!\n");
  else if ((f_numb = calc_fact(number)) > 0)
    printf("%d! = %d\n", number, f_numb);
  else
    printf("Sorry %d! is out of my range!\n", number);
}
/*
 *   Calculate the factorial number and return the result or return 0
 *   if value is out of range.
 */
long int
calc_fact(int n){
  long int        total = 1, last = 0;
  int             idx;
  for (idx = n; idx - 1; --idx) {
    total *= idx;
    if (total <= last)    /* Have we gone out of range?  */
      return (0);
    last = total;
  }
  return (total);
}
```

We would like to turn the factorial program into a client-server application, whereby the client could make a request for a factorial value from the remote *factorial* server. To accomplish this, we begin by writing the protocol definition file shown in Figure 9.19.

Fig. 9.19 The protocol definition file for the factorial program.

```
/*
 *  The protocol definition file for the factorial program
 */

program FACTORIAL {
  version ONE {
     long int CALC_FAC( int ) = 1;
  } = 1;
} = 0x2000049;
```

We then use **rpcgen** with the **-a** and **-c** flags to generate the header file, the client and server stub files, the client and server template files, and the application makefile. The details of and output from this process are shown in Figure 9.20.

Fig. 9.20 Using **rpcgen** with the **-a** and **-c** flags.

```
% ls *fact*
fact.x

% rpcgen -a -C fact.x

% ls *fact*
fact.h          fact_client.c     fact_server.c     makefile.fact
fact.x          fact_clnt.c       fact_svc.c
```

As shown, passing **rpcgen** the protocol definition file with the **-a** and **-c** flags will generate six files. The header file, fact.h, and the RPC stub files, fact_clnt.c and fact_svc.c, are similar in content and nature to those in the previous example. The three *new* files created by **rpcgen** bear further investigation. The client template file is fact_client.c. Again, **rpcgen** has used the file name of the protocol definition file as the root for the file name and added the _client.c suffix. The contents of the fact_client.c file are shown in Figure 9.21.

Fig. 9.21 The fact_client.c template client file generated by **rpcgen**.

```
/*
 * This is sample code generated by rpcgen.
 * These are only templates and you can use them
 * as a guideline for developing your own functions.
 */
#include "fact.h"
void
factorial_1(char *host)
{
```

```
          CLIENT *clnt;
          long  *result_1;
          int   calc_fac_1_arg;
#ifndef DEBUG
          clnt = clnt_create(host, FACTORIAL, ONE, "netpath");
          if (clnt == (CLIENT *) NULL) {
                  clnt_pcreateerror(host);
                  exit(1);
          }
#endif  /* DEBUG */
          result_1 = calc_fac_1(&calc_fac_1_arg, clnt);
          if (result_1 == (long *) NULL) {
                  clnt_perror(clnt, "call failed");
          }
#ifndef DEBUG
          clnt_destroy(clnt);
#endif          /* DEBUG */
}

main(int argc, char *argv[]){
          char *host;
          if (argc < 2) {
                  printf("usage:   %s server_host\n", argv[0]);
                  exit(1);
          }
          host = argv[1];
          factorial_1(host);
}
```

In the template file **rpcgen** has created a function called **factorial_1**. The function name is derived from the program name given in the protocol definition file with a suffix of **_1** (the version number). As shown, the **factorial_1** function is passed the host name. This function is used to make the RPC **clnt_create** call and the remote **calc_fac_1** function call. Notice that variables for the correct argument type and function return type have been placed at the top of the **factorial_1** function. By default, the nettype for the **clnt_create** call is specified as netpath (versus visible which was used in the previous example). The call to the remote **cal_fac_1** function is followed by a check of its return value. If the return value is NULL, the library function **clnt_perror** (Table 9.8) is called to display an error message.

The **clnt_perror** library call is passed the client handle from the **clnt_create** call and an informational message string. The **clnt_perror** message will have the informational message prefaced with an intervening colon.

A call to the library function, **clnt_destroy**, is also generated (Table 9.9). The **clnt_destroy** function is used to return, to the system, the resources allocated by the **clnt_create** function.

As would be expected, once a client RPC handle has been destroyed, it is undefined and can no longer be referenced.

To facilitate testing, **rpcgen** has also placed a series of preprocessor directives in the template file. However, it seems to overlook the fact that the call to **clnt_perror** requires the network library and thus should also be commented out when debugging the application. As in the previous example, if the **-c** option for **rpcgen** has been specified, and a call to the remote factorial function (**calc_fac_1**) is to be made in a debug

Table 9.8 Summary of the `clnt_perror` library call.

Include File(s)	`<rpc/rpc.h>`		Manual Section	**3N**

Summary	`void`
	`clnt_perror( const CLIENT *clnt,`
	`            const char *s );`			

Return	Success	Failure	Sets errno	
	Print message to standard error indicating why the RPC call failed			

Table 9.9 Summary of the `clnt_destroy` library call.

Include File(s)	`<rpc/rpc.h>`		Manual Section	**3N**
Summary	`void clnt_destroy( CLIENT *clnt );`			
Return	Success	Failure	Sets errno	

setting, the function name should have the string, **_svc**, appended, and the `clnt` argument should be cast to the data type (svc_req *).

We can now edit the `fact_client.c` program and add the appropriate code from the function **main** in our initial `fact.c` example. The modified `fact_client.c` program is shown in Figure 9.22. Note the change in the call to the **calc_fact** function to the **factorial_1 function**.

Fig. 9.22 The `fact_client.c` template file with modifications.

```
/*
 * This is sample code generated by rpcgen.
 * These are only templates and you can use them
 * as a guideline for developing your own functions.
 */
#include "fact.h"
#include <unistd.h>          /* added because we will call exit */
long int                     /* now returns a long vs void      */
factorial_1(int calc_fac_1_arg, char *host)

/*      ... same as before  */
  return *result_1;          /* return factorial to main        */
}
main(int argc, char *argv[ ]){
  char          *host;
```

```
/*
 *        Add own declarations here
 */
long int        f_numb;
int             number;

 if (argc < 2) {
    printf("usage:  %s server_host\n", argv[0]);
    exit(1);
  }  host = argv[1];

/*
 *        This is the code from the previous main in program fact.c
 */
 printf("Factorial Calculator\n");
 printf("Enter a positive integer value ");
 scanf("%d", &number);
 if (number < 0)
   printf("Positive values only!\n");
 else if ((f_numb=factorial_1(number, host)) > 0) /* generated fnct */
   printf("%d! = %d\n", number, f_numb);
 else
   printf("Sorry %d! is out of my range!\n", number);
}
```

The server template file generated by **rpcgen** is shown in Figure 9.23.

Fig. 9.23 Server template file `fact_server.c` generated by **rpcgen**.

```
/*
 * This is sample code generated by rpcgen.
 * These are only templates and you can use them
 * as a guideline for developing your own functions.
 */

#include "fact.h"
long *
calc_fac_1_svc(int *argp, struct svc_req *rqstp)
{
        static long  result;

        /*
         * insert server code here
         */

        return (&result);
}
```

As with the client template file, we now can modify the server template to incorporate the code for the remote procedure. The modified `fact_server.c` file is shown in Figure 9.24.

Fig. 9.24 The `fact_server.c` template file with modifications.

```
/*
 * This is sample code generated by rpcgen.
 * These are only templates and you can use them
 * as a guideline for developing your own functions.
 */

#include "fact.h"

long int            *
calc_fac_1_svc(int *argp, struct svc_req * rqstp)
{
  static long int    result;
  /*
   * insert server code here
   */
  long int          total = 1, last = 0;
  int               idx;
  for (idx = *argp; idx - 1; --idx) {
    total *= idx;
    if (total <= last) {      /* Have we gone out of range?  */
      result = 0;
      return (&result);
    }
    last = total;
  }
  result = total;
  return (&result);
}
```

The makefile generated by **rpcgen** is shown in Figure 9.25.

Fig. 9.25 The makefile, `makefile.fact`, generated by **rpcgen**.

```
# This is a template makefile generated by rpcgen
# Parameters

CLIENT = fact_client
SERVER = fact_server

SOURCES_CLNT.c =
SOURCES_CLNT.h =
SOURCES_SVC.c =
SOURCES_SVC.h =
SOURCES.x = fact.x

TARGETS_SVC.c = fact_svc.c fact_server.c
TARGETS_CLNT.c = fact_clnt.c fact_client.c
TARGETS = fact.h    fact_clnt.c fact_svc.c fact_client.c fact_server.c

OBJECTS_CLNT = $(SOURCES_CLNT.c:%.c=%.o) $(TARGETS_CLNT.c:%.c=%.o)
OBJECTS_SVC = $(SOURCES_SVC.c:%.c=%.o) $(TARGETS_SVC.c:%.c=%.o)

# Compiler flags

CFLAGS += -g
LDLIBS += -lnsl
RPCGENFLAGS = -C
```

```
# Targets

all : $(CLIENT) $(SERVER)

$(TARGETS) : $(SOURCES.x)
         rpcgen $(RPCGENFLAGS) $(SOURCES.x)

$(OBJECTS_CLNT) : $(SOURCES_CLNT.c) $(SOURCES_CLNT.h) $(TARGETS_CLNT.c)

$(OBJECTS_SVC) : $(SOURCES_SVC.c) $(SOURCES_SVC.h) $(TARGETS_SVC.c)

$(CLIENT) : $(OBJECTS_CLNT)
       $(LINK.c) -o $(CLIENT) $(OBJECTS_CLNT) $(LDLIBS)

$(SERVER) : $(OBJECTS_SVC)
       $(LINK.c) -o $(SERVER) $(OBJECTS_SVC) $(LDLIBS)

 clean:
       $(RM) core $(TARGETS) $(OBJECTS_CLNT) $(OBJECTS_SVC) $(CLIENT) $(SERVER)
```

While the makefile can be used pretty much as generated, you may want to modify some of the entries in the compiler flag section. For example, you may want to add the **-c** flag to RPCGENFLAGS, or indicate the math library should be linked by adding **-lm** to LDLIBS. If a compiler other than the default compiler (**cc** on most systems) is to be used, you would add the notation in this section (e.g., CC = **gcc** for the GNU compiler or CC = **cc** for Sun's C++ compiler). The **make** utility will assume the makefile it is to process is called makefile. As **rpcgen** creates a makefile whose name is makefile with a period "." root name of the protocol definition file (**fact**) appended, the user is left with two remedies. First, rename the generated makefile to makefile by using the **mv** command, or second, use the **-f** flag for **make**. If the **-f** flag is used with **make**, then the name of the file for **make** to use should immediately follow the **-f** flag.

Figure 9.26 presents the sequence of events on a local system when the **make** utility with the **-f** flag is used to generate the factorial application.

Fig. 9.26 Using the makefile.fact file.

```
% make -f makefile.fact
cc -g    -c fact_clnt.c -o fact_clnt.o
cc -g    -c fact_client.c -o fact_client.o
cc -g    -o fact_client  fact_clnt.o fact_client.o  -lnsl
cc -g    -c fact_svc.c -o fact_svc.o
"fact_svc.c", line 70: warning:  rlim_t assigned to  int
"fact_svc.c", line 55: warning:  sig not used
"fact_svc.c", line 195: warning:  rlim_t assigned to  int
"fact_svc.c", line 32: warning:  ::_rpcpmstart defined but not used
cc -g    -c fact_server.c -o fact_server.o
"fact_server.c", line 10: warning:  rqstp not used
cc -g    -o fact_server  fact_svc.o fact_server.o  -lnsl
```

Figure 9.27 shows a sequence for running the factorial client-server application.

Fig. 9.27 Running the factorial client-server application.

```
morpheus % fact_server
morpheus % ps -ef | grep gray
    gray   283    273 56 03:11:07 term/2      0:02 -csh
    gray  2685    283 37 11:02:33 term/2      0:00 ps -ef
    gray  2686    283  5 11:02:33 term/2      0:00 grep gray
    gray  2680      1 31 11:00:30 ?           0:00 fact_server
morpheus % fact_client morpheus
Factorial Calculator
Enter a positive integer value 11
11! = 39916800
morpheus % fact_client morpheus
Factorial Calculator
Enter a positive integer value 15
Sorry 15! is out of my range!

morpheus % rlogin obiwan

obiwan % cd BOOK/rpc/ex1
obiwan % ps -ef | grep gray
    gray 22135 22082 26 11:02:20 pts/0        0:00 ps -ef
    gray 22136 22082  7 11:02:20 pts/0        0:00 grep gray
    gray 22082 22080 80 11:01:22 pts/0        0:03 -csh

obiwan % fact_client morpheus
Factorial Calculator
Enter a positive integer value 9
9! = 362880

obiwan % fact_client morpheus
Factorial Calculator
Enter a positive integer value 98
Sorry 98! is out of my range!
obiwan % logout
```

In the previous example, the factorial server program is invoked on the workstation called morpheus. The **ps** command verifies the presence of the **fact_server** process. The factorial client program is invoked and passed the name of the host that is running the factorial server process. The client process requests the user to input an integer value. The user enters the value 11. The client process makes a remote call to the server process, passing it the value 11. The server process responds by calculating the factorial value and returning it to the client. The client process displays the returned result. The client process is invoked a second time and passed a value of 15. The value 15! is beyond the storage range for an integer on the server. Thus, the server returns the value 0, indicating it was unable to complete the calculation. The client displays the corresponding error message. Next, the user logs onto another workstation on the same network (obiwan) and changes to the directory where the executables for the factorial application reside. The **ps** command is used to check if the factorial server process is present on this workstation—it is not. The factorial client is invoked again and passed the name of the workstation running the server process (morpheus). The client program requests an integer value (entered as 9). This value is passed, via the remote procedure call, to the server process on the workstation morpheus. The factorial value is calculated by the server process on morpheus and returned to the client process which displays the results to the screen.

E X E R C I S E   9 – 5

Write an RPC-based client-server application that evaluates, in a single pass, in left to right order (ignoring operator precedence) a simple expression that consists of a series of single digit operands and the binary operators: +, -, / (integer division) and *. The client should process the expression and call the server application to perform the needed arithmetic operations. The server should have a *separate* procedure for each of the four operations. Try your application with the following input sequences (be sure to check for division by 0):

2 * 3 / 2 + 5 - 8

6 + 8 - 4 / 3

7 - 9 / 0

Hint: To pass multiple parameters, you should either make use of the **-N** option for **rpc-gen**, or place the parameters to be passed in a structure and then pass the reference to the structure.

9.7 ENCODING AND DECODING ARBITRARY DATA TYPES

For RPCs to pass data between systems with differing architectures, data is first converted to a standard XDR format. The conversion from a native representation to XDR format is called *serialization*. When the data is received in XDR format it is converted back to the native representation for the recipient process. The conversion from XDR format to native format is called *deserialization*. To be transparent the conversion process must take into account such things as native byte order[9], integer size, representation of floating-point values and the representation of character strings. Some of these differences may be hardware dependent, while others may be programming language dependent. Once the data is converted, it is assumed that individual bytes of data (each consisting of eight bits) are in themselves portable from one platform to another. Data conversion for standard simple data types (such as integers, floats, characters, etc.) are implemented via a series of predefined XDR primitive type library routines[10] which are sometimes called **filters**. These filters return a boolean value of TRUE (of type **bool_t**) if they successfully convert the data, other-

---

9. For example, with a 4-byte (32-bit) number the most significant byte (MSB) is always left-most and the least significant byte (LSB) right-most. If the sequence of bytes composing the number is ordered from left to right, as in the SPARC, the order is called big-endian. If the byte sequence is numbered from right to left, as in the 80x86 processor line, the order is called little-endian.

10. For more details, see the manual pages for **xdr_simple** in section 3N of the manual.

wise they return a value of FALSE. Each primitive routine takes a pointer to the result and a pointer to the XDR handle. The primitive routines are incorporated into more complex routines for complex data types,[11] such as arrays. The specifics of how the data conversion is actually done, while interesting, is beyond the scope of a one-chapter overview of RPC. However, it is important to keep in mind that such routines are necessary and that when passing data with RPCs, the proper conversion routines must be selected. Fortunately when using **rpcgen**, the references for the appropriate XDR conversion routines are automatically generated and placed in another C source file the application can reference. This file, containing the conversion routines for both the client and server, will have the suffix _xdr.c appended to the protocol definition file name.

To illustrate how data conversion is done, we will create an application that performs a remote directory tree listing. When the server for this application is passed a valid directory name, it will traverse the indicated directory and produce an indented listing of all of the directory's underlying subdirectories. For example, say we have the directory structure shown in Figure 9.28.

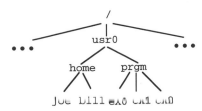

Fig. 9.28 A hypothetical directory structure.

If we request the application to produce a directory tree of the directory /usr0, the output returned from the directory tree application would be similar to that shown in Figure 9.29.

Fig. 9.29 The directory tree listing of /usr0.

```
/usr0:
    home
        joe
        bill
    prgm
        ex0
        ex1
        ex2
```

The directory traversed is listed with a trailing colon. Following this, each subdirectory displayed is indented to indicate its relationship to its parent directory and

---

11. See **xdr_complex** in manual section 3N for additional details.

sibling subdirectories. The subdirectories `home` and `prgm` are at the same level and thus are indented the same number of spaces. The subdirectories `joe` and `bill` which are beneath the `home` directory are indented to the same level as are the subdirectories `ex0`, `ex1` and `ex2` which are beneath the `prgm` directory.

   As written, the application will pass from the client to the server the name of the directory to be traversed on the server. The server will allocate an array of a fixed size[12] to store the tree directory listing and will return the contents of the array if it is successful. If the server fails, it will return a NULL value. The array is filled with the directory tree information by the server using the following high level algorithm. The passed directory reference is opened. While the directory reference is not NULL, each entry is checked to determine if it is accessible. Note that, if the server process does not have root privileges, this may cause some entries to be skipped. If the entry is accessible, and is a directory reference (versus a file reference) but not a dot entry (we are looking to skip the "." and ".." entries for obvious reasons), the entry is stored with the proper amount of indenting in the allocated array. For display purposes, each stored entry has an appended newline (\n) to separate it from the following entry. Since directory structures are recursive in nature, after processing an accessible directory entry, the **tree** display routine will call itself again passing the name of the *new* directory entry. Once the entire contents of a directory have been processed, the directory is closed. When all directories and subdirectories have been processed, the array, with the contents of the directory tree, is returned to the client process which will display its contents. The partial contents of the returned array for the previous example is shown in Figure 9.30.

Fig. 9.30 A partial listing of the directory tree array for `/usr0`.

The protocol definition file `tree.x` for the tree program is shown in Figure 9.31.

Fig. 9.31 The protocol definition file, `tree.x`.

```
/*
        Tree protocol definition file
*/
const   MAX   = 4096;   /* Upper limit on packet size is 8K.       */
const   DELIM = "\n";   /* To separate each directory entry.       */
const   INDENT= 5;      /* # of spaces to indent for one level.    */
const   DIR_1 = 128;    /* Maximum length of any one dir entry.    */

typedef char line[MAX]; /* A storage location for all the entries. */
```

---

12. I know, I know, this is *not* the *best* way to do this—a dynamic allocation would be more appropriate here as we do not know in advance how much storage room we will actually need. What is presented is a pedagogical example. The modification of the text example to use dynamic memory allocation is addressed in the exercise section.

```
typedef line *line_ptr; /* A reference to the storage location.    */
                        /* If no errors return reference else return
                           void                                    */
union dir_result
  switch( int errno ) {
  case 0:
      line *line_ptr;
  default:
      void;
};
/*
 * The do_dir procedure will take a reference to a directory and return
 * a reference to an array containing the directory tree.
 */
program TREE {
  version one{
     dir_result do_dir( string ) = 1;
  } = 1;
} = 0x2000001;
```

In the protocol definition file there is a series of constants. These constants will be mapped into #define statements by the **rpcgen** compiler. Following the constant section are two type declarations. The first, typedef char line[MAX], declares a *new* type called line that is an array of MAX number of characters. To translate this type, **rpcgen** creates a routine named **xdr_line** which it places in the tree_xdr.c file. The contents of this routine are shown in Figure 9.32.

Fig. 9.32 The **xdr_line** XDR conversion routine created by **rpcgen**.

```
bool_t
xdr_line(register XDR *xdrs, line objp){
register long *buf;
if (!xdr_vector( xdrs,
                 (char *)objp,
                  MAX,
                  sizeof (char),
                  (xdrproc_t) xdr_char))
        return (FALSE);
return (TRUE);
}
```

The generated **xdr_line** routine calls the predefined **xdr_vector** routine, which in turn invokes the **xdr_char** primitive. It is the **xdr_char** primitive that is found in both the client and server stub files that does the actual translation. A similar set of code is generated, as well, for the line pointer (**line_ptr**) declaration and the discriminated union that declares the type to be returned by the user defined remote **do_dir** procedure. If we examine the tree.h file produced by **rpcgen** from the tree.x file, we find the discriminated union is mapped to a structure that contains a union (as shown in Figure 9.33). The single argument for the **do_dir** procedure is a string (a special XDR data type) which is mapped to a pointer to a pointer to a character. The argument to **do_dir** will be the directory to *examine*.

Fig. 9.33 The structure generated by **rpcgen** from the discriminated union in tree.x.

```
struct dir_result {
        int errno;
        union {
                line *line_ptr;
        } dir_result_u;
};
typedef struct dir_result dir_result;
```

The code for the client portion (tree_client.c) of the tree program is shown in Program 9.6 and the server portion (tree_server.c) is shown in Program 9.7.

Program 9.6 The directory tree client program tree_client.c.

```
/*
#####  #####  ######  ######  ####   #       #   ######  #    #   #####
  #    #    # #    #  #      #    #  #       #   #       ##   #  #
  #    #    # #       #####  #       #       #   #####   # #  #  #
  #    #####  #       #      #       #       #   #       #  # #  #
  #    #   #  #    #  #      #    #  #       #   #       #   ##  #
  #    #    # ######  ######  ####   ######  #   ######  #    #   #
*/
#include "local.h"
#include "tree.h"
void
tree_1(char *host, char *the_dir ) {
  CLIENT        *client;
  dir_result    *result;

#ifndef DEBUG
  client = clnt_create(host, TREE, one, "tcp");
  if (client == (CLIENT *) NULL) {
    clnt_pcreateerror(host);
    exit(2);
  }
  result = do_dir_1(&the_dir, client);
#else
  result = do_dir_1_svc(&the_dir, (svc_req *) client);
#endif                              /* DEBUG */
  if (result == (dir_result *) NULL) {
#ifndef DEBUG
    clnt_perror(client, "call failed");
#else
    perror("Call failed");
#endif                                /* DEBUG */
    exit(3);
  } else                              /* display the whole array   */
    printf("%s:\n\n%s\n",the_dir,result->dir_result_u.line_ptr);
#ifndef DEBUG
  clnt_destroy(client);
#endif                                /* DEBUG */
}
main(int argc, char *argv[]) {
  char          *host;
  static char   directory[DIR_1];  /* Name of the directory   */
```

```
    if (argc < 2) {
      fprintf(stderr, "Usage %s server [directory]\n", argv[0]);
      exit(1);
    }
    host = argv[1];                          /* Assign the server      */
    if (argc > 2)
      strcpy(directory, argv[2]);
    else
      strcpy(directory , ".");
    tree_1(host, directory);                 /* Give it a shot!        */
}
```

The bulk of the `tree_client.c` program contains code that is either similar in nature to previous RPC examples or is self-documenting. The one statement that may bear further explanation is the **printf** statement that displays the directory tree information to the screen. Remember, the remote procedure returns a pointer to a *string*. This string is already in display format in that each directory entry is separate from the next with a newline. The reference to the string is written as `result->dir_result_u.line_ptr`. The proper syntax for this reference is obtained by examining the `tree.h` file produced by **rpcgen**:

Program 9.7 The directory tree client program `tree_server.c`.

```
/*
#####  #####  ######  ######  ####  ######  #####  #   #  ######  #####
  #      #    #    #  #    #  #   #    #    #    #  #   #  #       #   #
  #      #    #    #  #####   #####   ####  #####   # # #  #       #####
  #      #    #    #  #       #   #     #   #        #####  #       #   #
  #      #    #    #  #       # # #   # #   #       #   #  #        #####
  #      #    #    #  #       #   #  #   #  #       #   #  #        #   #
  #      #    ######  ######  ####  ######  #       #   #  #        #   #
*/
#include "local.h"
#include "tree.h"

static int cur = 0,                    /* Index into output array   */
       been_allocated = 0,             /* Has array been allocated? */
       depth = 0;                      /* Indenting level           */

dir_result       *
do_dir_1_svc( char **f, struct svc_req * rqstp) {
  static dir_result result;             /* Either array or void      */
  struct stat       statbuff;           /* For status check of entry */
  DIR               *dp;                /* Directory entry           */
  struct dirent     *dentry;            /* Pointer to current entry  */
  char              *current;           /* Position in output array  */
  int               length;             /* Length of current entry   */
  static char       buffer[DIR_1];      /* Temp storage location     */
  if (!been_allocated)                  /* If not done then allocate */
    if ((result.dir_result_u.line_ptr=(line *)malloc(sizeof(line))) == NULL)
      return (&result);
    else{
      been_allocated = 1;               /* Record allocation         */
  } else if ( depth == 0 )  {           /* Clear 'old' contents.     */
    memset(result.dir_result_u.line_ptr, 0, sizeof(line));
    cur = 0;                            /* Reset index position      */
  }
```

```
if ((dp = opendir(*f)) != NULL) {   /* If successfully opened   */
  chdir(*f);                         /* Change to the directory  */
  dentry = readdir(dp);             /* Read first entry         */
  while (dentry != NULL) {
    if (stat(dentry->d_name, &statbuff) != -1) /* If accessible */
      if ((statbuff.st_mode & S_IFMT) == S_IFDIR &&
                                           /* & a directory */
          dentry->d_name[0] != '.') {      /* & not . or .. */
        depth += INDENT;                   /* adjust indent */
        /*
         * Store the entry in buffer - then copy buffer into
         * larger array.
         */
        sprintf(buffer, "%*s %-10s\n", depth, " ", dentry->d_name);
        length = strlen(buffer);
        memcpy((char *)result.dir_result_u.line_ptr + cur,
               buffer, length);
        cur += length;                /* update ptr to ref next loc */
        current = dentry->d_name;     /* the new directory         */
        (dir_result *)do_dir_1_svc(&current, rqstp);
        chdir("..");                  /* back to previous level    */
        depth -= INDENT;              /* adjust the indent level   */
      }
    dentry = readdir(dp);            /* Read the next entry       */
  }
  closedir(dp);                      /* Done with this one        */
}
return (&result);                    /* Pass back the result      */
}
```

In the `tree_server.c` program, there are several static integers that are used either as counters or flags. The `cur` identifier references the current offset into the output array where the next directory entry should be stored. Initially the offset is set to 0. The `been_allocated` identifier acts as a flag to indicate whether or not an output buffer has been allocated. Initially this flag is set to 0 (FALSE). The last static identifier, `depth`, is used to track the current indent level. It is also set to 0 at the start.

The `do_dir_1_svc` procedure is passed a reference to a string (actually a character array) and a reference to an RPC client handle. Within the procedure, a series of local identifiers are allocated to manipulate and access directory information. Following this is an **if** statement that is used to test the `been_allocated` flag. If an output buffer has not been allocated, a call to **malloc** generates it. The allocated buffer is cast appropriately and is referenced by the `line_ptr` member of the `dir_result_u` structure. Once the buffer has been allocated, the `been_allocated` flag is set to 1 (TRUE). If the output buffer has already been allocated and this is the first call to this procedure, i.e., depth is at 0 (remember this is a recursive procedure), a call to **memset** is used to clear the previous output contents by filling the buffer with NULL values. When the contents of the output buffer are cleared, the `cur` index counter is reset to 0.

The procedure then attempts to open the referenced directory. If it is successful, a call to **chdir** is issued to change the directory (this was done to eliminate the need to construct and maintain a fully qualified path when checking the current directory). Next, the first entry for the directory is obtained with the **readdir** function. A while loop is used to cycle through the directory entries. Those entries for which the process has access permission are tested to determine if they reference a directory. If they do, and the directory does not start with a dot (.), the depth counter is incremented. The formatted directory entry is temporarily constructed in a buffer using the **sprintf** string function. The format descriptors direct **sprintf** to use the **depth** value as a dynamic indicator of the number of blanks it should insert prior to the directory entry. Each entry has a newline appended to it. The formatted entry is then copied (using **memcpy**) to the proper location in the output buffer using the value of cur as an offset. The directory name is then passed back to the **do_dir_1_svc** procedure via a call to itself. Upon return from parsing a subdirectory the procedure returns up one level via a call to **chdir** and decrements the depth counter accordingly. Once the entire directory is processed, the directory file is closed. When the procedure finishes, it returns the reference to output buffer.

An output sequence for the directory tree client-server application is shown in Figure 9.34. In this example, the directory tree server, **tree_server**, is run on the workstation called morpheus. A remote shell command, **rsh**, is issued a remote command on the workstation faust. faust is directed to run the directory tree client program, (**tree_client**). The name of the workstation that is running the serving process, morpheus, along with the directory to evaluate are also passed in the remote command.

Fig. 9.34 A sample run of the directory tree application.

```
morpheus% tree_server
morpheus% rsh faust $cwd/tree_client morpheus /etc/lp
/etc/lp:
        fd
        classes
        forms
        interfaces
        logs
```

E X E R C I S E   9 – 6

On most UNIX systems the **spell** utility uses a file of words as a base for its spell checking. On our system this file is /usr/share/lib/dict/words (check the **man** page for the **spell** command to find the exact location on your system). Write an RPC-based client-server application in which the client requests a word from the server. To process the request, the server should generate a random number (within the range of the number of words in the source word file). The server should then read and return the word at the random offset in the source file.

E X E R C I S E   9 – 7

Modify the directory tree example so that the server process allocates, on the fly, a node (structure) for each directory entry. A list of the nodes should be returned to the client (versus the fixed array in the example). Be sure to dispose of all allocated memory once the application is finished with it.

9.8 USING BROADCASTING TO SEARCH FOR AN RPC SERVICE

It is possible for a user to send a message to all **rpcbind** daemons on a local network requesting information on a specific service. The request is generated using the **rpc_broadcast** network call. The broadcast requests are sent using connectionless UDP transport. When sent, multiple responses may be obtained from the same server and from multiple servers. As each response is obtained the **rpc_broadcast** call will invoke a predefined routine. Table 9.10 provides the syntax details of the **rpc_broadcast** call.

Table 9.10 Summary of the **rpc_broadcast** library call.

Include File(s)	<rpc/rpc.h>		Manual Section	**3N**
Summary	<pre>enum clnt_stat rpc_broadcast(
const u_long prognum,
const u_long versnum,
const u_long procnum,
const xdrproc_t inproc,
const caddr_t in,
const xdrproc_t outproc,
caddr_t out,
const resultproc_t eachresult,
const char *nettype
);</pre>			
Return	**Success**	**Failure**	**Sets errno**	
	An enumerated type value RPC_SUCCESS indicating the success of the broadcast call	Use clnt_perrno for error message	Yes	

The **rpc_broadcast** call is similar in nature to the **rpc_call** function. The first three arguments are the program, version and procedure numbers of the service. The parameters, inproc and in, reference the encoding procedure and the address of its argument(s) while outproc and out reference the decoding procedure and the address of where to place the decoding output if it is successful. Every time the **rpc_broadcast** call receives a response, it will call the function reference by the eachresult parameter. The eachresult prototype is:

```
bool_t
eachresult( caddr_t out,
            const struct netbuf *addr,
            const struct netconfig *netconf );
```

Where the parameter out is the same as the one used for **rpc_broadcast**, addr is a reference to a netbuf structure containing information about the system that responded, and netconf is the network configuration structure, **netconfig**, of the transport on which the server responded. Every time the **eachresult** referenced function returns a 0 (FALSE), the **rpc_broadcast** call will continue to wait for additional replies. The **rpc_broadcast** call will eventually time-out (the user has no control over the amount of time). The nettype parameter is used to reference the nettype (see Table 9.5) and, if set to NULL, will cause the call to default to the type netpath.

Program 9.8 demonstrates the use of the **rcp_broadcast** call.

Program 9.8 Program broad.c, sending a broadcast request.

```
#include <stdio.h>
#include <string.h>
#include <unistd.h>
#include <stdlib.h>
#include <ctype.h>
#include <rpc/rpc.h>
#include <rpc/rpcent.h>
#include <netdir.h>

static bool_t
who_responded(void *out, struct netbuf * addr, struct netconfig * netconf) {
  char            *host, *port;
  int             i = 0, pnum = 0;                   /* Map to universal   */
  if ((host = taddr2uaddr(netconf, addr)) != NULL) {  /* addr format */
    port = host;
    while (port && i++ < 4)                          /* Move to 4th dot    */
      port - strchr(port, ' ') + 1;
    *(port - 1) = 0;                                 /* Chop into 2 parts  */
    pnum = atoi(port)*256;                           /* MSB of port #      */
    port = strchr(port,'.')+1;
    pnum += atoi(port);                              /* LSB of port #      */
    fprintf(stderr, "host %+12s\tport % 6d\n", host, pnum);
    return (FALSE);
  }
  fprintf(stderr, "Universal net address translation error\n");
  exit(4);
}
main(int argc, char *argv[]) {
  enum clnt_stat   rpc_stat;
  u_long           program_number, version;
  struct rpcent   *rpc_entry;
  if (argc != 3) {
    fprintf(stderr, "usage: %s RPC_service_[name | number]  version\n", *argv);
    exit(1);
  }
  ++argv;                            /* Step past your own prog name  */
  if (isdigit(**argv))               /* Check to see if # was passed  */
    program_number = atoi(*argv);    /* If # passed use it otherwise  */
  else {                             /* obtain RPC entry information   */
    if ((rpc_entry = getrpcbyname(*argv)) == NULL) {
      fprintf(stderr, "Unknown service: %s\n", *argv);
      exit(2);
    }
    program_number = rpc_entry->r_number;   /* prgm # for service    */
  }
  ++argv;                                      /* Move to the version #  */
```

```
version = atoi(*argv);
rpc_stat = rpc_broadcast(program_number, version, NULLPROC,
                        xdr_void, (caddr_t) NULL,
                        xdr_void, (caddr_t) NULL,
                        (resultproc_t) who_responded, (char *)NULL);
if (rpc_stat != RPC_SUCCESS)
 if (rpc_stat != RPC_TIMEDOUT) {              /* If error is not time out    */
  fprintf(stderr, "Broadcast failure : %s\n", clnt_sperrno(rpc_stat));
  exit(3);
 }
}
```

The program checks the command line for the number of arguments. It expects to be passed the name (or number) of the service to check and its version number. The first character of the first argument is checked. If it is a digit, it is assumed that the number for the service was passed and the **atoi** function is used to convert the string representation of the number into an integer value. If the name of the service was passed, the **getrpcbyname** network call is used to obtain details about the specified service. Table 9.11 summarizes the **getrpcbyname** network call.

Table 9.11 Summary of the **getrpcbyname** network call.

Include File(s)	`<rpc/rpcent.h>`		Manual Section	**3N**
Summary	`struct rpcent` `*getrpcbyname(const char * name);`			
Return	Success	Failure	Sets errno	
	A reference to the **rpcent** structure for the service	NULL		

The **getrpcbyname** call has one parameter, a reference to a character array containing the service name. If successful, the call will return a pointer to the **rpcent** structure for the service. The **rpcent** structure is defined as:

```
struct rpcent {
        char *r_name;          /* name of this rpc service */
        char **r_aliases;      /* zero-terminated list of
                                  alternate names */
        long r_number;         /* rpc program number */
    };
```

The program then converts the second command line argument into a version number. The **rpc_broadcast** call is used to garner responses. Each time a server responds to a broadcast request, the user-defined function **who_responded** is automatically invoked.

In the **who_responded** function, another network call, **taddr2uaddr**, is to obtain a pointer to a string containing the *universal* address of the respondent. The universal address is a dotted notation of the form N1.N2.N3.N4.P1.P2 whereby the first four N octets are the network or IP address and the last two P octets reference the specific port. If the conversion is not possible, which is a non-fatal condition, the **taddr2uaddr** returns a NULL value. Table 9.12 provides the syntax specifics for the **taddr2uaddr** network call.

Table 9.12 Summary of the **taddr2uaddr** network call.

Include File(s)	<netdir.h>		Manual Section	**3N**

Summary	char *taddr2uaddr(
	    const struct netconfig *config,
	    const struct netbuf *addr);			

Return	Success	Failure	Sets errno	
	A reference to a string with the *universal* address	NULL		

Once the universal address is obtained, it is broken into an IP address string by placing a NULL at the location of the fourth dot (.) and the remaining string, indicating the port, is turned into an integer value for display purposes. The program is compiled and linked with the network library (i.e., **-lnsl**) as it makes use of a number of network calls. A sample run of the program requesting information about the **walld** service, version 1, is shown in Figure 9.35.

Fig. 9.35 Output of the broad.c program showing servers providing **walld** service.

```
morpheus % broad walld 1
host   137.49.1.22      port   32820
host   137.49.1.22      port   32820   ◊ same host same port
host   137.49.1.98      port   1536
host    137.49.1.6      port   32804   ◊ different host different port
host    137.49.1.6      port   32804
host    137.49.1.8      port   1043
host    137.49.1.3      port   1043
host    137.49.1.4      port   1043
host    137.49.1.9      port   1043   ◊ different hosts same port
host   137.49.1.14      port   32789
host   137.49.1.14      port   32789
host   137.49.1.22      port   32820
host   137.49.1.22      port   32820
host   137.49.1.98      port   1536
host    137.49.1.6      port   32804
host    137.49.1.6      port   32804
host   137.49.1.14      port   32789
host   137.49.1.14      port   32789
host    137.49.1.8      port   1043
host    137.49.1.3      port   1043
host    137.49.1.9      port   1043
host    137.49.1.4      port   1043
```

Notice that before the broadcast call timed-out, some servers responded more than once. Also note that the service can be associated with different ports on different hosts. This output should be somewhat similar to the output produced by the **rpcinfo** command when called as:

```
% rpcinfo -b walld 1
```

EXERCISE   9 – 8

Modify the `broad.c` program to display the name (versus the IP address) of the host that responds to the broadcast. *Hint:* Check into the **gethostbyaddr** network function that, when passed an address, will return a structure that contains a reference to the host name.

9.9 SUMMARY

Programming with RPC allows the programmer to write distributed applications whereby a process residing on one workstation can request another "remote" workstation to execute a specified procedure. Because of their complexity most RPC-based programs make use of a protocol compiler such as Sun Microsystems's **rpcgen**. A protocol compiler provides the basic programming framework for the RPC-based application. In RPC applications the client and server processes do not need to know the details of underlying network protocols. Data passed between the processes is converted to/from an external data representation (XDR) format by predefined filters. Beneath the covers, RPC-based programs make use of the socket interface to carry out their communications. While not discussed in this chapter, RPC does support authentication techniques to facilitate secure client-server communications.

Sockets

10.1 INTRODUCTION

One of the nice things about UNIX is that it uses a common interface for the access of files and devices that reside on a single host. By using a file descriptor generated by an **open** system call, the user can easily read data from, and write data to, the file descriptor without being overly concerned with the underlying mechanics of the process, and without knowing to which device the descriptor has been mapped (e.g., the screen, a file on disk, etc.). When we discussed the use of **pipes**, we saw a similar approach. With pipes, we could have two-way (duplex) communications using **read** and **write** system calls as long as the processes were related. Again, the processes *communicated* by using **read** and **write** system calls as if they were dealing with files. When we discussed System V-based *message queues, semaphores* and *shared memory* as interprocess communication techniques, we began to stray from the read/write paradigm. We found that while we could use some of these techniques for interprocess communication, even with unrelated processes, each technique had its own special way of sending and receiving information. Unfortunately, while these techniques are powerful, and certainly have their place, their arcane syntax is somewhat restrictive. In the last chapter, we examined remote procedure calls. We noted that RPC mechanisms are used for interprocess communications. The RPC API (Application Program Interface) was developed to ease the burden of writing applications that required communication between unrelated processes residing in a distributed environment. However, in attempting to make things *easier*, the developers of RPCs have, in some cases, made things more complex and restrictive. RPC applications, by nature, have a large number of ancillary files whose contents and relationships may, at times, obscure their functionality. In an RPC-based application, it is easy to lose touch with, and control of, the mechanics of the communication process. It would seem that what is needed is an extension of the read/write paradigm with the inclusion of sufficient networking semantics to permit unrelated processes, on different hosts, to communicate as if they were reading and writing to a local file. This sort of *intermediate level* of interprocess communications would lie somewhere in between pipes, message queues, shared memory techniques and RPC applications. Fortunately, in UNIX, there are several application interfaces that allow this type of communication and are, in fact, the underlying basis for the RPC interface.

The most common APIs that provide remote interprocess communications are the Berkeley socket interface, introduced in the early 1980s, and Transport Level Interface (TLI) programming implemented by AT&T in the mid-1980s. There is much discussion as to which of these offers the better solution for remote interprocess communication. As the Berkeley socket interface preceded TLI, a majority of existing remote interprocess communication coding is done with sockets. However, sockets are not transport independent and must be used with caution in a multithreaded processing environment. On the other hand, TLI was designed to be transport independent. Unfortunately, to date, not all transport protocols support every TLI service. Unlike sockets, TLI is STREAMS-based, requiring that the application push a special module on the stream before performing reads and writes. The concept of privileged ports (a Berkeley concept) is not supported with TLI. In addition, broadcasting is not transport independent.

In this chapter we will explore the Berkeley socket interface. A socket is an abstract data structure that is used to create a channel (connection point) to send and receive information between unrelated processes. Once a channel is established, the connected processes can use generalized file system type access routines for communication. For the most part, when using a socket-based connection, the server process creates a socket, maps the socket to a local address, and waits (listens) for requests from clients. The client process creates its own socket and determines the location specifics (such as a host name and port number) of the server. Depending upon the type of transport/connection used, the client process will begin to send and receive data, either with or without receiving a formal acknowledgment (acceptance) from the server process.

10.2 COMMUNICATION BASICS

To understand how sockets work, a basic understanding of some of the details of process communications in a networked environment, and its associated terminology, is needed.

10.2.1 Network Addresses

Every host on a network has, at a minimum, two *unique* addresses. The first *unique* address is a 48-bit *ethernet* address. This address is assigned by the manufacturer of the ethernet hardware. Ethernet addresses are written in hexadecimal notation. An ethernet address is broken into six eight-bit numbers with intervening colons ":". When using hexadecimal, each eight-bit number will be, at most, two digits each consisting of 0-9, A-F. The case of the alphabetic digits is not important, and leading 0s are usually not included. On most systems the file /etc/ethers will contain ethernet addresses for local hosts. Figure 10.1 shows the partial contents of a local /etc/ethers file.

Fig. 10.1 Some ethernet addresses found in a local /etc/ethers file.

```
0:60:8c:c2:7c:5f      backroom            # Backroom 386 (509)
2:60:8c:43:42:32      wangfu              # Backroom 286 (503)
2:60:8c:3c:bb:14      office-1            # Bev's PC in office
2:60:8c:43:42:2c      office-2            # Marilyn's PC in office
2:60:8c:43:60:46      office-3            # D230 Office Backroom
```

The second *unique* address is a 32-bit Internet (IP) address. Internet addresses are assigned by the NIC (Network Information Center) which maintains a registry. The 32-bit IP address is broken into four eight-bit numbers each separated by a dot ".". Written in decimal notation, each of the four subnumbers can range from 0-255 (although the number 0 or 255 in the last grouping often has special meaning, such as a broadcast address).

The Internet address may be subdivided into a network and local portion. The network portion, or netid, occupies the leftmost portion of the IP address and the local portion, or hostid, the rightmost portion. Using the netid value networks can be divided into three classes. Each class is identified by its leading bit sequence(s), that is, Class A bit 0 is 0, Class B where the first two bits are 10, and Class C where the first 3 bits are 110. The netid portion of the address is assigned by NIC and indicates your network association. The content of the hostid portion is determined by the local network administrator and specifies your individual host (workstation) within your network. As can be seen in Figure 10.2, the range of hostids that a local network

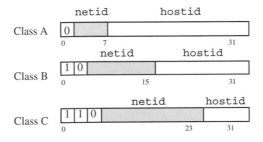

Fig. 10.2 Network class numbering scheme.

administrator can assign is directly related to the class of the network. In general, small sites are assigned Class C network addresses, larger sites Class B, etc. When this numbering scheme was initiated, it was not anticipated that the range of available network addresses would be restrictive.

It is the responsibility of the system to map a specific Internet address to its corresponding ethernet (hardware) address. This process, called address resolution, uses its own protocol called address resolution protocol (ARP). You can use the command, arp -a, to obtain a listing of recently resolved Internet/ethernet address pairs on your current host.

In discussing sockets, when we make reference to an address, unless otherwise noted, we are referring to its Internet (IP) address.

E X E R C I S E   1 0 – 1

Using the number scheme described above, how many unique Class C network numbers can be assigned? How many more possible ethernet addresses are there than possible Internet addresses?

10.2.2 Domains—Network and Communication

While IP addresses are a handy way to reference a specific host, we often map a dotted IP address into a more easily understood notation using the domain name system. In this schema, all Internet addresses are divided into a set of high-level organizational and geographical domains. Each organizational domain has an identifying code (usually three lowercase letters), such as com (commercial), edu (education), gov (government), etc. Each geographical domain consists of a two-letter country code, such as fi (Finland), ca (Canada), us (United States), etc. Within each of these high-level domains are subdomains. For example, within the edu domain is the subdomain hartford (for the University of Hartford). Within the hartford domain there may be further subdomains, or just an individual host's name. While there appears to be no established limit, usually the maximum number of levels for domain names is four to five. By using the domain naming system we can now reference a host as being, say, morpheus.hartford.edu versus 137.49.1.22. When reading names in this format the domain with the broadest scope is listed on the far right. As you move to the left, each domain found is within the domain to its right. The last name in the sequence (the leftmost) is the name of the host. Most networks run software (such as DNS [Domain Name Service] or NIS+ [Network Information Service]) that will dynamically map a domain-named reference to its corresponding Internet (IP) address.

E X E R C I S E   1 0 – 2

Explore the **nslookup** command by reading its manual page. Invoke **nslookup** and set the server to ucla.edu. What is the IP address of this server? Issue the **ls** command (while in **nslookup**). Are there any subdomains at ucla.edu?

The term "domain" is utilized again in reference to the communication type for a socket interface. When we create the socket, we specify its *communication* domain. The two types of socket communication domains that we will discuss are:

1. **UNIX domain.** In this domain, when sockets are created, they have actual file (path) names. These sockets can only be used with processes that reside on the same host. UNIX domain sockets are sometimes used as the first step in the development of socket-based communications as, due to their locality, they are somewhat easier to debug.

2. **Internet domain.** These sockets allow unrelated processes on different hosts to communicate.

While it should be clear by the context of the discussion, most often when we speak of domain, we will be talking about the communication domain of the socket, not the domain name of a host.

10.2.3 Protocol Families

Processes must also agree upon a set of rules and conventions for their communications. A set of such rules and conventions is called a *protocol*. Protocols, which can be quite complex in their entirety, are designed in layers. The layering of protocols facilitates a certain degree of isolation that permits changes to one layer to not affect the functionality of adjacent layers. The International Standards Organization (ISO) Open Systems Interconnect (OSI) Reference Model is often used as a generalized *guide* for how this layering should occur[1]. Figure 10.3 shows the standard OSI model.

Fig. 10.3 The ISO/OSI layer cake.

	Layer	Functionality
Higher Level	Application	Provides processes access to interprocess facilities.
	Presentation	Responsible for data conversion—text compression and reformatting, encryption.
	Session	Addresses the synchronization of process dialog.
Protocol Family	Transport	Responsible for maintaining an agreed-upon level of data exchange. Determines type of service, flow control, etc.
	Network	Concerned with the routing of data from one network to another—establishing, maintaining, and terminating connections.
	Data Link	Insures error-free transmission of data.
Lower Level	Physical	Addresses physical connections and transmission of raw data stream.

---

1. Some protocols, such as TCP, preceded the OSI model and thus do not cleanly map to its layering.

A grouping of layers, most commonly the *transport* and *network* layer, forms a *protocol family* or *suite*. As can be seen, a protocol family encompasses such things as data formats, addressing conventions, type of service information, flow control and error handling. There are a number of protocol families, including the following:

☞ **SNA**—IBM's Systems Network Architecture

☞ **UUCP**—UNIX-to-UNIX copy

☞ **XNS**—Xerox Network System

☞ **NETBIOS**—IBM's Network Basic Input/Output System

☞ **TCP/IP**—DARPA (Defense Advanced Research Projects Agency) Internet

Our discussion will center on the TCP/IP protocol family, Internet domain, which is composed of:

☞ **TCP**—Transmission Control Protocol. TCP is reliable, full-duplex and connection-oriented. Data is transmitted as a byte stream.

☞ **IP**—Internet Protocol. Provides delivery of packets. IP is usually called by TCP, UDP and ICMP.

☞ **ARP/RARP**—Address/Reverse Address Resolution Protocol. These protocols are used to resolve Internet/hardware addressing.

☞ **UDP**—User Datagram Protocol. UDP is non-reliable, full-duplex and connectionless. Data is transmitted as a series of packets.

☞ **ICMP**—Internet Control Message Protocol. Used for error handling and flow control.

Within the TCP/IP family, we will focus on TCP and UDP. When we create a socket we will specify its protocol family to be either PF_UNIX (UNIX[2]) or PF_INET (TCP/IP).

10.2.4 Socket Types

For processes to communicate in a networked setting, data must be transmitted and received. We can consider the communicated data to be in a *stream*, i.e., a sequence of bytes, or in *datagram* format. Datagrams are small, discrete packets that, at a gross level, contain header information (such as addresses), data and trailer information (error correction, etc.). As datagrams are small in size, communications between processes may consist of a series of datagrams.

When we create a socket, its type will determine how communications will be

---

2. Technically, UNIX is not a true communications protocol, but will be treated as such for our socket discussions.

carried on between the processes using the socket. Sockets must be of the same type to communicate. There are two[3] basic socket types the user can specify:

1. **Stream sockets.** These sockets are *reliable*. When using these sockets, data is delivered in order, in the same sequence in which it was sent. There is no duplication of data, and some type of error checking and flow control is usually present. Stream sockets allow *bi-directional* (full duplex) communication. Stream sockets are *connection oriented*. That is, a logical connection is created by the two processes using the socket. Information concerning the connection is established prior to the transmission of data and is maintained by each end of the connection during the communication. Data is transmitted as a stream of bytes. In a very limited fashion, these sockets will also permit the user to place a higher priority urgent message ahead of the data in the current stream.

2. **Datagram sockets.** Datagram sockets are potentially *unreliable*. Thus, with these sockets, received data *may* be out of order. Datagram sockets support *bi-directional* communications but are considered *connectionless*. There is no logical connection between the sending and receiving processes. Each datagram is sent, and processed, independently. Individual datagrams may take different routes to the same destination. With connectionless service there is no flow control. Error control, when specified, is minimal. Datagram packets are normally small and fixed in size.

There is an often-given analogy that compares stream socket communication to that of a phone conversation and datagram communication with communication (correspondence) via postcards. While the analogy is not entirely accurate, it does capture the spirit of the two types of communication.

10.3 IPC USING SOCKETPAIR

As a warm-up, we begin our exploration of sockets with the generation of a pair of UNIX domain sockets. The **socketpair** network call, shown in Table 10.1, is used to create the pair of sockets.

The **socketpair** network call takes four arguments. The first argument, `family`, is an integer value that specifies the address family. In general, the address family for socket-based network calls should be specified as one of the defined constants found in the header file `<sys/socket.h>`. When we look in this file, we find two sets of defined constants that can be used to indicate the `family`. One set of constants begins with AF_ (denoting address family) and the second set begins with PF_ (indicating protocol

---

3. Again a slight fudge—there are other socket types, such as raw and sequenced packet sockets. Raw sockets are for those with superuser access who wish to design and implement their own network protocol. Currently, sequenced packet sockets have not been implemented for any protocol. We will not address using raw or sequenced packet sockets.

Table 10.1 Summary of the `socketpair` network call.

Include File(s)	`<sys/types.h>` `<sys/socket.h>`		Manual Section	**3N**

Summary	`int socketpair( int   family,`
	`              int   type,`
	`              int   protocol,`
	`              int   sv[2] );`			

Return	Success	Failure	Sets `errno`	
	0 and two open socket descriptors	-1	Yes	

family). The PF_ set of constants is defined in terms of the AF_ constants. This mish-mash occurs as the concept of address families preceded that of protocol families. As we are heading toward the use of protocol families, the PF_ designated constants are more appropriate to use. However, at present, both the AF_ and PF_ versions of the constants reference identical values. The current set of *all* defined protocol families, as found in the `<sys/socket.h>` file, is shown in Table 10.2.

Table 10.2 Protocol family constants.

Value	Constant	Reference
0	PF_UNSPEC	Unspecified
1	PF_UNIX	Local to host (pipes, portals)
2	PF_INET	Internetwork: UDP, TCP, etc.
3	PF_IMPLINK	Arpanet imp addresses
4	PF_PUP	Pup protocols: e.g. BSP
5	PF_CHAOS	MIT CHAOS protocols
6	PF_NS	XEROX NS protocols
7	PF_NBS	NBS protocols
8	PF_ECMA	European computer manufacturers
9	PF_DATAKIT	Datakit protocols
10	PF_CCITT	CCITT protocols, X.25 etc.
11	PF_SNA	IBM SNA
12	PF_DECnet	DECnet
13	PF_DLI	Direct data link interface
14	PF_LAT	LAT

Table 10.2 Protocol family constants. (Continued)

Value	Constant	Reference
15	PF_HYLINK	NSC Hyperchannel
16	PF_APPLETALK	Apple Talk
17	PF_NIT	Network Interface Tap
18	PF_802	IEEE 802.2, also ISO 8802
19	PF_OSI	Umbrella for all families used
20	PF_X25	CCITT X.25 in particular
21	PF_OSINET	AFI = 47, IDI = 4
22	PF_GOSIP	U.S. Government OSI

Note that most of the socket-based network calls only work with a limited subset of address/protocol families. The **socketpair** network call is only implemented for the PF_UNIX family, thus restricting it to same host communications.

The second argument for the socketpair network call, type, indicates the socket type. The defined constant SOCK_STREAM can be used to indicate a stream socket or the defined constant SOCK_DGRAM to indicate a datagram-based socket. The third argument, protocol, is used to indicate the protocol within the specified family. In most cases, this argument is set to 0, which will indicate to the system that it should select the protocol. With Internet domain communications, the system will use, by default, UDP for connectionless sockets and TCP for connection-oriented sockets. If necessary, the IPPROTO_TCP and IPPROTO_UDP constants found in the header file <netinet/in.h> can be used to directly select the protocol within a specific family. The fourth argument, sock, is the base address of an integer array that will reference the two socket descriptors that will be created if the call is successful. Each descriptor is bi-directional and is available for both reading and writing. If the **socketpair** call fails, it will return a -1 and set **errno**. The value **errno** may take and an interpretation of each value are shown in Table 10.3.

Table 10.3 **socketpair** error messages.

#	Constant	perror **Message**	Explanation
12	ENOMEM	Not enough space	When creating a socket, insufficient memory available.
24	EMFILE	Too many open files	This process has reached the limit for open file descriptors.
63	ENOSR	Out of streams resources	Insufficient STREAMS resources for specified operation.

Table 10.3 `socketpair` error messages. (Continued)

#	Constant	`perror` **Message**	**Explanation**
120	EPROTONOSUPPORT	Protocol not supported	Requested `protocol` not supported on this system.
122	EOPNOTSUPP[*]	Operation not supported on socket	Specified `protocol` does not support socket pairs.
124	EAFNOSUPPORT	Address family not supported by protocol family	Cannot use indicated address family with specified `protocol` family.

[*] Some versions of Sun manual pages incorrectly state this constant as EOPNOSUPPORT.

Program 10.1 creates a socket pair, **forks** a child process, and uses the created sockets to communicate information between the parent and child processes. When this program was compiled, the socket library was passed to the compiler as **-lsocket**. In earlier versions of UNIX, many of the network calls resided in the standard C library and did not require the linking of a special library.

Program 10.1 Creating and using a socket pair.

```
/*
 *  Program 10.1 Creating a socket pair
 */
#include <stdio.h>
#include <stdlib.h>
#include <unistd.h>
#include <sys/types.h>
#include <sys/socket.h>
#define BUF_SZ 10

main(void) {
  int             sock[2],       /* The socket pair              */
                  cpid, i;
  static char     buf[BUF_SZ];   /* Temporary buffer for message */
  if (socketpair(PF_UNIX, SOCK_STREAM, 0, sock) < 0) {
    perror("Generation error");
    exit(1);
  }
  switch (cpid = (int) fork()) {
  case -1:
    perror("Bad fork");
    exit(2);
  case 0:                        /* The child process            */
    close(sock[1]);
    for (i = 0; i < 10; i += 2) {
      sleep(1);
      sprintf(buf, "c: %d\n", i);
      write(sock[0], buf, sizeof(buf));
      read(sock[0], buf, BUF_SZ);
      printf("c-> %s", buf);     /* Message from parent          */
    }
    close(sock[0]);
```

```
      break;
   default:                        /* The parent process          */
      close(sock[0]);
      for (i = 1; i < 10; i += 2) {
         sleep(1);
         read(sock[1], buf, BUF_SZ);
         printf("p-> %s", buf);     /* Message from child          */
         sprintf(buf, "p: %d\n", i);
         write(sock[1], buf, sizeof(buf));
      }
      close(sock[1]);
   }
   return 0;
}
```

The program begins by creating, with a single call, a pair of UNIX stream sockets. The program then forks, producing a child process. When in the child, the program closes the socket descriptor referenced as sock[1]. It then enters a loop, from 0 to 9 counting in steps of 2, where it does the following. The process **sleep**s for one second to slow down its output display sequence. It then creates, in a temporary buffer, a message to be sent to the parent process. The message contains the character sequence c:, to label it as from the child, followed by the current integer loop counter value. The contents of the temporary buffer are then written to socket descriptor 0, (sock[0]) using the **write** system call. Following the write to the socket, the child process reads from the *same* socket descriptor to obtain the message generated by the parent process. The child process then displays the message from the parent on the screen.

The parent process follows a similar set of steps. However, it closes sock[0] and does its socket reading and writing from sock[1]. When this program is run it will produce the output shown in Figure 10.4.

Fig. 10.4 The output of Program 10.1.

```
morpheus % CC p10_1.c -lsocket
morpheus % a.out
p-> c: 0
c-> p: 1
p-> c: 2
c-> p: 3
p-> c: 4
c-> p: 5
p-> c: 6
c-> p: 7
p-> c: 8
c-> p: 9
```

Before the process forks, both sock[0] and sock[1] descriptors are available in the parent for reading and writing. After the fork, the child process closes sock[1] and reads and writes with sock[0]. The parent closes sock[0] and reads and writes with sock[1]. At the kernel level the sockets are still one and the same. Thus, what the child process writes to sock[0] can be read by the parent process from sock[1] and vice versa. Figure 10.5 presents a diagrammatic representation of this relationship.

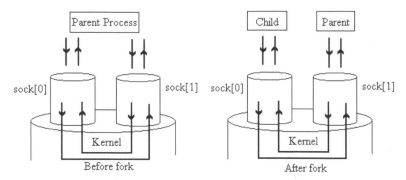

Fig. 10.5 The **socketpair** before and after the process forks.

EXERCISE   10 – 3

What happens when you adjust the sleep times in the child/parent processes in Program 10.1 (don't forget to reference the socket library as **-lsocket** when compiling)? Will the parent/child processes wait for each other no matter what the time differential? Why? Why not? If the socket type is changed to datagram SOCK_DGRAM is it possible to get the information sent to be out of order? (Be sure to experiment with messages of larger sizes.) Why? Why not?

10.4 SOCKETS—THE CONNECTION-ORIENTED PARADIGM

When using sockets for interprocess communications, we can specify the socket type as either connection-oriented (type SOCK_STREAM) or connectionless (type SOCK_DGRAM). The sequence of events that must occur for connection-oriented communications is shown in Figure 10.6. In a connection-oriented setting, the process initiating the connection is the client process and the process receiving the connection is the server.

As shown, both the client and server processes use the **socket** network call to create a new instance of a socket. The socket will act as a queuing point for data exchange. The summary for the **socket** network call is shown in Table 10.4.

The **socket** network call accepts three arguments. The arguments parallel those for the **socketpair** network call without the fourth integer array/socket pair reference. In short, the **socket** call takes an integer value (one of the defined constants in the <sys/sockets.h> file) that indicates the address/protocol family as its first argument. At present, only PF_UNIX (for internal UNIX protocol) and PF_INET (TCP/IP Internet protocols) are implemented. The second argument, type, denotes the socket

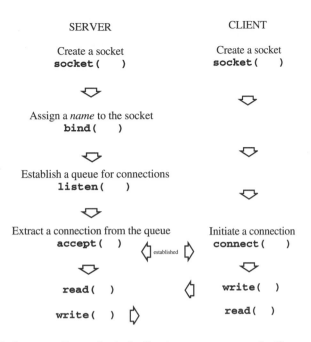

Fig. 10.6 A connection-oriented, client-server communication sequence.

Table 10.4 Summary of the **socket** network call.

Include File(s)	`<sys/types.h>` `<sys/socket.h>`		Manual Section	**3N**

Summary	`int socket( int family,`
	`            int type,`
	`            int protocol );`			

Return	Success	Failure	Sets errno	
	0 and an open socket descriptor	-1	Yes	

type (such as, SOCK_STREAM or SOCK_DGRAM). The third argument, `protocol`, is the specific protocol to be used within the indicated address/protocol family. As with the **socketpair** network call, we will most often set this value to 0 to let the system choose the protocol based on the protocol family. If the **socket** call is successful, it will return an integer value that can be used to reference the socket descriptor. If the call fails, it will return a -1 and set **errno**. The value for **errno**, and an interpretation of the error message, is shown in Table 10.5.

When a **socket** call is made in a program, the *socket* library must be specifically linked at compile time, i.e., **-lsocket**.

Table 10.5 `socket` error messages.

#	Constant	`perror` **Message**	**Explanation**
12	ENOMEM	Not enough space	When creating a socket, insufficient memory available.
13	EACCES	Permission denied	Cannot create a socket of the specified type/protocol.
24	EMFILE	Too many open files	This process has reached the limit for open file descriptors.
63	ENOSR	Out of streams resources	Insufficient STREAMS resources for specified operation.
120	EPROTONOSUPPORT	Protocol not supported	Requested `protocol` not supported on this system.

E X E R C I S E   1 0 – 4

Generate a three-column list of all the network calls found in the `libsocket.a` library. *Hint:* Use the **ar** command and pipe its output to the **pr** utility.

Initially the socket is unbound, i.e., there is no name or address/port number pair associated with the socket. If the process creating the socket is to act as a server, the socket must be bound. This is similar in concept to the assignment of a phone number to an installed phone or a street name, number, etc., to a mailing address. The **bind** network call is used to associate a name or address/port pair with a socket. If the socket is to be used in the UNIX domain, a file name must be provided. In the Internet domain, an address/port pair must be assigned. Table 10.6 provides a summary of the **bind** network call.

Table 10.6 Summary of the **bind** network call.

Include File(s)	`<sys/types.h>` `<sys/socket.h>`		Manual Section	**3N**

Summary	`int bind( int    socket,`
	`const struct sockaddr *name,`
	`int    namelen);`			

Return	Success	Failure	Sets `errno`	
	0	-1	Yes	

The first argument for **bind** is an integer value that has been returned from a successful **socket** call. The second argument, a reference to a `sockaddr` structure, is a real gem. It is a reference to a *generic* address structure defined in the header file `<sys/socket.h>` as:

```
struct sockaddr {
        u_short sa_family;
        char    sa_data[14];
};
```

We will use this structure definition to *standardize* our address references. We will come back to the use of this structure in a few paragraphs.

Keep in mind that **bind** can be used for both UNIX and Internet domain sockets. For UNIX domain sockets, a reference to a file must be bound to the socket. A UNIX socket domain address is defined in the header file <sys/un.h> [4] as:

```
struct   sockaddr_un {
        short   sun_family;             /* AF_UNIX    */
        char    sun_path[108];          /* path name  */
};
```

When using this structure, the sockaddr_un.sun_family member is usually assigned the defined constant AF_UNIX to indicate UNIX addressing is being used. The second member, sun_path, is the path (absolute or relative) to the file name to be bound to the socket. In the UNIX domain, **bind** will create a file entry for the socket. If the file is already present, an error will occur. When listing a directory in long format with the **ls** command, a file that is bound to the socket will have the letter p or s as its file type indicating it is a *pipe* or *socket*. The number of bytes in the file will be listed as 0. The maximum length for the sun_path member, *including* the NULL terminator, is 108 characters.

If the socket is to be used in the Internet domain, the addressing structure found in the file <netinet/in.h> is used. As with UNIX domain sockets, if we are working with Internet domain sockets, this file must be in the include list of the program. This structure is defined as:

```
struct sockaddr_in {
        short   sin_family;         /* AF_INET                          */
        u_short sin_port;           /* 16 bit port #                    */
        struct  in_addr sin_addr;   /* reference to address structure   */
        char    sin_zero[8];        /* future expansion                 */
};
```

Remember that, in the Internet domain, we must map the socket to an Internet address/port number pair. To accomplish this, we use the sockaddr_in structure shown above. The first member of the structure, like the sockaddr_un structure, is a short integer value that indicates the address family. In this scenario, this member is assigned the value AF_INET. The second member, sin_port, indicates the port number for the service. The port number is a 16-bit value that acts as an *offset*[5] to the indicated Internet address, and references the actual endpoint for the communication. A list of assigned port numbers can be obtained by viewing the contents of the /etc/services file. A partial excerpt from a local /etc/services file is shown in Figure 10.7.

---

4. If we are working with UNIX domain sockets, this file *must* be in the include list of the program.
5. Sticking with our phone system analogy for connection-oriented protocol, this would be similar to an extension for a given phone number.

Fig. 10.7 Partial contents of a local /etc/services file.

```
% cat /etc/services
#ident    "@(#)services    1.8      93/08/27 SMI"   /* SVr4.0 1.8   */
#
# Network services, Internet style
#
tcpmux            1/tcp
echo              7/tcp
echo              7/udp
discard           9/tcp          sink null
discard           9/udp          sink null
systat           11/tcp          users
daytime          13/tcp
daytime          13/udp
netstat          15/tcp
chargen          19/tcp          ttytst source
chargen          19/udp          ttytst source
ftp-data         20/tcp
ftp              21/tcp
telnet           23/tcp
...
```

As can be seen, each service has a name, such as **telnet**, is associated with a specific port (e.g., 23) and uses a specific protocol (e.g., tcp). Ports with values less than 1024 are *reserved* (can only be used by processes whose effective ID is root). Many of these low-numbered ports are considered to be *well-known*, that is, they consistently have the same value, and are always associated with the same type of service using the same protocol. A port can be associated with more than one protocol.

The third member of the sockaddr_in structure, sin_addr, is a reference to an in_addr structure. This structure holds the actual 32-bit host Internet address value (with adjustments for byte-orderings, i.e., little-endian versus big-endian). The fourth field, sin_zero[8], is for future expansion and is currently unused. We will present the details of how to fill in the sockaddr_in structure in the example section.

We are now ready to come back to the *generic* sockaddr structure, which is the second argument of the **bind** call. There are two members in the *generic* sockaddr structure. The first member, sa_family, is a short (u_short) integer value used to indicate the address family. The second member, sa_data, is a reference to the *actual* address. To make **bind** work, we first fill in the addressing structure (sockaddr_un or sockaddr_in) with appropriate values. Then, when passing the structure as an argument, **cast** the reference (struct sockaddr *) to *convince* **bind** that we are passing a reference to the proper structure type. The third argument to **bind**, which provides the size of the address structure, helps to resolve things such as being able to pass a UNIX domain address with a 108-byte file/path reference. Again, the details of how to calculate the size of the address structure will be presented in the example section.

If **bind** is successful, it will return a 0; otherwise, it will return a -1 and set the value of **errno**. Table 10.7 summarizes the errors associated with a failure of **bind**.

While our main concern will be with Internet domain protocols, a UNIX domain socket may also be *bound*. In the UNIX domain, an actual file entry will be generated that must be removed (unlinked) when the user is done with the socket. If **bind** expe-

Table 10.7 `bind` error messages.

#	Constant	`perror` Message	Explanation
9	EBADF	Bad file number	`socket` reference is invalid.
13	EACCES	Permission denied	Cannot create a socket of the specified type/protocol.
22	EINVAL	Invalid argument	• `namelength` is invalid. • socket already bound to an address
63	ENOSR	Out of streams resources	Insufficient STREAMS resources for specified operation.
95	ENOTSOCK	Socket operation on non-socket	`socket` is a file descriptor not a socket descriptor.
125	EADDRINUSE	Address already in use	Specified address already in use.
126	EADDRNOTAVAIL	Can't assign request address	The specified address is not available on the local system.

riences difficulty with a UNIX domain socket, the error codes that can be returned are shown in Table 10.8. Because **bind** creates a file entry, many of these codes are similar to the ones returned by the failure of a file **open**.

Remaining with the server process in the connection-oriented setting, the next network call issued is to **listen**. This call will create a queue for incoming connection requests. If the queue is full, the client process generating the request will receive the error, ECONNREFUSED, from the server. The summary for **listen** is given in Table 10.9.

Table 10.8 Additional **bind** error messages for UNIX domain sockets.

#	Constant	`perror` Message	Explanation
2	ENOENT	No such file or directory	Component of the path for the file name entry does not exist.
5	EIO	I/O error	I/O error when creating the directory entry.
13	EACCES	Permission denied	Search access denied for part of the path specified by name.
20	ENOTDIR	Not a directory	Component of the path for the file name entry is not a directory.
21	EISDIR	Is a directory	NULL path name specified.
30	EROFS	Read-only file system	File would reside on a read-only file system.
90	ELOOP	Symbolic link loop	Too many symbolic links found in file name entry.

Table 10.9 Summary of the `listen` network call.

Include File(s)	`<sys/types.h>` `<sys/socket.h>`		Manual Section	**3N**
Summary	`int listen( int    socket,` `            int    backlog );`			
Return	Success	Failure	Sets errno	
	0	-1	Yes	

The first argument of the **listen** network call is a valid integer socket descriptor. The second argument, `backlog`, denotes the maximum size of the queue. Current documentation indicates that there is no limit to the value for `backlog`. However, in many versions of UNIX the limit is set to five for any `backlog` value greater than five.

Should the **listen** network call fail, it will set **errno** and return one of the values shown in Table 10.10.

Table 10.10 `listen` error messages.

#	Constant	perror **Message**	**Explanation**
9	EBADF	Bad file number	socket reference is invalid.
95	ENOTSOCK	Socket operation on non-socket	socket is a file descriptor not a socket descriptor.
122	EOPNOTSUPP	Operation not supported on socket	Socket type (such as SOCK_DGRAM) does not support **listen** operation.

At this juncture, the server is ready to accept a connection from a client process. By default, the **accept** call will *block*, if there are no pending requests for connections. The summary for the **accept** network call is given in Table 10.11.

Table 10.11 Summary of the **accept** network call.

Include File(s)	`<sys/types.h>` `<sys/socket.h>`		Manual Section	**3N**
Summary	`int accept( int socket,` `            struct sockaddr *addr,` `            int *addrlen );`			
Return	Success	Failure	Sets errno	
	Positive integer **new** socket descriptor value	-1	Yes	

The first argument is a socket descriptor that has been *previously bound* to an address with the **bind** network call and is currently **listen**ing for a connection. If one or more client connections are pending, the first connection in the queue is returned by the **accept** call. The second argument for **accept**, *addr, is a pointer to a generic sockaddr structure. This structure is returned to the server once the connection with the client has been established. Its actual format, as in the **bind** network call, is dependent upon the domain in which the communication will occur. The structure the addr pointer will reference will contain the client's address information. The third argument, *addrlen, will contain a reference to the length, in bytes, of the previous sockaddr structure. If **accept** is successful, it will return a *new* socket descriptor that can be used for reading and writing. This new descriptor will be associated with the descriptor passed as the first argument to the **accept** network call. The original socket remains as it was and can, in some settings, still continue to **accept** additional connections. If the **accept** call fails, it returns a value of -1 and sets the value of **errno** to one of the values shown in Table 10.12.

Table 10.12 accept error messages.

#	Constant	perror **Message**	Explanation
4	EINTR	Interrupted system call	A signal was received during the **accept** process.
9	EBADF	Bad file number	socket reference is invalid.
11	EWOULDBLOCK	Resource temporarily unavailable	socket is set to non-blocking and no connections are pending.
12	ENOMEN	Not enough core	Insufficient memory to perform operation.
19	ENODEV	No such device	Specified protocol family/type not found in the netconfig file.
63	ENOSR	Out of streams resources	Insufficient STREAMS resources for specified operation.
71	EPROTO	Protocol error	An error in protocol has occurred.
95	ENOTSOCK	Socket operation on non-socket	socket is a file descriptor not a socket descriptor.
122	EOPNOTSUPP	Operation not supported on socket	socket is not of type SOCK_STREAM.

In the connection-oriented setting, the child process initiates the connection with the server process with the **connect** network call. The summary of the **connect** network call is shown in Table 10.13.

The first argument is a valid integer socket descriptor. The second argument, *name, is handled differently depending upon whether the referenced socket is connection-oriented (type SOCK_STREAM) or connectionless (type SOCK_DGRAM). In the

Table 10.13 Summary of the **connect** network call.

Include File(s)	`<sys/types.h>` `<sys/socket.h>`		Manual Section	**3N**

Summary	`int connect( int socket,`
	`            struct sockaddr *name,`
	`            int namelength );`			

Return	Success	Failure	Sets errno	
	0	-1	Yes	

connection-oriented setting, *name references the address of the socket with which it wants to communicate (i.e., the serving processes' address). For a connectionless socket, *name will reference where (the address) the datagrams are to be sent. Normally, a stream socket is **connect**ed only once, while a datagram socket can be **connect**ed several times. Further, if the protocol domain is UNIX, *name will reference a path/file name, while in the Internet domain, i.e., AF_INET, *name will reference an Internet address/port number pair. In either case, the reference should be cast to a *generic* sockaddr structure reference. Clear as mud, right? Hopefully, the section with the client-server examples will help to clarify the details of the **connect** network call.

As there are a number of ways in which the **connect** call can fail, the list of errors that **connect** can generate is quite extensive. A list of **connect** errors is found in Table 10.14.

Table 10.14 **connect** error messages.

#	Constant	`perror` **Message**	**Explanation**
2	ENOENT	No such file or directory	• Part of path prefix for *name does not exist. • Socket referenced by *name does not exist.
4	EINTR	Interrupted system call	A signal was received during **connect** process.
5	EIO	I/O error	I/O error while reading from/writing to the socket.
9	EBADF	Bad file number	socket reference is invalid.
13	EACCES	Permission denied	Search permission denied for part of path referenced by *name.
20	ENOTDIR	Not a directory	Part of path prefix is not a directory.
22	EINVAL	Invalid argument	namelength is not correct for address referenced by *name.
63	ENOSR	Out of streams resources	Insufficient STREAMS resources for specified operation.

Table 10.14 `connect` error messages. (Continued)

#	Constant	`perror` **Message**	**Explanation**
95	ENOTSOCK	Socket operation on non-socket	• `socket` is a file descriptor not a socket descriptor. • `*name` does not reference a socket.
98	EPROTOTYPE	Protocol wrong type for socket	Conflicting protocols, `socket` versus `*name` reference.
124	EAFNOSUPPORT	Address family not supported by protocol family	Address referenced by `*name` cannot be used with this `socket`.
125	EADDRINUSE	Address already in use	Address referenced by `*name` already in use.
126	EADDRNOTAVAIL	Can't assign requested address	Address referenced by `*name` not available on remote system.
128	ENETUNREACH	Network is unreachable	Cannot reach specified system.
130	ECONNABORTED	Software caused connection abort	Socket connection aborted—`socket` closed or removed.
133	EISCONN	Socket already connected	`socket` already connected.
145	ETIMEDOUT	Connection timed out	Could not establish a connection within time limits.
146	ECONNREFUSED	Connection refused	Connect attempt rejected. Close calling socket descriptor and reissue **socket** call before reconnecting.
149	EALREADY	Operation already in progress	Socket is non-blocking and no previous connection completed.

Once the connection between the client and server has been established, they can communicate using standard I/O calls such as **read** and **write**, or one of a number of specialized *send/receive* type network calls covered in a following section. When the processes are finished with the socket descriptor, they issue a standard **close**, which, by default, will attempt to send remaining queued data should the protocol for the connection (such as TCP) specify reliable delivery.

10.4.1 A UNIX Domain Stream Socket Example

In the following example, Programs 10.2 and 10.3, we will create a server and client process that uses a UNIX domain, connection-oriented (SOCK_STREAM) socket for communication. The server will create the socket, bind it to an address, generate a wait queue, accept a connection and, when data is available, **read** from the socket and display the results to the screen. The client process will create a socket, connect to the server, and generate ten messages which it writes to the socket for the server process to read.

Program 10.2 UNIX domain connection-oriented **server**.

```
/*
 Server - UNIX domain, connection-oriented
*/
#include <stdio.h>
#include <unistd.h>
#include <stdlib.h>
#include <string.h>
#include <sys/types.h>
#include <sys/socket.h>
#include <sys/un.h>            /* as we are using UNIX protocol       */
#define NAME "my_sock"

main( void ) {
    int            orig_sock, /* Original socket descriptor in server */
                   new_sock,  /* New socket descriptor from connect   */
                   clnt_len,  /* Length of client address             */
                   i;         /* Loop counter                         */
    static struct sockaddr_un
                   clnt_adr,  /* UNIX addresses of client-server      */
                   serv_adr;
    static char    buf[10];       /* Buffer for messages              */
    void clean_up( int, char *);  /* Close socket and remove routine  */

    if ((orig_sock = socket(AF_UNIX, SOCK_STREAM, 0)) < 0) {/* SOCKET */
      perror("generate error");
      exit(1);
    }
    serv_adr.sun_family = AF_UNIX; /* Set tag appropriately           */
    strcpy(serv_adr.sun_path,NAME);/* Assign name (108 chars max)     */
    unlink(NAME);                   /* Remove old copy if present      */

    if (bind( orig_sock, (struct sockaddr *) &serv_adr,    /* BIND    */
            sizeof(serv_adr.sun_family)+strlen(serv_adr.sun_path)) < 0) {
      perror("bind error");
      clean_up(orig_sock, NAME);
      exit(2);
    }
    listen(orig_sock, 1);                                 /* LISTEN   */
    clnt_len = sizeof(clnt_adr);
    if ((new_sock = accept( orig_sock, (struct sockaddr *) &clnt_adr,
                       &clnt_len)) < 0) {                  /* ACCEPT   */
      perror("accept error");
      clean_up(orig_sock, NAME);
      exit(3);
    }
    for (i = 1; i <= 10; i++) {                           /* Process  */
      sleep(1);
      read(new_sock, buf, sizeof(buf));
      printf("s-> %s", buf);
    }
    close(new_sock);
    clean_up(orig_sock, NAME);
    exit(0);
}
void
clean_up( int sd, char *the_file ){
    close( sd );                                          /* close it */
    unlink( the_file );                                   /* rm it    */
}
```

Notice the call to **bind** in the server program (10.2). As written, the third argument, which is the length of the address structure, is an expression. The expression calculates the total size by adding the size of the sun_family member of the address structure to the string length of the sun_path member. If we just applied the **sizeof** operator to the whole address structure, on most platforms the size returned would be 110 (say, two bytes for the sun_family member plus the 108 bytes for the sun_path member).

The client program is shown in Program 10.3.

Program 10.3 UNIX domain connection-oriented **client**.

```
/*
 *Client - UNIX domain, connection-oriented
 */
#include <stdio.h>
#include <unistd.h>
#include <stdlib.h>
#include <string.h>
#include <sys/types.h>
#include <sys/socket.h>
#include <sys/un.h>
#define NAME "my_sock"
main( void ) {
   int              orig_sock, /* Original socket descriptor in client*/
                    i;         /* Loop counter                        */
   static struct sockaddr_un
                    serv_adr;  /* UNIX address of the server process  */
   static char      buf[10];   /* Buffer for messages                 */
if ((orig_sock = socket(AF_UNIX, SOCK_STREAM, 0)) < 0) { /* SOCKET   */
   perror("generate error");
   exit(1);
}
serv_adr.sun_family = AF_UNIX;   /* Set tag appropriately            */
strcpy(serv_adr.sun_path, NAME);/* Assign name                      */

if (connect( orig_sock, (struct sockaddr *) &serv_adr, /* CONNECT */
         sizeof(serv_adr.sun_family)+strlen(serv_adr.sun_path)) < 0) {
   perror("connect error");
   exit(1);
}
for (i = 1; i <= 10; i++) {                             /* Send msgs  */
   sprintf(buf, "c: %d\n", i);
   write(orig_sock, buf, sizeof(buf));
}
close(orig_sock);
exit(0);
}
```

We run the client-server pair by placing the server process in the background. We then run the client process in the foreground. The compilation sequence and the output generated by the client-server programs are shown in Figure 10.8.

Fig. 10.8 UNIX domain client-server program output.

```
caribou % CC p10.2.c -o server -lsocket
caribou % CC p10.3.c -o client -lsocket
caribou % server &
[1] 874                                          ─── Is the socket present ? Yes, as a pipe
caribou %ls -l my_sock ◄────                          when the type is SOCK_STREAM.
p---------  1 gray       users           0 Jan 12 09:46 my_sock
caribou % client
caribou % s-> c: 1
s-> c: 2
. . .
s-> c: 10
[1]    Done                      server
```

On the command line, the presence of the socket can also be confirmed by using the **netstat** command. This command, which has numerous options, can be used to display information about socket-based communications. Figure 10.9 shows part of the output of **netstat** on a local system after the UNIX domain server program has been placed in the background.

Fig. 10.9 Sample output from the **netstat** command.

```
TCP
    Local Address          Remote Address      Swind Send-Q Rwind Recv-Q  State
------------------    --------------------    ----- ------ ----- ------ -------
caribou.32788         caribou.32771           16384      0 16384      0 ESTABLISHED
. . .
Active UNIX domain sockets
Address  Type         Vnode       Conn Addr
fc35ce00 stream-ord   54938          0 my_sock
```

E X E R C I S E   1 0 - 5

If we place the server process in the background, and attempt to run multiple (say three) client processes, we get the error messages and output sequence shown below:

```
    caribou % server &
    [1] 962
    caribou % client & ; client & ; client
    [2] 963
    [3] 964
    [2]    Done                      client
    connect error: Connection refused
    caribou % s-> c: 1
    s-> c: 2
    . . .
    s-> c: 10
    connect error: Software caused connection abort
    [3]    Exit 1                    client
    [1]    Done                      server
```

> Rewrite the server program (10.2) so that it will accept, and process, multiple (three) simultaneous client connections *without* generating any error messages.

10.4.2 An Internet Domain Stream Socket Example

In the Internet domain, processes must have address and port information to communicate. An application may *know* the name of a host (such as caribou or morpheus) with which it wants to communicate, but lack specifics about the host's fully qualified name, Internet address, services offered (on which ports), etc. There are a number of network information calls that can be used to return this information.

The **gethostbyname** network call will return information about a specific host when passed its name. Table 10.15 presents a summary of the **gethostbyname** network call.

Table 10.15 Summary of the **gethostbyname** network call.

Include File(s)	`<sys/types.h>` `<sys/socket.h>` `<netdb.h>` `<netinet/in.h>`		Manual Section	**3N**
Summary	`struct hostent` `*gethostbyname( const char *name );`			
Return	Success	Failure	Sets errno	
	Reference to a hostent structure	NULL	Yes	

The **gethostbyname** network call takes a single character string reference that contains the name of the host. The call queries the local network database[6] to obtain information about the indicated host. If the host name is found, the call will return a reference to a hostent structure. The hostent structure is defined in the include file `<netdb.h>` as:

```
struct  hostent {
        char  *h_name;        /* official name of host     */
        char  **h_aliases;    /* alias list                */
        int   h_addrtype;     /* host address type         */
        int   h_length;       /* length of address         */
        char  **h_addr_list⁷;  /* list of addresses from
                                  name server              */
```

---

6. Information may come from any of the sources for services specified in the `/etc/nss-witch.conf` file (see `nsswitch.conf` in section 4 of the manual pages).

7. Note, in some manual pages on **gethostbyname**, one level of indirection is missing in the description of the h_addr_list member.

```
#define h_addr   h_addr_list[0] /* address, for backward
                                   compatibility                 */
};
```

If the host name is not found, the call will return a NULL. Should the call encounter an error situation it will set a global variable called **h_error** (not **errno**) to indicate the error. The values **h_error** can take, and the associated defined constants (found in the include file <netdb.h>) are shown in Table 10.16.

Table 10.16 **gethostbyname** error messages.

#	Constant	Explanation
1	HOST_NOT_FOUND	Authoritative answer not found/no such host.
2	TRY_AGAIN	Non-authoritative host not found or SERVERFAIL.
3	NO_RECOVERY	Non-recoverable error.
4	NO_DATA	Valid name but no data record of requested type.

The object code for the **gethostbyname** network call resides in the libnsl.a archive. When using this call, the switch **-lnsl** must be added to the compilation line.

Program 10.4 uses the **gethostbyname** network call to obtain information about a host.

Program 10.4 Obtaining host information with **gethostbyname**.

```
/*
 *Checking host entries
 */
#include <stdio.h>
#include <sys/types.h>
#include <string.h>
#include <sys/socket.h>
#include <netinet/in.h>
#include <arpa/inet.h>
#include <netdb.h>

main( void ) {
  struct hostent *host;
  static char who[10];
  printf("Enter host name to look up: ");
  scanf("%10s", who);
  host = gethostbyname( who );
  if ( host != (struct hostent *) NULL ) {
    printf("Here is what I found about %s :\n", who);
    printf("Official name : %s\n", host->h_name);
    printf("Aliases        : ");
    while ( *host->h_aliases ) {
      printf("%s  ", *host->h_aliases );
      ++host->h_aliases;
      }
    printf("\nAddress type  : %i\n", host->h_addrtype);
```

```
    printf("Address length: %i\n", host->h_length);
    printf("Address list  : ");
    while ( *host->h_addr_list ) {
      struct in_addr in;
      memcpy( &in.s_addr, *host->h_addr_list, sizeof (in.s_addr));
      printf("[%s] = %s  ", *host->h_addr_list, inet_ntoa(in));
      ++host->h_addr_list;
    }
    printf("\n");
  }
}
```

In Program 10.4, the **gethostbyname** network call is used to obtain network database information on a host. When run, the user is asked for the name of a host (as written, the name can be at most nine characters). If the **gethostbyname** call is successful, the official database entry name of the host is displayed. This is followed by a list of aliases (alternate names). The address type and length is displayed next. In an Internet domain setting, we can expect these values to be 2 (the value of AF_INET) and 4 (the number of bytes needed to store an integer value). The last part of the program displays the Internet address of the host. It uses an additional network call, **inet_ntoa**, to *translate* the character encoded network address referenced by the h_addr_list member into the more standard dotted notation. The manual page on **inet_ntoa** provides a good explanation of how the character string argument to the call is translated. A compilation and run of Program 10.4 is shown in Figure 10.10.

Fig. 10.10 A run of Program 10.4.

```
caribou % CC p10.4.c -o p10.4 -lnsl
caribou % p10.4
Enter host name to look up: caribou
Here is what I found about caribou :
Official name : caribou
Aliases      :
Address type  : 2
Address length: 4
Address list  : [         1H] = 137.49.1.200
```

E X E R C I S E   1 0 – 6

There is a call similar to **gethostbyname** that returns host entry information when passed the Internet address of the host. Write a program based on Program 10.4 that requests the Internet address of a host. Then use the **gethostbyaddr** network call to display the host's information.

In addition to knowing the server's 32-bit Internet address, the client must also be able to make reference to a particular service at a given port on the server. As noted previously, there are some TCP- and UDP-based *well-known ports* which have standard services, such as **echo**, associated with them. The ports with numbers less than

1024 are reserved for processes with an effective ID of root. Ports 1024 and above are considered *ephemeral*, and may be used by any system user. An application can issue the **getservbyname** network call (see Table 10.17) to obtain information about a particular service/port.

Table 10.17 Summary of the **getservbyname** network call.

Include File(s)	<netdb.h>		Manual Section	**3N**
Summary	struct servent *getservbyname(const char *name, char *proto);			
Return	Success	Failure	Sets errno	
	Reference to a servent structure	NULL		

The **getservbyname** network call is passed the name of the host and protocol (e.g., tcp). If successful, it will return a reference to a servent structure. The servent structure is defined in <netdb.h> as:

```
struct   servent {
         char    *s_name;        /* official service name */
         char    **s_aliases8;   /* alias list            */
         int     s_port;         /* port #                */
         char    *s_proto;       /* protocol to use       */
};
```

If the call fails, it will return a NULL value. Program 10.5 uses the **getservbyname** network call to return information about a selected service type for a given protocol.

Program 10.5 Obtaining service information on a host using getservbyname.

```
/*
 *Checking service -- port entries for a host
 */
#include <stdio.h>
#include <netdb.h>
#include <netinet/in.h>

main( void ) {
  struct servent *serv;
  static char protocol[10], service[10];
  printf("Enter service to look up : ");
  scanf("%9s", service);
```

---

8. Again, some pages leave off one level of indirection for the s_aliases member when describing the servent structure.

```
printf("Enter protocol to look up: ");
scanf("%9s", protocol);
serv = getservbyname( service, protocol );
if ( serv != (struct servent *)NULL ) {
  printf("Here is what I found \n");
  printf("Official name  : %s\n", serv->s_name);
  printf("Aliases        : ");
  while ( *serv->s_aliases ) {
    printf("%s  ", *serv->s_aliases );
    ++serv->s_aliases;
    }
  printf("\nPort number    : %i\n", htons(serv->s_port));
  printf("Protocol Family: %s\n\n", serv->s_proto);
} else
  printf("Service %s for protocol %s not found\n",service,protocol);
}
```

When the port number is displayed, it is first passed to the network function **htons**. This is one of a group of functions that are used to insure byte ordering is maintained when converting 16- and 32-bit integer values that represent host and network addresses. The summary for **htons** is shown in Table 10.18.

Table 10.18 Summary of the **htons** network call.

Include File(s)	<sys/types.h> <netinet/in.h>		Manual Section	**3N**
Summary	u_short htons(u_short hostshort);			
Return	Success	Failure	Sets errno	
	The argument in proper byte order for the network			

The inverse of the **htons** call is **ntohs** (notice the switch of the letters h and n). The letter s indicates the argument is a short (16-bit) integer, as is the returned value. There are two similar routines, **htonl** and **ntohl**, that accept and return long (32-bit) integers. If byte ordering is not necessary for the given platform, these calls act as a no-op.

A sample run of Program 10.5 and a copy of the corresponding /etc/services entry are shown in Figure 10.11.

EXERCISE   10 – 7

The manual page for **getservbyname** includes a description of a network function called **getservent**. The **getservent** call can be used to enumerate all services on a host. Write a program that requests the protocol type and uses the **getservent** network call to display all services on the host that use the indicated protocol. Be sure to call **setservent** prior to issuing the **getservent** call.

Fig. 10.11 A run of Program 10.5.

```
ren % p10.5
Enter service to look up : mail
Enter protocol to look up: tcp
Here is what I found
Official name  : smtp
Aliases        : mail
Port number    : 25
Protocol Family: tcp
ren % grep mail /etc/services
smtp              25/tcp            mail
```

We now have *most* of the basic tools to write a client-server application that uses Internet protocol with a connection-oriented socket. In this next example, the server process will receive messages from the client process. As each message is received, the server will change the case of the message and return it to the client. Communication will terminate when the client sends a string that has a dot "." in column one. For each connection initiated by a client, the server process will **fork** a child process that will run concurrently and carry on communications.

Both the client and server programs share a common header file called `local.h`. The contents of `local.h` are shown in Figure 10.12.

Fig. 10.12 The `local.h` include file for the Internet domain, connection-oriented application.

```
#include <stdio.h>
#include <string.h>
#include <ctype.h>
#include <stdlib.h>
#include <unistd.h>
#include <sys/types.h>
#include <sys/socket.h>
#include <netdb.h>
#include <netinet/in.h>
#include <arpa/inet.h>

#define  PORT   6996
static char       buf[BUFSIZ];           /* Buffer for messages    */
```

The `local.h` file contains references to the include files needed by both the server and client programs. The defined constant PORT is an arbitrary integer port number that we will use with this application. The value for the port should be one that is currently *not in use* and is greater than or equal to 1024. An alternate approach would be to add an entry for the port in the `/etc/services` file. If the port is in the `/etc/services` file, the port information could then be obtained dynamically with the **getservbyname** network call. However, most users do not have the required root access to add an entry. The character array `buf` will be used as a temporary storage location for characters.

The server program, Program 10.6, is presented first.

Program 10.6 The Internet domain, connection-oriented **server.**

```c
/*
 *      Internet domain, connection-oriented SERVER
 */
#include "local.h"
main( void ) {
  int            orig_sock, /* Original socket descriptor in server */
                 new_sock,  /* New socket descriptor from connect   */
                 clnt_len;  /* Length of client address             */
  struct sockaddr_in
                 clnt_adr,  /* Internet address of client & server  */
                 serv_adr;
  int            len, i;    /* Misc counters, etc.                  */
  if ((orig_sock = socket(AF_INET, SOCK_STREAM, 0)) < 0) {/* SOCKET */
    perror("generate error");
    exit(1);
  }
  memset( &serv_adr, 0, sizeof(serv_adr) );       /* Clear structure   */
  serv_adr.sin_family      = AF_INET;             /* Set address type  */
  serv_adr.sin_addr.s_addr = htonl(INADDR_ANY); /* Any interface     */
  serv_adr.sin_port        = htons(PORT);         /* Use our fake port */
                                                  /* BIND              */
  if (bind( orig_sock, (struct sockaddr *) &serv_adr,
            sizeof(serv_adr)) < 0){
    perror("bind error");
    close(orig_sock);
    exit(2);
  }
  if (listen(orig_sock, 5) < 0 ) {                /* LISTEN            */
    perror("listen error");
    exit(3);
  }
  do {
    clnt_len = sizeof(clnt_adr);
    if ((new_sock = accept( orig_sock, (struct sockaddr *) &clnt_adr,
                       &clnt_len)) < 0) {          /* ACCEPT    */
      perror("accept error");
      close(orig_sock);
      exit(4);
    }
    if ( fork( ) == 0 ) {                          /* In CHILD process  */
      while ( (len=read(new_sock, buf, BUFSIZ)) > 0 ){
        for (i=0; i < len; ++i)                    /* Change the case   */
          buf[i] = toupper(buf[i]);
        write(new_sock, buf, len);                 /* write it back     */
        if ( buf[0] == '.' ) break;                /* are we done yet ? */
      }
      close(new_sock);                             /* In CHILD process  */
      exit( 0 );
    } else close(new_sock);                        /* In PARENT process*/
  } while( 1 );                                    /* FOREVER           */
}
```

The server program contains a few new bells and whistles that were not in our previous examples. Notice the use of the **memset** library function to *clear* the structure before its contents are assigned[9]. When assigning the address member of the server structure, the address is first passed to **htonl**. In this example, the server passes the defined constant INADDR_ANY, found in the header file <netinet/in.h>, to **htonl**. This constant, which is mapped to the value 0, indicates to the server that *any* address of socket type (SOCK_STREAM) will be acceptable.

The client program is shown in Program 10.7.

Program 10.7 The Internet domain, connection-oriented **client**.

```
/*
 *    Internet domain, connection-oriented CLIENT
 */
#include "local.h"
main( int argc, char *argv[] ) {
  int              orig_sock, /* Original socket descriptor in client */
                   len;        /* Length of server address            */
  struct sockaddr_in
                   serv_adr;  /* Internet address of server           */
  struct hostent  *host;      /* The host (server)                    */

  if ( argc != 2 ) {          /* Expect name of host on cmd line      */
    fprintf(stderr, "usage: %s server\n", argv[0]);
    exit(1);
  }
  host = gethostbyname(argv[1]);              /* Get the host info    */
  if (host == (struct hostent *) NULL ) {
    perror("gethostbyname ");
    exit(2);
  }
  memset(&serv_adr, 0, sizeof( serv_adr));    /* Clear the structure */
  serv_adr.sin_family = AF_INET;              /* Set address type    */
  memcpy(&serv_adr.sin_addr, host->h_addr, host->h_length);  /* Adr  */
  serv_adr.sin_port   = htons( PORT );        /* Use our fake port   */

  if ((orig_sock = socket(AF_INET, SOCK_STREAM, 0)) < 0) {/* SOCKET  */
    perror("generate error");
    exit(3);
  }
/* CONNECT                                                           */
  if (connect( orig_sock,(struct sockaddr *)&serv_adr,
               sizeof(serv_adr)) < 0) {
    perror("connect error");
    exit(4);
  }
  do {
    write(fileno(stdout),"> ", 3);                    /* Prompt user */
    if ((len=read(fileno(stdin), buf, BUFSIZ)) > 0) { /* Get input   */
      write(orig_sock, buf, len);                     /* Write to sck*/
      if ((len=read(orig_sock, buf, len)) > 0 )       /* If returned */
```

---

9. An alternate approach is to use **bzero**, a strictly BSD string function, to fill the location with NULL bytes. If the **bzero** function is used the library **ucb** usually found in /usr/ucblib, or the library **iberty** usually found in /usr/local/lib, may need to be specified to the linker when compiling (use **-L** pathname to indicate the path).

```
        write(fileno(stdout), buf, len);              /* display it. */
    }
  } while( buf[0] != '.' );
  close(orig_sock);
  exit(0);
}
```

The client program expects the name of a server (host) to be passed on the command line. The **gethostbyname** network call is used to obtain specific host addressing information. The returned information, stored in the `hostent` structure, is referenced by *host. This information is used, in part, to fill the server Internet address information stored in the `serv_adr` structure. The `serv_adr` structure is cleared using the **memset** library function. The address family is set to AF_INET. The **memcpy** library function is used to copy the obtained host address to the server address member. The **memcpy** function is used, as it will copy a specified number of bytes even if the referenced locations contain non-standard strings (i.e., contain NULLs, or do not end in a NULL). The assignment of the port number is similar to what was done in the server.

Next, a socket is created and a connection to the server process established. The client process then enters an endless loop. In the loop it requests user input with a "> " prompt. The user's input is read from the device mapped to standard input (most likely the keyboard). This input is then written to the socket where the server will read and process it (capitalize). The socket descriptor is then read by the client to obtain the processed string. The contents of this string (stored in the buf array) are written to the device mapped to standard output (usually the screen). The client continues to loop until a string that begins with a "." is entered.

A sample run of the Internet domain, connection-oriented client-server application is shown in Figure 10.13.

Fig. 10.13 A run of the Internet domain, connection-oriented client-server application.

```
caribou % ps
    PID TTY        TIME COMD
   5155 pts/3      0:00 ps
   3435 pts/3      0:07 csh
caribou server &   ◄─────────────────────── Server placed in background.
[1] 5156
caribou % server
bind error: Address already in use
caribou % client
usage: client server
caribou % telnet ren
...
ren % client caribou  ◄─────────────────── We run the client. It works, so we
> How is this?                              place it in background with ^Z and
HOW IS THIS?                                check what processes are running.
> ^Z
Stopped (user)
ren % rsh caribou ps
    PID TTY        TIME COMD
   5156 pts/3      0:00 server  ◄────────── Now two server processes—the
   3435 pts/3      0:08 csh                 initial one and one child process.
```

```
    5162 pts/3          0:00 server
    5163 pts/3          0:00 ps
ren % fg
client caribou
this is ok
THIS IS OK
> and this?
AND THIS?
> .
    .
```

In this sequence, the user has logged on to the host `caribou` and issued the **ps** command. The output of the command verifies that no server process is present. The server process is then invoked and placed in the background with the "&" (note, unlike the server programs that we developed in the RPC environment, we must explicitly place this server program in the background). When the server is invoked a second time, the error message `bind error: Address already in use` is displayed. This message is generated because the previous invocation of the server program has already bound the port. The user then **telnet**s to another host on the network and changes to the directory where the client-server application resides. The client program is invoked and passed the name of the host running the server program (in this case, `caribou`). When the prompt appears, a line of text is entered. The server process, on the remote host, `caribou`, processes the line of text and returns it to the client process on host `ren`. The client process displays the line (the initial line which now is in all capitals). The user then places the client program into the background with the keystrokes ^Z (ctrl-z). A second **ps** command is issued on `caribou` (a **rsh**, remote shell, command is used with the **ps**, as we are currently on a different host). The output of this second **ps** command shows that there are two server processes running on `caribou`. The initial server process and the second child process (ID 5162) which was **fork**ed when the connection from the host `ren` was established. The user then returns to the current process on `ren` via the **fg** command. A few more lines of text are entered and the application terminates with the entry of a line starting with a single period ".".

E X E R C I S E   1 0 – 8

Modify Programs 10.6 and 10.7 to play a remote game of tic-tac-toe. The client (the user) will play against the server (the computer). The client will request the user enter a row/column pair which is sent to the server along with the current board. The server then generates a valid row/column pair for its move which it sends to the client. The client displays the server move and the current status of the board, etc. While it is less than optimal, both the client and server will need to be able to determine if a win, loss or tie has occurred. The server should have separate routines to produce winning moves and to block. The server should determine if the user's intended move is valid before accepting it. If the user's move is invalid the server should request another move from the user. The server always generates valid moves. The server should create a separate process for each connected client.

Further modify the tic-tac-toe game to allow two users to play against one another by connecting to a separate tic-tac-toe arbitrator process (server). Off-load some of the common functions, such as the checking for a win, loss or tie, who goes first, whose turn is next, etc., to the arbitrator process.

10.5 SOCKETS—THE CONNECTIONLESS PARADIGM

The sequence of events for connectionless client-server communication has some common elements with connection-oriented communication. Both the client and server still generate sockets using the **socket** network call. However, the server and, most often, the client, will **bind** their sockets to an address. In the connection-oriented sequence, *only* the server performed this step. The client process does not use **connect** to establish a connection with the server. Instead, both the server and client will send/ receive datagram packets to/from a specified address. The server process sends its packets to the client address, and the clients to the server's address. These events are shown in Figure 10.14.

In this setting, we have used the **sendto** and **recvfrom** network calls for data exchange. The **sendto** network call in the client is somewhat similar in function to the **connect–write** sequence we saw in the initial Internet domain connection-oriented example. The **recvfrom** network call is analogous to the **accept–read** sequence we used for the server in the same example.

The **sendto** network call is one of several alternate ways to write data to a socket. Table 10.19 provides a summary of three network calls that can write data to a socket descriptor.

The **send** network call, since it contains no destination addressing information, can only be used with connected (SOCK_STREAM) sockets. The **sendto** and **sendmsg**

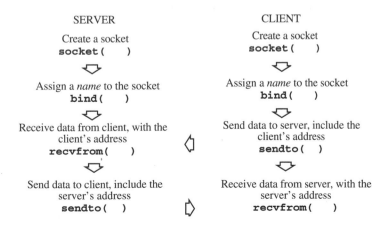

Fig. 10.14 A connectionless, client-server communication sequence.

Table 10.19 Summary of the **send,** **sendto** and **sendmsg** network calls.

Include File(s)	`<sys/types.h>` `<sys/socket.h>` `<sys/uio.h>`		Manual Section	**3N**
Summary	`int send(  int socket, const char *msg,` `            int len, int flags );` `int sendto( int socket, const char *msg,` `            int len, int flags,` `      const struct sockaddr *to,` `      int tolen );` `int sendmsg( int socket,` `        const struct msghdr *msg,` `      int flags );`			
Return	Success	Failure	Sets errno	
	Number of bytes sent	-1	Yes	

calls can be used with either socket type but are most commonly used with datagram sockets (SOCK_DGRAM). The **send** and **sendto** calls *send* a sequence of bytes. The **sendmsg** call is used to transmit data that resides in non-contiguous (scattered) memory locations (such as in a structure).

In all three calls, the integer argument, **socket**, references a valid socket descriptor. The *msg argument references the message to be sent. In the **sendmsg** call, the reference is to the structure msghdr that contains additional addressing/messaging information[10]. This structure is defined as:

```
struct msghdr {
  caddr_t msg_name;           /* optional address */
  int     msg_namelen;        /* size of address */
  struct  iovec *msg_iov;     /* scatter/gather array */
  int     msg_iovlen;         /* # elements in msg_iov */
  caddr_t msg_accrights;      /* access rights sent/received */
  int     msg_accrightslen;
};
```

where the type iovec (found in the header file <sys/uio.h>) is:

```
typedef struct iovec {
        caddr_t iov_base;
        int     iov_len;
} iovec_t;
```

The len argument is the length of the message to send. Message size is limited by the underlying protocol. The **sendto** network call contains an argument that refer-

---

10. As its use is rather complex, we will only mention **sendmsg** (and its reciprocal **recvmsg**) in passing (no pun intended!).

ences the address structure with the information of where to send the message. In the **sendto** call, the address argument is followed by an argument containing the size of the addressing structure. If **sendto** is used with a connection-oriented socket, these two arguments are ignored. All three calls have an integer-based **flag** argument. The **flag** value is obtained by ORing the value 0 with one or more of the defined constants in Table 10.20.

Table 10.20 Flags for the **send**, **sendto** and **sendmsg** network calls.

Flag	Meaning
MSG_OOB	**M**essage **O**ut **O**f **B**and. At present this flag is valid only for Internet stream-based sockets. Specifying MSG_OOB allows the process to send *urgent* data. The receiving process can choose to ignore the message.
MSG_DONTROUTE	Bypass routing tables and attempt to send message in one hop. This is often used for diagnostics purposes.

When using any of the above calls, the network and socket library should be specified to the linker (i.e., **-lnsl -lsocket**). These calls return the number of bytes sent or, in case of error, a -1, setting **errno** to one of the values found in Table 10.21. Data sent to an unbound socket is discarded.

Table 10.21 **send**, **sendto** and **sendmsg** error messages.

#	Constant	perror Message	Explanation
4	EINTR	Interrupted system call	A signal was received by process before data was sent.
9	EBADF	Bad file number	socket reference is invalid.
11	EWOULDBLOCK	Resource temporarily unavailable	socket is set to non-blocking and no connections are pending.
12	ENOMEN	Not enough core	Insufficient memory to perform operation.
22	EINVAL	Invalid argument	tolen argument contains incorrect value.
63	ENOSR	Out of streams resources	Insufficient STREAMS resources for specified operation.
71	EPROTO	Protocol error	An error in protocol has occurred.
97	EMSGSIZE	Message too long	Socket type requires message be atomic (all one) and message sent is too long.
95	ENOTSOCK	Socket operation on non-socket	socket is a file descriptor not a socket descriptor.

Other than **read**, there are three *send* comparable network calls for *receiving* data from a socket descriptor. These calls are **recv, recvfrom** and **recvmsg**. Unless otherwise specified (such as with **fcntl**), these calls will *block* if no message has arrived at the socket. Table 10.22 provides a summary of these network calls.

Table 10.22 Summary of the **recv**, **recvfrom**, and **recvmsg** network calls.

Include File(s)	`<sys/types.h>`
	`<sys/socket.h>`
	`<sys/uio.h>`
			Manual
			Section
				3N

Summary	`int recv(  int socket, char *buffer,`
	`            int len, int flags );`
	`int recvfrom( int socket, char *buffer,`
	`            int len, int flags,`
	`            const struct sockaddr *from,`
	`            int *fromlen );`
	`int recvmsg( int socket,`
	`            const struct msghdr *msg,`
	`            int flags );`			

Return	Success	Failure	Sets errno	
	Number of bytes received	-1	Yes	

Since it contains no sender address information, the **recv** network call should only be used with connection-oriented (SOCK_STREAM) sockets. The **recvfrom** and **recvmsg** calls can be used with connection-oriented or connectionless sockets. Usually, when data is written to a socket with **send**, **sendto** and **sendmsg**, it is read with the corresponding **recv**, **recvfrom** and **recvmsg** call.

In each call, the integer argument socket is a valid socket descriptor. The *buffer argument references the location where the received message will be stored. The user is responsible for allocating the storage space for the received message. As with the **sendmsg** network call, the *msg argument for **recvmsg** references the msghdr structure found in the `<sys/socket.h>` file. The len argument is the length of the receive message buffer. Remember that the message size is limited by the underlying protocol and exceedingly long messages may be truncated. The *receive* call returns the actual number of bytes received. If the *from argument for the **recvfrom** call is not NULL, it will reference a sockaddr structure containing the address information of the host that sent the message. The *fromlen argument will reference the length of this addressing structure. The flag argument is formed by ORing the value 0 with one or more of the defined flags shown in Table 10.23.

When using any of the above *receive* calls, the network and socket library should be specified to the linker (i.e., **-lnsl -lsocket**). In cases of error, these calls will return a -1 and set **errno** to one of the values found in Table 10.24.

Table 10.23 Flags for the `recv`, `recvfrom` and `recvmsg` network calls.

Flag	Meaning
MSG_OOB	**M**essage **O**ut **O**f **B**and. At present, this flag is valid only for Internet, stream-based sockets. Specifying MSG_OOB allows the process to read *urgent* out of band data.
MSG_PEEK	Look at the current data but do not consume it. Subsequent **read**–receive type calls will retrieve the same *peeked*-at data.

Table 10.24 `recv`, `recvfrom` and `recvmsg` error messages.

#	Constant	perror **Message**	Explanation
4	EINTR	Interrupted system call	A signal was received by process before data was received.
5	EIO	I/O error	I/O during file read or write.
9	EBADF	Bad file number	`socket` reference is invalid.
11	EWOULDBLOCK	Resource temporarily unavailable	`socket` is set to non-blocking and no connections are pending.
12	ENOMEN	Not enough core	Insufficient memory to perform operation.
63	ENOSR	Out of streams resources	Insufficient STREAMS resources for specified operation.
95	ENOTSOCK	Socket operation on non-socket	`socket` is a file descriptor not a socket descriptor.
151	ESTALE	Stale NFS file handle	A stale NFS (network file system) file handle was found.

10.5.1 A UNIX Domain Datagram Socket Example

Our UNIX domain datagram socket example will be similar in function to the stream socket example presented in section 10.4. In this example, the server will create a datagram socket (SOCK_DGRAM) in the UNIX domain and bind it to an address (file name). The client will also create a datagram socket and bind it to an address (using a different file name, unique to each client). The client and server will use the **sendto** and **recvfrom** network calls for communication. The client will generate ten messages which will be sent to the server. The server will display the messages that it has received. The code for the server process is shown in Program 10.8.

Program 10.8 The UNIX domain, connectionless **server**.

```
/* SERVER - UNIX domain - connectionless                          */
#include <stdio.h>
#include <stdlib.h>
#include <unistd.h>
```

```
#include <string.h>
#include <sys/types.h>
#include <sys/socket.h>
#include <sys/un.h>              /* as we are using UNIX protocol        */
#define  SERVER_FILE "server_socket"
main( void ) {
  int             orig_sock, /* Original socket descriptor in server */
                  clnt_len,  /* Length of client address             */
                  i;         /* Loop counter                         */
  static struct sockaddr_un
                  clnt_adr, /* UNIX adr of client and server        */
                  serv_adr;

  static char     buf[10];      /* Buffer for messages              */
  void clean_up( int, char *);  /* Close socket and remove routine  */
  if ((orig_sock = socket(AF_UNIX, SOCK_DGRAM, 0)) < 0) {/* SOCKET  */
    perror("generate error");
    exit(1);
}
  serv_adr.sun_family = AF_UNIX;           /* Set tag appropriately   */
  strcpy(serv_adr.sun_path,SERVER_FILE);/* Assign name               */
  unlink( SERVER_FILE);                    /* Remove leftovers        */
  if (bind(orig_sock, (struct sockaddr *) &serv_adr,     /* BIND     */
          sizeof(serv_adr.sun_family)+strlen(serv_adr.sun_path)) < 0) {
    perror("bind error");
    clean_up(orig_sock, SERVER_FILE);
    exit(2);
  }
  for (i = 1; i <= 10; i++) {
    recvfrom(orig_sock, buf, sizeof(buf), 0,     /* RECEIVE it        */
          (struct sockaddr *) &clnt_adr, &clnt_len);
    printf("s-> %s", buf);
  }
  clean_up(orig_sock, SERVER_FILE);
  exit(0);
}
void
clean_up( int sd, char *the_file ){
  close( sd );
  unlink( the_file );
}
```

The code for the client process is shown in Program 10.9.

Program 10.9 The UNIX domain, connectionless **client**.

```
/*
 *     CLIENT - UNIX domain - connectionless  */
 */
#include <stdio.h>
#include <stdlib.h>
#include <unistd.h>
#include <string.h>
#include <sys/types.h>
#include <sys/socket.h>
#include <sys/un.h>
#include <unistd.h>
#define  SERVER_FILE "server_socket"
main( void ) {
  int             orig_sock, i;
  static struct sockaddr_un
```

```
                    clnt_adr,
                    serv_adr;
  static char       buf[10],
                    client_file[15];
  void clean_up( int, char * );

  serv_adr.sun_family = AF_UNIX;
  strcpy(serv_adr.sun_path, SERVER_FILE);

  if ((orig_sock = socket(AF_UNIX, SOCK_DGRAM, 0)) < 0) {
    perror("generate error");
    exit(1);
  }
  sprintf(client_file,"%07d_socket",getpid());
  clnt_adr.sun_family = AF_UNIX;
  strcpy(clnt_adr.sun_path, client_file);

  if (bind(orig_sock, (struct sockaddr *) &clnt_adr,    /* BIND     */
           sizeof(clnt_adr.sun_family)+strlen(clnt_adr.sun_path)) < 0) {
    perror("bind error");
    exit(2);
  }
  for (i=1; i <= 10; i++) {
    sleep(1);                               /* Slow down the client */
    sprintf(buf, "c: %d\n", i);             /* create message       */
    sendto(orig_sock, buf, sizeof(buf), 0,  /* SEND it              */
           (struct sockaddr *) &serv_adr, sizeof(struct sockaddr));
  }
  clean_up( orig_sock, client_file);
  exit(0);
}
void
clean_up( int sd, char *the_file ){
  close( sd );
  unlink( the_file );
}
```

In the client, the **sprintf** function is used in conjunction with the **getpid** system call to generate a unique file name to be bound to the client's socket. An alternate, more typical way to generate a unique file name would be to use the standard I/O function **tmpnam**. If there are multiple clients communicating with the server, it is *imperative* that each have its own unique file name for binding.

A standard compilation/output sequence using this client-server pair is shown in Figure 10.15.

Fig. 10.15 Running the UNIX domain, connectionless client-server application.

```
caribou % CC p10.8.c -lnsl -lsocket -o server
caribou % CC p10.9.c -lnsl -lsocket -o client
caribou % server &
[1] 527
caribou % client
s-> c: 1
. . .
s-> c: 9
s-> c: 10
caribou %
[1]    Done                    server
```

Figure 10.16 shows what happens if we run two clients and use the **ls** command to check for the file names to which the client and server sockets are bound. Notice that the server still processes ten messages. However, it receives half of the messages from one client and half from the other. No error message is generated when the clients continue to send their data to the unbound (closed) server socket.

Fig. 10.16 Running the same application with multiple clients.

```
caribou % server &
[1] 522
caribou % client &; client &; ls -l *socket
[2] 524
[3] 525
p---------   1 gray       users        0 Jan 18 10:23 0000524_socket
p---------   1 gray       users        0 Jan 18 10:23 0000525_socket
p---------   1 gray       users        0 Jan 18 10:23 server_socket
caribou % s-> c: 1
s-> c: 1
s-> c: 2
s-> c: 2
s-> c: 3
s-> c: 3
s-> c: 4
s-> c: 4
s-> c: 5
s-> c: 5
[1]     Done                server
[2]     Done                client
[3]     Done                client
caribou %
```

EXERCISE   10 – 10

Frick and Frack were discussing UNIX domain connectionless sockets. Frick noted that he thought that the code for the client, in Program 10.9, was *excessive*. Frick's client code is shown below.

```
/*   Frick's CLIENT - UNIX domain, connectionless   */
#include <stdio.h>
#include <string.h>
#include <stdlib.h>
#include <sys/types.h>
#include <sys/socket.h>
#include <sys/un.h>
#include <unistd.h>
#define   SERVER_FILE "server_socket"
main( void ) {
    int             orig_sock, i;
    static struct sockaddr_un
                    serv_adr;
    static char     buf[10];
    if ((orig_sock = socket(AF_UNIX, SOCK_DGRAM, 0)) < 0) {
```

```
            perror("generate error");
            exit(1);
        }
        serv_adr.sun_family = AF_UNIX;
        strcpy(serv_adr.sun_path, SERVER_FILE);
    for (i=1; i <= 10; i++) {
        sprintf(buf, "c: %d\n", i);
        sendto(orig_sock, buf, sizeof(buf), 0,
                (struct sockaddr *) &serv_adr,
                sizeof(struct sockaddr));
    }
        exit(0);
    }
```

Does Frick's client code work with the server? Why? If Frick's code works, what are its limitations? If it does not work, what must be done to make it work?

10.5.2 An Internet Domain Datagram Socket Example

In the next example, we will create a client-server application that uses connectionless sockets. This application will act like a rudimentary chat program. A user running the server process can interactively **read** messages from, and **write** messages to, the user running the client program and vice versa. When running this application the server program is invoked first and remains in the *foreground*. At start up, the server will display the port to which the client should **bind**. The client program, run in the foreground on a *different* host or in a *separate* window on the same host, is passed on the command line the name of the host where the server process is executing and the port number. Once this is done, the user on the client enters a line of text and presses enter. The client's input is displayed on the screen of the server. The user running the server process then enters a response which is displayed on the screen of the client, etc. In a regimented, lock-step, send/receive manner, the two users can carry on a form of interactive communication[11]. The client process terminates when the user enters a ^D. The server, which is iterative, continues until removed with a **kill** command. The program for the server process is shown in Program 10.10.

Program 10.10 Internet domain connectionless **server**.

```
/*
 *   Program 10.10 - SERVER - Internet Domain - connectionless
 */
#include "local.h"
main( void ) {
    int             sock, n,
                    server_len, client_len;
```

---

11. Granted this will never replace the **talk** utility, or **IRC,** but this *could* serve as a base for a more sophisticated application.

```
struct sockaddr_in server,              /* Address structures */
                   client;              /* create the SOCKET  */
if ((sock = socket(AF_INET, SOCK_DGRAM, 0)) < 0) {
  perror("SERVER socket ");
  exit(1);
}                                       /* set svr adr info   */
server.sin_family      = AF_INET;       /* Address family     */
server.sin_addr.s_addr = htonl(INADDR_ANY); /* use any adr    */
server.sin_port        = htons(0);      /* pick a free port   */
                                        /* BIND the socket    */
if (bind(sock, (struct sockaddr *) &server,
    sizeof(server) ) < 0) {
  perror("SERVER bind "); exit(2);
}                                       /* obtain chosen adr  */
if (getsockname(sock, (struct sockaddr *) &server,
    &server_len) < 0) {
  perror("SERVER getsocketname "); exit(3);
}                                       /* display port #     */
printf("Server using port %d\n", ntohs(server.sin_port));
while ( 1 ) {
  client_len = sizeof(client);          /* estimate length  */
  memset(buf, 0, BUFSIZ);               /* clear the buffer */
  if ((n=recvfrom(sock, buf, BUFSIZ, 0, /* the clnt message */
      (struct sockaddr *) &client, &client_len)) < 0){
   perror("SERVER recvfrom ");
   close(sock); exit(4);
  }
  write(fileno(stdout), buf, n);        /* show msg to server */
  memset(buf, 0, BUFSIZ);               /* clear the buffer   */
  if (fgets(buf, BUFSIZ, stdin) != NULL ){/* server's msg    */
    if ((sendto(sock, buf, strlen(buf) ,0,/* send to client  */
      (struct sockaddr *) &client, client_len)) <0){
      perror("SERVER sendto ");
      close(sock); exit(5);
    }
  }
 }
}
```

Keep in mind that for communications to occur between cooperating processes, a unique association must be established. In the Internet domain, the association is characterized by a quintuple consisting of:

protocol, local address, local port, remote address, remote port

In the server program, a datagram (connectionless) socket is created with the **socket** call. The address family is set to AF_INET, and, by default, the protocol (which was set to 0) will be UDP. The addressing information for the server is assigned next. The defined constant INADDR_ANY, a *wild-card* address, indicates the server can use (receive messages at) any valid address for this protocol. Setting the port number to 0 directs the system to select a port. When passed a 0 value, the system will pick a port that is not in use, and is greater than IPPORT_USERRESERVED (the lower limit for ports for non-privileged processes which is defined in <netinet/in.h>). The **getsock-name** call is issued to determine which port the system selected. The port number is displayed so a user running a client process will know which port to specify. The

server program then enters an endless loop. It clears a receiving buffer and issues a
recvfrom call. The **recvfrom** call will, by default, cause the server process to block
until information is received. Once information is received, the remaining parts of the
association, the remote address and port, are realized as this information is contained
in the message. The received data is written to standard output (the screen). The
server then clears the buffer and collects the user's response with a call to **fgets**.
Again, **fgets** will cause the serving process to block while awaiting input. If the user
enters a non-null response, the **sendto** call is used to *send* the response to the address/
port of the client from which the message was received. The server process remains
active until removed with a **kill** command.

As noted, when the client program is invoked, the name of the host running the
server process and the port on the server are passed on the command line. The client
then uses the **gethostbyname** call to obtain additional information about the server.
This information, along with the passed port number, is stored in the server socket
address structure of the client. In an Internet domain setting, a datagram socket is
created next, the client addressing information is set, and a call to **bind** is issued. At
this juncture, the client process has sufficient information to initiate communications
with the server process. The client enters a loop. The **fgets** call is used to obtain user
input. If user input does not indicate an end-of-file condition (i.e., the user has not
entered ^D), the input is *sent* to the serving process with the **sendto** call. The receiving buffer is then cleared, and a call to **recvfrom** retrieves the response from the user
running the server program. The response is displayed to the screen, the buffer
cleared, and the loop repeated. If the user running the client process enters ^D, the
processing loop is exited, the socket is closed, and the client process terminates.

In this example, the conventions for client-server communications are *extremely*
regimented. The server process is always started first. The client process must be
passed the name of the host running the server process and the proper port number.
The client process obtains its user input first, which it then sends to the server. The
user running the server process then responds. The user running the client responds
to this response, etc. As can be seen, there is a lot of room for improvement in this
application!

The code for the client is shown in Program 10.11 and the contents of the
local.h file in Figure 10.17.

Program 10.11 Internet domain connectionless **client**.

```
/*
 *Program 10.11 - CLIENT - Internet Domain - connectionless */
 */
#include "local.h"
main(int argc, char *argv[]){
  int             sock, n,
                  server_len;
  static struct sockaddr_in              /* Address structures */
                  server, client;
  struct hostent *host;                  /* For host info     */
  if ( argc < 3 ) {                      /* need server & port */
    fprintf(stderr, "usage: %s server port_#\n", argv[0]);
```

```
      exit(1);
   }
   if (!(host=gethostbyname(argv[1]))){  /* get server info    */
      perror("CLIENT gethostname ");  exit(2);
   }                                    /* set svr adr info    */
   server.sin_family = AF_INET;         /* address family      */
                                        /* actual address      */
   memcpy(&server.sin_addr, host->h_addr, host->h_length);
   server.sin_port   = htons(atoi(argv[2]));/* @ passed port # */
                                        /* create a SOCKET     */
   if ((sock=socket(AF_INET, SOCK_DGRAM, 0)) < 0 ) {
      perror("CLIENT socket "); exit(3);
   }                                    /* set clnt adr info   */
   client.sin_family      = AF_INET;    /* address family      */
   client.sin_addr.s_addr = htonl(INADDR_ANY);/* use any adr   */
   client.sin_port        = htons( 0 ); /* pick free port      */
                                        /* BIND the socket     */
   if (bind(sock, (struct sockaddr *) &client,
       sizeof(client)) < 0 ) {
      perror("CLIENT bind "); exit(4);
   }
   while( fgets(buf, BUFSIZ, stdin) != NULL ){/* get clnt's msg  */
     server_len=sizeof(server);             /* guess at length */
     if (sendto( sock, buf, strlen(buf), 0,   /* send msg to srvr*/
       (struct sockaddr *) &server, server_len) < 0 ){
         perror("CLIENT sendto ");
         close(sock); exit(5);
     }
     memset(buf,0,BUFSIZ);                 /* clear the buffer    */
     if ((n=recvfrom(sock, buf, BUFSIZ, 0, /* server's message    */
         (struct sockaddr *) &server, &server_len)) < 0){
       perror("CLIENT recvfrom ");
       close(sock);  exit(6);
     }
     write(fileno(stdout),buf,n);          /* show msg to clnt    */
     memset(buf,0,BUFSIZ);                 /* clear the buffer    */
   }
   close(sock);
   exit(0);
}
```

Fig. 10.17 Contents of the header file `local.h`.

```
#include <stdio.h>
#include <string.h>
#include <stdlib.h>
#include <unistd.h>
#include <sys/types.h>
#include <sys/socket.h>
#include <netdb.h>
#include <netinet/in.h>
#include <arpa/inet.h>
static char       buf[BUFSIZ];  /* Buffer for messages          */
```

A sample run of this application is shown in Figure 10.18.

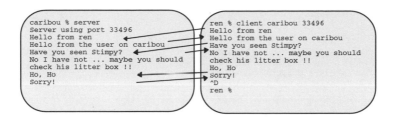

Fig. 10.18 A run of Programs 10.10 and 10.11 in two separate windows.

E X E R C I S E   1 0 – 1 1

Run the chat application presented in Program 10.10 and 10.11 with multiple clients. To accomplish this you will need either access to multiple hosts or the ability to create multiple windows on one host to simulate a multiple host configuration. Can the user running the server program still communicate with each individual client process? Modify code for the client so that it initially requests a three-letter ID (handle) from the user. Add the handle to the beginning of all messages sent from the client to the server.

10.6 MULTIPLEXING I/O WITH SELECT

It is clear from the last example that when processes communicate, they need a way to coordinate their activities other than blocking (waiting) for the recipient process to respond. One approach would be to change the socket from its default of blocking to non-blocking. The process could then perform its own polling/checking at some designated interval to determine if I/O is pending. This technique is shown in the modified server Program 10.12. The sections of code that have been added, or significantly modified, are indicated in gray areas.

Program 10.12 Internet domain connectionless **server**, non-blocking.

```
/*    Program 10.12 - SERVER Internet Domain - connectionless -
 *    non-blocking
 */
#include "local.h"
#include <sys/filio.h>
#include <errno.h>
extern errno;
main( void ) {
  int            sock, n, server_len, client_len,
                 errcount=0, flag = 1;
  struct sockaddr_in server,
                 client;

  if ((sock = socket(AF_INET, SOCK_DGRAM, 0)) < 0) {
    perror("S:socket ");
    exit(1);
  }
```

```
  if (ioctl(sock, FIONBIO, &flag) < 0 ) {
    perror("S:ioctl ");
    exit(2);
  }
  server.sin_family       = AF_INET;
  server.sin_addr.s_addr = htonl(INADDR_ANY);
  server.sin_port         = htons(0);
  if (bind(sock, (struct sockaddr *) &server, sizeof(server) ) < 0) {
    perror("S:bind ");
    exit(3);
  }
  if (getsockname(sock, (struct sockaddr *) &server,
      &server_len) < 0) {
    perror("S:getsocketname ");
    exit(4);
  }
  printf("Server using port %d\n", ntohs(server.sin_port));
  while ( 1 ) {
    client_len = sizeof(client);
    memset(buf, 0, BUFSIZ);
if ((n=recvfrom(sock, buf, BUFSIZ, 0,
        (struct sockaddr *) &client, &client_len)) < 0){
    if ( errcount++ > 3 || errno != EWOULDBLOCK ) {
      perror("S:recvfrom ");
      close(sock);
      exit(5);
    }
    sleep(errcount * 2);
    continue;
    }
    errcount = 0;
    write(fileno(stdout), buf, n);                /* display message      */
    memset(buf, 0, BUFSIZ);
    if (fgets(buf, BUFSIZ, stdin) != NULL ){
      if ((sendto(sock, buf, strlen(buf) ,0,
        (struct sockaddr *) &client, client_len)) <0){
        perror("S:sendto ");
        close(sock);
        exit(6);
      }
    }
  }
}
```

In this example, the **ioctl** system call is used to change the socket to non-block-ing. The **ioctl** call performs a wide variety of file control operations[12]. Its actions are described fully in two sections of the manual: section 2, **ioctl,** and section 7, **streamio** (**ioctl**'s action on STREAM files). The **ioctl** call is not the only way to set the socket to non-blocking. An alternate approach would be to use the **fcntl** (file control) system call. If **fcntl** is used the syntax would be:

---

12. I realize that this is a departure from the normal approach (i.e., a full explanation of the system call once it is encountered/used). The **ioctl** system call is complex, and as we will be only using it in passing, the details of its syntax and use have been omitted.

```
#include <sys/types.h>
#include <fcntl.h>
• • •
if (fcntl(sock, F_SETFL, FNDELAY) < 0 ) {
    perror("S:fcntl ");    exit(2);
}
```

In Program 10.12, the file, <sys/filio.h>, is added to the include section. This file contains defined constants used by the **ioctl** system call. In the program we also reference **errno** (which necessitates its external declaration at the top of the program) and use one of the defined constants found in the include file, <errno.h>. Once the socket is created, the **ioctl** call is employed to change the socket status to non-blocking. The **ioctl** call is passed the socket descriptor, the defined constant FIONBIO (signifying file I/O non-blocking I/O) and the address of an integer flag. If the **ioctl** call is successful, it returns a non-negative value.

The processing loop of the server is modified to introduce a limited form of polling. If a message is not available, and fewer than four receive attempts have been made, the process will **sleep** and try again. When the socket is set to non-blocking, the **recvfrom** call will return immediately if no message is available. When this occurs, the external variable **errno** is set to EWOULDBLOCK indicating the call *would have* blocked. As written, when the error code returned by **recvfrom** is EWOULDBLOCK, and the number of attempts to receive a message is less than four, the process issues a call to **sleep**. The amount of sleep time, in seconds, is calculated by multiplying the current error count by two. As the number of receive attempts increases, the sleep time continually doubles. Once a message is received, the error count is reset to 0 and the message is processed as before. If **recvfrom** returns an error code other than EWOULDBLOCK, or the number of attempts to receive a message exceeds three, an error message is generated and the process is exited. The number of times to retry, and the amount of sleep time, is somewhat arbitrary and can be adjusted by trial and error to meet specific needs.

While the above approach is both interesting and functional, it has all the drawbacks of any code that implements its own polling. It would seem that communication coordination would be greatly improved if a process could somehow *notify* a recipient process that a message was available. For example, we could signal a process when a socket has data to be read. To do this, the process receiving the signal would need to establish a signal handler for the SIGIO signal. Second, it must associate its process ID with the socket. Third, the socket must be set to allow asynchronous I/O. While all this is possible (using the **signal** and **fcntl** system calls), it, too, is less than desirable. Signals can get lost, and should multiple processes be involved in the communication process, coding can become quite complex. It is best to allow the system to handle the details of notifying processes that I/O is pending. The **select** library call can be used for this purpose. The **select** call, as shown in Table 10.25, is fairly complex.

The **select** library call uses a series of file descriptor *masks* to determine which files it should check for pending I/O. These references indicate file descriptors for reading (*readfds), for writing (*writefds) and those to be checked for exceptions (message out of band) (*exceptfds). The initial argument, nfds, is the number of bits in

Table 10.25 Summary of the **select** library call.

Include File(s)	`<sys/time.h>` `<sys/types.h>`		Manual Section	**3c**

Summary	`int select( int nfds, fd_set *readfds,`
	`                fd_set *writefds,`
	`                fd_set *exceptfds,`
	`                struct timeval *timeout );`			

Return	Success	Failure	Sets errno	
	Number of ready file descriptors	-1	Yes	

the masks that will be processed. As these masks are 0-based, passing the value 4 indicates the first four bits, representing descriptors 0–3, are to be used. The final **select** argument, *timeout, references a timeval structure that contains information about the length of time the system should wait before completing the **select** call.

When we trace down the data type for fd_set for the file descriptor masks, we find its definition actually resides in the `<sys/select.h>` file, which is an include in the `<sys/types.h>` file, as:

```
#ifndef FD_SETSIZE
#define FD_SETSIZE      1024
#endif
#ifndef NBBY        /* number of bits per byte */
#define NBBY 8
#endif

typedef long    fd_mask;
#define NFDBITS (sizeof (fd_mask) * NBBY) /* bits / mask */

#ifndef howmany
#define howmany(x, y)    (((x)+((y)-1))/(y))
#endif

typedef struct fd_set {
        fd_mask fds_bits[howmany(FD_SETSIZE, NFDBITS)];
} fd_set;
```

As shown, the read, write and exception file descriptor[13] masks are actually arrays of long integers. On the system shown, the number of file descriptors, FD_SETSIZE, that can be represented by a mask is 1024 (descriptors 0-1023). The first bit in the first element of the array is for file descriptor 0, the second bit for file descriptor 1, etc. If the process does not need to check any descriptors for pending

---

13. These are file descriptors, not file pointers. When using **select**, a socket descriptor is treated the same as a file descriptor.

reads, the read descriptor mask may be set to NULL. This also applies for the write and exception masks.

To simplify referencing a specific file descriptor represented by a single bit, several macros are available. These macros, whose descriptions are most often found on the manual page for **select**, are:

```
void FD_ZERO(fd_set &fdset);
void FD_SET(int fd, fd_set &fdset);
void FD_CLR(int fd, fd_set &fdset);
int  FD_ISSET(int fd, fd_set &fdset);
```

Each macro must be passed a reference (the address of the file descriptor mask) to manipulate. The FD_ZERO macro will zero (set to all zeros) the referenced mask. The FD_SET macro will set the appropriate bit for the passed file descriptor value. The FD_CLEAR macro will clear the bit for the passed file descriptor. The FD_ISSET macro will return, without changing its state, the status of the bit for the passed file descriptor (0 for not set and 1 for set). In practice, the FD_ISSET macro is used when the **select** call returns to determine which descriptors are actually ready for the indicated I/O event.

The last argument for **select** specifies the amount of time the call should wait before completing its action and returning. This argument references the timeval structure shown below:

```
struct timeval {
        long    tv_sec;         /* seconds */
        long    tv_usec;        /* and microseconds */
};
```

If this argument is set to NULL, the **select** call will wait (block) indefinitely until one of the specified descriptors is ready for I/O. If the tv_sec member *and* the tv_usec member are both set to 0, the **select** call will poll the specified descriptors and return immediately with their status. If the timeval members are non-zero, the system will wait the indicated number of seconds/microseconds for an I/O event to occur *or* return immediately if one of the indicated events occurs prior to the expiration of the specified time.

If **select** is successful, it will return the number of ready file descriptors. If the call has timed out, it will return a 0. If the call fails, it will return a -1 and will set **errno** to one of the values shown in Table 10.26. The file descriptor masks are modified to reflect the current status of the descriptors when the **select** call is successful or has timed out. The masks are not modified in the event of an error.

A closing note about **select**: the first argument, which indicates the number of bits that **select** will process in the file descriptor mask(s), must be set to the value of the largest file (socket) descriptor value plus **1** (*remember references are 0-based*).

Program 10.13, which shows how the **select** call can be used, is a modification of the original Internet domain connectionless server program (10.10). Modified statements, and new lines of code, are placed in gray.

Table 10.26 `select` error messages.

#	Constant	`perror` Message	Explanation
4	EINTR	Interrupted system call	A signal was received by process before any of the indicated events occurred or time limit expired.
9	EBADF	Bad file number	One of the file descriptor masks references an invalid file descriptor.
22	EINVAL	Invalid argument	One of the time limit values is out of range: $0 \leq$ tv_sec $\leq 10^8$, $0 \leq$ tv_usec $\leq 10^6$.

Program 10.13 Using `select` to multiplex I/O in the server program.

```
/*
 * Program 10.13 - SERVER - Internet Domain - connectionless
 */
#include "local.h"
#include <sys/time.h>
main( void ) {
  int               sock, n,
                    server_len, client_len,
                    n_ready, need_rsp;
struct sockaddr_in server,                    /* Address structures */
                    client;

  fd_set            read_fd;
  struct timeval    time_2_wait;

                                              /* create the SOCKET  */
  if ((sock = socket(AF_INET, SOCK_DGRAM, 0)) < 0) {
    perror("SERVER socket ");
    exit(1);
  }                                           /* set svr adr info   */
  server.sin_family      = AF_INET;           /* Address family     */
  server.sin_addr.s_addr = htonl(INADDR_ANY); /* use any address    */
  server.sin_port        = htons(0);          /* pick a free port   */
                                              /* BIND the socket    */
  if (bind(sock, (struct sockaddr *) &server, sizeof(server) ) < 0) {
    perror("SERVER bind "); exit(2);
  }                                           /* obtain chosen adr  */
  if (getsockname(sock, (struct sockaddr *) &server,
      &server_len) < 0) {
    perror("SERVER getsocketname "); exit(3);
  }                                           /* display port #     */
  printf("Server using port %d\n", ntohs(server.sin_port));

  time_2_wait.tv_sec = 5;

  while ( 1 ) {
    FD_ZERO( &read_fd );                      /* zero all bits      */
    FD_SET( sock, &read_fd );                 /* the one to read    */
    if ( (n_ready=select( sock + 1, &read_fd, (fd_set *) NULL,
                     (fd_set *) NULL, &time_2_wait)) < 0 ) {
      perror("SERVER read socket select "); continue;
    }
    if ( FD_ISSET( sock, &read_fd ) ) {
```

```
        client_len = sizeof(client);                 /* estimate length  */
        memset(buf, 0, BUFSIZ);                       /* clear the buffer */
        if ((n=recvfrom(sock, buf, BUFSIZ, 0,        /* the clnt message */
          (struct sockaddr *) &client, &client_len)) < 0){
          perror("SERVER recvfrom ");
          close(sock); exit(4);
        }
        write(fileno(stdout), buf, n);               /* show msg to server */
        memset(buf, 0, BUFSIZ);                       /* clear the buffer */
        need_rsp = 1;
      }

    if ( need_rsp ) {
      FD_ZERO( &read_fd );                           /* zero all bits    */
      FD_SET( fileno(stdin), &read_fd );             /* the one to read  */
      if ( (n_ready=select( fileno(stdin) + 1, &read_fd,
          (fd_set *) NULL,(fd_set *) NULL, &time_2_wait)) < 0 ) {
        perror("SERVER read stdin select "); continue;
      }
      if ( FD_ISSET( fileno(stdin), &read_fd ) ) {
        if (fgets(buf, BUFSIZ, stdin) != NULL ){/* get server msg   */
          if ((sendto(sock, buf, strlen(buf) ,0,/* send to client   */
            (struct sockaddr *) &client, client_len)) <0){
            perror("SERVER sendto ");
            close(sock); exit(5);
          }
        need_rsp = 0;
      }
    }
  }
}
}
```

The modified server program adds the include file <sys/time.h> since it makes reference to the timeval structure. Two integer variables have also been added. The n_read variable will be assigned the number of ready I/O descriptors found by the **select** call. In this setting, this variable should only contain the value 0 or 1. The second variable, need_rsp, is used as a flag to keep track of whether or not the server has responded to a received message. As the address of the process sending the message is included with the message, a **sendto** call to respond to the message cannot be issued until a message address pair has been received. The mask that represents the descriptors for reading, read_fd, is allocated next. A structure to hold the time to wait for the **select** call is allocated and set arbitrarily to five seconds.

In the processing loop, the read descriptor mask is zeroed and the bit to indicate the socket to process is set. The **select** call is used to determine the status of the socket. Since we are only interested in reading, the remaining descriptor masks are set to NULL (note that each is cast appropriately). When the **select** call returns, the FD_ISSET macro determines if the socket is actually available for reading. If the socket is ready, the message is received, via **recvfrom**, and displayed. Once the message is displayed, the need_rsp variable is set to 1 to flag the reception.

After checking for received messages, and having either received a message or timed-out waiting, the server looks to send a response. The need_rsp variable is checked to determine if a response to a message should be generated. If a response is

needed, the read_fd mask is reset to reference **stdin** and a call to **select** is made to
determine if any input (in this setting, from the keyboard) is available for reading. If
the user running the server process has entered information, it is **read** and sent to the
client. After a message has been sent, the need_rsp variable is set to 0 to indicate a
response was generated and sent.

While these changes help the server process to better handle asynchronous communications with the client process, it does not resolve all of the communication problems. The client process must also be changed in a similar manner to allow for non-
blocking asynchronous communications. In addition, if there are multiple clients and
the user on the server does not respond in a timely manner, how does the server *know*
(keep track of) to whom it should send its response once it receives additional messages from another client (user)?

10.7 PEEKING AT DATA

The **recv, recvfrom** and **rcvmsg** calls allow the user to look at received data without
consuming it (the data will still be available for the next *receive*-type call). This is
handy should the receiving process need to examine a message to, say, perhaps act
upon it, rather than pass it on to another process. To implement a non-consumptive
receive the user must set the integer flags argument for the *receive* call to the defined
constant MSG_PEEK. A modified Internet domain server program (Program 10.6)
shows how this can be done. The processing loop of the program (where a child process
is generated to handle the connection from the client) is modified to include a peek at
the incoming message. These modifications are shown in Program 10.14.

Program 10.14 Internet domain connection-oriented **server** using MSG_PEEK.

```
/*
 *   Internet domain, connection-oriented SERVER - MSG_PEEK
 */
    •
    •                      /* same as Program 10.6          */
    •
if ( fork( ) == 0 ) {                          /* In CHILD process     */
      while ( (len=recv(new_sock, buf, BUFSIZ, MSG_PEEK)) > 0 ){
         write( fileno(stdout),"Peeked and found: ",20);
         write( fileno(stdout), buf, len);  /* show peeked message  */
         if ( !strncmp(buf, ".done", len-1) ) break;
         len=recv(new_sock, buf, BUFSIZ, 0 ); /* retrieves same msg */
         write( fileno(stdout), "Re-read buffer  : ",20);
         write( fileno(stdout), buf, len);
      }
      write( fileno(stdout),"Leaving child process\n",23);
      close(new_sock);                         /* In CHILD process     */
      exit( 0 );
   } else close(new_sock);                      /* In the PARENT process*/
 } while( 1 );                                  /* FOREVER              */
}
```

The modifications to the client program (Program 10.7) are shown in the partial listing Program 10.15. As both the server and client make use of the **strncmp** function, the file <string.h> must be added to the files included in the local.h header file.

Program 10.15 Internet domain connection-oriented **client** using MSG_PEEK.

```
/*
 *    Internet domain, connection-oriented CLIENT -- MSG_PEEK
 */
 •
 •                  /* same as Program 10.7
 •
do {
    write(fileno(stdout),"> ", 3);                     /* Prompt the user */
    if ((len=read(fileno(stdin), buf, BUFSIZ)) > 0) { /* user input  */
      write(fileno(stdout), "Sending ", 9);
      write(fileno(stdout), buf, len);
      send(orig_sock, buf, len, 0);
    }
  } while( strncmp(buf, ".done", len-1) );
  close(orig_sock);
  exit(0);
 }
```

When these modified programs are compiled and run (as shown in Figure 10.19), it is easy to see that the server process can peek at the received data by specifying MSG_PEEK. When the second receive call is made, the peeked-at data is received again.

```
caribou % server                    caribou % client caribou
Peeked and found: hello             > hello
Re-read buffer  : hello             Sending hello
Peeked and found: this              > this
Re-read buffer  : this              Sending this
Peeked and found: is                > is
Re-read buffer  : is                Sending is
Peeked and found: peeking           > peeking
Re-read buffer  : peeking           Sending peeking
Peeked and found: .done             > .done
Leaving child process               Sending .done
^C                                  caribou %
caribou %
```

Fig. 10.19 Peeking at messages.

10.8 OUT OF BAND MESSAGES

There are occasions when a sending process needs to notify the recipient process of an urgent message. The MSG_OOB (message out of band) flag is used with the *send* and *receive* calls to indicate and process urgent messages. At present, only stream-based sockets will support out of band messaging.

As with MSG_PEEK, we can modify Program 10.6 to show how the server process might process an urgent message that has been sent by a client. Since the modifications are somewhat more extensive, the entire server program is shown in Program 10.16. Modified sections of code are in gray.

Program 10.16 Internet domain connection-oriented **server** using MSG_OOB.

```
/*
 *       Internet domain, connection-oriented SERVER - MSG_OOB
 */
#include "local.h"
main( void ) {
    int             orig_sock, /* Original socket descriptor in server */
                    new_sock,  /* New socket descriptor from connect   */
                    clnt_len;  /* Length of client address             */
    struct sockaddr_in
                    clnt_adr,  /* Internet address of client & server  */
                    serv_adr;
    int             len, i,    /* Misc counters, etc.                  */
                    urg, mark; /* flag reception of OOB message, and   */
                               /* note its location in the stream ...  */
    if ((orig_sock = socket(AF_INET, SOCK_STREAM, 0)) < 0) {/* SOCKET  */
      perror("generate error");
      exit(1);
    }
    memset( &serv_adr, 0, sizeof(serv_adr) );  /* Clear the structure  */
    serv_adr.sin_family      = AF_INET;        /* Set address type     */
    serv_adr.sin_addr.s_addr = htonl(INADDR_ANY); /* Any interface     */
    serv_adr.sin_port        = htons(PORT);       /* Use our fake port */
                                                  /* BIND              */
    if (bind( orig_sock, (struct sockaddr *) &serv_adr,
        sizeof(serv_adr)) < 0){
      perror("bind error");
      close(orig_sock);
      exit(2);
    }
    if (listen(orig_sock, 1) < 0 ) {                      /* LISTEN     */
      perror("listen error");
      exit(3);
    }
do {
    clnt_len = sizeof(clnt_adr);
    if ((new_sock = accept( orig_sock, (struct sockaddr *) &clnt_adr,
                            &clnt_len)) < 0) {            /* ACCEPT     */
      perror("accept error");
      close(orig_sock);
      exit(4);
    }
    if ( fork( ) == 0 ) {                      /* In CHILD process      */
      urg = mark = 0;
      do {
        sleep(3);                              /* slow down the server  */
        if ( (len=recv(new_sock, buf, BUFSIZ, MSG_OOB)) > 0) {
          write( fileno(stdout), "URGENT msg pending\n", 19);
          urg = 1;
        }
```

```
          if ( urg ) ioctl(new_sock, SIOCATMARK, &mark);
          if ( mark ) {
            write( fileno(stdout), " <-- the URGENT msg\n",20);
            mark = urg = 0;
          }
          if ((len-recv(new_sock, buf, BUFSIZ, 0)) > 0) {
            if ( !strncmp(buf, ".done", len-1) ) break;
            write( fileno(stdout), buf, len);
          }
        } while( 1 );
        write( fileno(stdout),"Leaving child process\n",23);
        close(new_sock);                        /* In CHILD process     */
        exit( 0 );                              /* In the PARENT process*/
      } else close(new_sock);                   /* FOREVER              */
    } while( 1 );
}
```

In the server program (10.16), the integer variables urg and mark have been
added to facilitate the processing of urgent messages. These variables will act as flags
to indicate when an urgent message has been received (urg) and actually processed
(mark). In the processing loop of the server, these variables are initially set to 0. An
inner **do–while** loop starts with a call to **sleep**. The **sleep** call is added to slow down
the server process. When we run this program we will see that the notification of the
receipt of an urgent message is received prior to messages that have already been
sent, but not yet received. A **recv** call with the flags argument set to MSG_OOB is
made next. If notification of an urgent message has been received, this call will return
a value greater than 0 (i.e., 1). When the server receives notification, it will display, to
standard output, the message URGENT msg pending and set the urg variable to 1. Following this, the urg variable is checked. If it is set (i.e., is non-zero), a call to **ioctl** is
made. With the addition of the **ioctl** call, we must include the header file <sys/
ioctl.h> in the local.h file. The **ioctl** call is passed the socket descriptor, the flag
SIOATMARK[14], and the address of the mark variable. With this argument set, the
ioctl call will assign the variable mark a positive value if the next I/O call will process
data that is beyond the urgent data; otherwise, it will assign mark a 0 value. The contents of the mark variable are tested next. If the server is beyond the processing of the
urgent message data the string <-- the URGENT msg is appended to the data currently
displayed, and the mark and urg variables cleared by resetting them to 0. In either
event, a second call to **recv** is made to receive and process pending messages from the
client. If a message is not the string .done, the message is displayed; otherwise, a
message indicating the child process is exiting is generated, the socket descriptor is
closed, and the child process exits.

The code for the client must be changed minimally. If the first character of the
data entered by the user is an exclamation mark (!), the remaining data is considered
urgent and sent with the flag argument set to MSG_OOB; otherwise, the data is sent
with the flag argument set to 0. Program 10.17 shows the modified 10.7 client program.

---

14. Defined in the <sys/sockio.h> file which also is included in the local.h file.

Program 10.17 Internet domain connection-oriented **client** using MSG_OOB.

```
/*     Internet domain, connection-oriented CLIENT - MSG_OOB      */
•
•         /* same as Program 10.7      */
•
do {
    write(fileno(stdout),"> ", 3);                   /* Prompt the user */
    if ((len=read(fileno(stdin), buf, BUFSIZ)) > 0) {   /* Get input  */
      if ( buf[0] == '!' ){
        write(fileno(stdout), "URGENT msg sent\n", 16);
        send(orig_sock, buf, len, MSG_OOB );
      } else
        send(orig_sock, buf, len, 0 );
    }
  } while( strncmp(buf, ".done", len-1) );
  close(orig_sock);
  exit(0);
 }
```

Figure 10.20 shows what occurs when this MSG_OOB client-server application is run.

The server process is established first, then the client. The user running the client program enters the letters a-d, the string !help followed by the letters e-f and then the string .done. The server process begins to process the messages from the client (remember, we added a call to **sleep** in the server to slow it down). After it has processed the initial message, it receives notice that an urgent message is pending. However, it does not actually receive the urgent message at this time. The urgent message, which is eventually received and flagged by the server process with the words <-- URGENT msg, is received in its proper order. If we want to obtain the urgent message at the time of notification, we must either buffer the intervening messages or discard them.

Fig. 10.20 Using MSG_OOB in two separate windows on the same host.

EXERCISE 10-12

Further refine the chat program to allow multiple users on different clients to communicate with one another in a manner similar in function to a *party line* or *conference* conversation. In this implementation, each user chooses a chat-name, which identifies all messages subsequently typed by that user. The chat-name is prefaced by the host name. A chat conversation might look like this:

```
[beta:fred] What did you think of the test yesterday?
[xi:zippo]  Ok, but I didn't like the question about efficiency!
[rho:joe]   Yeah, more or less efficient—we should have got the points
            on that one.
```

The options for invoking this version of chat are:

chat	Invoke chat for eavesdropping—i.e., no talking allowed—just view messages
chat fred	Invoke chat with the chat-name fred

When in **chat**, the user should be able to issue commands that are acted upon rather than sent as a message to others. For example some chat commands (lines beginning with either a . or !) might be:

.re jokes	Read file jokes—contents appear in the conversation
.wr cstuff	Write a copy of the conversation in a file called cstuff
.ap cstuff	Append a copy of the conversation to a file called cstuff
.en	End recording of conversation to output file
!cmd	Escape chat temporarily and execute the command cmd
.wn rho:joe	Whisper (talk only) to chat-name joe at host rho
.wf	Turn whisper off
.lo	Leave chat
.wo	Display the names of all chat participants

The chat program should make use of sockets. Implement some form of non-blocking I/O to prevent possible deadlock situations. To complete the assignment, you will need to write two programs: a server program which facilitates communications between clients and runs continuously in the background, and a client program that runs in the foreground. You will need to decide whether or not the server should **fork** child processes to manage communications with individual clients, or keep information in some sort of table arrangement. When the client program is invoked by the user, it connects to the chat server. As broadcasting is frowned upon, the client program should read the environment variable, CHAT, to find the name of the chat server. If the entry cannot be made in the /etc/services file for the chat port, an environment variable, such as PORT, should be used to hold the number of the port. You may want to use the MSG_PEEK option to peek at data to determine if it is a command or a message. Some commands should be processed locally by the client, while others might best be done by the server with the information returned to the appropriate client.

10.9 SUMMARY

Sockets provide the user with a means of interprocess communication whereby the processes involved can reside on different workstations across a network. The most common socket types are **stream** sockets, which provide a logical connection between processes and support the reliable exchange of data, and **datagram** sockets, which are connectionless and may be unreliable. The actual encoding of data and its transport are further dependent upon the selection of a specific transport protocol.

A series of socket network system calls are used to establish socket-based communications. The `socket` system call is used to create a socket of a specific type using a particular protocol. The `bind` system call establishes a relationship between the socket and a system address. In a stream-based setting (connection-oriented), the serving process then creates a queue for incoming connections using the `listen` system call. When a connection from a client process is made the server then uses the `accept` system call to generate a *new* socket which will be used for actual communications. The connection-oriented client process creates its own socket and uses the `connect` system call to initiate a connection with the server process. Once a connection is established the processes involved can use `read`–`write` systems calls or specialized network *send/receive* calls to exchange data.

If the communication is datagram-based (connectionless) both the client and server processes generate a socket and bind it. Communication is carried out using a `connect`–`write` / `accept`–`read` sequence or with specialized *send/receive* network calls. In a connectionless setting, addressing specifics are incorporated within the message.

The `select` system call can be used to multiplex socket-based communications. In a stream-based setting a process can peek at arriving data without consuming it and can be notified of a pending urgent message.

Using UNIX Manual Pages

A.1 Manual Page Sections

The on-line manual pages found in UNIX provide a wealth of information. The manual pages are loosely grouped by category into the following sections and subsections:

1   User commands and application programs.

       1B   SunOS/BSD compatibility package commands.

       1C   Communication commands.

       1F   Form and menu language interpreter (FMLI) commands.

       1M System maintenance commands.

       1S   SunOS specific commands.

2   System calls. A complete list of system calls can be found in Table A.1 at the end of this appendix.

3   Library functions—these functions do not directly invoke kernel primitives.

       3B   SunOS/BSD compatibility library functions. The user must specify the option `-lucb`[1] for the C compiler to link the object code for these functions.

---

1. Not only must the object code library for the function be specified at compile time, the proper header file(s) containing the declaration for the function must also be included in the source program.

3C   C library functions. These functions, along with the system calls found in section 2 and the standard I/O functions found in section 3S, form the standard C library. By default, the object code for the standard C library (found in the archive /usr/lib/libc.a) is automatically linked by the C compiler at compile time. A list of C library functions can be found in Table A.2 at the end of this appendix.

3E   Extensible Linking Format (ELF) access functions. The user must specify the option -lelf for the C compiler to link the object code for these functions.

3F   FORTRAN library routines. On some systems the FORTRAN routines may not be a separate section; instead the manual page sections for the FORTRAN routines are sublabeled with the letter "F", e.g., 3/3F.

3G   String pattern-matching and pathname manipulation functions. The user must specify the option -lgen for the C compiler to link the object code for these functions.

3I   Wide character (multibyte) manipulation functions. The user must specify the option -lintl or -lw (as needed) for the C compiler to link the object code for these functions.

3K   Kernel access functions. The user must specify the option -lucb for the C compiler to link the object code for these functions. Due to privilege limitations these functions are of limited use to the normal user.

3M   Math functions. The user must specify the option -lm for the C compiler to link the object code for these functions.

3N   Network services functions. The user must specify the option -lnsl for the C compiler to link the object code for these functions. Most of the functions discussed in the chapters on remote procedure calls and socket-based communications are to be found here.

3R   POSIX.4 real-time functions. The user must specify the option -lposix4 for the C compiler to link the object code for these functions.

3S   Standard I/O functions. The object code for these functions is automatically linked when compiling with the C compiler. A list of the standard I/O functions can be found in Table A.3 at the end of this appendix.

3T   Multithreaded functions. The user must specify the option -lthread for the C compiler to link the object code for these functions.

3X   Specialized functions (not Xlib functions). Many of these require the user to link in specialized object code libraries (see the specified manual page for details).

4   File formats[2]. The include files, found in the `/usr/include` and `/usr/include/sys` subdirectories, often contain the structure declarations for accessing these files.

    4B   Miscellaneous file formats.

5   Headers, tables and macros. This section of the manual contains information on a variety of miscellaneous items such as character set tables.

6   Games and demonstrations.

7   Special files and commands.

9   Device Driver Interface (DDI) and Driver Kernel Interface (DKI).

    9E   DDI and DKI entry point functions.

    9F   DDI and DKI kernel functions.

    9S   DDI and DKI data structures.

Each section (i.e., 1,2,3 ... 7 and 9) has a manual page called **intro** that provides an overview of the section. To obtain the proper **intro** manual page for a section the `-s` command option must be used with the **man** command to specify the section. For example, the **intro** manual page for section 2 (system calls) would be specified as:

```
% man -s2 intro
```

A.2 MANUAL PAGE FORMAT

Individual manual pages follow a standard format. Across the top of the manual page is a title line. On the left and right sides of the title line is the name of the manual page item immediately followed by parentheses, which contain the manual section/subsection. Centered between these entries is a brief description of the manual section (e.g., User Commands, Multithread Functions, etc.) similar to the section divisions listed in the previous outline. The title entry for the library function **perror** is shown below:

```
perror(3C)          C Library Functions          perror(3C)
```

Following the title line is a series of subdivisions delineated by uppercase labels. The subdivisions common to most system call/library function manual pages are:

NAME   The name of the item is followed by a one-line description. The description is often similar, if not the same, to the one-line

---

2. If you are searching for manual page information for a specific file, you can use the **-f** command option with **man**. For example, the command `% man -f wtmp` would return the manual page on the wtmp file.

description returned when a `man -k` (know) query for a specific topic is made[3]. For example, the manual page on **pipe** has the following NAME entry:

```
NAME
pipe - create an interprocess channel
```

The `man -k pipe` command returns all manual page summaries for any item (system call, library function, etc.) that references *"pipe"*.

```
% man -k pipe

p2close   p2open (3g)  - open,close pipes to and from a command
p2open    p2open (3g)  - open,close pipes to and from a command
pclose    popen (3s)   - initiate pipe to/from a process
pipe      pipe (2)     - create an interprocess channel
pipemod   pipemod (7)  - STREAMS pipe flushing module
popen     popen (3s)   - initiate pipe to/from a process
```

SYNOPSIS

This provides the syntactical information for the correct use of the item. In the case of a system call/library function, the requisite include file(s), external variables referenced and prototype are given. The data type of the return value of the system call/library function can be obtained from the prototype definition. For example, the manual page for the system calls **brk** and **sbrk** (used to change the amount of allocated space for the data segment of a process) has the following SYNOPSIS:

```
SYNOPSIS
  #include <unistd.h>
  int brk(void *endds);
  void *sbrk(int incr);
```

This indicates that to use either the **brk** or **sbrk** system call, the header file <unistd.h> must be included. The **brk** system call accepts a single argument, endds, which is a pointer to type void. The return value for **brk** is of type int. The **sbrk** system call also accepts a single argument, incr, which is of type int. The **sbrk** system call returns a pointer to type void. A discussion of the specifics, such as the details of what individual arguments reference, and how they are interpreted by

---

3. The **-k** command option for **man** uses the windex database created by running the **catman** program. If **catman** has not been run by the system administrator, the **-k** option for **man** will not work correctly.

the system call/library function, are found in the following
DESCRIPTION subdivision.

Be sure to note arguments that are pointers (references).
These arguments must reference the correct data type (e.g.,
char, int, etc.). If information is to be passed to the system
call/library function, the referenced object must be set to the
proper initial value. In addition, if information is to be
returned via the reference, the programmer *must* allocate sufficient space for the referenced item prior to the call.

MT-LEVEL   An indication of whether or not this item is safe to use in a
                multithread setting.

DESCRIPTION   This subdivision contains a detailed narration of what the sys-
                tem call/library function does. For example, the DESCRIP-
                TION entry for the manual page on **brk** and **sbrk** states:

```
DESCRIPTION

    brk() and sbrk() are used to change dynamically  the  amount
    of  space  allocated  for the calling process's data segment
    (see  exec(2)).   The  change  is  made  by  resetting   the
    process's  break value and allocating the appropriate amount
    of space.  The break value is the address of the first loca-
    tion  beyond  the  end  of  the data segment.  The amount of
    allocated space increases  as  the  break  value  increases.
    Newly allocated space is set to zero.  If, however, the same
    memory space is reallocated to the same process its contents
    are undefined.

    When a program begins execution using execve() the break  is
    set  at  the highest location defined by the program and data
    storage areas.

    The getrlimit(2) function may be used to determine the  max-
    imum  permissible  size  of the data segment; it will not be
    possible to set the break beyond the rlim_max value returned
    from  a  call  to  getrlimit(),  that  is to say, "etext +
    rlim.rlim_max."  (See  end(3C)  for  the  definition  of
    etext().)

    brk() sets the break value to endds and  changes  the  allo-
    cated space accordingly.

    sbrk() adds incr bytes to the break value  and  changes  the
    allocated space accordingly.  incr can be negative, in which
    case the amount of allocated space is decreased.
```

RETURN   The value(s) the system call/library function returns and how
VALUES   to interpret them. The RETURN VALUES entry will indicate
                whether or not **errno** is set.

ERRORS   When present (i.e., **errno** is set), this entry will list the error codes generated by the system call/library function if it fails. A short explanation of how to interpret each error code is given.

EXAMPLE   Short sections of code showing the correct use of the system call/library function.

FILES   Files accessed/modified by the system call/library function.

SEE ALSO   Other items of interest such as related system calls/library functions.

NOTES   A catch-all containing additional pertinent information that does not fall into any particular category.

There are a number of other manual page divisions, which, like those above, are usually self-explanatory (e.g., BUGS, WARNINGS, DIAGNOSTICS, etc.). On occasion small flashes of humor are encountered. The following is from a Sun BSD UNIX Version 4.1 manual page on the system command **tunefs** (used for file system tuning) " ... *You can tune a file system, but you can't tune a fish.*" Unfortunately, as UNIX becomes more standardized, such frivolities are becoming less common.

A.3 STANDARD C LIBRARY SYSTEM CALLS/LIBRARY FUNCTIONS

Table A.1 Section 2: System calls.

_exit	fchmod	munmap	shmop
_lwp_cond_broadcast	fchown	nice	sigaction
_lwp_cond_signal	fchroot	open	sigaltstack
_lwp_cond_timedwait	fcntl	p_online	sighold
_lwp_cond_wait	fork	pathconf	sigignore
_lwp_continue	fork1	pause	signal
_lwp_create	fpathconf	pipe	sigpause
_lwp_exit	fstat	plock	sigpending
_lwp_getprivate	fstatvfs	poll	sigprocmask
_lwp_kill	getaudit	pread	sigrelse
_lwp_makecontext	getauid	priocntl	sigsend
_lwp_mutex_lock	getcontext	priocntlset	sigsendset
_lwp_mutex_trylock	getdents	processor_bind	sigset
_lwp_mutex_unlock	getegid	processor_info	sigsuspend
_lwp_self	geteuid	profil	sigwait

Table A.1 Section 2: System calls. (Continued)

_lwp_sema_init	getgid	ptrace	stat
_lwp_sema_post	getgroups	putmsg	statvfs
_lwp_sema_wait	getitimer	putpmsg	stime
_lwp_setprivate	getmsg	pwrite	swapctl
_lwp_suspend	getpgid	read	symlink
_lwp_wait	getpgrp	readlink	sync
access	getpid	readv	sysfs
acct	getpmsg	rename	sysinfo
adjtime	getppid	rmdir	time
alarm	getrlimit	sbrk	times
audit	getsid	semctl	uadmin
auditon	getuid	semget	ulimit
auditsvc	ioctl	semop	umask
brk	kill	setaudit	umount
chdir	lchown	setauid	uname
chmod	link	setcontext	unlink
chown	llseek	setegid	ustat
chroot	lseek	seteuid	utime
close	lstat	setgid	utimes
creat	mincore	setgroups	vfork
dup	mkdir	setitimer	vhangup
exec	mknod	setpgid	wait
execl	mmap	setpgrp	waitid
execle	mount	setrlimit	waitpid
execlp	mprotect	setsid	write
execv	msgctl	setuid	writev
execve	msgget	shmat	yield
execvp	msgop	shmctl	
exit	msgrcv	shmdt	
fchdir	msgsnd	shmget	

Table A.2 Section 3C: C library functions.

_tolower	fpgetsticky	hdestroy	mlock	stdipc
_toupper	fpsetmask	hsearch	mlockall	strcasecmp
a641	fpsetround	initgroups	modf	strcat
abort	fpsetsticky	insque	modff	strchr
abs	free	isalnum	monitor	strcmp
addseverity	frexp	isalpha	mrand48	strcoll
alloca	fsetpos	isascii	msync	strcpy
ascftime	fsync	isastream	munlock	strcspn
asctime	ftok	isatty	munlockall	strdup
asctime_r	ftruncate	iscntrl	nextafter	strerror
atexit	ftw	isdigit	nftw	strftime
atof	gcvt	isgraph	nl_langinfo	string
atoi	getcwd	islower	nrand48	strlen
atol	getdate	isnan	offsetof	strncasecmp
atoll	getenv	isnand	opendir	strncat
bsearch	getgrent	isnanf	perror	strncmp
calloc	getgrent_r	isprint	psiginfo	strncpy
catclose	getgrgid	ispunct	psignal	strpbrk
catgets	getgrgid_r	isspace	ptsname	strrchr
catopen	getgrnam	isupper	putenv	strsignal
cftime	getgrnam_r	isxdigit	putmntent	strspn
clock	gethrtime	jrand48	putpwent	strstr
closedir	gethrvtime	l64a	putspent	strtod
conv	getlogin	labs	pututline	strtok
crypt	getlogin_r	lckpwdf	pututxline	strtok_r
ctime	getmntany	lcong48	qsort	strtol
ctime_r	getmntent	ldexp	raise	strtoll
ctype	getopt	ldiv	rand	strtoul
difftime	getpass	lfind	rand_r	strtoull
directory	getpw	llabs	readdir	strxfrm
div	getpwent	lldiv	readdir_r	swab

Table A.2 Section 3C: C library functions. (Continued)

drand48	getpwent_r	lltostr	realloc	swapcontext
dup2	getpwnam	localeconv	realpath	sysconf
ecvt	getpwnam_r	localtime	remove	tcsetpgrp
edata	getpwuid	localtime_r	remque	tdelete
encrypt	getpwuid_r	lockf	rewinddir	telldir
end	getspent	logb	scalb	tfind
endgrent	getspent_r	longjmp	seed48	toascii
endpwent	getspnam	lrand48	seekdir	tolower
endspent	getspnam_r	lsearch	select	toupper
endutent	getsubopt	major	setgrent	truncate
endutxent	gettimeofday	makecontext	setjmp	tsearch
erand48	gettxt	makedev	setkey	ttyname
etext	getutent	malloc	setlocale	ttyname_r
exit	getutid	mbchar	setpwent	ttyslot
fattach	getutline	mblen	setspent	twalk
fcvt	getutmp	mbstowcs	settimeofday	tzset
fdetach	getutmpx	mbstring	setutent	tzsetwall
ffs	getutxent	mbtowc	setutxent	ulckpwdf
fgetgrent	getutxid	memalign	sigaddset	ulltostr
fgetgrent_r	getutxline	memccpy	sigdelset	unlockpt
fgetpos	getvfsany	memchr	sigemptyset	unordered
fgetpwent	getvfsent	memcmp	sigfillset	updwtmp
fgetpwent_r	getvfsfile	memcpy	sigismember	updwtmpx
fgetspent	getvfsspec	memmove	siglongjmp	utmpname
fgetspent_r	gmtime	memory	sigsetjmp	utmpxname
finite	gmtime_r	memset	sigsetops	valloc
fmtmsg	grantpt	minor	sleep	wcstombs
fpclass	gsignal	mkfifo	srand	wctomb
fpgetmask	hasmntopt	mktemp	srand48	
fpgetround	hcreate	mktime	ssignal	

Table A.3 Section 3S: Standard I/O functions.

clearerr	fprintf	gets	setvbuf
ctermid	fputc	getw	sprintf
ctermid_r	fputs	pclose	sscanf
cuserid	fread	popen	stdio
fclose	freopen	printf	system
fdopen	fscanf	putc	tempnam
feof	fseek	putc_unlocked	tmpfile
ferror	ftell	putchar	tmpnam
fflush	funlockfile	putchar_unlocked	tmpnam_r
fgetc	fwrite	puts	ungetc
fgets	getc	putw	vfprintf
fileno	getc_unlocked	rewind	vprintf
flockfile	getchar	scanf	vsprintf
fopen	getchar_unlocked	setbuf	

UNIX Error Messages

Errors, generated by the failure of a system call or library function, can be displayed using the **perror** library function call (see the section on **Managing System Call Failures**). The error messages returned by **perror** on a UNIX system can be displayed in their entirety by the program listed in Program B.1.

Program B.1 Displaying **perror** messages.

```
#include <stdio.h>
#include <errno.h>
#include <stdlib.h>

extern int sys_nerr;
extern int errno;

main(void){
char buf[6];

  for ( errno = 1; errno < sys_nerr; ++errno ){
    sprintf(buf,"%3d  ",errno);
    perror(buf);
  }
  exit(0);
}
```

As the output of the program will fill more than one screen, it may be helpful to redirect the output to either a file, for future reference, or to the **more** command to allow viewing at a controlled pace. The output from **perror** is written to standard error, not standard out. To capture the output of the program in a file called emessages (in a BSD/C shell environment) the command sequence would be:

```
% a.out >& emessages
```

Likewise, if you want the output to be piped to **more,** the command sequence would be:

```
% a.out |& more
```

The messages generated by **perror** are sometime slightly different in wording from the *commented* descriptions listed in the include file <sys/errno.h>. The <sys/errno.h> file contains the definitions for the symbolic constants and is included when the include file <errno.h> is referenced.

The table that follows lists the error number, its symbolic name, the *commented* description in <sys/errno.h> and the actual message generated by **perror**. Where there are inconsistencies in the descriptions the entry is shaded. Some error numbers have not been officially assigned a description. Breaks in sequence are denoted with a double line.

Table B.1 Error messages.

Error #	Symbolic Constant	Description in <sys/errno.h>	Message Generated by perror
1	**EPERM**	Not superuser	Not owner
2	**ENOENT**	No such file or directory	No such file or directory
3	**ESRCH**	No such process	No such process
4	**EINTR**	Interrupted system call	Interrupted system call
5	**EIO**	I/O error	I/O error
6	**ENXIO**	No such device or address	No such device or address
7	**E2BIG**	Arg list too long	Arg list too long
8	**ENOEXEC**	Exec format error	Exec format error
9	**EBADF**	Bad file number	Bad file number
10	**ECHILD**	No children	No child processes
11	**EAGAIN**	Resource temporarily unavailable	Resource temporarily unavailable
12	**ENOMEM**	Not enough core	Not enough space
13	**EACCES**	Permission denied	Permission denied
14	**EFAULT**	Bad address	Bad address

Table B.1 Error messages. (Continued)

Error #	Symbolic Constant	Description in <sys/errno.h>	Message Generated by perror
15	**ENOTBLK**	Block device required	Block device required
16	**EBUSY**	Mount device busy	Device busy
17	**EEXIST**	File exists	File exists
18	**EXDEV**	Cross-device link	Cross-device link
19	**ENODEV**	No such device	No such device
20	**ENOTDIR**	Not a directory	Not a directory
21	**EISDIR**	Is a directory	Is a directory
22	**EINVAL**	Invalid argument	Invalid argument
23	**ENFILE**	File table overflow	File table overflow
24	**EMFILE**	Too many open files	Too many open files
25	**ENOTTY**	Inappropriate ioctl for device	Inappropriate ioctl for device
26	**ETXTBSY**	Text file busy	Text file busy
27	**EFBIG**	File too large	File too large
28	**ENOSPC**	No space left on device	No space left on device
29	**ESPIPE**	Illegal seek	Illegal seek
30	**EROFS**	Read-only file system	Read-only file system
31	**EMLINK**	Too many links	Too many links
32	**EPIPE**	Broken pipe	Broken pipe
33	**EDOM**	Math arg out of domain of func.	Argument out of domain
34	**ERANGE**	Math result not representable	Result too large
35	**ENOMSG**	No message of desired type	No message of desired type
36	**EIDRM**	Identifier removed	Identifier removed
37	**ECHRNG**	Channel number out of range	Channel number out of range
38	**EL2NSYNC**	Level 2 not synchronized	Level 2 not synchronized

Table B.1 Error messages. (Continued)

Error #	Symbolic Constant	Description in <sys/errno.h>	Message Generated by perror
39	**EL3HLT**	Level 3 halted	Level 3 halted
40	**EL3RST**	Level 3 reset	Level 3 reset
41	**ELNRNG**	Link number out of range	Link number out of range
42	**EUNATCH**	Protocol driver not attached	Protocol driver not attached
43	**ENOCSI**	No CSI structure available	No CSI structure available
44	**EL2HLT**	Level 2 halted	Level 2 halted
45	**EDEADLK**	Deadlock condition	Deadlock situation detected/avoided
46	**ENOLCK**	No record locks available	No record locks available
47	**ECANCELED**	Operation canceled	Error 47
48	**ENOTSUP**	Operation not supported	Error 48
50	**EBADE**	Invalid exchange	Bad exchange descriptor
51	**EBADR**	Invalid request descriptor	Bad request descriptor
52	**EXFULL**	Exchange full	Message tables full
53	**ENOANO**	No anode	Anode table overflow
54	**EBADRQC**	Invalid request code	Bad request code
55	**EBADSLT**	Invalid slot	Invalid slot
56	**EDEADLOCK**	File locking deadlock error	File locking deadlock
57	**EBFONT**	Bad font file fmt	Bad font file format
60	**ENOSTR**	Device not a stream	Not a stream device
61	**ENODATA**	No data (for no delay I/O)	No data available
62	**ETIME**	Timer expired	Timer expired
63	**ENOSR**	Out of streams resources	Out of streams resources
64	**ENONET**	Machine is not on the network	Machine is not on the network
65	**ENOPKG**	Package not installed	Package not installed
66	**EREMOTE**	The object is remote	Object is remote

Table B.1 Error messages. (Continued)

Error #	Symbolic Constant	Description in <sys/errno.h>	Message Generated by perror
67	**ENOLINK**	The link has been severed	Link has been severed
68	**EADV**	Advertise error	Advertise error
69	**ESRMNT**	Surmount error	Surmount error
70	**ECOMM**	Communication error on send	Communication error on send
71	**EPROTO**	Protocol error	Protocol error
74	**EMULTIHOP**	Multihop attempted	Multihop attempted
77	**EBADMSG**	Trying to read unreadable message	Not a data message
78	**ENAMETOOLONG**	Path name is too long	File name too long
79	**EOVERFLOW**	Value too large to be stored in data type	Value too large for defined data type
80	**ENOTUNIQ**	Given log. name not unique	Name not unique on network
81	**EBADFD**	f.d. invalid for this operation	File descriptor in bad state
82	**EREMCHG**	Remote address changed	Remote address changed
83	**ELIBACC**	Can't access a needed shared lib.	Can not access a needed shared library
84	**ELIBBAD**	Accessing a corrupted shared lib.	Accessing a corrupted shared library
85	**ELIBSCN**	.lib section in a.out corrupted	.lib section in a.out corrupted
86	**ELIBMAX**	Attempting to link in too many shared libraries	Attempting to link in more shared libraries than system limit
87	**ELIBEXEC**	Attempting to exec a shared library	Cannot exec a shared library directly
88	**EILSEQ**	Illegal byte sequence	Error 88
89	**ENOSYS**	Unsupported file system operation	Operation not applicable

Table B.1 Error messages. (Continued)

Error #	Symbolic Constant	Description in <sys/errno.h>	Message Generated by perror
90	ELOOP	Symbolic link loop	Number of symbolic links encountered during path name traversal exceeds MAXSYMLINKS
91	ERESTART	Restartable system call	Error 91
92	ESTRPIPE	If pipe/FIFO, don't sleep in stream head	Error 92
93	ENOTEMPTY	Directory not empty	Directory not empty
94	EUSERS	Too many users (for UFS)	Too many users
95	ENOTSOCK	Socket operation on non-socket	Socket operation on non-socket
96	EDESTADDRREQ	Destination address required	Destination address required
97	EMSGSIZE	Message too long	Message too long
98	EPROTOTYPE	Protocol wrong type for socket	Protocol wrong type for socket
99	ENOPROTOOPT	Protocol not available	Option not supported by protocol
120	EPROTONOSUPPORT	Protocol not supported	Protocol not supported
121	ESOCKTNOSUPPORT	Socket type not supported	Socket type not supported
122	EOPNOTSUPP	Operation not supported on socket	Operation not supported on transport endpoint
123	EPFNOSUPPORT	Protocol family not supported	Protocol family not supported
124	EAFNOSUPPORT	Address family not supported by protocol family	Address family not supported by protocol family
125	EADDRINUSE	Address already in use	Address already in use
126	EADDRNOTAVAIL	Can't assign requested address	Cannot assign requested address
127	ENETDOWN	Network is down	Network is down
128	ENETUNREACH	Network is unreachable	Network is unreachable

Table B.1 Error messages. (Continued)

Error #	Symbolic Constant	Description in <sys/errno.h>	Message Generated by perror
129	**ENETRESET**	Network dropped connection because of reset	Network dropped connection because of reset
130	**ECONNABORTED**	Software caused connection abort	Software caused connection abort
131	**ECONNRESET**	Connection reset by peer	Connection reset by peer
132	**ENOBUFS**	No buffer space available	No buffer space available
133	**EISCONN**	Socket is already connected	Transport endpoint is already connected
134	**ENOTCONN**	Socket is not connected	Transport endpoint is not connected
135	**EUCLEAN**	Structure needs cleaning	Structure needs cleaning
137	**ENOTNAM**	Not a XENIX named type file	Not a name file
138	**ENAVAIL**	No XENIX semaphores available	Not available
139	**EISNAM**	Is a named type file	Is a name file
140	**EREMOTEIO**	Remote I/O error	Remote I/O error
141	**EINIT**	Reserved for future	Reserved for future use
142	**EREMDEV**	Error 142	Error 142
143	**ESHUTDOWN**	Can't send after socket shutdown	Cannot send after socket shutdown
144	**ETOOMANYREFS**	Too many references: can't splice	Too many references— cannot splice
145	**ETIMEDOUT**	Connection timed out	Connection timed out
146	**ECONNREFUSED**	Connection refused	Connection refused
147	**EHOSTDOWN**	Host is down	Host is down
148	**EHOSTUNREACH**	No route to host	No route to host
149	**EALREADY**	Operation already in progress	Operation already in progress
150	**EINPROGRESS**	Operation now in progress	Operation now in progress

Table B.1 Error messages. (Continued)

Error #	Symbolic Constant	Description in <sys/errno.h>	Message Generated by perror
151	**ESTALE**	Stale NFS file handle	Stale NFS file handle
EAGAIN	**EWOULDBLOCK**	Resource temporarily unavailable	Resource temporarily unavailable

RPC Syntax Diagrams

C.1 INTRODUCTION

The correct syntax for the RPC language (XDR with the addition of the **program** and **version** types) can be obtained by tracing through the syntax diagrams[1] following the flow indicated by the arrows. In each diagram, the words or symbols that are listed in boxes with rounded corners should be entered exactly as shown. Items in boxes with square corners that contain entries that are *not italicized* reference further syntax diagrams. *Italicized* entries reference "common" items. These items consist of:

- ☞ identifiers (e.g., const-ident, type-ident, etc.), which adhere to standard syntax for C identifiers;
- ☞ types, which reference standard C data types (e.g., int, double, etc.) with the addition of three special XDR language data types: bool (boolean), string (a sequence of characters terminated by a NULL) and opaque (untyped data); and
- ☞ values, which reference standard C values (e.g., integer constants, literals, etc.).

The **rpcgen** compiler will convert all RPC definitions into standard C. Statements that have a % in the first column will be passed through without interpretation.

---

1. While I would like to be able to note that these syntax diagrams follow defined standards, they do not exactly. However, they are close enough in format and style that most should find no difficulty interpreting them.

The RPC language consists of a series of RPC definitions delineated by semicolons:

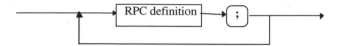

which can be divided into six categories or definitions.

C.2 RPC DEFINITIONS

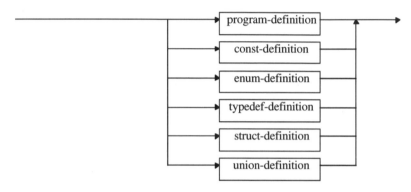

C.2.1 Program-definition

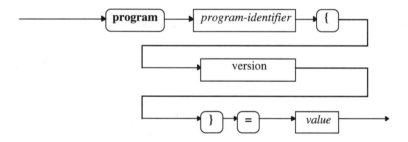

C.2.1.1 Version

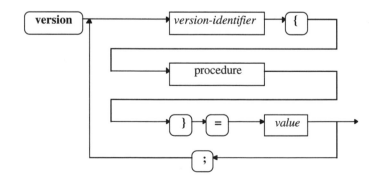

C.2.1.2 Procedure

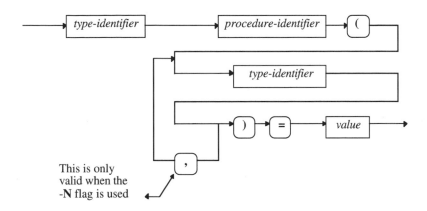

This is only
valid when the
-N flag is used

C.2.2 Const-definition

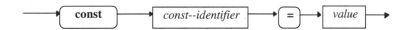

C.2.3 Enum-definition

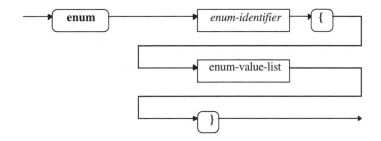

C.2.3.1 Enum-value-list

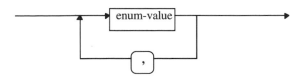

C.2.3.2 Enum value

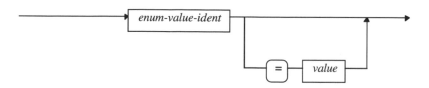

C.2.4 Typedef-definition

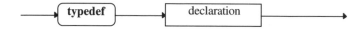

C.2.4.1 Declaration[2]

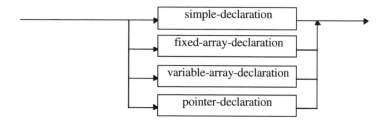

C.2.4.2 Simple declaration

C.2.4.3 Fixed array declaration

---

2. These are **type** declarations, not variable declarations (e.g., int my_number) which are unsupported by **rpcgen**.

C.2.4.4 Variable array declaration[3]

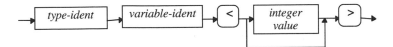

C.2.4.5 Pointer declaration[4]

C.2.5 Structure-definition

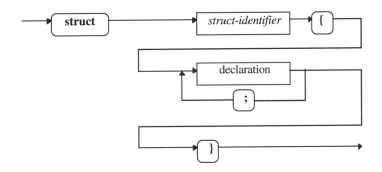

C.2.6 Union-definition[5]

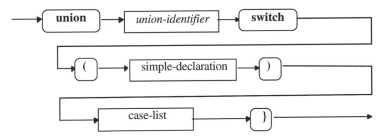

---

3. The integer value in angle brackets indicates a maximum size or, if empty, an array of any size.

4. Not actually an address. Technically called optional-data; often used for references to linked structures.

5. In RPC, unions are closer in syntax (and spirit) to variant records in Pascal than standard C unions.

C.2.6.1 Case-list

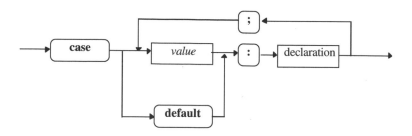

C.3 RPC KEYWORDS

The following RPC keywords have special meaning and cannot be used as identifiers.

bool	const	enum	int	string	typedef
char	double	hyper	quadruple	switch	unsigned
void	case	default	float	struct	union

C.4 SOME RPC EXAMPLES

In the examples below, each set of entries in an RPC ".x" file are followed by a sequence of statements in gray, which are those produced by the **rpcgen** compiler.

```
/*
 ****************     const    ********************
 */
const MAX = 1024;
const DELIMITER = "@";

/* is converted to:                                  */
```

```
#define MAX 1024
#define DELIMITER "@"
```
The equal sign and semicolon is removed and **const** is replaced with **# define**.

```
/*
 ***************     enum    ********************
 */
enum primary { red, yellow = 4, blue  };

/* is converted to:                                  */
```

```
enum primary {
        red = 0,
        yellow = 4,
        blue = 4 + 1
};
typedef enum primary primary;
```
Notice how the assignment is handled. The duplicate use of primary is acceptable as the C compiler stores these identifiers in different name spaces.

```
/*
 ****************        typedef ******************/
typedef colors strange;          /* simple              */
typedef char line[80];           /* fixed length array  */
typedef string var_line<80>;     /* variable len array with max */
typedef int some_ints< >;        /* variable len array - NO max */
typedef var_line  *line_ptr;     /* pointer       */

/* is converted to:                                 */
```

```
typedef colors strange;
typedef char line[80];
typedef char *var_line;
typedef struct {
        u_int some_ints_len;
        int *some_ints_val;
} some_ints;
typedef var_line *line_ptr;
```

The variable length array is mapped to a structure with two members. The first stores the number of items in the array. The second references the base address of the array. Note how the members are named using the array name as a base.

```
/*
 ****************        struct  *********************
 */
struct record {
        var_line   name;
        int        age;
};

/* is converted to:                                 */
```

```
struct record {
        var_line name;
        ⎡⎡⎡ ▪□▪;
};
typedef struct record record;
```

```
/*
 ****************        union  *********************
 */
union ret_value switch( extern errno ) {
case 0:
        line answer;
default:
        void;
};

/* is converted to:                                 */
```

```
struct ret_value {
        extern errno;
        union {
                line answer;
        } ret_value_u;
};
typedef struct ret_value ret_value;
```

The union is mapped to a structure containing a union whose element is the "larger" (storage-wise) of the initially listed members.

Bibliography

Bach, M. J., *The Design of the UNIX Operating System,* Englewood Cliffs, NJ: Prentice Hall, 1986.

Bloomer, J., *Power Programming with RPC.* Sebastopol, CA: O'Reilly & Associates, Inc., 1992.

Brown, C., *UNIX Distributed Programming.* Englewood Cliffs, NJ.: Prentice Hall, 1994.

Dijkstra, E. W., "Cooperating Sequential Processes," Technological University, Eindhoven, Netherlands, 1965.

Ditel, H. M., *Operating Systems.* Reading, MA: Addison-Wesley, 1990.

Kernighan, B. W., and Pike, R., *The UNIX Programming Environment.* Englewood Cliffs, NJ: Prentice Hall, 1984.

Kochan, S. G., and Wood, P. H., *UNIX®, Networking.* Indianapolis, IN: Hayden Books, 1989.

Krol, E., *The Whole Internet Users Guide and Catalog.* Sebastopol, CA: O'Reilly & Associates, Inc., 1993.

Leach, R. J., *Advanced Topics in UNIX®, Processes, Files, and Systems.* New York: John Wiley & Sons, Inc., 1994.

Leffler, S. J., McKusick, M. K., and Quaterman, J. S., *The Design and Implementation of the 4.3 BSD UNIX Operating System.* Reading, MA: Addison-Wesley, 1989.

Rago, S. A., *UNIX System V Network Programming.* Reading, MA: Addison-Wesley, 1993.

Rieken, B., and Weiman, L., *Adventures in UNIX™ Network Applications Programming.* New York: John Wiley & Sons, Inc., 1992.

Rochkind, M. J., *Advanced UNIX Programming*. Englewood Cliffs, NJ: Prentice Hall, 1985.

Silberschatz, A., and Peterson, J. L., *Operating System Concepts*. Reading, MA: Addison-Wesley, 1989.

Stevens, W. R., *Advanced Programming In the UNIX®, Environment*. Reading, MA: Addison-Wesley, 1992.

Stevens, W. R., *UNIX®, NETWORK Programming*. Englewood Cliffs, NJ: Prentice Hall, 1990.

SunSoft, *SunOS™ Network Interfaces Programmer's Guide*. Mountain View, CA: Sun Microsystems, 1992.

SunSoft, *SunOS™ Reference Manual, Section 2. System Calls*. Mountain View, CA: Sun Microsystems, 1993.

SunSoft, *SunOS™ Reference Manual, Section 3. Library Routines (A-M)*. Mountain View, CA: Sun Microsystems, 1993.

SunSoft, *SunOS™ Reference Manual, Section 3. Library Routines (N-Z)*. Mountain View, CA: Sun Microsystems, 1993.